Thriving at UNCG and Beyond

Customized Version of *Thriving at College and Beyond* by Joseph Cuseo, Viki Sox Fecas and Aaron Thompson, Designed Specifically for Foundations for Learning at The University of North Carolina at Greensboro

Twelfth Edition

The University of North Carolina at Greensboro
Students First Office

Edited by
Brandy S. Propst & Shakima M. Clency

Kendall Hunt
publishing company

Kendall Hunt
publishing company

www.kendallhunt.com
Send all inquiries to:
4050 Westmark Drive
Dubuque, IA 52004-1840

ISBN 978-1-4652-7756-5

Contents

Acknowledgments

It is with extreme gratitude that I thank my colleagues, Dr. Bryan Terry of Enrollment Management; Dana Saunders, Shakima Clency, Holly Grabowski, Jalonda Thompson, Heather Kern, Elena Medeiros and Kate Jessup in the Students First Office; Shawn O'Neil in the Student Success Center; Erin Lawrimore in UNCG Libraries; and Peer Academic Leader, Astrid Hacker, for their chapter contributions, support, and feedback regarding the customization of this book. I greatly value the teamwork and passion that our office exhibits in creating an exceptional experience for UNCG students.

In addition, I would like to acknowledge the *Your First Year* initiative coordinated by New Students & Spartan Family Programs for collaborating with FFL in our efforts to provide a successful transition for first-year students. I would also like to thank Katie Wendler of Kendall/Hunt Publishing for the guidance and assistance with making this customization a reality.

Last but not least, I would like to thank our students, who keep us on our toes, make us laugh and cry, and motivate us to come to work each day. May this book serve as a guide for your first year at UNCG, and beyond!

—*Brandy S. Propst*

Introduction Welcome Letter

Dear First Year Student,

Welcome to The University of North Carolina at Greensboro (UNCG)! My name is Bryan Terry and I am the Associate Provost for Enrollment Management at UNCG. Our unit is comprised of several offices: Undergraduate Admissions, Financial Aid, University Registrar's Office, UNCG Guarantee, Student Success Center and the Students First Office. We are delighted by your decision to join the UNCG community. It is our mission to provide you with the necessary resources to support your transition to UNCG from enrollment to graduation.

Courtesy of UNCG Relations Office

By enrolling in Foundations for Learning (FFL) you have taken the first of many steps to ensure your success as a UNCG student. It is our hope that what you learn in this course will pave the way for a smooth first-year experience and beyond. FFL is designed to help you explore the purpose of higher education and your individual role in the educational experience. Working with your instructor, fellow students, and your Peer Academic Leader (PAL), you will become familiar with all of the resources that are available to assist you throughout your undergraduate journey.

Through courses like FFL and many other campus programs, there is indeed a wealth of opportunity and support at your fingertips at UNCG, and many offices and people ready to assist you. As with most things in life, your experience at UNCG and with this course will depend on you and the effort you put into it. Take ownership of your education, ask questions, connect with faculty and staff, get involved and be sure to take advantage of all that UNCG has to offer. Your time here will be one of the best experiences of your life. Best of luck as you start this memorable journey—few experiences will be quite as exciting as your first year!

Sincerely,

Bryan Terry

Dr. Bryan Terry
Associate Provost for Enrollment Management

Introduction

Congratulations and welcome! We applaud your decision to continue your education. Your previous enrollment in school was required; however, you're decision to continue your education in college is entirely *your choice*. You've chosen to enter "higher education," where you will be learning and thinking at a higher level than you did in high school. You are about to begin a new and exciting journey; your time in college has the potential to be the most enriching experience of your life. It's probably safe to say that after your experience in college, you'll never again be a member of an organization or community with as many resources and services that are intentionally designed to promote your learning, development, and success. If you capitalize on the campus resources available to you, and if you utilize effective college-going strategies (such as those suggested in this book), you can create a life-changing experience for yourself that will enrich the quality of your life for the remainder of your life. (See **Box I.1** for a snapshot summary of the multiple, lifelong benefits of a college education and college degree.)

Snapshot Summary

I.1

Why College Is Worth It: The Economic and Personal Benefits of a College Education

Less than 30 percent of Americans have earned a 4-year college degree (U.S. Census Bureau). When individuals who attend college are compared with people from similar social and economic backgrounds who did not continue their education beyond high school, research reveals that college is well worth the investment. College graduates experience numerous long-lasting benefits, such as those summarized in the following list.

1. **Career Benefits**
   - Career Security and Stability—lower rates of unemployment
   - Career Versatility and Mobility—more flexibility to move out of a position and into other positions

- Career Advancement—more opportunity to move up to higher professional positions
- Career Interest—more likely to find their work stimulating and challenging
- Career Autonomy—greater independence and opportunity to be their own boss
- Career Satisfaction—enjoy their work more and feel that it allows them to use their special talents
- Career Prestige—hold higher-status positions (i.e., careers that more socially desirable and respected)

2. **Economic Advantages**
   - Make better consumer choices and decisions
   - Make wiser long-term investments

- Receive greater pension benefits
- Earn higher income: The gap between the earnings of high school and college graduates is *growing*. Individuals with a bachelor's degree now earn an average annual salary of about $50,000 per year, which is 40 percent higher than high school graduates—whose average salary is less than $30,000 per year. When these differences are calculated over a lifetime, families head by people with a bachelor's degree will take in about 1.6 million more than families headed by people with a high school diploma.

> ### Student Perspective
>
> "I am coming from a household that does not have a high standard of living—I want to do better than just getting by."
>
> –First-year student, quoted in Franklin, et al. (2002)

"

"A bachelor's degree continues to be a primary vehicle of which one gains an advantaged socioeconomic position in American society."

–Ernest Pascarella & Patrick Terenzini, *How College Affects Students*

"

"If you think education is expensive, try ignorance."

–Derek Bok, former President, Harvard University

3. **Advanced Intellectual Skills**
   - Greater knowledge
   - More effective problem-solving skills
   - Better ability to deal with complex and ambiguous (uncertain) problems
   - Greater openness to new ideas

- More advanced levels of moral reasoning
- Clearer sense of self-identity—more awareness and knowledge of personal talents, interests, values, and needs
- Greater likelihood to continue learning throughout life

4. **Better Physical Health**
   - Better health insurance—more comprehensive coverage and more likely to be covered
   - Better dietary habits
   - Exercise more regularly
   - Lower rates of obesity
   - Live longer and healthier lives

5. **Social Benefits**
   - Higher social self-confidence
   - Understand and communicate more effectively with others
   - Greater popularity
   - More effective leadership skills
   - Greater marital satisfaction

> ### Student Perspective
>
> "I noticed before when I wasn't going to college, they [my family] didn't look at me as highly as a person. But now since I have started college, everybody is lifting me up and saying how proud the [are] of me."
>
> –First-year student, quoted in Franklin, et al. (2002)

6. **Emotional Benefits**
   - Lower levels of anxiety
   - Higher levels of self-esteem
   - Greater sense of self-efficacy—believe they have more influence and control over their life
   - Higher levels of psychological well-being
   - Higher levels of personal happiness

7. **Effective Citizenship**
   - Greater interest in national issues—both social and political
   - Greater knowledge of current affairs
   - Higher voting participation rates
   - Higher rates of participation in civic affairs and community service

8. **Higher Quality of Life for Their Children**
   - Less likely to smoke during pregnancy
   - Provide better health care for their children
   - Spend more time with their children
   - More likely to involve their children in educational activities that stimulate their mental development
   - More likely to save money for their children to go to college
   - More likely that their children will graduate from college
   - More likely that their children will attain high-status and higher-paying careers

Student Perspectives

"My 3-month old boy is very important to me, and it is important that I graduate from college so my son, as well as I, live a better life."

–First-year student responding to the question, "What is most important to you?"

"Being a first-generation college student, seeing how hard my parents worked these past 18 years to give all that they can to get me to where I am now, I feel I cannot let them down. It is my responsibility to succeed in school and life and to take care of them in their old age."

–First-year college student, quoted in Nunez (2005)

References

Astin, A. W. (1993). *What Matters in College?* San Francisco: Jossey-Bass.

Bowen, H. R. (1977, 1997). *Investment in Learning: The Individual & Social Value of American Higher Education.* Baltimore: The Johns Hopkins University Press.

College Board (2006). *Education pays update.* Washington, D. C.: Author.

Dee, T. (2004). Are there civic returns to education? *Journal of Public Economics,* 88, 1697-1720.

Feldman, K. A., & Newcomb, T. M. (1969, 1994). *The impact of college on students.* San Francisco: Jossey-Bass.

Pascarella, E. T., & Terenzini, P. T. (1991). *How college affects students: Findings and Insights from Twenty Years of Research.* San Francisco: Jossey-Bass.

Pascarella, E. T., & Terenzini, P. T. (2005). *How college affects students: A third decade of research* (volume 2). San Francisco: Jossey-Bass.

Tomasho, R. (2009, April 22.). Study tallies education gap's effect on GDP. *Wall Street Journal*

U.S. Census Bureau (2008). *Bureau of Labor Statistics.* Washington, D.C.: Author.

"Getting the [college] degree meant more to me than an NCAA title, being named All-American or winning an Olympic gold medal."

–Patrick Ewing, Hall of Fame basketball player, and college graduate (Georgetown University)

◆ The Importance of the First Year of College

Your movement into higher education represents an important life transition. Somewhat similar to an immigrant moving to a new country, you're moving into a new culture with different expectations, regulations, customs, and language (Chaskes, 1996) (See the Glossary and Dictionary of College Vocabulary at the end of this book for "translations" of the new language that is used in the college culture.)

Pause for Reflection

Why have you decided to attend college?

Why did you decide to attend the college or university you're enrolled in now?

The *first* year of college is undoubtedly the most important year of the college experience because it's a stage of *transition*. During the first year of college, students report the most change, the most learning, and the most development (Flowers, et al., 2001; Doyle, Edison, & Pascarella, 1998; Light, 2001). Other research suggests that the academic habits students establish in their first year of college are likely to persist throughout their remaining years of college (Schilling, 2001). When graduating seniors look back at their college experience, many of them say that the first year was the time of greatest change and the time during which they made the most significant improvements in their approach to learning. Here is how one senior put it during a personal interview:

Interviewer: What have you learned about your approach to learning [in college]?

Student: I had to learn how to study. I went through high school with a 4.0 average. I didn't have to study. It was a breeze. I got to the university and there was no structure. No one took attendance to make sure I was in class. No one checked my homework. No one told me I had to do something. There were no quizzes on the readings. I did not work well with this lack of structure. It took my first year and a half to learn to deal with it. But I had to teach myself to manage my time. I had to teach myself how to study. I had to teach myself how to learn in a different environment (Chickering & Schlossberg, 1998, p. 47).

In many ways, the first-year experience in college is similar to ocean surfing or downhill skiing: it can be filled with many exciting thrills, but there's also a risk of taking some dangerous spills. The first year is also the stage of the college experience during which students experience the most stress, the most academic difficulties, and the highest withdrawal rate (American College Testing, 2009; Bartlett, 2002; Sax, Bryant, & Gilmartin, 2004). The ultimate goal of downhill skiing and surfing is to experience the thrills, avoid the spills, and finish the run while you're still standing. The same is true for the first year of college; studies show that if you can complete your first-year experience in good standing, your chances for successfully completing college improve dramatically (American College Testing, 2009).

In a nutshell, your college success will depend on what you for yourself and how you take advantage of what your college can do for you. You'll find that the research cited and the advice provided in this book point to one major conclusion: Success in college depends on you—you make it happen by what you do and how well you capitalize on the resources available to you.

After reviewing 40 years of research on how college affects students, two distinguished researched the following conclusion:

> *The impact of college is largely determined by individual effort and involvement in the academic, interpersonal, and extracurricular [co-curricular] offerings on a campus. Students are not passive recipients of institutional efforts to "educate"*

"*What students do during college counts more than who they are or where they go to college.*"

–George Kuh, author, *Student Success in College*

"*Some people make things happen, while others watch things happen or wonder what has happened.*"

–Author unknown

or "change" them, but rather bear major responsibility for any gains they derive from their postsecondary [college] experience (Pascarella & Terenzini, 2005, p. 602).

Pause for Reflection

In order to succeed in college, what do you think you'll have to do differently than you've done in the past?

Compared to your previous schooling, college will provide with a broader range of courses, more resources to capitalize on, more freedom of choice, and more decision-making opportunities. Your own college experience will differ from any other college student because you have the freedom to actively shape or create it in a way that is uniquely your own. Don't let college happen *to* you; make it happen *for* you—take charge of your college experience and take advantage of the college resources that are at your command.

◆ Importance of a Student Success Course (also known as a First-Year Experience Course)

If you're reading this book, you are already beginning to take charge of your college experience because you're enrolled in a course that's designed to promote your college success. Research strongly indicates that new students who participate in student-success courses are more likely to stay continue in college until they complete their degree and perform at a higher level. These positive effects have been found for:

- All types of students (under-prepared and well-prepared, minority and majority, residential and commuter, male and female),
- Students at all types of colleges (2-year and 4-year, public and private),
- Students attending college of different sizes (small, mid-sized, and large), and
- Students attending college in different locations (urban, suburban, and rural).

(References: Barefoot et al., 1998; Boudreau & Kromrey, 1994; Cuseo & Barefoot, 1996; Fidler & Godwin, 1994; Glass & Garrett, 1995; Grunder & Hellmich, 1996; Hunter & Linder, 2005; Porter & Swing, 2006; Shanley & Witten, 1990; Sidle & McReynolds, 1999; Starke, Harth, & Sirianni, 2001; Thomson, 1998; Tobolowski, 2005).

There has been more carefully conducted research on student-success or college-success courses, and more evidence supporting their effectiveness for promoting success, than there is for any other course in the college curriculum. You're fortunate to be enrolled in this course, so give it your best effort and take full advantage of what it has to offer. If you do, you'll be taking an important first step toward thriving in college and beyond.

Enjoy the trip!

Student Perspective

"I am now one of the peer counselors on campus, and without this class my first semester, I don't think I could have done as well, and by participating in this class again (as a teaching assistant), it reinforced this belief."

—First-year student comment made when evaluating a first-year seminar (college success course)

"Every first-semester freshman needs a class like this—whether they think so or not."

—First-year student comment made when evaluating a first-year seminar (college success course)

Student Perspective

"I could really relate to everything we talked about. It is a great class because you can use it in your other classes."

—First-year student comment made when evaluating a first-year seminar (college success course)

Liberal Arts

The Meaning, Purpose, and Value of General Education

Before you launch into this chapter, do your best to answer the following question:

Which one of the following statements represents the most accurate meaning of the term *liberal arts*?

1. Learning to be less politically conservative
2. Learning to be more artistic
3. Learning ideas rather than practical skills
4. Learning to spend money more freely
5. Learning skills for freedom

LEARNING GOAL

To appreciate the meaning, purpose, and benefits of the liberal arts and to develop a strategic plan for making the most out of general education.

Personal Story

I was once advising a first-year student (Laura) who intended to major in business. While helping her plan the courses she needed to complete her degree, I pointed out to Laura that she still needed to take a course in philosophy. Here's how our conversation went after I made this point.

Laura (in a somewhat irritated tone): Why do I have to take philosophy? I'm a business major.

Dr. Cuseo: Because philosophy is an important component of a liberal arts education.

Laura (in a very agitated tone): I'm not liberal and I don't want to be a liberal. I'm conservative and so are my parents; we all voted for Ronald Reagan in the last election!

—Joe Cuseo

◆ The Meaning and Purpose of a Liberal Arts Education

If you're uncertain about what the term "liberal arts" means, you're not alone. Most first-year students don't have the foggiest idea what a liberal arts education represents (Hersh, 1997). If they were to guess, they may mistakenly say that it's something impractical or related to liberal politics.

Laura probably would have picked option 1 as her answer to the multiple-choice question posed at the start of this chapter. That would not have been the right choice; option 5 is the correct answer. Literally translated, the term "liberal arts" derives from the Latin words liberales—meaning to "liberate" or "free," and artes—meaning "skills." Thus, "skills for freedom" is the most accurate meaning of the term "liberal arts."

The roots of the term "liberal arts" date back to the origin of modern civilization—to the ancient Greeks and Romans, who argued that political power in a democracy rests with the people because they choose (elect) their own leaders. In a democracy, people are liberated from uncritical dependence on a dictator or autocrat. To preserve their political freedom, citizens in a democracy must be well educated and critical thinkers so that they can make wise choices about whom they elect as their leaders and lawmakers (Bishop, 1986; Cheney, 1989).

Many students (and their parents) do not know what the term *"liberal arts"* truly means.

"Knowledge will forever govern ignorance; and a people who mean to be their own governors must arm themselves with the power which knowledge gives."

–James Madison, fourth president of the United States and cosigner of the American Constitution and first author of the Bill of Rights

"It is such good fortune for people in power that people do not think."

–Adolf Hitler, German dictator

The political ideals of the ancient Greeks and Romans were shared by the founding fathers of the United States who also emphasized the importance of an educated citizenry for preserving America's new democracy. As Thomas Jefferson, third president of the United States, wrote in 1801 (Ford, 1903, p. 278):

I know of no safe depository of the ultimate powers of a society but the people themselves; and if we think them not enlightened enough to exercise control with a wholesome discretion [responsible decision-making], the remedy is not to take power from them, but to inform their discretion by education.

Thus, the liberal arts are rooted in the belief that education is the essential ingredient for preservation of democratic freedom. When people are educated in the liberal arts, they gain the breadth of knowledge and depth of thinking to vote wisely, preserve democracy, and avoid autocracy (dictatorship).

The importance of a knowledgeable, critical-thinking citizenry for making wise political choices is still relevant today. Contemporary political campaigns are using more manipulative media advertisements. These ads rely on short sound bites, one-sided arguments, and powerful visual images that are intentionally designed to appeal to emotions and discourage critical thinking (Goleman, 1992).

Over time, the term "liberal arts" has acquired the more general meaning of liberating or freeing people to be self-directed individuals who make personal choices and decisions that are determined by their own, well-reasoned ideas and values, rather than blind conformity to the ideas and values of others (Gamson, 1984). Self-directed critical thinkers are empowered to resist manipulation by politicians and other societal influences, including:

- Authority figures (e.g., they question excessive use or abuse of authority by parents, teachers, or law enforcers);
- Peers (e.g., they resist peer pressure that's unreasonable or unethical); and
- Media (e.g., they detect and reject forms of advertisements designed to manipulate their self-image and material needs).

A liberal arts education encourages you to be your own person and to ask "Why?" It's the component of your college education that supplies you with the mental tools needed to be an independent thinker with an inquiring mind that questions authority and resists conformity.

◆ The Liberal Arts Curriculum

The first liberal arts curriculum (collection of courses) was designed with the belief that individuals who experienced these courses would be equipped with (a) a broad base of knowledge that would ensure they would be well informed in various subjects and (b) a range of mental skills that would enable them to think deeply and critically. Based on this educational philosophy of the ancient Greeks and Romans, the first liberal arts curriculum was developed during the Middle Ages and consisted of the following subjects: logic, language, rhetoric (the art of argumentation and persuasion), music, mathematics, and astronomy (Ratcliff, 1997; Association of American Colleges & Universities, 2002).

The purpose of the original liberal arts curriculum has withstood the test of time. Today's colleges and universities continue to offer a liberal arts curriculum designed to provide students with a broad base of knowledge in multiple subject areas and equip them with critical skills. The liberal arts curriculum today is often referred to as general education—representing skills and knowledge that are general rather than narrowly specialized. General education is what all college students learn, no matter what their major or specialized field of study may be (Association of American Colleges & Universities, 2002).

On some campuses, the liberal arts are also referred to as the core curriculum, with "core" standing for what is central or essential for all students to know and do because of their importance for effective performance in any field, or as breadth requirements, referring the their broad scope that spans a range of subject areas.

> **! Remember**
>
> Whatever term is used to describe the liberal arts, the bottom line is that they are the foundation of a college education upon which all academic specializations (majors) are built; they are what all college graduates should be able to know and do for whatever occupational path they choose to pursue; they are what distinguishes college education from vocational preparation; and they define what it means to be a well-educated person.

◆ Major Divisions of Knowledge and Subject Areas in the Liberal Arts Curriculum

Pause for Reflection

For someone to be successful in any major and career, what do you think that person should:

1. Know; and

2. Be able to do?

The divisions of knowledge in today's liberal arts curriculum have expanded to include more subject areas than those included in the original curriculum that was based on the work of the ancient Greeks and Romans. The liberal arts' divisions, and the courses that make up each division, vary somewhat from campus to campus. Campuses also vary in terms of the nature of courses required within each division of knowledge and the range of courses from which students can choose to fulfill their general educational requirements. On average, about one-third of a college graduate's course credits were required general education courses selected from the liberal arts curriculum (Conley, 2005).

Despite campus-to-campus variation in the number and nature of courses required, the liberal arts curriculum on every college campus represents the areas of knowledge and the types of skills that all students should possess, no matter what their particular major may be. It allows you to stand on the shoulders of intellectual giants from a range of fields and capitalize on their collective wisdom.

On most campuses today, the liberal arts curriculum typically consists of general divisions of knowledge and related subject areas similar to those listed in the sections that follow. As you read through these divisions of knowledge, highlight any subjects in which you've never had a course.

Humanities

Courses in the humanities division of the liberal arts curriculum focus on the human experience and human culture, asking the important questions that arise in the life of humans, such as "Why are we here?" "What is the meaning or purpose of our existence?" "How should we live?" "What is the good life?" and "Is there life after death?"

The following are the primary subject areas in the humanities division:

- **English Composition.** Writing clearly, critically, and persuasively;
- **Speech.** Speaking eloquently and persuasively;
- **Literature.** Reading critically and appreciating the artistic merit of various literary genres (forms of writing), such as novels, short stories, poems, plays, and essays;
- **Languages.** Listening, speaking, reading and writing languages other than the student's native tongue;

- **Philosophy.** Thinking rationally, developing wisdom (the ability to use knowledge prudently), and living an ethically principled life;
- **Theology.** Understanding how humans conceive of and express their faith in a transcendent (supreme) being.

Fine Arts

Courses in the fine arts division focus largely on the art of human expression, asking such questions as "How do humans express, create, and appreciate what is beautiful?" and "How do we express ourselves aesthetically (through the senses) with imagination, creativity, style, and elegance?"

The primary subject areas of the fine arts division are as follows:

- **Visual Arts.** Creating and appreciating human expression through visual representation (drawing, painting, sculpture, photography, and graphic design);
- **Musical Arts.** Appreciating and creating rhythmical arrangements of sounds;
- **Performing Arts.** Appreciating and expressing creativity through drama and dance.

Mathematics

Courses in the mathematics division are designed to promote skills in numerical calculation, quantitative reasoning and problem solving.

Mathematics has the following primary subject areas:

- **Algebra.** Mathematical reasoning involving symbolic representation of numbers in a language of letters that vary in size or quantity;
- **Statistics.** Mathematical methods for summarizing; estimating probabilities; representing and understanding numerical information depicted in graphs, charts, and tables; and drawing accurate conclusions from quantitative data;
- **Calculus.** Higher mathematical methods for calculating the rate at which the quantity of one entity changes in relation to another and for calculating the areas enclosed by curves.

Natural Sciences

Courses in the natural sciences division of the liberal arts curriculum are devoted to systematic observation of the physical world and the explanation of natural phenomena, asking such questions as "What causes physical events that take place in the natural world?" "How can we predict and control these events?" and "How do we promote symbiotic interaction between humans and the natural environment that sustains the survival of both?"

The following are the primary subject areas of the natural sciences division:

- **Biology.** Understanding the structure and underlying processes of all living things;
- **Chemistry.** Understanding the composition of natural and synthetic (manmade) substances and how these substances may be changed or developed;
- **Physics.** Understanding the properties of physical matter, the principles of energy and motion, and electrical and magnetic forces;

"Never mistake knowledge for wisdom.

One helps you make a living; the other helps you make a life."

–Sandra Carey, lobbyist to the California State Assembly

"Dancing is silent poetry."

–Simonides, ancient Greek poet

© El Greco, 2010. Under license from Shutterstock, Inc.

"The universe is a grand book which cannot be read until one learns to comprehend the language and become familiar with the characters of which it is composed. It is written in the language of mathematics."

–Galileo Galilei, seventeenth-century Italian physicist, mathematician, astronomer, and philosopher

The natural sciences division of the liberal arts curriculum focuses on the observation of the physical world and the explanation of natural phenomena.

"Science is an imaginative adventure of the mind seeking truth in a world of mystery."

–Cyril Herman Hinshelwood, Nobel Prize–winning English chemist

"Man, the molecule of society, is the subject of social science."

–Henry Charles Carey, nineteenth-century American economist

"To eat is a necessity, but to eat intelligently is an art."

–La Rochefoucauld, seventeenth-century French author

- **Geology.** Understanding the composition of the earth and the natural processes that have shaped its development;
- **Astronomy.** Understanding the makeup and motion of celestial bodies that comprise the universe.

Social and Behavioral Sciences

Courses in the division of social and behavioral sciences focus on the observation of human behavior, individually and in groups, and ask such questions as "What causes humans to behave the way they do?" and "How can we predict, control, or improve human behavior and human interaction?"

This division has the following primary subject areas:

- **Psychology.** Understanding the human mind, its conscious and subconscious processes, and the underlying causes of human behavior;
- **Sociology.** Understanding the structure, interaction, and collective behavior of organized social groups and institutions or systems that comprise human society (e.g., families, schools, and social services);
- **Anthropology.** Understanding the cultural and physical origin, development, and distribution the human species;
- **History.** Understanding past events, their causes, and their influence on current events;
- **Political Science.** Understanding how societal authority is organized and how this authority is exerted to govern people, make collective decisions, and maintain social order;
- **Economics.** Understanding how the monetary needs of humans are met through allocation of limited resources and how material wealth is produced and distributed;
- **Geography.** Understanding how the place (physical location) where humans live influences their cultural and societal development and how humans have shaped and been shaped by their surrounding physical environment.

Physical Education and Wellness

Courses in the physical education and wellness division of the liberal arts curriculum focus on the human body, how to best maintain health, and how to attain peak performance levels of performance. They ask such questions as "How does the body function most effectively?" and "What can we do to prevent illness, promote wellness, and improve the physical quality of our lives?"

These primary subject areas fall under this division:

- **Physical Education.** Understanding the role of human exercise for promoting health and peak performance;
- **Nutrition.** Understanding how the body uses food as nourishment to promote health and generate energy;
- **Sexuality.** Understanding the biological, psychological, and social aspects of sexual relations;
- **Drug Education.** Understanding how substances that alter the body and mind affect physical health, mental health, and human performance.

© Laurence Gough, 2010. Under license from Shutterstock, Inc.

Most of your liberal arts requirements will be taken during your first 2 years of college. Don't be disappointed if some of these requirements seem similar to courses you recently had in high school, and don't think you'll be bored because these are subjects you've already studied. College courses will not be videotape replays of high school courses because you will examine these subjects in greater depth and breadth and at a higher level of thinking (Conley, 2005). Research shows that most of the higher-level thinking gains that students make in college take place during their first 2 years—the years during which they're taking most of their liberal arts courses (Pascarella & Terenzini, 2005).

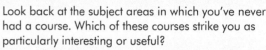

Pause for Reflection

Look back at the subject areas in which you've never had a course. Which of these courses strike you as particularly interesting or useful?

Why?

◆ Transferable Learning Skills That Last a Lifetime

A liberal arts education promotes success in your major, career, and life by equipping you with a set of lifelong learning skills with two powerful qualities:

- **Transferability.** These skills can be transferred and applied to a range of subjects, careers, and life situations.
- **Durability.** These skills are long lasting and can be continually used throughout your lifetime.

To use an athletic analogy, what the liberal arts do for the mind is similar to what cross-training does for the body. Cross-training engages the body in a range of exercises to promote total physical fitness and develop a range of physical skills (e.g., strength, endurance, flexibility, and agility), which can be applied to improve performance in any sport or athletic endeavor. Similarly, the liberal arts engage the mind in a range of subject areas (e.g., arts, sciences, and humanities), which develop a range of mental skills that can be applied to improve performance in any academic field or professional career.

> "You know you've got to exercise your brain just like your muscles."
>
> –Will Rogers, Native American humorist and actor

! Remember

The liberal arts not only provide you with academic skills needed to succeed in your chosen major but also equip you with skills to succeed in whatever career or careers you decide to pursue. Don't underestimate the importance of these transferable and durable skills. Work hard at developing them, and take seriously the general education courses that promote their development.

A major difference exists between learning factual knowledge and learning transferable skills. A transferable skill can be applied to different situations or contexts. The mental skills developed by the liberal arts are transportable across academic subjects you'll encounter in college and work positions you'll assume after college. It could be said that these lifelong learning skills are a mental gift that keeps on giving.

The transferable skills developed by the liberal arts are summarized in **Box 1.1**.

As you read them, rate yourself on each of the skills using the following scale:

> "If you give a man a fish, you feed him for a day.
>
> If you teach a man how to fish, you feed him for life."
>
> –Author unknown

4 = very strong, 3 = strong, 2 = needs some improvement,
1 = needs much improvement

Take Action!

Transferable Lifelong Learning Skills Developed by the Liberal Arts

1. Communication Skills. Accurate comprehension and articulate expression of ideas. Five particular types of communication skills are essential for success in any specialized field of study or work:

- Written communication skills. Writing in a clear, creative, and persuasive manner;
- Oral communication skills. Speaking concisely, confidently, and eloquently;
- Reading skills. Comprehending, interpreting, and evaluating the literal meaning and connotations of words written in various styles and subject areas;
- Listening skills. Comprehending spoken language accurately and sensitively;
- Electronic communication skills. Using computer and technology-mediated communication skills effectively.

2. Information literacy skills. Effectively and efficiently accessing, retrieving, and evaluating information from various sources, including in-print and online (technology-based) systems.

> " *"Ability to recognize when information is needed and have the ability to locate, evaluate, and use it effectively."*
>
> –Definition of "information literacy," American Library Association Presidential Committee on Information Literacy

3. Computation skills. Accurate calculation, analysis, summary, interpretation, and evaluation of quantitative information or statistical data.
4. Higher-level thinking skills. Learning deeply and thinking at a more advanced level than simply acquisition and memorization of factual information.

1.1

Pause for Reflection

Reflect on the four skill areas developed by a liberal arts education (communication, information literacy, computation, and higher-level thinking). Which one do you think is most important or most relevant to your future success?

Write a one-paragraph explanation about why you chose this skill.

Students often see general education as something to get out of the way and get behind them so they can get into their major and career (Association of American Colleges & Universities, 2007). Don't take the view that general education as a series of obstacles along the way to a degree; instead, view it as a learning process from which you can take a set of powerful skills that are:

1. **Portable.** Travel well across work situations and life roles; and
2. **Stable.** Remain relevant and useful across changing times.

! Remember

When you acquire lifelong *learning* skills, you're also acquiring lifelong *earning* skills.

The skills developed by a liberal arts education are strikingly similar to the types of skills that employers seek in new employees. In numerous national surveys and in-depth interviews, employers and executives in both industry and government consistently report that they seek employees with skills that fall into the following three categories:

1. **Communication skills** (e.g., listening, speaking, writing, and reading; Business–Higher Education Forum, 1999; National Association of Colleges & Employers, 2003; Peter D. Hart Research Associates, 2006):

   "There is such a heavy emphasis on effective communication in the workplace that college students who master these skills can set themselves apart from the pack when searching for employment." Marilyn Mackes, executive director of the National Association of Colleges and Employers (Mackes, 2003, p. 1).

2. **Thinking skills** (e.g., problem solving and critical thinking; Business–Higher Education Forum, 1999; Peter D. Hart Research Associates, 2006; Van Horn, 1995):

    "We look for people who can think critically and analytically. If you can do those things, we can teach you our business." Paul Dominski, store recruiter for the Robinson-May Department Stores Company (Indiana University, 2004, p. 1).

3. **Lifelong learning skills** (e.g., learning how to learn and how to continue learning; Conference Board of Canada, 2000):

    "Employers are virtually unanimous that the most important knowledge and skills the new employee can bring to the job are problem solving, communication, and 'learning to learn' skills. The workers of the future need to know how to think and how to continue to learn." David Kearns, former chief executive officer (CEO) for the Xerox Corporation (Kearns, 1989, p. 8).

The remarkable resemblance between the work skills sought by employers and the academic skills developed by a liberal arts education isn't surprising when you think about the typical duties or responsibilities of working professionals. They need good communication skills because they must listen, speak, describe, and explain ideas to co-workers and customers. They read and critically interpret written and statistical reports, and they write letters, memos, and reports. They need highly developed thinking skills to analyze problems, construct well-organized plans, generate innovative ideas and solutions to problems (creative thinking), and evaluate whether their plans and strategies will be effective (critical thinking).

A Liberal Arts Education Is Preparation for Your Major

Don't assume that liberal arts courses you're taking as general education requirements have nothing to do with your specialized field of interest. Liberal arts courses provide a relevant foundation for success in your major. Recall our story at the start of the chapter about Laura, the first-year student with a business major who questioned why she had to take a course in philosophy. Laura needed to take philosophy because she will encounter topics in her business major that relate either directly or indirectly to philosophy. In her business courses, she will likely encounter philosophical issues relating to (a) the logical assumptions and underlying values of capitalism, (b) business ethics (e.g., hiring and firing practices), and (c) business justice (e.g., how profits should be fairly or justly distributed to workers and shareholders). Philosophy will equip her with the fundamental logical thinking and ethical reasoning skills to understand these issues deeply and respond to them humanely.

As with the field of business, liberal arts subjects are relevant to successful performance in any major and career. For example, historical and ethical perspectives are needed for all fields because all of them have a history and none of them are value free.

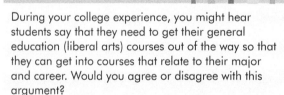

The academic skills developed by a liberal arts education are also *practical* skills that contribute to successful performance in *any career.*

Learning from the collective wisdom of diverse disciplines provides you with a broad base of knowledge that enables you to view issues and solve problems from multiple angles or vantage points. Although you may specialize in a particular field of study in college (your major), real-life issues and challenges are not divided neatly into specialized majors. Important and enduring issues, such as effective leadership, improving race relations, and preventing international warfare, can neither be fully understood nor effectively solved by using the thinking tools of a single academic discipline. Approaching multidimensional issues such as these from the perspective of a single, specialized field of study is likely to result in single-minded and over-simplified attempt to solve a complex problem.

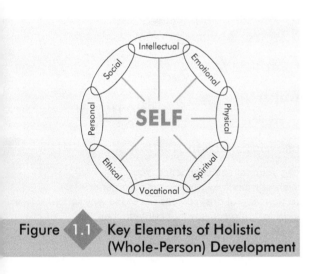

Figure 1.1 Key Elements of Holistic (Whole-Person) Development

The Liberal Arts Promote Self-awareness and Development of the Whole Person

One of the most emphasized intended outcomes of a liberal arts education is to "know thyself" (Cross, 1982). The ability to turn inward and become aware of your self is a form of intelligence that has been referred to as intrapersonal intelligence (Gardner, 1999), and it's essential for beginning any quest for personal growth and self-fulfillment.

To become self-aware requires awareness of all elements that comprise the self. As illustrated in **Figure 1.1**, the human self is composed of multiple dimensions that join together to form the whole person.

◆ Key Dimensions of the Self

Each of the following elements of self plays an influential role in promoting human health, success, and happiness:

1. **Intellectual.** Knowledge, perspectives, and ways of thinking;
2. **Emotional.** Feelings, self-esteem, emotional intelligence, and mental health;
3. **Social.** Interpersonal relationships;
4. **Ethical.** Values, character, and moral convictions;
5. **Physical.** Bodily health and wellness;
6. **Spiritual.** Beliefs about the meaning or purpose of life and the hereafter;

7. **Vocational.** Occupational or career development and satisfaction;
8. **Personal.** Identity, self-concept, and self-management.

Research strongly suggests that quality of life depends on attention to and development of all elements of the self. It's been found that people who are healthy (physically and mentally) and successful (personally and professionally) are those who attend to and integrate dimensions of their self, enabling them to lead well-rounded and well-balanced lives (Covey, 1990; Goleman, 1995; Heath, 1977).

In Figure 1.1, these diverse dimensions of the self are joined or linked to represent how they are interrelated and work not independently but interdependently to affect an individual's development and well-being (Love & Love, 1995).

These elements are discussed separately in this chapter to keep them clear in your mind. In reality, they do not operate independently of one another; they are interconnected and influence one another. (This is why the elements the self in Figure 1.1 are depicted as links in an interconnected chain.) Thus, the self is a diverse, multidimensional entity that has the capacity to develop along various interdependent dimensions.

One of the primary goals of the liberal arts is to provide a well-rounded education that promotes development the whole person (Kuh, Shedd, & Whitt, 1987). Research on college students confirms that their college experience affects them in multiple ways and promotes the development of multiple dimensions of self (Bowen, 1997; Feldman & Newcomb, 1994; Pascarella & Terenzini, 1991).

Since wholeness is essential for wellness, success, and happiness, carefully read the following descriptions and skills associated with each of the eight elements of holistic development. As you are read the skills and qualities listed beneath each of the eight elements, place a checkmark in the space next to any skill that is particularly important to you. You may check more than one skill within each area.

◆ Skills and Qualities Associated with Each Element of Holistic (Whole-Person) Development

1. **Intellectual development.** Acquiring knowledge and learning how to learn deeply and think at a higher level.
   Goals and skills:
   ☑ Becoming aware of your intellectual abilities, interests, and learning styles
   ☑ Maintaining attention and concentration
   ☑ Improving your ability to retain knowledge (long-term memory)
   ☑ Moving beyond memorization to higher levels of thinking
   ☑ Acquiring effective research skills for accessing information from various sources and systems
   ☑ Viewing issues from multiple angles or viewpoints (psychological, social, political, economic, etc.) to attain a balanced, comprehensive perspective
   ☑ Evaluating ideas critically in terms of their truth and value
   ☑ Thinking creatively or imaginatively
   ☑ Responding constructively to differing viewpoints or opposing arguments
   ☑ Detecting and rejecting persuasion tactics that appeal to emotions rather than reason

Know Thyself

Self-awareness is the first step to overcoming personal prejudices and developing intrapersonal intelligence.

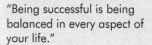
Student Perspective

"Being successful is being balanced in every aspect of your life."

—First-year college student

"The research portrays the college student as changing in an integrated way, with change in any one area appearing to be part of a mutually reinforcing network or pattern of change in other areas."

—Ernest Pascarella and Pat Terenzini, How College Affects Students (XXXX)

"Intellectual growth should commence at birth and cease only at death."

—Albert Einstein, Nobel Prize–winning physicist

2. **Emotional development.** Strengthening skills for understanding, controlling, and expressing emotions.

Goals and skills:

☑ Dealing with personal emotions in an honest, nondefensive manner
☑ Maintaining a healthy balance between emotional control and emotional expression
☑ Responding with empathy and sensitivity to emotions experienced by others
☑ Dealing effectively with depression
☑ Dealing effectively with anger
☑ Using effective stress-management strategies to control anxiety and tension
☑ Responding effectively to frustrations and setbacks
☑ Dealing effectively with fear of failure and poor performance
☑ Accepting feedback in a constructive, nondefensive manner
☑ Maintaining optimism and enthusiasm

3. **Social development.** Enhancing the quality and depth of interpersonal relationships.

Goals and skills:

☑ Developing effective conversational skills
☑ Becoming an effective listener
☑ Relating effectively to others in one-to-one, small-group, and large-group situations
☑ Collaborating effectively with others when working in groups or teams
☑ Overcoming shyness
☑ Developing more meaningful and intimate relationships
☑ Resolving interpersonal conflicts assertively, rather than in aggressively or passively
☑ Providing feedback to others in a constructive and considerate manner
☑ Relating effectively with others from different cultural backgrounds and lifestyles
☑ Developing leadership skills

4. **Ethical development.** Developing a clear value system for guiding life choices and decisions and building moral character, or the ability to make and act on ethical judgments and to demonstrate consistency between convictions (beliefs) and commitments (actions).

Goals and skills:

☑ Gaining deeper self-awareness of personal values and ethical assumptions
☑ Making personal choices and life decisions based on a meaningful value system
☑ Developing the capacity to think and act with personal integrity and authenticity
☑ Using electronic technology in an ethical and civil manner
☑ Resisting social pressure to act in ways that are inconsistent with personal values
☑ Treating others in an ethical manner
☑ Knowing how to exercise individual freedom without infringing on the rights of others
☑ Developing concern and commitment for human rights and social justice
☑ Developing the courage to confront those who violate the rights of others
☑ Becoming a responsible citizen

"It's not stress that kills us, it is our reaction to it."

–Hans Selye, Canadian endocrinologist and author of *Stress Without Distress*

Chi rispetta sara rippetato.

("Respect others and you will be respected.")

–Italian proverb

"The moral challenge is simply to abide by the knowledge we already have."

–Soren Kierkegaard, nineteenth-century Danish philosopher and theologian

"If you don't stand for something you will fall for anything."

–Malcolm X, African American Muslim minister, public speaker, and human rights activist

5. **Physical development.** Applying knowledge about how the human body functions to prevent disease, preserve wellness, and promote peak performance.
   Goals and skills:
   - ☑ Maintaining awareness of your physical condition and state of health
   - ☑ Applying knowledge about exercise and fitness training to promote physical and mental health
   - ☑ Understanding how sleep patterns affect health and performance
   - ☑ Maintaining a healthy balance among work, recreation and relaxation
   - ☑ Applying knowledge of nutrition to reduce the risk of illness and promote optimal performance
   - ☑ Becoming knowledgeable about nutritional imbalances and eating disorders
   - ☑ Developing a positive physical self-image
   - ☑ Becoming knowledgeable about the effects of drugs and their impact on physical and mental well-being
   - ☑ Being knowledgeable about human sexuality and sexually transmitted diseases
   - ☑ Understanding how biological differences between the sexes affect male–female relationships and gender orientation

6. **Spiritual development.** Searching for answers to the big questions, such as the meaning or purpose of life and death, and exploring nonmaterial issues that transcend human life and the physical world.
   Goals and skills:
   - ☑ Developing a personal philosophy or worldview about the meaning and purpose of human existence
   - ☑ Appreciating what cannot be completely understood
   - ☑ Appreciating the mysteries associated with the origin of the universe
   - ☑ Searching for the connection between the self and the larger world or cosmos
   - ☑ Searching for the mystical or supernatural—that which transcends the boundaries of the natural world
   - ☑ Being open to examining questions relating to death and life after death
   - ☑ Being open to examining questions about the possible existence of a supreme being or higher power
   - ☑ Being knowledgeable about different approaches to spirituality and their underlying beliefs or assumptions
   - ☑ Understanding the difference and relationship between faith and reason
   - ☑ Becoming aware and tolerant of religious beliefs and practices

7. **Vocational development.** Exploring career options, making career choices wisely, and developing skills needed for lifelong career success.
   Goals and skills:
   - ☑ Understanding the relationship between college majors and careers
   - ☑ Using effective strategies for exploring and identifying potential careers
   - ☑ Selecting career options that are consistent with your personal values, interests, and talents
   - ☑ Acquiring work experience in career fields that relate to your occupational interests
   - ☑ Developing an effective résumé and portfolio

"A man too busy to take care of his health is like a mechanic too busy to take care of his tools."

–Spanish proverb

Student Perspective

"You may think I'm here, living for the 'now' . . . but I'm not. Half of my life revolves around the invisible and immaterial. At some point, every one of us has asked the Big Questions surrounding our existence: What is the meaning of life? Is my life inherently purposeful and valuable?"

–College student (Dalton, Eberhardt, Bracken, & Echols, 2006)

"Everyone is a house with four rooms: a physical, a mental, an emotional, and a spiritual. Most of us tend to live in one room most of the time but unless we go into every room every day, even if only to keep it aired, we are not complete."

–Native American proverb

"Your work is to discover your work and then with all your heart to give yourself to it."

–Hindu Siddhartha Prince Gautama Siddharta, a.k.a. Buddha, founder of the philosophy and religion of Buddhism

- ☑ Adopting effective strategies for identifying individuals to serve as personal references and for improving the quality of personal letters of recommendation
- ☑ Acquiring effective job-search strategies
- ☑ Using effective strategies for writing letters of inquiry and applications to potential employers
- ☑ Developing strategies for performing well in personal interviews
- ☑ Acquiring effective networking skills for developing personal contacts with potential employers

8. **Personal development.** Developing positive self-beliefs, personal attitudes, and personal habits.
Goals and skills:

- ☑ Developing a strong sense of personal identity and a coherent self-concept (e.g., "Who am I?")
- ☑ Finding a sense of purpose direction in life (e.g., "Who will I become?")
- ☑ Developing self-respect and self-esteem
- ☑ Increasing self-confidence
- ☑ Developing self-efficacy, or the belief that events and outcomes in life are influenced or controlled by personal initiative and effort
- ☑ Setting realistic personal goals and priorities
- ☑ Becoming self-motivated and self-disciplined
- ☑ Developing the perseverance and persistence to reach long-range goals
- ☑ Acquiring practical skills for managing personal affairs effectively and efficiently
- ☑ Becoming independent and self-reliant

> "Remember, no one can make you feel inferior without your consent."
>
> –Eleanor Roosevelt, UN diplomat and humanitarian

> "I'm a great believer in luck and I find the harder I work, the more I have of it."
>
> –Thomas Jefferson

◆ The Cocurriculum: Using the Whole Campus to Develop the Whole Person

To maximize the impact of a liberal arts education, you need to take advantage of the total college environment. This includes not only the courses you take in the college curriculum, but also the learning experiences you have outside the classroom, known as the cocurriculum. Cocurricular experiences include all educational discussions you have with your peers and professors outside the classroom, as well as your participation in the various events and programs offered on your campus. As mentioned, research clearly indicates that out-of-class learning experiences are as important to your overall development as the course curriculum (Kuh, 1995; Kuh, Douglas, Lund, & Ramin-Gyurnek, 1994), hence the term "co"-curriculum.

The learning that takes place in college courses is primarily vicarious—that is, you learn from or through somebody else—by listening to professors in class and by reading outside of class. While this type of academic learning is valuable, it needs to be complemented by experiential learning (i.e., learning directly through firsthand experiences). For example, leadership cannot be developed solely by listening to lectures and reading books about

Pause for Reflection

Look back and count the number of checkmarks you've placed by each of the eight areas of self-development. Did you find that you placed roughly the same number of checkmarks in all eight areas, or were there large discrepancies across the eight areas?

Based on the checkmarks that you placed in each area, would you say that your interests in self-development are balanced across elements of the self, or do they suggest a strong interest in certain dimensions of yourself, with little interest in others?

Do you think you will eventually develop a more balanced set of interests across these different dimensions of self-development?

leadership. To fully develop your leadership skills, you need to have leadership experiences, such as those developed by "leading a [discussion] group in class, holding office in student government or by being captain of a sports team" (Association of American Colleges & Universities, 2002, p. 30). Fully using campus resources is one of the keys to college success, so take advantage of your whole college to develop yourself as a whole person.

Listed in **Snapshot Summary 1.1** are some programs and services included in a cocurriculum, accompanied by the primary dimension of the self that they are designed to develop.

> "To educate liberally, learning experiences must be offered which facilitate maturity of the whole person. These are goals of student development and clearly they are consistent with the mission and goals of liberal education."
>
> −Theodore Berg, "Student Development and Liberal Education"

Snapshot Summary   1.1

Cocurricular Programs and Services Promoting Dimensions of Holistic Development

Intellectual Development
- Academic advising
- Learning center services
- College library
- Tutoring services
- Information technology services
- Campus speakers
- Concerts, theater productions, and art shows

Emotional and Social Development
- Student activities
- Student clubs and organizations
- Counseling services
- Peer counseling
- Peer mentoring
- Residential life programs
- Commuter programs

Ethical Development
- Judicial Review Board
- Student government
- Integrity committees and task forces

Physical Development
- Student health services
- Wellness programs
- Campus athletic activities and intramural sports

Spiritual Development
- College chaplain
- Campus ministry
- Peer ministry

Vocational Development
- Career development services
- Internships programs
- Service learning experiences
- Work–study programs
- Major and career fairs

Personal Development
- Financial aid services
- Campus workshops on self-management (e.g., managing time or money)

Note: This list represents just a sample of the total number of programs and services that may be available on your campus. As you can see from the list's length, colleges and universities are organized to promote your development in multiple ways. The power of the liberal arts is magnified when you combine coursework and cocurricular experiences to create a college experience that contributes to your development as a whole person.

> **Remember**
>
> A liberal arts education includes both the curriculum and the cocurriculum; it involves strategic use of the total college environment, both inside and outside the classroom.

◆ Broadening Your Perspective of the World Around You

You should know more than yourself; you should know your world. The liberal arts education helps you move beyond yourself and expands your perspective to include the wider world around you (Braskamp, 2008). The components of this larger perspective are organized and illustrated in **Figure 1.2**.

In Figure 1.2, the center circle represents the self. Fanning out to the right of the self is a series of arches that encompasses the *social–spatial perspective*; this perspective includes increasingly larger social groups and more distant places, ranging from the narrowest perspective (the individual) to the widest perspective (the universe). The liberal arts liberate you from the narrow tunnel vision of a self-centered (egocentric) perspective, providing a panoramic perspective of the world that enables you to move outside yourself and see yourself in relation to other people and other places.

To the left of the self in Figure 1.2 are three arches labeled the *chronological perspective*; this perspective includes the three dimensions of time: past (historical), present (contemporary), and future (futuristic). The liberal arts not only widen your perspective but also lengthen it by stretching your vision beyond the present—enabling you to see yourself in relation to humans who've lived before you and will live after you. The chronological perspective gives you hindsight to see where the world has been, insight into the world's current condition, and foresight to see where the world may be going.

It could be said that the chronological perspective provides you with a mental time machine for flashing back to the past and flashing forward to the future, and the social–spatial perspective provides you with a conceptual telescope for viewing people and places that are far away. Together, these two

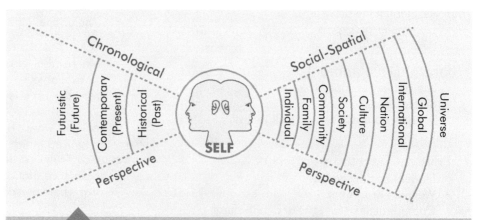

Figure 1.2 Multiple Perspectives Developed by the Liberal Arts

broadening perspectives of the liberal arts enable to you to appreciate the experience of anyone living anywhere at any time.

The elements that comprise each of these broadening perspectives are provided in the next sections.

◆ Elements of the Social–Spatial Perspective

The Family Perspective

Moving beyond the perspective of your individual self, you are part of a larger social unit—your family. The people with whom you were raised have almost certainly influenced the person you are today and how you got to be that way. Moreover, your family hasn't only influenced you; you've also influenced your family. For example, your decision to go to college may make your parents and grandparents proud and may influence the decision of other members of your family to attend college. In addition, if you have children, graduating from college will have a positive influence on their future welfare. As mentioned in the introduction to this book, children of college graduates experience improved intellectual development, better physical health, and greater economic security (Bowen, 1977, 1997; Pascarella & Terenzini, 1991, 2005).

The Community Perspective

Moving beyond the family, you are also a member of a larger social unit—your community. This wider social circle includes friends and neighbors at home, at school, and at work. These are communities where you can begin to take action to improve the world around you. If you want to make the world a better place, this is the place to start—through civic engagement in your local communities.

Civically responsible people also demonstrate civic concern by stepping beyond their narrow self-interests to selflessly volunteer time and energy to help members of their community, particularly those in need. They demonstrate their humanity by being humane (they show genuine compassion for others who are less fortunate than they are) and by being humanitarian (they work to promote the welfare of other humans).

> "Think globally, act locally."
> —Patrick Geddes, Scottish urban planner and social activist

> "Get involved. Don't gripe about things unless you are making an effort to change them. You can make a difference if you dare."
> —Richard C. Holbrooke, former director of the Peace Corps and American ambassador to the United Nations

The Societal Perspective

Moving beyond our local communities, we are also members of a larger society that includes people from different regions of the country, cultural backgrounds, and social classes.

In human societies, groups of people are typically stratified into social classes with unequal levels of resources, such monetary wealth. According to U.S. Census (2000) figures, the wealthiest 20 percent of the American population controls approximately 50 percent of the total American income, while the 20 percent with the lowest level of income controls 4 percent of the nation's wealth. Sharp differences in income level exist among people of different race, ethnicity, and gender. A recent survey revealed that Black households had the lowest median income in 2007 ($33,916), compared to a median income of $54,920 for non-Hispanic White households (Current Population Survey Annual Social and Economic Supplement, 2008).

> "[Liberal arts education] shows you how to accommodate yourself to others, how to throw yourself into their state of mind, how to come to an understanding of them. You are at home in any society; you have common ground with every class."
> —John Henry Newman

"It is difficult to see the picture when you are inside the frame."

–Author unknown

"A progressive society counts individual variations as precious since it finds in them the means of its own growth. A democratic society must, in consistency with its ideal, allow intellectual freedom and the play of diverse gifts and interests."

–John Dewey, U.S. educator, philosopher, and psychologist

"A liberal [arts] education frees a person from the prison-house of class, race, time, place, background, family, and nation."

–Robert Hutchins, former dean of Yale Law School and president of the University of Chicago

"Treat the Earth well. It was not given to you by your parents. It was loaned to you by your children."

–Kenyan proverb

The Cultural Perspective

Culture can be broadly defined as a distinctive pattern of beliefs and values that are learned by a group of people who share the same social heritage and traditions. In short, culture is the whole way in which a group of people has learned to live (Peoples & Bailey, 2008); it includes their customary style of speaking (language), fashion, food, art, music, values, and beliefs.

Intercultural awareness is one of the outcomes of a liberal arts education (Wabash National Study, 2007). Being able to step outside of your own culture and see issues from a broader worldview enables you to perceive reality and evaluate truth from diverse vantage points. This makes your thinking more comprehensive and less ethnocentric (centered on your own culture).

The National Perspective

Besides being a member of society, you're also a citizen of a nation. Having the privilege of being a citizen in a free nation brings with it the responsibility of participating in your country's governance through the process of voting. As a democracy, the United States is a nation that has been built on the foundation of equal rights and freedom of opportunity, which are guaranteed by its constitution.

Exercise your right to vote, and when you do vote, be mindful of political leaders who are committed to ensuring equal rights, social justice, and political freedom. When the personal rights and freedom of any of our fellow citizens are threatened by prejudice and discrimination, the political stability and survival of any democratic nation is threatened.

The International Perspective

Moving beyond your particular country of citizenship, you are also a member of an international world that includes close to 200 nations (Rosenberg, 2009). Communication and interaction among citizens of different nations is greater today than at any other time in world history, largely because of rapid advances in electronic technology (Dryden & Vos, 1999; Smith, 1994). The World Wide Web is making today's world a small one indeed, and success in today's world requires an international perspective. Our lives are increasingly affected by events beyond our national borders because boundaries between nations are breaking down as a result of international travel, international trading, and multinational corporations. Employers of college graduates are placing higher value on prospective employees with international knowledge and foreign language skills (Fixman, 1990; Office of Research, 1994). By learning from and about different nations, you become more than a citizen of your own country: you become cosmopolitan—a citizen of the world.

The Global Perspective

Broader than an international perspective is the global perspective. It extends beyond the relations among citizens of different nations to include all life forms that inhabit the earth and the relationships between these diverse life forms and the earth's natural resources (minerals, air, and water). Humans share the earth and its natural resources with approximately 10 million animal species (Myers, 1997) and more than 300,000 forms of vegetative life (Knoll, 2003).

As inhabitants of this planet and as global citizens, we have an environmental responsibility to address global warming and other issues that require balancing our industrial–technological progress with the need to sustain the earth's natural resources and preserve the life of our planet's cohabitants.

The Universal Perspective

Beyond the global perspective is the broadest of all perspectives—the universe. The earth is just one planet that shares a solar system with seven other planets and is just one celestial body that shares a galaxy with millions of other celestial bodies, including stars, moons, meteorites, and asteroids (Encrenaz et al., 2004).

Just as we should guard against being ethnocentric (thinking that our culture is the center of humanity), we should guard against being geocentric (thinking that we are at the center of the universe). All heavenly bodies do not revolve around the earth; our planet revolves around them. The sun doesn't rise in the east and set in the west; our planet rotates around the sun to produce our earthly experiences of day and night.

"In astronomy, you must get used to viewing the earth as just one planet in the larger context of the universe."

–Physics professor (Donald, 2002)

"The sun, with all those planets revolving around it and dependent on it, can still ripen a bunch of grapes as if it had nothing else in the universe to do."

–Galileo Galilei

◆ Elements of the Chronological Perspective

The Historical Perspective

A historical perspective is critical for understanding the root causes of our current human condition and world situation. Humans are products of both a social and a natural history. Don't forget that the earth is estimated to be more than 4.5 billion years old and our human ancestors date back more than 250,000 years (Knoll, 2003). Thus, our current lives represent a small frame of time in a long chronological reel. Every modern convenience we now enjoy reflects the collective efforts and cumulative knowledge of diverse human groups that have accumulated over thousands of years of history. By studying the past, we can build on our ancestors' achievements and avoid their mistakes. For example, by understanding the causes and consequences of the Holocaust, we can reduce the risk that an atrocity of that size and scope will ever happen again.

Pause for Reflection

Look back at the broadening perspectives developed by a liberal arts education. What college course would develop each perspective? If you're unsure or cannot remember whether a course is designed to develop any of these perspectives, look at the course's goals described in your college catalog (in print or online).

The Contemporary Perspective

The contemporary perspective focuses on understanding the current world situation and the events that comprise today's news. One major goal of a liberal arts education is to increase your understanding the contemporary human condition so that you may have the wisdom to improve it (Miller, 1988). For example, despite historical progress in the nation's acceptance and appreciation of different ethnic and racial groups, the Unites States today remains a nation that is deeply divided with respect to culture, religion, and social class (Brooking Institute, 2008).

The current technological revolution is generating information and new knowledge at a faster rate than at any other time in human history (Dryden &

"Those who cannot remember the past are damned to repeat it."

–George Santayana, Spanish-born American philosopher

"Yesterday is gone. Tomorrow has not yet come. We have only today. Let us begin."

–Mother Teresa of Calcutta, Albanian, Catholic nun and winner of the Nobel Peace Prize

"The only person who is educated is the one who has learned how to learn and change."

–Carl Rogers, humanistic psychologist and Nobel Peace Prize nominee

"In times of change, learners inherit the Earth . . . [they] find themselves beautifully equipped to deal with a world that no longer exists."

–Eric Hoffer, author of *The Ordeal of Change* (XXXX) and recipient of the Presidential Medal of Freedom

"The future is literally in our hands to mold as we like. But we cannot wait until tomorrow. Tomorrow is now."

–Eleanor Roosevelt

"We all inherit the past. We all confront the challenges of the present. We all participate in the making of the future."

–Ernest Boyer and Martin Kaplan, *Educating for Survival*

Pause for Reflection

In light of the information you've read in this chapter, how would you interpret the following statement: "We can't know where we're going until we know where we've been"?

"A truly great intellect is one which takes a connected view of old and new, past and present, far and near, and which has an insight into the influence of all these on one another, without which there is no whole, and no center."

–John Henry Newman, *The Idea of a University* (1852)

Vos, 1999). Knowledge quickly becomes obsolete when there is rapid creation and communication of new information (Naisbitt, 1982). Workers in the today's complex, fast-changing world need to continually update their skills to perform their jobs and advance in their careers (Niles & Harris-Bowlsbey, 2002). This creates a demand for workers who have learned how to learn, a hallmark of the liberal arts.

The Futuristic Perspective

The futuristic perspective allows us to flash forward and envision what our world will be like years from now. This perspective focuses on such questions as "Will we leave the world a better or worse place for humans who will inhabit after our departure, including our children and grandchildren?" and "How can humans living today avoid short-term, shortsighted thinking and adopt a long-range vision that anticipates the consequences of their current actions on future generations of humans?"

To sum up, a comprehensive chronological perspective brings the past, present, and future into focus on a single screen. It enables us to see how the current world is a single segment of a temporal sequence that's been shaped by events that preceded it and will shape future events.

Remember

By embracing the perspectives of different times, places, and people, you're embracing the diversity promoted by a liberal arts education. These diverse perspectives liberate or emancipate you from the here and now and empower you to see things long ago and far away.

◆ The Synoptic Perspective: Integrating Diverse Perspectives to Form a Unified Whole

A liberal arts education helps you not only appreciate multiple perspectives but also integrate them into a meaningful whole (King, Brown, Lindsay, & VanHencke, 2007). Understanding of how the perspectives of time, place, and person interrelate to form a unified whole is sometimes referred to as a synoptic perspective (Cronon, 1998; Heath, 1977). The word derives from a combination of two roots: syn, meaning "together" (as in the word "synthesize"), and optic, meaning "to see." Thus, a "synoptic" perspective literally means to "see things together" or "see the whole." It enables you to see how all the trees come together to form the forest.

A liberal arts education helps you step beyond yourself to see the wider world and connects you with it. By seeing yourself as an integral part of humankind, you become integrated with the whole of humanity; you're able to see how you, as an individual, fit into the big picture—the larger scheme of things (Heath, 1968). When we view ourselves as nested within a web of interconnections with other places, cultures, and times, we become aware of the common humanity we all share. This increased sense of connection with humankind decreases our feelings of personal isolation or alienation (Bellah, Madsen, Sullivan, Swidler, & Tipton, 1985). In his book The Perfect Education, Kenneth Eble (1966, pp. 214–215) skillfully describes this benefit of a liberal arts education:

> It can provide that overarching life of a people, a community, a world that was going on before the individual came onto the scene and that will continue on after [s]he departs. By such means we come to see the world not alone. Our joys are more intense for being shared. Our sorrows are less destructive for our knowing universal sorrow. Our fears of death fade before the commonness of the occurrence.

> "Without exception, the observed changes [during college] involve greater breadth, expansion, and appreciation for the new and different. These changes are eminently consistent with values of a liberal [arts] education, and the evidence for their presence is compelling."
>
> –Ernest Pascarella and Pat Terenzini, How College Affects Students

!

Remember

A liberal arts education launches you on a quest for two forms of wholeness: (a) an *inner* wholeness in which elements of self become connected to form a *whole person*, and (b) an *outer* wholeness in which your individual self becomes connected with the *whole world*. This inner and outer quest will enable you to lead a richer, more fulfilling life that's filled with greater breadth, balance, and wholeness.

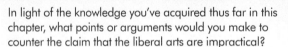

Pause for Reflection

In light of the knowledge you've acquired thus far in this chapter, what points or arguments would you make to counter the claim that the liberal arts are impractical?

◆ Educating You for Life

Research shows that the primary reasons students go to college are to prepare for a career and get a better job (Sax, Lindholm, Astin, Korn, & Mahoney, 2004). While these are important reasons and your career is an important element of your life, a person's vocation or occupation represents just one element of the self. It also represents just one of many roles or responsibilities that you are likely to have in life.

Similar to global issues, personal issues and challenges that individuals face in their everyday lives are multidimensional, requiring perspectives and skills that go well beyond the boundaries of a single academic field or career specialization. Your occupational role represents just one of many roles you assume in life, which include the roles of family member, friend, co-worker, community member, citizen, and possibly, mother or father. A liberal arts education provides you with the breadth of knowledge and the variety skills needed to successfully accommodate the multiple roles and responsibilities you face in life.

> "Virtually all occupational endeavors require a working appreciation of the historical, cultural, ethical, and global environments that surround the application of skilled work."
>
> –Robert Jones, "Liberal Education for the Twenty-First Century: Business Expectations"

> "The finest art, the most difficult art, is the art of living."
>
> –John Albert Macy, American author, poet, and editor of Helen Keller's autobiography

Personal Story

One life role that a liberal arts education helped prepare me for was the role of parent. Courses that I took in psychology and sociology proved to be useful in helping me understand how children develop and how a parent can best support them at different stages of their development. Surprisingly, however, there was one course I took in college that I never expected would ever help me as a parent. That course was statistics, which I took to fulfill a general education requirement in mathematics. It was not a particularly enjoyable course; some of my classmates sarcastically referred to it as "sadistics" because they felt it was a somewhat painful or torturous experience. However, what I learned in that course became valuable to me many years later when, as a parent, my 14-year-old son (Tony) developed a life-threatening disease, leukemia, which is a form of cancer that attacks blood cells. Tony's form of leukemia was a particularly perilous one because it had only a 35 percent average cure rate; in other words, 65 percent of those who develop the disease don't recover and eventually die from it. This statistic was based on patients that received the traditional treatment of chemotherapy, which was the type of treatment that my son began receiving when his cancer was first detected.

Another option for treating Tony's cancer was a bone-marrow transplant, which involved using radiation to destroy all of his own bone marrow (that was making the abnormal blood cells) and replace it with bone marrow donated to him by another person. My wife and I got opinions from doctors at two major cancer centers—one from a center that specialized in chemotherapy, and one from a center that specialized in bone-marrow transplants. The chemotherapy doctors felt strongly that drug treatment would be the better way to treat and cure Tony, and the bone-marrow transplant doctors felt strongly that his chances of survival would be much better if he had a transplant. So, my wife and I had to decide between two opposing recommendations, each made by a respected group of doctors.

To help us reach a decision, I asked both teams of doctors for research studies that had been done on the effectiveness of chemotherapy and bone-marrow transplants for treating my son's particular type of cancer. I read all of these studies and carefully analyzed their statistical findings. I remembered from my statistics course that when an average is calculated for a general group of people (e.g., average cure rate for people with leukemia), it tends to lump together individuals from different subgroups (e.g., males and females or young children and teenagers). Sometimes, when separate statistics are calculated for different subgroups, the results may be different from the average statistic for the whole group. So, when I read the research reports, I looked for any subgroup statistics that may have been calculated. I found two subgroups of patients with my son's particular type of cancer that had a higher rate of cure with chemotherapy than the general (whole-group) average of 35 percent. One subgroup included people with a low number of abnormal cells at the time when the cancer was first diagnosed, and the other subgroup consisted of people whose cancer cells dropped rapidly after their first week of chemotherapy. My son belonged to both of these subgroups, which meant that his chance for cure with chemotherapy was higher than the overall 35 percent average. Furthermore, I found that the statistics showing higher success rate for bone-marrow transplants were based only on patients whose body accepted the donor's bone marrow and did not include those who died because their body rejected the donor's bone marrow. So, the success rates for bone-marrow patients were not actually as high as they appeared to be, because the overall average did not include the subgroup of patients who died because of transplant rejection. Based on these statistics, my wife and I decided to go with chemotherapy and not the transplant operation.

Our son has now been cancer free for more than 5 years, so we think we made the right decision. However, I never imagined that a statistics course, which I took many years ago to fulfill a general education requirement, would help me fulfill my role as a parent and help me make a life-or-death decision about my own son.

—Joe Cuseo

Remember

The liberal arts education not only prepares you for a career but also prepares you for life.

◆ Summary and Conclusion

General education represents the foundation of a college education upon which all academic majors are built. It promotes success in any major and career by supplying students with a set of lifelong learning skills that can be applied in multiple settings and that can be continually used throughout life.

General education promotes development of the whole person (intellectual, emotional, social, physical, spiritual, etc.) and broadens your perspective on the world by expanding (a) your social–spatial perspective to include increasingly larger social groups and more distant places, from the individual to the universe; and (b) your chronological perspective to include the past, present, and future.

Despite popular beliefs the contrary, the liberal arts have many practical benefits, including promoting career mobility and career advancement. Most importantly, a liberal arts education prepares you for life roles other than an occupation, including roles such as family member, community member, and citizen. In short, a liberal arts education prepares you for than a career; it prepares you for life.

Learning More Through the World Wide Web

Internet-Based Resources for Further Information on Liberal Arts Education

For additional information related to the ideas discussed in this chapter, we recommend the following Web sites:

Liberal Arts Education: **www.aacu.org/resources/liberaleducation/index.cfm**

Liberal Arts Resources: **www.eace.org/networks/liberalarts.html**

1.1 Planning Your Liberal Arts Education

Since general education is an essential component of your college experience, it should be intentionally planned. This exercise will leave you with a flexible plan that capitalizes on your educational interests while ensuring that your college experience has both breadth and balance.

1. Use your course catalog (bulletin) to identify the general education requirements at your college. The requirements should be organized into general divisions of knowledge similar to those discussed in this chapter (humanities, fine arts, natural sciences, etc.) Within each of these liberal arts divisions, you'll find specific courses listed that fulfill the general education requirements for that particular division. (Catalogs can sometimes be difficult to navigate; if you encounter difficulty or doubt about general education requirements, seek clarification from an academic advisor on campus).

2. You'll probably have some freedom to choose courses from a larger group of courses that fulfill general education requirements within each division. Use your freedom of choice to choose courses whose descriptions capture your curiosity or pique your interest. You can take liberal arts courses not only to fulfill general education requirements but also to test your interest and talent in fields that you may end up choosing as a college major or minor.

3. Highlight the courses in the catalog that you plan to take to fulfill your general education requirements in each division of the liberal arts, and use the form that follows to pencil in the courses you've chosen. (Use pencil because you will likely make some adjustments to your plan.) Remember that the courses you're taking this term may be fulfilling certain general education requirements, so be sure to list them on your planning form.

1.2 General Education Planning Form

Division of the Liberal Arts Curriculum: _____

General education courses you're planning to take to fulfill requirements in this division (record the course number and course title):

_____   _____

_____   _____

_____   _____

Division of the Liberal Arts Curriculum: _____

General education courses you're planning to take to fulfill requirements in this division (record the course number and course title):

_____   _____

_____   _____

_____   _____

Division of the Liberal Arts Curriculum: _____

General education courses you're planning to take to fulfill requirements in this division (record the course number and course title):

_____   _____

_____   _____

_____   _____

Division of the Liberal Arts Curriculum: _____

General education courses you're planning to take to fulfill requirements in this division (record the course number and course title):

_____   _____

_____   _____

_____   _____

Division of the Liberal Arts Curriculum: _____

General education courses you're planning to take to fulfill requirements in this division (record the course number and course title):

_____   _____

_____   _____

_____   _____

4. Look back at the general education courses you've listed and identify the broadening perspectives developed by the liberal arts that each course appears to be developing. Use the form that follows to ensure that your overall perspective is comprehensive and that you have no blind spots in your liberal arts education. For any perspective that's not covered in your plan, find a course in the catalog that will enable you to address the missing perspective.

Broadening Social–Spatial Perspectives

Perspective	Course Developing This Perspective
Self	_____
Family	_____
Community	_____
Society	_____
Culture	_____
Nation	_____
International	_____
Global	_____
Universe	_____

Broadening Chronological Perspectives

Perspective	Course Developing This Perspective
Historical	_____
Contemporary	_____
Futuristic	_____

5. Look back at the general education courses you've listed and identify what element of holistic (whole-person) development each course appears to be developing. Use the form that follows to ensure that your course selection didn't overlook any element of the self. For any element that's not covered in your plan, find a course in the catalog or a cocurricular experience program that will enable you to address the missing area. For cocurricular learning experiences (e.g., leadership and volunteer experiences), consult your student handbook or contact someone in the Office of Student Life.

Dimensions of Self	Course or Cocurricular Experience Developing This Dimension of Self (Consult your student handbook for cocurricular experiences.)
Intellectual	_____
Emotional	_____
Social	_____
Ethical	_____
Physical	_____
Spiritual	_____
Vocational	_____
Personal	_____

Remember

This general education plan is not set in stone; it may be modified as you gain more experience with the college curriculum and campus life. Its purpose is not to restrict your educational exploration or experimentation but to give it some direction, breadth, and balance.

Dazed and Confused: General Education versus Career Specialization

Joe Tech was really looking forward to college because he thought he would have freedom to select the courses he wanted and the opportunity to get into the major of his choice (computer science). However, he's shocked and disappointed with his first-term schedule of classes because it consists mostly of required general education courses that do not seem to relate in any way to his major. He's frustrated further because some of these courses are about subjects that he already took in high school (English, history, and biology). He's beginning to think he would be better off quitting college and going to a technical school where he could get right into computer science and immediately begin to acquire the knowledge and skills he'll need to prepare him for his intended career.

Reflection and Discussion Questions

1. Can you relate to this student, or do you know of students who feel the same way as Joe does?

2. If Joe decides to leave college for a technical school, how do you see it affecting his future: (a) in the short run and (b) in the long run?

3. Do you see any way Joe might strike a balance between pursuing his career interest and obtaining his college degree so that he could work toward achieving both goals at the same time?

Promoting Self-Awareness—Create Your "I Am" Poem

The "I Am" Poem provides you an opportunity to reflect on your life and become aware of the different dimensions of the self. You will write unique information about yourself to help develop further insight regarding things that are important to you; it may also point out the things that inspire and provoke you. This poem will serve as a starting point in helping you to understand elements of your holistic development.

The "I Am" Poem begins with you describing two things about yourself; write two special things that other people might not know about you. Avoid obvious and ordinary characteristics, such as: "I am exciting and personable." Instead, think of things about yourself that are distinctive, such as: "I am someone who lives life to the fullest and enjoys being around positive people." The second example above is better because it gives a sense of your uniqueness. Dare to be different—because you are!

Below you will find a line-by-line guide to follow. The first two words of each line are required for your poem; you construct the rest of the line (the words in parentheses) based on your own thoughts, feelings and/or experiences. This poem is most effective when written based on the first thoughts that come to mind; therefore, set a time limit to complete the poem.

I Am
I am (describe two interesting characteristics about yourself).
I notice (describe something you study or observe in other people).
I see (describe something you see—real or imaginary).
I feel (describe the way you feel about something or someone in your life).
I say (describe something you say out loud or to yourself).
I touch (describe something that you touch—real or imaginary).
I need (describe something that you MUST have).
I yearn (describe something positive you want from other people).
I love (describe something or someone you have a deep love for).
I am (describe something unique about yourself).

I pretend (describe something that you pretend to do).
I cry (describe something that makes you cry).
I worry (describe something you worry about).
I understand (describe something you accept or know to be true).
I hear (describe a sound you hear—real or imaginary).
I wonder (describe something you are curious about).
I imagine (describe a "picture" or "image" you have in your head about life).
I believe (describe something you believe could happen to you).
I plan (describe how you want to make a difference in the world).
I am (describe something positive about you that you give or share with others).

I value (describe something that's very important to you).
I want (describe a change you want to see in the world).
I will (describe one thing that you will do to make a change in your life).
I appreciate (describe something that you're grateful for or thankful for).
I cherish (describe something that you hold close to your heart or something you treasure).
I desire (describe something you actually long for/crave).
I dream (describe something you dream about).
I wish (describe something you want to come true).
I hope (describe something you hope for others).
I am (describe how you feel right now as you complete this exercise).

Adapted from William H. Johnson, Jr., Office of Life Planning & Personal Development, The University of North Carolina at Greensboro.

I Am Poem

I am _____

I notice _____

I see _____

I feel _____

I say _____

I touch _____

I need _____

I yearn _____

I love _____

I am _____

I pretend _____

I cry _____

I worry _____

I understand _____

I hear _____

I wonder _____

I imagine _____

I believe _____

I plan _____

I am _____

I value _____

I want _____

I will _____

I appreciate _____

I cherish _____

I desire _____

I dream _____

I wish _____

I hope _____

I am _____

Adapted from William H. Johnson, Jr., Office of Life Planning & Personal Development, The University of North Carolina at Greensboro.

Examples

I am a simple and complicated person.	I am a person who champions cultural diversity, and enjoys creative expression.
I notice how similar and different people can be.	I notice when people smile with their eyes.
I see something good in nearly everyone I meet.	I see artistic inspiration every day.
I feel like I'm always waiting for something better out of life.	I feel happy when someone I respect compliments me.
I say a lot of things with sarcasm.	I say "Make time, not excuses."
I touch soft things as I walk through stores.	I touch others by encouraging them with positive energy.
I need alone time to reflect every once in a while.	I need to challenge myself by stepping out of my comfort zone.
I yearn for complete acceptance from another person.	I yearn for genuine companionship.
I love to make grand Italian dinners.	I love the positive feelings of accomplishment and productivity.
I am musically and academically talented.	I am most creative when I feel completely engulfed in my emotions.
I pretend that everything is fine until I can't suppress it anymore.	I pretend that I always have *it* together.
I cry when I watch romantic movies.	I cry when my efforts are futile.
I worry about my family's finances.	I worry about missing opportunities or being oblivious of critical moments.
I understand that my past experiences have shaped me.	I understand that emotions can get the best of people.
I hear popular songs as marching band music.	I hear a musical beat everywhere.
I wonder what people and life are like in other countries.	I wonder how many people actually understand 'regret'.
I imagine multiple scenarios for every situation I come across.	I imagine having my own classroom to teach.
I believe that my future holds success, marriage, and children.	I believe I will always have a thirst for knowledge.
I plan on sharing my joy with the world.	I plan on encouraging others to always accept, respect, and love.
I am a good listener.	I am a very motivated person who wants to inspire others.
I value not always being serious.	I value creativity, education, and the pursuit of knowledge.
I want society to put less emphasis on trivial matters.	I want people to live more and text less.
I will never forget the importance of God.	I will choose the path that best suits me.
I appreciate the opportunities and gifts that life has given me.	I appreciate meaningful relations that foster personal growth and true happiness.
I cherish my relationships with family and friends.	I cherish personal connections.
I desire to feel like time isn't flying by.	I desire to be fluent in many languages.
I dream about crazy, random things.	I dream about success and fulfillment in my life.
I wish the world was a more peaceful place.	I wish for a career in education.
I hope for others to find true happiness.	I hope others will see the good in everybody else.
I am myself and no one else.	I am excited about life.

Adapted from William H. Johnson, Jr., Office of Life Planning & Personal Development, The University of North Carolina at Greensboro.

UNCG'S History

From the 19th to the 21st Century

Betty H. Carter

Edited by Erin Lawrimore, University Archivist,
University Libraries

In the 1880s, the state of North Carolina was poverty-stricken, struggling to recover from the Civil War just 20 years before. There were no public school systems, although several communities had established "graded schools," which were considered innovative for the time. The vast majority of the schools were "subscription" schools, formed when parents in a particular neighborhood pooled their resources to provide a school and teacher for their children. Unfortunately, these schools were usually very small, poorly equipped, and open, on average, less than three months during the year. A number of social leaders across the state argued that a more robust public education system was the key to moving North Carolina—and the entire South—out of postwar poverty.

◆The Normal

In 1883, a group of leading educators in the state formed the North Carolina Teachers Assembly. Led by Charles Duncan McIver and Edwin Alderman, the members of this organization supported the establishment of a state-supported "normal school," a school designed to train teachers. A committee from the Teachers Assembly approached the General Assembly of North Carolina in 1887 asking that a state-supported, coeducational normal school be established. This effort failed, as did a similar effort in 1889; however, on the third try, in 1891, a teacher training school exclusively for women was created and named the State Normal and Industrial School.

In May 1891, Greensboro was chosen as the site of the new school, and Charles Duncan McIver was selected as its first president. Opening a week behind schedule, on October 5, 1892, the new school enrolled 176 girls on the first day. By the end of the month, enrollment had risen to 198 students before reaching 223 by the end of the first school year.

Lula Martin McIver, wife of the new president of the school, described the campus on that first day as having two buildings, ten acres of mud, and one tree. She was partially correct. There were two main buildings: the Main Building and Brick Dormitory. It was quite muddy after heavy rain, so wooden boards had been put down to protect the girls' dresses. There was one tree on the front campus, but since the campus was on the edge of the city in a farming area, there were many cornstalks. The campus did, however, have more than two buildings. In addition to the Main Building and the Brick Dormitory, the school had a second dormitory, known as Wooden Dormitory; the McIver home; a laundry shed; and a stable for the McIver horse and buggy. The only building to survive from this original campus is the Main Building, known today as the Foust Building.

The school benefited from McIver's national reputation and contacts, and opened with an excellent faculty. At Mrs. McIver's insistence, the campus also had a female medical doctor on campus at all times for the girls. Three main areas of curriculum were available for study: commercial (typing, shorthand, and accounting), domestic science (a predecessor to home economics), and pedagogy (teaching). Graduation from the Normal in the area of pedagogy would give the graduate a lifelong license to teach in North Carolina.

Opponents of the Normal did not believe that it was the state's business to educate women, and questioned whether women could handle such academic topics. It has been suggested that much of this opposition was due to the fact that the Normal gave college-bound students another option for education, taking students away from church-supported and other private colleges.

The Normal thrived from the beginning, even though it experienced several catastrophes within its first 15 years. In the fall of 1899, a typhoid epidemic closed the school for over two months. Thirteen students and one staff member died. In January 1904, Brick Dormitory burned, leaving over 300 girls without housing or anything other than the clothing they were wearing. Perhaps the greatest tragedy of all, however, occurred in September 1906, when President Charles McIver suffered a stroke and died ten days short of his 46th birthday.

Julius Isaac Foust was named acting president in 1906 and made president in 1907. He had come to the school in 1902 as head of the Department of Pedagogy and been named dean of the Normal in 1904. Foust was well liked by students and is remembered as a successful president; he was also the longest-serving chief executive of the school, holding the office for 28 years.

North Carolina College for Women (NCCW)

Foust has been called the "builder" of the campus. While he was president, at least 30 buildings or major building additions were added to the campus, most of them during the 1920s. The prelude to the construction boom began in 1909 with the opening of the first section of the first McIver Building. A large infirmary was completed in 1912, followed shortly by two dormitories: Woman's and Kirkland.

During the 1920s, new buildings seemed to appear overnight, including the seven dormitories in the Quad, Rosenthal Gym, Aycock Auditorium, the Brown Building, the first part of the Stone Building, and new additions to the first McIver Building and the Carnegie Library, known today as the Forney Building. Since faculty members were having problems finding appropriate housing, Foust ordered seven Aladdin House kits, which were built on the edge of the campus. The Chancellor's Residence was completed in 1923. During the 1920s, Spring Garden Street, College Avenue, and other streets on and near the College were paved.

In addition to a growth in campus construction, Foust's tenure saw the growth of the faculty and campus activities. Several well-known faculty members, some later to have buildings named in their legacy, came during Foust's tenure, including Harriet Wiseman Elliott, Walter Clinton Jackson, Wade Brown, Raymond Taylor, and Mary Channing Coleman. The *Alumnae News* began in 1912; the Student Government was established on campus in 1914; the *Carolinian*, the student newspaper, began in 1919; and the literary magazine known as the *State Normal Magazine* was renamed *Coraddi* in the same year. The first master's degree was awarded in 1922. Also during Foust's administration, the school earned accreditation in 1921 from the Association of Secondary Schools and Colleges of the Southern States. Only three North Carolina colleges were accredited earlier—Duke, UNC at Chapel Hill, and Davidson. Meredith and Wake Forest also gained accreditation in 1921.

The WC

The school's name changed twice during the Foust years. In 1919, it became the North Carolina College for Women (NCCW), and in 1931, it became the Woman's College of the University of North Carolina, commonly referred to as the "WC."

Only a year after becoming the WC, however, the school admitted its first group of male students. During the Great Depression years of 1932–1933, 80 young men from Greensboro attended the Woman's College because they could not afford to go anywhere else. Foust was hoping that these men would provide the opening wedge for the school to become co-ed, but the experiment lasted only one school year.

Walter Clinton Jackson became the school's chief executive in 1934 upon the retirement of President Foust. He had come to the Normal in 1909, served as head of the History Department, and had a reputation as an excellent

teacher. Jackson dealt with the usual campus problems as well as two extraordinary events of the time: the continuing Great Depression and World War II. During the 1930s, the student body decreased, and faculty salaries were slashed. Three dormitories were closed. Although enrollment returned to normal levels by the early 1940s, it would be several years before faculty salaries fully recovered.

By 1942, the WC was the largest residential women's college in the nation, attracting girls from North Carolina, the Southeast, and all along the eastern seaboard. The three most popular majors during this time were secretarial administration, home economics, and education. A few major buildings appeared on the campus during Jackson's years—the Alumni House, the Petty Building, Weil-Winfield, and the new library (which would be named for Jackson in 1960). Jackson's tenure also saw controversy in the closing of a stretch of Walker Avenue in September of 1948. The school sought to have the street closed for the safety of the students as well as for the location for a new library. For the daily commuters to downtown Greensboro, the closing of the street was not greeted with enthusiasm.

From 1891 to 1950 (59 years), the school had prospered under very stable leadership, with only three chief executives of the school (McIver, Foust, and Jackson). During the 1950s and 1960s, the school would continue to prosper, but under five different leaders. Suddenly, the chancellor's office had a revolving door. Edward Kidder Graham served from 1950 to 1956, Gordon Williams Blackwell served from 1957 to 1960, and Otis Arnold Singletary served from 1961 to 1966. William Whatley Pearson also served as acting chancellor for two separate one-year terms from 1956–1957 and 1960–1961. In 1967, with the tenure of James Sharbrough Ferguson, stability was restored to the office.

Despite these administrative upheavals, several important historical events occurred during these two decades. In the fall of 1956, the first African American students were admitted to the school—Bettye Davis Tillman and JoAnne Smart. Three more African American students came in 1957, and five more enrolled in 1958. Today, UNCG is the leader in the UNC system in minority enrollment among predominantly white institutions. JoAnne Smart Drane became a member of the UNCG Board of Trustees in 1996.

The civil rights movement also affected the WC campus. In February 1960, a landmark event occurred in Greensboro—the sit-ins at Woolworth's lunch counter located on Elm Street. Four students from North Carolina A&T College (now North Carolina A&T State University) sat at a "whites only" lunch counter and waited to be served. They were not served, but returned in the following days—with more students—to continue their nonviolent sit-in to protest the segregated lunch counter. At least four white WC students participated in these sit-ins wearing their WC class jackets, removing all doubt as to which school they attended. WC school officials worked feverishly with Greensboro city leaders and administrators from North Carolina A & T College to defuse the situation, and the WC students were reprimanded. However, the Greensboro sit-ins led to desegregation of the Woolworth's lunch counter and a spread of the nonviolent sit-in movements throughout the South.

◆ UNCG

With the creation of the UNC system in 1963, the institution known for 30 years as the Woman's College became The University of North Carolina at Greensboro (UNCG). Following this name change, men would finally be admitted as undergraduate residential students in the fall of 1964. In addition to admitting its first male students, the University also began awarding doctoral degrees during this time period. The University awarded its first PhD degree in May 1963, and by the end of Ferguson's term as chancellor in 1979, the PhD was offered in 12 areas and the master's degree in 65 areas.

Fortunately, the UNCG campus escaped the violence that hit many campuses during the turbulent 1960s and 1970s. Chancellor Ferguson safely navigated through anti-war protests, civil rights marches, a campus strike by cafeteria workers, a Black Power Forum, hippies, and streaking. In his last annual report, he said that the two greatest needs for the campus were a student recreation center and parking space.

William E. Moran served as chancellor from 1979 to 1994. His time in office was one of great growth in physical facilities, academic offerings, student life, and financial support. Seven new buildings appeared on campus, including the first parking deck, a state-of-the-art soccer stadium, and Tower Village, the first residential area built for students in 25 years.

The athletic program was upgraded from NCAA Division III to Division I in 1991, social sororities and fraternities were approved for the campus in the early 1980s, and five bachelor's, 12 master's, and four doctoral degrees were added during Moran's 15 years. Finally, the University endowment increased from $3.7 million to $42.5 million.

Moran retired in August of 1994, and Debra Stewart served a four-month term as interim chancellor. In January of 1995, Patricia A. Sullivan, the first female chancellor of the institution, began her term of office. Under Sullivan's leadership, UNCG was transformed into a high-level research university, gaining the Carnegie classification as a Research University with High Research Activity. She led this transformation, and also enhanced the school's rich heritage as a student-centered university. Enrollment grew to over 17,000 students, and over 33,000 students received degrees during her years. Graduate programs grew significantly, including nine new doctoral programs. Cam-

pus growth was supported in large part by a successful $3.1 billion NC Higher Education Bonds referendum as well as two fundraising drives on the UNCG campus. Over $500 million in renovations and new construction took place during her time at UNCG, including the Gatewood Studio Arts Building, the Moore Humanities and Research Administration Building, and the Sullivan Science Building. The campus became a more beautiful place under her leadership with the addition of the Spring Garden Streetscape, the College Avenue Pedestrian Corridor, and the Peabody Park Bridge.

In 2008, Chancellor Sullivan retired, and Linda P. Brady (our current chancellor) was selected as the tenth chief executive for the school.

Despite the many changes that have occurred since that first October in 1892, UNCG is still known for high-quality instruction, groundbreaking research, and caring faculty. A strong tradition in the liberal arts, the sciences, and excellent professional preparation is still a point of pride for the institution today.

During its history, the school has had five different names:

- 1892–1897: State Normal and Industrial School
- 1897–1919: State Normal and Industrial College
- 1919–1932: North Carolina College for Women
- 1932–1963: Woman's College of the University of North Carolina
- 1963–Present: The University of North Carolina at Greensboro

Chapter 2 Exercises

2.1 History of UNCG Quiz

1. UNCG was established in 1891 as a _____, or a school designed to train teachers.
   a. Boarding school
   b. Finishing school
   c. Normal school
   d. Trade school

2. The first president of UNCG was:
   a. Charles McIver
   b. Edwin Alderman
   c. Julius Isaac Foust
   d. Walter Clinton Jackson

3. One of the original buildings still stands at UNCG today. It is:
   a. McIver
   b. Foust
   c. Curry
   d. Petty

4. Which of the following was *not* a part of the original curriculum?
   a. Commercial (typing, shorthand, accounting)
   b. Domestic science (home economics)
   c. Business (management, economics)
   d. Pedagogy (teaching)

5. Between 1899 and 1906, the Normal experienced several catastrophes. Which event in the list below did not occur at UNCG?
   a. A typhoid epidemic closed the school for over two months
   b. Brick Dormitory burned
   c. A winter storm shut down the school for a week
   d. Charles McIver suffered a stroke and died

6. TRUE or FALSE? Julius Isaac Foust was the longest-serving president of the school.

7. TRUE or FALSE? The Woman's College admitted men on a temporary basis in 1932–1933 during the Great Depression.

8. Walter Clinton Jackson succeeded Foust as president in 1934. The most controversial event to occur during his administration was:
   a. Rapid campus growth
   b. Faculty salaries slashed
   c. The closing of three dormitories
   d. The closing of Walker Avenue

9. In February of 1960, a landmark event of the civil rights era occurred in Greensboro. It was:
   a. The integration of the residence halls at the WC (Women's College of the University of North Carolina)
   b. The first African American students were admitted to the WC
   c. The sit-ins at the Woolworth lunch counter
   d. The integration of the bus system in Greensboro

10. With the creation of the UNC system in 1963, the institution known for 30 years as the Woman's College became the _____.

Dear First-Year Student

Dear First Year Student,

 I want to start off by saying congratulations and welcome to UNCG! It may not have hit you yet but attending college is a huge accomplishment and reasons enough to be proud of yourself. During the first few weeks you might be filled with a variety of emotions as you deal with new situations, but it is nothing that you can't handle. The best way to meet new people and ensure success in your social and academic career in college is to get involved. Thankfully UNCG has plenty of opportunities for you to do just that.

Courtesy of UNCG Relations Office

From joining a student organization to taking a position as a student leader, getting involved is easy. I became a Peer Academic Leader (PAL) the first semester of my sophomore year in an effort to get more involved and share my experiences with first-year students. I was the shy freshman that didn't want to explore campus unless I had someone with me, however the more clubs I joined the more comfortable I became with my surroundings. When I was given the opportunity to become a PAL I took it because I wanted to assure the next class of incoming first-year students that their fears were something almost every student experiences and I wanted to help them successfully transition into the UNCG community. Becoming a PAL gave me opportunities to enhance my public speaking and communication skills, but most of all I gained the confidence in my abilities as a leader and role model.

I have talked with many students over the course of my time as a student at UNCG and the difference between the student that enjoys UNCG and the student that does not is whether or not they have gotten involved in the UNCG community. College is a life changer; it's where you make connections and friendships that last a lifetime, and learn that you are capable of more than you imagined. To put it simply, getting involved in college is the equivalent of carpe diem, it is seizing opportunities that will change the way that you view and approach life for years to come. I hope that you will use the information presented in this chapter to learn more about the resources and opportunities available to help you.

Good luck and Go Spartans!

Sincerely,

Astrid Hacker
Peer Academic Leader

Getting Connected at UNCG

3

Kate Jessup

With Contributions by Holly Hebard and Jalonda Thompson

THOUGHT STARTERS

1. How do you think college will be different from high school?

2. How do you plan to get involved at UNCG? What groups or student organizations do you plan to join?

3. What offices/programs/resources will you utilize to be successful?

One of the best parts of being a student at UNCG is the tremendous number of opportunities available to you. In addition to the multitude of ways to become involved on campus, there are numerous campus and academic resources available to support you throughout your undergraduate experience. Sometimes it can be overwhelming to try and take advantage of all the new experiences awaiting you, but with some intentional focus, you will be able to find the offices, organizations, resources, and people that will be beneficial in helping you make the most of your Spartan experience. Remember, while you will inevitably learn a lot in your classroom experiences at UNCG, there are many cocurricular opportunities that will also be essential to your learning and personal growth. This chapter includes a brief introduction to many of the resources, services, and opportunities for involvement you will want to consider. Take a look and then reflect on those that will be most valuable to your personal efforts in becoming a member of the UNCG community!

◆ Getting Involved at UNCG

Resources outlined here will help you find ways to get connected to other students in the UNCG community based on your personal interests. You will also find contact information for each resource at the end of this chapter.

Athletics

UNCG Athletics is affiliated with the Southern Conference of the NCAA Division I and offers a variety of intercollegiate athletic activities for both men and women. Students are given free admission to all regular-season contests (with the exception of preseason and postseason contests) for all sports, including men's basketball games at the Greensboro Coliseum, when they present a valid UNCG ID. All fans receive free admission to all Olympic sports' regular-season home contests. The University also supports a pep band, dance team, and coed cheerleading squad.

◆ Campus Activities and Programs (CAP)

Campus Activities and Programs provides a wealth of opportunities for students to get involved in different organizations throughout UNCG. Core responsibilities of the office include:

* Managing major campus events
* Coordinating student group recognition
* Providing student leadership training and development
* Advising SGA, CAB, and the Greek Governing Councils

To learn more about UNCG events, please visit cap.uncg.edu/campus-events/.

Campus Recreation

Campus Recreation fosters various healthy and active endeavors designed to improve your overall well-being. Programs include:

* *Informal Recreation*—access to cardio- and weight-training equipment
* *Intramural Sports*—a combination of team and individual sports
* *Outdoor Adventures*—access to the Edge Indoor Climbing Wall
* *Group Fitness and Personal Training*—classes and consultations
* *Club Sports*—competitive and instructional sporting activities
* *Team QUEST*—experiential learning for campus groups

Elliott University Center (EUC)

The Elliott University Center has been literally and symbolically identified as the center of UNCG since it opened in 1953. It is a familiar home base for students, faculty, and staff; a meeting place for activities, events, and ceremonies; and a greeting place for campus visitors. The EUC houses a 480-seat auditorium, the Multicultural Resource Center, a meditation room, an art gallery, meeting rooms with state-of-the-art technology, open lounge areas, and meeting and office spaces for student organizations and offices including the Office of the EUC, Campus Activities and Programs, the Career Services Center, the Office of Accessibility and Resources Services, New Student and Spartan Family Programs, the Office of Intercultural Engagement, the Dean of Students Office, and the Office of Leadership and Service-Learning. The UNCG SpartanCard Center and the UNCG Bookstore are also housed within the EUC.

Office of Intercultural Engagement (OIE)

The Office of Intercultural Engagement provides opportunities for students to increase cultural awareness and respect for differences. OIE also enhances the ability to appreciate one's own cultural identity within a multicultural society. A variety of opportunities for students include:

- Education and training (including Safe Zone)
- Advocacy and outreach
- Programs and activities

Office of Leadership and Service-Learning (OLSL)

Through civic engagement, community partner collaboration, and personal reflection, the Office of Leadership and Service-Learning prepares students for a life of active citizenship. Programs coordinated within OLSL include:

- *Leadership Challenge*—The Leadership Challenge Program is an institution-wide commitment to offer all UNCG students leadership education, training, and development through curricular and cocurricular experiences to enhance a personal philosophy of leadership that includes understanding of self, others, and community.
- *Leadership Conferences*—OLSL hosts an on-campus, one-day leadership conference in each of the fall and spring semester. Each conference is an opportunity for students to hone specific skills that will improve their capacity to create positive change in their world.
- *The LeaderShape® Institute*—More than a program. It's a vision. A Movement. A Cause. The LeaderShape® Institute is an intensive and energizing six-day program. It is open to any student interested in producing extraordinary results.
- *Service Trips*—Service Trips immerse students in regional communities and engage them in quality, direct service that promotes education of social and environmental issues. Students reflect on their experiences and are challenged to grow personally and become active citizens.
- *Peer Leadership Educators and Training Workshops*—Well-trained and motivated students facilitate in-class modules and create workshops for group or class needs.

Student Media: *The Carolinian, Coraddi*, WUAG

UNCG's student newspaper, *The Carolinian*, is published weekly during the academic year except during holidays and examination periods. It is a teaching newspaper organized and produced by UNCG students. *The Carolinian* covers all campus, local, state, and national news of relevance and interest to the campus. Look for *The Carolinian* distribution bins around campus or visit them at http://www.carolinianuncg.com.

Coraddi, UNCG's student literary magazine published twice during the academic year, features works by students in the fields of poetry, fiction, art, and photography. *Coraddi* provides experience and training in a nonacademic setting to those students interested in editing, illustration, design, layout, and the entire field of magazine publishing. For information on joining the *Coraddi* staff or submitting works for publication, visit them online at http://www. thecoraddi.info.

WUAG 103.1 FM is UNCG's primarily student-operated radio station, broadcasting at 103.1 FM. WUAG is on the air seven days a week, offering indie rock, hip-hop, electronic, and a variety of other musical genres broadcast in a noncommercial format. WUAG strives to entertain and inform students about events on campus and around the community and to provide academic extracurricular radio experience for students interested in broadcasting. WUAG news, programming, music, production, and programming departments are open to all UNCG students. For more information, visit their website at http://www.wuag.net or call (336) 334-4308.

Music, Theatre, and Dance

Throughout the year, the School of Music, Theatre, and Dance hosts or cosponsors numerous on-campus events for the mutual benefit of musical, dance, and theatre organizations, public schools, and UNCG. Such events include ensemble and solo performances, competitions, auditions, professional meetings, and specialized workshops. Performances held throughout the school year include performances by the UNCG Wind Ensemble, North Carolina Dance Festival,

Symphony Orchestra, Jazz Ensemble, Chamber Singers, Old Time Ensemble, Dance Faculty, North Carolina Theatre for Young People, and many more. In addition to its opera workshop presentations, the Music department mounts a major grand opera and one or two chamber operas each year. Each fall, the Music and Theatre departments produce a complete staging of a major Broadway musical.

Weatherspoon Art Museum

The Weatherspoon Art Museum, located at the corner of Spring Garden and Tate Street, is one of our most prized cultural arts centers. As a university art museum, Weatherspoon serves the UNCG community along with regional and national audiences by collecting, preserving, presenting, and interpreting visual art. Weatherspoon is the largest collection of modern and contemporary American art in the Southeast.

Weatherspoon presents more than 15 exhibitions annually, including exhibitions curated from the museum's permanent collection of works by such artists as Henri Matisse, Henry Ossawa Tanner, Willem de Kooning, Andy Warhol, Louise Nevelson, and Cindy Sherman. A year-round calendar is available to share educational programs such as artist talks, family days, films, and concerts. Admission and parking are free.

◆ Getting Connected for Academic Success

UNCG cares about you and your academic success. Departments and resources listed here are specifically intended to help you achieve your educational goals as a student at UNCG.

College or School	Advising Center	Advising Process	Location/Website
College of Arts and Sciences	CASA	Most students who have declared a major in the College of Arts and Sciences and have not earned 24 credit hours will be advised in CASA. After completing 24 credit hours, students will be assigned a faculty advisor within their major department.	103 Foust Building uncg.edu/casa/
Bryan School of Business and Economics	Undergraduate Student Services	Most students who have declared a major within the Bryan School will be advised on course selection and academic goals through the Office of Undergraduate Student Services.	301 Bryan Building http://bae.uncg.edu/advise/
School of Education	Office of Student Services	Students who have declared Education as a major are advised in the Office of Student Services in the School of Education.	142 School of Education Building http://oss.uncg.edu
School of Health and Human Sciences	HHS Student Advising Center	Students who have been formally admitted to a major within the School of Health and Human Sciences will be advised by a faculty advisor. The Health and Human Sciences Student Advising Center advises pre-majors and those who have not been formally admitted to HHS majors.	221 McIver Building uncg.edu/hhs/student-advising-center.html
School of Music, Theatre, and Dance	Student Resources	The Director of Undergraduate Advising for the School of Music, Theatre, and Dance advises all undergraduate Music majors and minors. Theatre and Dance majors are advised by departmental faculty and staff advisors.	220 Music Building/various http://performingarts.uncg.edu/current/advising/music Various websites for theatre and dance
School of Nursing	Advising Center	Freshmen students who have declared Nursing as a major are advised by one of two faculty advisors in addition to the School of Nursing's Director of Undergraduate Advising.	123 Moore Nursing Building nursing.uncg.edu/undergraduate/advising
Exploratory Majors	Students First Office	All Exploratory Majors are advised in SFO until declaring a major.	061 McIver Building Studentsfirst.uncg.edu

Academic Advising Centers

Your academic advisor will be one of your most valuable academic resources at UNCG. Over time, you will build a professional relationship with your academic advisor that will aid you in progressing toward your educational and career goals. Students at UNCG are assigned an academic advisor based on their academic major; however, each of the University's professional schools and the College of Arts and Sciences also has a general academic advising center that can provide major-specific information regarding advising at UNCG. Additionally, the Students First Office serves as the centralized advising center for all Exploratory Majors. The following chart provides general information about the seven academic advising centers at UNCG. You can also find more information on academic advising at UNCG in Chapter 11.

Students First Office (SFO)

The Students First Office (SFO) fosters a learner-centered experience for undergraduate success by serving as one of the first lines of response in helping UNCG students address any number of academic issues they may experience at the University. The office coordinates intervention processes across different academic and administrative units to help students determine the best possible success strategies for addressing academic concerns. In collaboration with other support services across campus, SFO serves as an academic one-stop shop for assisting students with academic advising, academic recovery, academic transition, appeals, and graduation planning. In addition, SFO coordinates:

- Academic advising for exploratory (undecided) students
- Resources for students on academic warning, academic probation, or in academic recovery
- Support for students who are considering withdrawal from one of all of their courses
- The Starfish program
  - Starfish EARLY ALERT is a support system that allows instructors to raise Starfish flags to let students know they may need additional support in a class. In addition, instructors can raise *kudos* to congratulate students on their academic success.
  - Starfish CONNECT allows students to easily make appointments with instructors, program coordinators, academic advisors, and the Starfish Outreach Team in the Students First Office.
- Foundations for Learning (FFL) 100 and 250, transition courses designed to foster students' academic and personal success, holistic development, and seamless transition throughout their undergraduate experience at UNCG.

The Students First Office website (http://studentsfirst.uncg.edu) is also a valuable resource, providing students with a UNCG GPA calculator, steps for looking up academic advisors, the ability to chat online with one of the advisors, and detailed information about academic policies, appeals, and resources. The Students First Office also offers walk-in assistance Monday through Friday from 1:00 to 3:00 pm along with extended evening hours on Tuesdays from 4:00 to 7:00 pm (walk-ins and appointments available).

Career Services Center (CSC)

The Career Services Center provides professional guidance and resources to undergraduate students for their lifelong career development. Programs and services assist with career planning and decision-making, as well as employment search activities. In addition to sponsoring etiquette dinners, career fairs, and networking events, CSC staff can help students:

- Explore career paths
- Find internships
- Learn interview and networking skills
- Prepare for graduate school
- Write resumes and cover letters

The Digital ACT Studio

The Digital ACT (Action, Consultation, and Training) Studio supports students, faculty, and staff in their effective creation or incorporation of digital media into projects. Consultants act as a trained, engaged audience, providing feedback on slide presentations, video projects, podcasts, digital photography, websites, and blogs by offering collaborative, dialog-based consultations.

International Programs Center (IPC)

The International Programs Center helps students at UNCG explore Study Abroad opportunities and navigate the exciting world of Study Abroad and Exchanges. IPC also helps international students discover UNCG and all it has to offer. The IPC oversees the programs in the International House in Hawkins Residence Hall and serves as the administrative advisor for the International Students Association. The IPC also serves as the liaison between international students and U.S. Citizenship and Immigration Services (USCIS) and acts as a campus advocate for international student concerns.

The International House (I-House)

The International House is home to international students and students from the United States interested in developing a global perspective and learning about other cultures. Students who are interested in, or returning from, a Study Abroad experience often find the I-House appealing, as do those who hope to work in international business or communications. I-House offers a variety of social activities, travel adventures, and events that highlight exposure to cultures from around the world. Students must apply to live in I-House through the IPC. Every attempt is made to place international students and U.S. students as roommates to facilitate the cross-cultural learning process.

Lloyd International Honors College (LIHC)

Lloyd International Honors College offers two programs for highly motivated students.

The International Honors Program enhances general education studies by providing special internationally focused Honors courses, an opportunity to study abroad, and the benefit of learning a second language. *The Disciplinary Honors Program* is directed at current students who seek to deepen study in their declared academic major.

Advantages of the Honors College include:

- A sense of community
- Research, scholarship, and creative activities
- Priority registration
- Honors Residence at North Spencer
- Recognition of graduating with International Honors, Disciplinary Honors, or both

Office of Accessibility and Resources Services (OARS)

The Office of Accessibility and Resources Services provides, coordinates, and advocates for services that enable undergraduate students with disabilities to receive equal access to a college education and to all aspects of university life. Students admitted to the University with documented disabilities are strongly encouraged to inquire about registration with the UNCG's Office of Accessibility and Resources Services (OARS). In addition, students desiring further information may complete a "Voluntary Disability Disclosure" form located in the eligibility section of the OARS website, or the OARS may be contacted directly using the information below. Information submitted to or obtained by the OARS is strictly confidential.

Services include:

- Alternative testing
- Academic and organization assistance
- Adaptive technology/computer services
- Advocacy assistance
- Interpreter services
- Note-taker services
- Tutoring

Living-Learning Communities and Residential Colleges

The Office of Housing and Residence Life and the Residential Colleges at UNCG foster student learning through integrated experiences in and out of the classroom.

- *Residential Colleges*—Students in Residential Colleges live together while enrolling in common integrated courses. The Colleges provide students with meaningful connections to faculty mentors and long-standing College traditions.
- *Living-Learning Communities*—Students in Living-Learning Communities (LLCs) live together while enrolling in common integrated courses. LLCs focus on exploring UNCG with faculty and staff mentors within a discipline or interest area.

Student Success Center (SSC)

The SSC is composed of three academic support programs that assist students as they persist toward an undergraduate degree and develop into lifelong learners. Descriptions of the three academic support programs within the Student Success Center are as follows:

The Tutoring and Academic Skills Program (TASP) serves the entire undergraduate community by providing programming and services to help undergraduate students improve their academic performance and achieve their educational goals. Support services include group and individual tutoring; academic skills assessment and instruction; computer-assisted learning skills enhancement; academic skills workshops; and a resource computer lab. All services are available to any student at no cost.

Special Support Services (SSS) is a program jointly funded by the U.S. Department of Education and UNCG that assists students who are first-generation, are from modest income backgrounds, or have a disability, and who also demonstrate academic need for services. Specific support services include individualized peer and professional tutoring; academic skills assessment and instruction; writing and research writing instruction; comprehensive personal, academic, and career counseling; graduate/professional school guidance; financial literacy help; and opportunities to attend both educational and cultural events in order to help students to overcome academic, social, and cultural barriers to higher education.

The Supplemental Instruction Program (SIP) is an academic support program that targets historically difficult courses. Students enrolled in SIP-identified courses have the option to attend regularly scheduled, out-of-class review/discussion sessions. The sessions are focused on reviewing lecture notes, discussing course readings, and preparing for examinations. Students learn how to integrate course content with reasoning and study skills.

UNCG Bookstore

Visit the UNCG Bookstore for all things UNCG! Here you can purchase University apparel, textbooks, magazines, gift cards, software and computer accessories, and much more. Plus, a portion of all purchases support UNCG scholarships. Additionally, the bookstore also offers Bookstore Bucks in partnership with the SpartanCard Center. By adding funds to this account, you can make purchases in the bookstore using your UNCG ID card.

Undergraduate Research, Scholarship, and Creativity Office (URSCO)

At UNCG, there are many faculty, staff, and students involved in academic research. At its core, research means asking an original question and then using the tools of an academic discipline to answer the question. Research can be and is conducted in all academic disciplines. Research can be done in a variety of places, such as an art studio, the library, a field site, or a laboratory. The Undergraduate Research, Scholarship and Creativity Office (URSCO) supports undergraduate research on the UNCG campus in a variety of ways, including:

- Undergraduate research assistantships
- An annual undergraduate research expo
- Undergraduate research assistant travel awards

University Registrar's Office (URO)

The University Registrar's Office (URO) oversees adherence to academic policy and data integrity and is responsible for the registration of all students in academic credit courses offered by the University. Registration is web-based through the University's automated student information system, UNCGenie. The URO handles all aspects of registration, including the preparation of the semester schedule of courses, demographic updates, major changes, faculty advisor assignments, and registration scheduling and processing. In conjunction with registration, the URO is also responsible for grade processing at the close of each semester and maintains the official academic records (transcripts) for all current and former students.

The University Speaking Center

UNCG's Speaking Center provides one-on-one tutoring and instructional workshop services to students to help hone oral communication, confidence, and competence. Assistance is offered in the preparation and delivery of speeches, development of knowledge and skill in interpersonal communication, and group or team communication through:

- Workshops
- Consultations
- Orientations

The University Writing Center

UNCG's Writing Center assists students with papers, helping them clarify the goals of the paper and gain control of the writing process. Services that are offered include:

- Face-to-face consultations
- Online consultations via chat
- Online consultations via email

◆ Getting Connected for Your Personal Wellness

There will certainly be times in your collegiate career when you may benefit from additional support related to personal wellness. The following services and offices are here to support your general well-being during your time at UNCG.

Counseling Center

Every student needs a little additional support at some point during their collegiate experience. The campus environment can be exciting and challenging; however, it can also be highly stressful, as social and emotional concerns can interfere with effective functioning and academic performance. The Counseling Center provides a wide range of counseling and psychological services that focus on students' holistic wellness. Services provided to currently enrolled UNCG students include:

- Individual therapy
- Group therapy
- Crisis intervention
- Psychiatric services
- Outreach and support
- Training and consultation

Dean of Students Office

The Dean of Students Office provides support for all UNCG students by working together with families, faculty, and staff to create a culture of care at UNCG. In addition to services focused on student advocacy, education, and crisis response, the Dean of Students also coordinates the Student Code of Conduct and the Academic Integrity Policy. This office also sponsors a variety of programs and opportunities for students, including:

- UNCG Cares
- Geek Week
- PATHS (Partners Assisting the Homeless & Hungry Spartan)
- Student Conduct Team
- SMART Planning

Dining Services

Thanks to Dining Services, you will never go hungry with all the options that UNCG has to offer! Whether you are a residential student or a commuter, meal plans are reasonably priced and provide ample flexibility to satisfy your appetite. Plus, there are dining possibilities located throughout the campus, including:

- *EUC Food Court*—Papa John's, Ghassan's, Thai Garden, Salsarita's, Chick-fil-A
- *Moran Commons*—Fountain View Dining Hall, Taco Bell, Pizza Hut, Wing Street
- *Spartan's Place at EUC*—Wild Greens, Subway, and Jamba Juice
- *Bryan School Food Court*—Au Bon Pain

Student Health Services (SHS)

UNCG's Student Health Services provides collaborative health care designed to empower students to develop lifelong skills that enhance their physical, psychological, and wellness status.

The Medical Clinic

The Medical Clinic provides primary health-care services for students, such as pharmacy services, immunizations, allergy injections, flu shots, laboratory and X-ray services, and women's health services, including contraceptive management.

The Wellness Center

The Wellness Center provides a variety of programs and resources aimed at increasing students' knowledge of health and wellness concerns. Programming and other services are provided campus-wide and include:

- Wellness workshops
- Massage therapy and acupuncture
- Nutrition counseling and education
- Smoking cessation

- Alcohol Edu
- Peer Education
- BRAVE (Building Responsible Advocates for Violence Education)
- Sexual Violence Campus Advocacy (SVCA)
- Red Flag Campaign

UNCG Police Department

UNCG Campus Police is comprised of police officers, uniformed security officers, and other support personnel who work together to provide safety and security to UNCG's campus. Several support programs are in place for safety prevention, including:

- Pedestrian Safety Program
- Victim Assistance Program
- Partnerships for a Safer Campus
- Rape Aggression Defense
- Police Ride Along Program
- Campus Safety Escort

Veterans Resource Center

UNCG has a proud legacy of embracing student veterans and strives to create a welcoming atmosphere for veterans, active duty military personnel, and their dependents on campus. The Veterans Resource Center works to:

- Advocate for veterans' success and serve as liaisons when needed
- Answer questions regarding benefits or school concerns
- Create community between military and civilian populations
- Provide a quiet study space for military veterans and dependents

Financial Support and Other Resources

Cashiers and Student Accounts Office

The Cashiers and Student Accounts Office manages student accounts, loans, payment plans, and refunds. Additionally, the office also provides information on financial planning and budgets based on the schedule of tuition and fee charges for each semester.

Financial Aid Office

The Financial Aid Office assists students with the process of applying for financial aid. The financial aid staff is available to assist students with scholarship, loan, and work study information, as well as a financial aid checklist and important information about maintaining eligibility for financial aid.

Greensboro Community

Beyond campus, there are many things for college students to do in the Greensboro and Triad area, from shopping, movies, and sporting events to a variety of museum exhibits, concerts, and cultural events happening throughout the year. For information on events happening around town, visit the following websites:

www.news-record.com
www.greensborocoliseum.com
www.exploregreensboro.com
www.downtowngreensboro.net

Information Technology Services (ITS)

Information Technology Services manages and provides support for UNCG student accounts, passwords, and email. ITS operates the 10 computer labs that are available for students and also provides assistance with wireless computing and general troubleshooting on students' personal computers. Students can also purchase new business-class computer equipment at discounted prices.

Spartan Mail

Spartan Mail is available for all of your mail needs, accurately and efficiently handling inbound and outbound mail at UNCG. Services include postage sales; letter and package delivery; express, certified, and registered mail; money orders; international mail; and USPS mail supplies. If you live on campus, you can receive mail via the following address format:

Student Name (ex. Sparty Spartan)
iSpartan Username (ex.sspartan) at UNCG
Greensboro, NC 27413

SpartanCard Center

Your SpartanCard is your all-in-one campus ID card. In addition to serving as a student ID, the SpartanCard is also a library card, a meal card, and a convenient form of payment across campus. This card will play a large part in your campus life by allowing you access to University programs and services. If you choose to store money on your SpartanCard, you can use it for purchases at campus dining locations, the UNCG Bookstore, or other vendors across campus.

Student Employment Office (SEO)

The Student Employment Office (SEO) believes that part-time work experience can be a valuable part of career planning, skill building, and leadership development. The office aims to be a one-stop shop for all possible resources related to part-time employment.

SEO staff provides resources and advice for finding on-campus (work study and/or non-work-study) and off-campus work. The SEO manages all part-time job listings and the I-9 forms (employment verification) for all on-campus student employees. The SEO also organizes three part-time job fairs as well as the annual Student Employee of the Year celebration.

Table 1: Academic Resources

Office/Department Name	Location	Telephone Number	Website
Career Services Center (CSC)	1 Elliott University Center	(336) 334-5454	csc.uncg.edu
Digital ACT Studio	Lower Level, Jackson Library	(336) 256-1381	digitalactstudio.uncg.edu
International Program Center (IPC)	207 Foust Building	(336) 334-5404	uncg.edu/ipg/
International House (I-House)	Hawkins Residence Hall	(336) 334-5404	uncg.edu/ipg/ihouse.html
Lloyd International Honors College (LIHC)	205 Foust Building	(336) 334-5538	honorscollege.uncg.edu
Office of Accessibility and Resources Services (OARS)	Suite 215, Elliott University Center	(336) 334-5440	ods.uncg.edu
Students First Office (SFO)	061 McIver Building	(336) 334-5730	studentsfirst.uncg.edu
Student Success Center (SSC)	104 McIver Building	(336) 334-3878	success.uncg.edu
UNCG Bookstore	Elliott University Center	(336) 334-5563	bookstore.uncg.edu
Undergraduate Research, Scholarship and Creativity Office	136 McIver Building	(336) 334-4776	ursco.uncg.edu
University Registrar's Office (URO)	180 Mossman Building	(336) 334-5946	uncg.edu/reg/
The University Speaking Center	3211 Moore Humanities and Research Administration Building	(336) 256-1346	speakingcenter.uncg.edu
The University Writing Center	3211 Moore Humanities and Research Administration Building	(336) 334-3125	uncg.edu/eng/writingcenter/

Table 2: Cocurricular Resources

Office/Department Name	Location	Telephone Number	Website
Athletics	337 Health and Human Performance Building	(336) 334-5952	uncgspartans.com
Campus Activities and Programs (CAP)	Suite 221, Elliott University Center	(336) 334-5800	cap.uncg.edu
Campus Recreation	412 Student Recreation Center	(336) 334-5924	campusrec.uncg.edu
The Carolinian	Suite 236, Elliott University Center	(336) 334-5752	carolinianuncg.com
Coraddi Magazine	Various meeting locations	the.coraddi@gmail.com	thecoraddi.info
Elliott University Center (EUC)	Elliott University Center	(336) 334-5510	euc.uncg.edu
Office of Intercultural Engagement (OIE)	Suite 062, Elliott University Center	(336) 334-5090	oma.uncg.edu

Table 2: Continued

Office/Department Name	Location	Telephone Number	Website
Office of Leadership and Service-Learning (OLSL)	Suite 214, Elliott University Center	(336) 256-0538	olsl.uncg.edu
Music, Theatre, and Dance	Various Locations	(336) 334-5789	performingarts.uncg.edu
Weatherspoon Art Museum	The intersection of Spring Garden and Tate Street	(336) 334-5770	weatherspoon.uncg.edu
WUAG 103.1 FM	210 Brown Building	(336) 334-4308	http://wuag.net

Table 3: Personal Wellness and Support

Office/Department Name	Location	Telephone Number	Website
Counseling Center	Gove Student Health Center, Second Floor	(336) 334-5874	shs.uncg.edu/cc/
Dean of Students Office	Suite 210, Elliott University Center	(336) 334-5514	sa.uncg.edu/dean/
Dining Services	Dining Hall, Lower Level	(336) 334-4451	dineoncampus.com/UNCG/
Student Health Services (SHS)	Gove Student Health Center, Main Floor	(336) 334-5340	shs.uncg.edu
The Wellness Center	Gove Student Health Center, Ground Level	(336) 334-3190	shs.uncg.edu/wellness/
UNCG Police Department	1200 W. Lee St.	(336) 334-5963 or dial 4-4444 for all on-campus emergencies	police.uncg.edu
Veterans Resource Center	Above the Spartan Trader in the Spring Garden Apartments	(336) 334-4715	http://veterans.uncg.edu/veterans-resource-center/

Table 4: Financial Support and Other Resources

Office Name	Location	Telephone Number	Website
Cashier's and Student Accounts Office	151 Mossman Building	(336) 334-5831	csh.uncg.edu
Financial Aid Office	723 Kenilworth Street	(336) 334-5702	fia.uncg.edu
Information Technology Services	Forney Building	(336) 256-TECH (8324)	its.uncg.edu
Spartan Mail	Jefferson Suites Building	(336) 256-0147	postal.uncg.edu
Spartan Card Center	Suite 121, Elliott University Center	(336) 334-5651	spartancard.uncg.edu
Student Employment Office	UNCG's Career Services Center, 1 Elliott University Center	(336) 334-5454	csc.uncg.edu/students/studentemploymentoffice

3.1 What do you know about UNCG?

In the following chart, list the best campus resource(s) for helping you address common needs or issues you may need assistance with in your first semester.

Issue or Need	UNCG Office or Resource	Location
I am trying to decide on a major		
I need assistance in writing a paper for ENG 101		
I am interested in getting a tutor for PSY 121		
I am interested in participating in intramural basketball		
I want to find out how dropping a course might affect degree progress		
I am confused about my tuition bill		
I would like to explore career and internship options		
I need special accommodations for my learning disability		
I want to run for student government		
I would like to get an on-campus job		
I want to learn more about study abroad opportunities		
I want to learn to kayak		
I am feeling a little homesick		

3.2 UNCG Involvement Plan

Getting connected at UNCG will require you to be thoughtful and intentional about the different ways you would like to get involved in the campus community. Use the following reflection questions to start thinking about what you are passionate about, what campus activities interest you, and how you might integrate these opportunities into your first-year experience at UNCG.

- Why am I interested in getting involved with this activity or office? How does it fit into my personal success plan?
- What activities do I want to take advantage of right away? What activities can wait until later in my college career?
- Who at UNCG can help me find out more information on getting connected and getting involved? (PALs, upper-class students, faculty, or staff members)
- How much time will each of my activities require? Am I stretching myself too thin?
- How will each of these opportunities help me get connected with the UNCG community?

Personal Goal	UNCG Resource(s)	Action Steps	Timeline for Completion	Anticipated Outcomes
Explore leadership opportunities	Office of Leadership and Service-Learning Career Services FFL	1. Visit the UNCG resources 2. Choose two opportunities to pursue	9-1-15	*Become involved in a service organization* *Apply to be a PAL*

Adapted from Latino, J., & Powell, J. (Eds.) (2010). *Transitions. Building a new community.* Columbia, SC: University of South Carolina.

3.3 Mapping Your Activities and Academics

Have you ever created a *Mind Map*? This kind of diagram can help you think about and display the different relationships between cocurricular activities you are engaged in outside the classroom and the different things you are learning in your course work. In the given space, use your list of activities you are involved in (or plan to get involved in) and a list of classes you are taking to connect all the interrelated areas. Remember, you can have multiple connections for each. In fact, the more connections, the better!

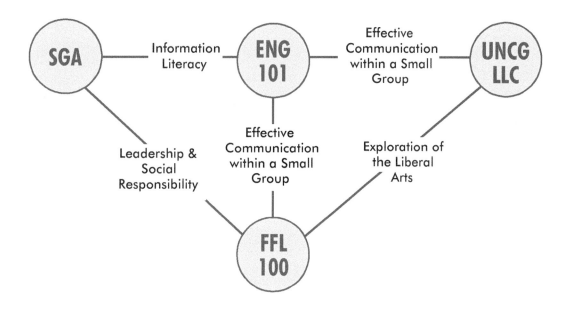

Adapted from Latino, J., & Powell, J. (Eds.) (2010). *Transitions. Building a new community.* Columbia, SC: University of South Carolina.

Your First Year Resources

The first year of college is an exciting and challenging time. We want you to have the best experience possible, so we've designed a website just for you. It's full of tips, tricks, and links to help you make the most of Your First Year! If you have questions or need help finding your way at UNCG, you can always email us at yfy@uncg.edu or visit yourfirstyear.uncg.edu.

At the end of each chapter there is a list of Your First Year (YFY) resources that are associated with offices, programs and/or services mentioned in each chapter. These resources and the YFY website, yourfirstyear.uncg.edu, will assist you with your transition to UNCG!

Goal Setting, Motivation, and Character

4

ACTIVATE YOUR THINKING — Journal Entry 4.1

1. How would you define the word "successful"?

LEARNING GOAL

To develop meaningful goals to strive for, along with strategies for maintaining motivation and building character to achieve those goals.

◆ What Does Being "Successful" Mean to You?

The word "success" means to achieve a desired outcome; it derives from the Latin root *successus*, which means "to follow or come after" (as in the word "succession"). Thus, by definition, success involves an order or sequence of actions that lead to a desired outcome. The process starts with identifying an end (goal) and then finding a means (sequence of steps) to reach that goal (achieving success). Goal setting is the first step in the process of becoming successful because it gives you something specific to strive for and ensures that you start off in the right direction. Studies consistently show that setting goals is a more effective self-motivational strategy than simply telling yourself that you should try hard or do your best (Boekaerts, Pintrich, & Zeidner, 2000; Locke & Latham, 1990).

By setting goals, you show initiative—you initiate the process of gaining control of your future and taking charge of your life. By taking initiative, you demonstrate what psychologists call an internal locus of control—you believe that the locus (location or source) of control for events in your life is *internal*, and thus inside of you and within your control, rather than *external*, or outside of you and beyond your control (controlled by such factors as luck, chance, or fate; Rotter, 1966).

Research has revealed that individuals with a strong internal locus of control display the following characteristics:

1. Greater independence and self-direction (Van Overwalle, Mervielde, & De Schuyer, 1995);
2. More accurate self-assessment (Hashaw, Hammond, & Rogers, 1990; Lefcourt, 1982);
3. Higher levels of learning and achievement (Wilhite, 1990); and
4. Better physical health (Maddi, 2002; Seligman, 1991).

> "You've got to be careful if you don't know where you're going because you might not get there."
>
> –Yogi Berra, Hall of Fame baseball player

> "There is perhaps nothing worse than reaching the top of the ladder and discovering that you're on the wrong wall."
>
> –Joseph Campbell, American professor and writer

> "Success is getting what you want. Happiness is wanting what you get."
>
> –Dale Carnegie, author of the best-selling book *How to Win Friends and Influence People* (1936) and founder of The Dale Carnegie Course, a worldwide program for business based on his teachings

> "The future is literally in our hands to mold as we like. But we cannot wait until tomorrow. Tomorrow is now."
>
> –Eleanor Roosevelt, UN diplomat and humanitarian

Pause for Reflection

You are not required by law or by others to attend college; you've made the decision to continue your education. Do you believe you are in charge of your educational destiny?

Why or why not?

An internal locus of control also contributes to the development of another positive trait that psychologists call self-efficacy—the belief that you have power to produce a positive effect on the outcomes of your life (Bandura, 1994). People with low self-efficacy tend to feel helpless, powerless, and passive; they think (and allow) things to happen to them rather than taking charge and making things happen for them. College students with a strong sense of self-efficacy believe they're in control of their educational success, regardless of their past or current circumstances.

If you have a strong sense of self-efficacy, you initiate action, put forth effort, and sustain that effort until you reach your goal. If you encounter setbacks or bad breaks along the way, you don't give up or give in; you persevere or push on (Bandura, 1986, 1997).

Students with a strong sense of academic self-efficacy have been found to:

1. Put great effort into their studies;
2. Use active-learning strategies;
3. Capitalize on campus resources; and
4. Persist in the face of obstacles (Multon, Brown, & Lent, 1991; Zimmeman, 1995).

Students with self-efficacy also possess a strong sense of personal responsibility. As the breakdown of the word "responsible" implies, they are "response" "able"—that is, they think they're able to respond effectively to personal challenges, including academic challenges.

Students with self-efficacy don't have a false sense of entitlement. They don't feel they're entitled to, or owed, anything; they believe that success is earned and is theirs for the taking. For example, studies show that students who convert their college degree into a successful career have two common characteristics: personal initiative and a positive attitude (Pope, 1990). They don't take a passive approach and assume a good position will fall into their lap; nor do they believe they are owed a position simply because they have a college degree or credential. Instead, they become actively involved in the job-hunting process and use various job-search strategies (Brown & Krane, 2000).

◆ Strategies for Effective Goal Setting

Motivation begins with goal setting. Studies show that people who neglect to set and pursue life goals are prone to feelings of "life boredom" and a belief that one's life is meaningless (Bargdill, 2000).

Goals may be classified into three general categories: long range, midrange, and short range, depending on the length of time it takes to reach them and the order in which they are to be achieved. Short-range goals need to be completed before a mid-range goal can be reached, and mid-range goals must be reached before a long-range goal can be achieved. For example, if your long-range goal is a successful career, you must complete the courses required for a degree that will allow you entry into a career (mid-range goals); to reach your mid-range goal of a college degree, you need to successfully complete the courses you're taking this term (short-range goals).

Setting Long-Range Goals

Setting effective long-range goals involves two processes: (a) self-awareness, or insight into who you are now, and (b) self-projection, or a vision of what you want to become. When you engage in both of these processes, you're able to see a connection between your short- and your long-range goals.

Long-range goal setting enables you to take an approach to your future that is proactive—acting beforehand to anticipate and control your future life rather than putting it off and being forced to react to it without a plan. Research shows that people who neglect to set goals for themselves are more likely to experience boredom with life (Bargdill, 2000). Setting long-range goals and planning ahead also help reduce feelings of anxiety about the future because you've given it forethought, which gives you greater power to control it (i.e., it gives you a stronger sense of self-efficacy). As the old saying goes, "To be forewarned is to be forearmed."

Remember that setting long-range goals and developing long-range plans doesn't mean you can't adjust or modify them. Your goals can undergo change as you change, develop skills, acquire knowledge, and discover interests or talents. Finding yourself and discovering your path in life are among the primary purposes of a college education. Don't think that the process of setting long-range goals means you will be locked into a premature plan and reduced options. Instead, it will give you something to reach for and some momentum to get you moving in the right direction.

Pause for Reflection

In what area or areas of your life do you feel that you've been able to exert the most control and achieve the most positive results?

In what area or areas of your life do you wish you had more control and were achieving better results?

What have you done in those areas of your life in which you've taken charge and gained control that might be transferred or applied to those areas in which you need to gain more control?

> "To fail to plan is to plan to fail."
>
> –Robert Wubbolding, internationally known author, psychologist, and teacher

◆ Steps in the Goal-Setting Process

Effective goal setting involves a four-step sequence:

1. **Awareness of yourself.** Your personal interests, abilities and talents, and values;

   ↓

2. **Awareness of your options.** The choices available to you;

   ↓

3. **Awareness of the options that best fit you.** The goals most compatible with your personal abilities, interests, values, and needs;

   ↓

4. **Awareness of the process.** The steps that you need to take to reach your chosen goal.

Discussed in the next sections are strategies for taking each of these steps in the goal-setting process.

> You have brains in your head. You have feet in your shoes. You can steer yourself any direction you choose.
>
> –Theodore Seuss Giesel, a.k.a. Dr. Seuss, author of children's books including *Oh the Places You'll Go*

Step 1. Gain Awareness of Yourself

The goals you choose to pursue say a lot about who you are and what you want from life. Thus, self-awareness is a critical first step in the process of goal setting. You must know yourself before you can choose the goals you want to achieve. While this may seem obvious, self-awareness and self-discovery are often overlooked aspects of the goal-setting process. Deepening your self-awareness puts you in a better position to select and choose goals and to pursue a personal path that's true to who you are and what you want to become.

> "Know thyself, and to thine own self be true."
>
> –Plato, ancient Greek philosopher

> ### Remember
>
> Self-awareness is the first, most important step in the process of making any important life choice or decision. Good decisions are built on a deep understanding of one's self.

No one is in a better position to know who you are, and what you want to be, than *you*. One effective way to get to know yourself more deeply is through self-questioning. You can begin to deepen your self-awareness by asking yourself questions that can stimulate your thinking about your inner qualities and priorities. Effective self-questioning can launch you on an inward quest or journey to self-discovery and self-insight, which is the critical first step to effective goal setting. For example, if your long-range goal is career success, you can launch your voyage toward achieving this goal by asking yourself thought-provoking questions related to your personal:

- **Interests.** What you like to do;
- **Abilities and talents.** What you're good at doing; and
- **Values.** What you believe is worth doing.

The following questions are designed to sharpen your self-awareness with respect to your interests, abilities, and values. As you read each question, briefly note what thought or thoughts come to mind about yourself.

"In order to succeed, you must know what you are doing, like what you are doing, and believe in what you are doing."

–Will Rogers, Native American humorist and actor

Your Personal Interests

1. What tends to grab your attention and hold it for long periods?

2. What sorts of things are you naturally curious about or tend to intrigue you?

3. What do you enjoy and do as often as you possibly can?

4. What do you look forward to or get excited about?

5. What are your favorite hobbies or pastimes?

6. When you're with your friends, what do you like to talk about or spend time doing together?

7. What has been your most stimulating or enjoyable learning experience?

8. If you've had previous work or volunteer experience, what jobs or tasks did you find most enjoyable or stimulating?

9. When time seems to fly by for you, what are you usually doing?

10. What do you like to read about?

11. When you open a newspaper or log on to the Internet, what do you tend to read first?

12. When you find yourself daydreaming or fantasizing about your future life, what do you most find yourself doing?

Pause for Reflection

From your responses to the preceding questions, identify a long-range goal you could pursue that's compatible with your personal interests. In the space that follows, note the goal and the interests that are compatible with it.

Your Personal Abilities and Talents

1. What seems to come easily or naturally to you?

2. What would you say is your greatest or talent or personal gift?

3. What do you excel at when you apply yourself and put forth your best effort?

4. What are your most advanced or well-developed skills?

5. What would you say has been the greatest accomplishment or achievement in your life thus far?

6. What about yourself are you most proud of or do you take the most pride in doing?

7. When others come to you for advice or assistance, what is it usually for?

"Never desert your line of talent. Be what nature intended you for and you will succeed."

–Sydney Smith, eighteenth-century English writer and defender of the oppressed

8. What would your best friend or friends say is your best quality, trait, or characteristic?

9. When you had a strong feeling of being successful after you had done something, what was it that you did?

10. If you've received awards or other forms of recognition, what have you received them for?

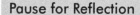

Pause for Reflection

From your responses to the preceding questions, identify a long-range goal you could pursue that's compatible with your personal abilities and talents. In the space that follows, note the goal and the abilities and talents that are compatible with it.

11. On what types of learning tasks or activities have you experienced the most success?

12. In what types of courses do you tend to earn the highest grades?

Your Personal Values

1. What matters most to you?

2. If you were to single out one thing you stand for or believe in, what would it be?

3. What would you say are your highest priorities in life?

4. What makes you feel good about what you're doing when you're doing it?

5. If there were one thing in the world you could change, improve, or make a difference in, what would it be?

> "Do what you value; value what you do."
>
> –Sidney Simon, author of *Values Clarification* (XXXX) and *In Search of Values*

6. When you have extra spending money, what do you usually spend it on?

7. When you have free time, what do you usually find yourself doing?

8. What does living a "good life" mean to you?

9. How would you define success? (What would it take for you to feel that you were successful?)

10. How would you define happiness? (What would it take for you to feel happy?)

11. Do you have any heroes or anyone you admire, look up to, or feel has set an example worth following? If yes, who and why?

Pause for Reflection

From your responses to the preceding questions, identify a long-range goal you could pursue that's compatible with your personal values. In the space that follows, note the goal and the values that are compatible with it.

12. How would you like others to see you? Rank these characteristics in the order of their priority for you (1 = highest, 4 = lowest).

- Smart   _____
- Wealthy   _____
- Creative   _____
- Caring   _____

Step 2. Gain Awareness of Your Options

The second critical step in the goal-setting process is to become aware of your long-range goal choices. For example, to effectively choose a career goal, you need to be aware of the careers options available to you and have a realistic understanding of the type of work done in these careers. To gain this knowledge, you'll need to capitalize on available resources, such as by doing the following:

1. Reading books about different careers
2. Taking career development courses
3. Interviewing people in different career fields
4. Observing (shadowing) people working in different careers

One characteristic of effective goal setting is to create goals that are realistic. In the case of careers, getting firsthand experience in actual work settings (e.g., shadowing, internships, volunteer services, and part-time work) would allow you to get a realistic view of what work is like in certain careers—as opposed to the idealized or fantasized way careers are portrayed on TV and in the movies.

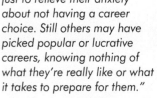

"Students [may be] pushed into careers by their families, while others have picked one just to relieve their anxiety about not having a career choice. Still others may have picked popular or lucrative careers, knowing nothing of what they're really like or what it takes to prepare for them."

–Lee Upcraft, Joni Finney, and Peter Garland, student development specialists

Step 3. Gain Awareness of the Options That Best Fit You

In college, you'll have many educational options and career goals from which to choose. To deepen your awareness of what fields may be a good fit for you, take a course in that field to test out how well it matches your interests, values, talents, and learning style. Ideally, you want to select a field that closely taps into, or builds on, your strongest skills and talents. Choosing a field that's compatible with your strongest abilities should enable you to master the skills required by that field more deeply and efficiently. You're more likely to succeed or excel in a field that draws on your talents, and the success you experience will, in turn, strengthen your self-esteem, self-confidence, and drive to continue with it. You've probably heard of the proverb "If there's a will, there's a way" (i.e., when you're motivated, you're more likely to succeed). However, it's also true that "If there's a way, there's a will" (i.e., when you know how to do something well, you're more motivated to do it).

Student Perspective

"Making good grades and doing well in school helps my ego. It gives me confidence, and I like that feeling."

–First-year college student (Franklin, 2002)

Step 4. Gain Awareness of the Process

The fourth and final step in an effective goal-setting process is becoming aware of the steps needed to reach your goal. For example, if you've set the goal of achieving a college degree in a particular major, you need to be aware of the course requirements for a degree in that major. Similarly, to set a career goal, you need to know what major or majors lead to that career because some careers require a specific major but other careers may be entered through various majors.

Pause for Reflection

Think about a career you're considering and answer the following questions:

1. Why are you considering this career? What led or caused you to become interested in this choice? Why or why not?

2. Would you say that your interest in this career is motivated primarily by intrinsic factors (i.e., factors "inside" of you, such as your personal abilities, interests, needs, and values)? Or would you say that your interest in the career is motivated more heavily by extrinsic factors (i.e., factors "outside" of you, such as starting salary, pleasing parents, and meeting family expectations or societal expectations for your gender or ethnicity)?

Remember

The four-step process for effective goal setting applies to more than just educational goals. It's a strategic process that could and should be applied to any goal you set for yourself in life, at any stage of your life.

◆ Motivation: Moving Toward Your Long-Range Goals

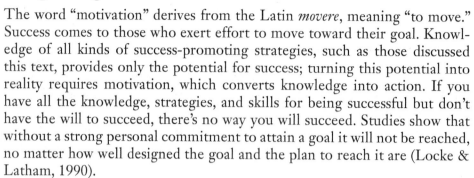

> "Mere knowledge is not power; it is only possibility. Action is power; and its highest manifestation is when it is directed by knowledge."
>
> –Francis Bacon, English philosopher, lawyer, and champion of modern science

> "You can lead a horse to water, but you can't make him drink."
>
> –Author unknown

> "Education is not the filling of a pail, but the lighting of a fire."
>
> –William Butler Yeats, Irish poet and playwright

> "Success comes to those who hustle."
>
> –Abraham Lincoln, 16th U.S. president and author of the Emancipation Proclamation, which set the stage for the abolition of slavery in the United States

The word "motivation" derives from the Latin *movere*, meaning "to move." Success comes to those who exert effort to move toward their goal. Knowledge of all kinds of success-promoting strategies, such as those discussed this text, provides only the potential for success; turning this potential into reality requires motivation, which converts knowledge into action. If you have all the knowledge, strategies, and skills for being successful but don't have the will to succeed, there's no way you will succeed. Studies show that without a strong personal commitment to attain a goal it will not be reached, no matter how well designed the goal and the plan to reach it are (Locke & Latham, 1990).

Motivation consists of three elements that may be summarized as the "three Ds" of motivation:

1. Drive
2. Discipline
3. Determination

Drive

Drive is the force within you that supplies you with the energy needed to overcome inertia and initiate action. Much like shifting into the drive gear is necessary to move your car forward, it takes personal drive to move forward and toward your goals.

People with drive aren't just dreamers: They're dreamers and doers. They take action to convert their dreams into reality, and they hustle—they go all out and give it their all, all of the time, to achieve their goals. College students with drive approach college with passion and enthusiasm. They don't hold back and work halfheartedly; they give 100 percent and put their whole heart and soul into the experience.

Discipline

Discipline includes such positive qualities as commitment, devotion, and dedication. These personal qualities enable you to keep going over an extended period. Successful people think big but start small—they take all the small steps and diligently do all the little things that need to be done, which in the long run add up to a big accomplishment: the achievement of their long-range goal.

People who are self-disciplined accept the day-to-day sweat, toil, and perspiration needed to attain their long-term aspirations. They're willing to tolerate short-term strain or pain for long-term gain. They have the self-control and self-restraint needed to resist the impulse for instant gratification or the temptation to do what they feel like doing instead of what they need to do. They're willing to sacrifice their immediate needs and desires in the short run to do what is necessary to put them where they want to be in the long run.

Pause for Reflection

Think about something that you do with drive, effort, and intensity. What thoughts, attitudes, and behaviors do you display when you do it?

Do you see ways in which you could apply the same approach to your college experience?

> "I long to accomplish some great and noble task, but it is my chief duty to accomplish small tasks as if they were great and noble."
>
> –Helen Keller, seeing- and hearing-impaired author and activist for the rights of women and the handicapped

The ability to delay short-term (and short-sighted) gratification is a distinctively human characteristic that differentiates people from other animals. As you can see in **Figure 4.1**, the upper frontal part of the brain that's responsible for long-range planning and controlling emotions and impulses is much larger in humans than it is in one of the most intelligent and human-like animals, the chimpanzee.

The part of the brain responsible for long-range planning and controlling emotions and impulses is much larger in humans than in other animals, including the highly intelligent chimpanzee.

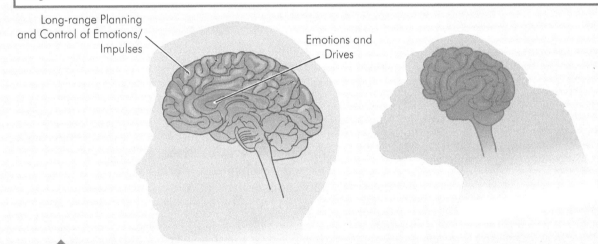

Long-range Planning and Control of Emotions/Impulses

Emotions and Drives

Figure 4.1   Where Thoughts, Emotions, and Drives are Experienced in the Brain

Personal Story   When I entered college in the mid-1970s, I was a first-generation student from an extremely impoverished background. Not only did I have to work to pay for part of my education, but I also needed to assist my family financially. I stocked grocery store shelves at night during the week and waited tables at a local county club on the weekends. Managing my life, time, school, and work required full-time effort. However, I always understood that my purpose was to graduate from college and all of my other efforts supported that goal. Thus, I went to class and arrived on time even when I did not feel like going to class. One of my greatest successes in life was to keep my mind and body focused on the ultimate prize of getting a college education. That success has paid off many times over.

—Aaron Thompson

Postponing immediate or impulsive satisfaction of material desires is a key element of effective college financing and long-term financial success.

Studies show that individuals with dedication—who are deeply committed to what they do—are more likely to report that they are healthy and happy (Maddi, 2002; Myers, 1993).

Determination

People who are determined pursue their goals with a relentless tenacity. They have the fortitude to persist in the face of frustration and the resiliency to bounce back after setbacks. If they encounter something on the road to their goal that's hard to do, they work harder and longer to do it. When they encounter a major bump or barrier, they don't let it stand in their way by giving up or giving in; instead, they dig deeper and keep going.

People with determination are also more likely to seek out challenges. Research indicates that people who continue to pursue opportunities for personal growth and self-development throughout life are more likely to report feeling happy and healthy (Maddi, 2002; Myers, 1993). Rather than remaining stagnant and simply doing what's safe, secure, or easy, they stay hungry and display an ongoing commitment to personal growth and development; they keep striving and driving to be the best they can possibly be in all aspects of life.

Student Perspective

"Why is it so hard when I *have* to do something and so easy when I *want* to do something?"

—First-year college student

"Self-discipline is the ability to make yourself do the thing you have to do, when it ought be done, whether you like it or not."

—Thomas Henry Huxley, nineteenth-century English biologist

! **Remember**

On the highway to success, you can't be a passive passenger; you're the driver and at the wheel. Your goal setting will direct you there, and your motivation will drive you there.

"*If you are going through hell, keep going.*"

—Winston Churchill

"*SUCCESS is peace of mind which is a direct result of self-satisfaction in knowing you made the effort to become the best that you are capable of becoming.*"

—John Wooden, college basketball coach and author of the *Pyramid of*

Strategies for Maintaining Motivation and Progress Toward Your Goals

Reaching your goals requires will and energy; it also requires skill and strategy. Listed here are strategies for maintaining your motivation and commitment to reaching your goals.

Put your goals in writing. When you put your goals in writing, they become visible and memorable. Doing so can provide you with a sense of direction, a source of motivation for putting your plan into action, or a written contract with yourself that makes you more accountable to following through on your commitment.

Create a visual map of your goals. Lay out your goals in the form a flowchart to show the steps you'll be taking from your short- through your mid- to your long-range goals. Visual diagrams can help you "see" where you want to go, enabling you to connect where you are now and where you want to be. Diagramming can be energizing because it gives you a sneak preview of the finish line and a maplike overview of how to get there.

Keep a record of your progress. Research indicates that the act of monitoring and recording progress toward goals can increase motivation to continue pursuing them (Matsui, Okada, & Inoshita, 1983). The act of keeping records of your progress probably increases your motivation by giving you frequent feedback on your progress and positive reinforcement for staying on track and moving toward your target (long-range goal) (Bandura & Cervone, 1983; Schunk, 1995). For example, you can keep a journal of the goals you've reached. Your entries can keep you motivated by supplying you with concrete evidence of your progress and commitment. You can also chart or graph your progress, which can sometimes provide a powerful visual display of your upward trends and patterns. Place it where you see it regularly to keep your goals in your sight and on your mind.

Develop a skeletal résumé of your goals. Include your goals as separate sections or categories that will be fleshed out as you complete them. Your to-be-completed résumé can provide a framework or blueprint for organizing, building, and tracking progress toward your goals. It can also serve as a visual reminder of the things you plan to accomplish and eventually showcase to potential employers. Furthermore, every time you look at your growing résumé, you'll be reminded of your past accomplishments, which can energize and motivate you to reach your goals. As you fill in and build up your résumé, you can literally see how much you've achieved, which boosts your self-confidence and motivation to continue achieving.

Reward yourself for making steady progress toward your long-range goals. Reward is already built into reaching your long-range goal because it represents the end of your trip, which lands you at your desired destination (e.g., in a successful career). However, short- and mid-range goals may not be desirable ends in themselves but rather means to a desirable end (your long-range goal). Consequently, you need to intentionally reward yourself for landing on these smaller stepping stones up the path to your long-range goal. When you complete these short- and mid-range goals, record and reward your accomplishments (e.g., celebrate your successful completion of midterms or finals by treating yourself to something you enjoy).

A habit of perseverance and persistence through all intermediate steps needed to reach a long-range goal, like any other habit, is more likely to continue if it's followed by a reward (positive reinforcement). Setting small goals, moving steadily toward them, and rewarding yourself for reaching them are components of a simple but powerful strategy. This strategy will help you maintain motivation over the extended period needed to reach a long-range goal.

Capitalize on available campus resources that can help you stay on track and move toward your goal. Research indicates that college success results from a combination of what students do for themselves (personal responsibility) and what they do to capitalize on the resources available to them (resourcefulness; Pascarella & Terenzini, 1991, 2005). Successful college students are resourceful students; they seek out and take advantage of college resources to help them reach their goals.

"Life isn't a matter of milestones but of moments."

—Rose Fitzgerald Kennedy, philanthropist and mother of John F. and Robert F. Kennedy

"Willpower is the personal strength and discipline, rooted in strong motivation, to carry out your plans. 'Waypower' is the exertion of willpower that helps you find resources and support."

—Jerry Pattengale, history professor and author of The Purpose-Guided Student: Dream to Succeed

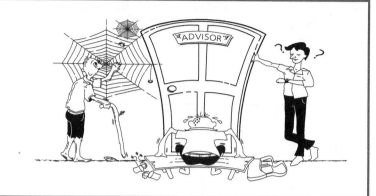

Don't only see your advisor during the mad rush of registration for the short-range purpose of scheduling next term's classes; schedule advisor appointments at less hectic times to discuss your long-range educational goals.

"Develop an inner circle of close associations in which the mutual attraction is not sharing problems or needs. The mutual attraction should be values and goals."

–Denis Waitley, former mental trainer for U.S. Olympic athletes and author of *Seeds of Greatness*

"I make progress by having people around who are smarter than I am."

–Henry Kaiser, successful industrialist known as the father of American shipbuilding

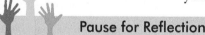

Pause for Reflection

What would you say is the biggest setback or obstacle you've overcome in your life thus far?

How did you overcome it? (What enabled you to get past it or prevented you from being blocked by it?)

"We are what we think."

–Hindu Prince Siddhartha Gautama, a.k.a. Buddha, founder of the philosophy and religion of Buddhism

For example, a resourceful student who's having trouble deciding what field of study to pursue for a degree will seek assistance from an academic advisor on campus. A resourceful student who's interested in a particular career but is unclear about the best educational path to take toward that career will use the Career Development Center as a resource.

Use your social resources. The power of social support groups for helping people achieve personal goals is well documented by research in various fields (Ewell, 1997; Moeller, 1999). You can use the power of people by surrounding yourself with peers who are committed to successfully achieving their educational goals and by avoiding "toxic" people who are likely to poison your plans or dampen your dreams.

For example, find a supportive and motivating friend and make a mutual pact to help each other reach your respective goals. This step could be taken to a more formal level by drawing up a "social contract" whereby you and your partner are "cowitnesses" or designated social-support agents whose role is to help each other stay on track and move toward long-range goals. Studies show that making a public commitment to a goal increases your commitment to it, probably because it becomes a matter of personal pride and integrity that's seen not only through your own eyes but also through the eyes of others (Hollenbeck, Williams, & Klein, 1989).

Convert setbacks into comebacks. The type of thoughts you have after experiencing a setback can affect your emotional reaction to it and the action you take in response. For instance, what you think about a poor performance (e.g., a poor test grade) can affect your emotional reaction to that grade and what action, or lack of action, you take in response to it. You can react to the poor grade by knocking yourself down with a putdown ("I'm a loser") or by building yourself back up with a positive pep talk ("I'm going to learn from my mistakes on this test and rebound with a stronger performance on the next one").

If a poor past performance is seen not as a personal failure but as learning opportunity, the setback may be turned into a comeback. Here are some notable people who turned early setbacks into successful comebacks:

- Louis Pasteur, famous bacteriologist, who failed his admission test to the University of Paris;
- Albert Einstein, Nobel Prize–winning physicist, who failed math in elementary school;

- Thomas Edison, prolific inventor, who was once expelled from school as "uneducable";
- Johnny Unitas, Hall of Fame football player, who was cut twice from professional football teams early in his career.

In response to their early setbacks, these successful people didn't get bitter; they got better. Getting mad or sad about a setback is likely to make you stressed or depressed and leave you focused on a past event that you can no longer control. By reacting rationally to a poor performance and using the results as feedback to improve your future performance, you gain control of it. You put yourself in the position to convert the setback into a comeback and turn a liability into an opportunity.

This can be a challenging task because when you have an experience, your response to it passes through emotional areas of the brain before it reaches areas of the brain involved in rational thinking and reasoning (see **Figure 4.2**; LeDoux, 1998).

Thus, your brain reacts to events emotionally before it does rationally. If the experience triggers intense emotions (e.g., anger, anxiety, or sadness after receiving a bad test grade), your emotional reaction has the potential to short-circuit or wipe out rational thinking. Thus, if you find yourself beginning to feel overwhelmed by negative emotions following a setback, you need to consciously and quickly block them by rational thoughts (e.g., thinking or saying to yourself, "Before I get carried away emotionally, let me think this through rationally"). This involves more than simply saying, "I have to think positively." Instead, you should develop a set of specific counterthinking strategies ready to use as soon as you begin to think negatively. Described here are thinking strategies that you can use to maintain motivation and minimize negative thinking in reaction to setbacks.

Whatever you do, don't let setbacks make you mad or sad, particularly at early stages in your college experience, because you're just beginning to learn what it takes to be successful in college. A bad performance can be turned into a good learning experience by using the results as an error detector for identifying sources or causes of your mistakes and as feedback for improving your future performance.

> "What happens is not as important as how you react to what happens."
> –Thaddeus Golas, *Lazy Man's Guide to Enlightenment*

> "When written in Chinese, the word 'crisis' is composed of two characters. One represents danger, and the other represents opportunity."
> –John F. Kennedy, 35th U.S. president

Information passes through the emotional center of the brain (lower, shaded area) before reaching the center responsible for rational thinking (upper area). Thus, people need to counteract their tendency to respond emotionally and irrationally to personal setbacks by making a conscious attempt to respond rationally and reflectively.

Figure 4.2 The Brain's Human Attention System

Remember

Don't let past mistakes bring you down emotionally or motivationally; however, don't ignore or neglect them either. Instead, inspect them, reflect on them, and correct them so that they don't happen again.

Maintain positive expectations. Just as your thoughts in reaction to something that's already taken place can affect your motivation, so can thoughts

"Whether you think you can or you can't, you're right."

–Henry Ford, founder of Ford Motor and one of the richest people of his generation

Pause for Reflection

Would you consider yourself to be an optimist or a pessimist?

In what situations are you more likely to think optimistically and pessimistically?

Why?

"A pessimist sees the difficulty in every opportunity; an optimist sees the opportunity in every difficulty."

–Winston Churchill

"Many people take no care of their money 'til they come nearly to the end of it, and others do just the same with their time."

–Johann Wolfgang von Goethe, German poet, dramatist, and author of the epic Faust

"You've got to think about 'big things' while you're doing small things, so that all the small things go in the right direction."

–Alvin Toffler, American futurologist and author who predicted the future effects of technology on our society

about what you expect to happen next affect what will occur. Your expectations of things to come can be either positive or negative. For example, before a test you could think, "I'm poised, confident, and ready to do it." Or you could think, "I know I'm going to fail this test; I just know it."

Expectations can lead to what sociologists and psychologists have called a self-fulfilling prophecy—a positive or negative expectation leads you to act in a way that is consistent with your expectation, which, in turn, makes your expectation come true. For instance, if you expect you're going to fail an exam ("What's the use? I'm going to fail anyway."), you're less likely to put as much effort into studying for the test. During the test, your negative expectation is likely reduce your test confidence and elevate you test anxiety; for example, if you experience difficulty with the first item on a test, you may get anxious and begin to think you're going to have difficulty with all remaining items and flunk the entire exam. All of this negative thinking is likely to increase the probability that your expectation of doing poorly on the exam will become a reality.

In contrast, positive expectations can lead to a positive self-fulfilling prophecy: If you expect to do well on an exam, you're more likely to demonstrate higher levels of effort, confidence, and concentration, all of which combine to increase the likelihood that you'll earn a higher test grade. Research shows that learning and practicing positive self-talk increase a sense of hope—a belief in the ability to reach goals and the ability to actually reach them (Snyder, 1994).

Keep your eye on the prize. Don't lose sight of the long-term consequences of your short-term choices and decisions. Long-range thinking is the key to reaching long-range goals. Unfortunately, however, humans are often more motivated by short-range thinking because it produces quicker results and more immediate gratification. It's more convenient and tempting to think in the short term ("I like it. I want it. I want it now."). Studies show that the later consequences occur, the less likely people are to consider those consequences when they make their decisions (Ainslie, 1975; Elster & Lowenstein, 1992; Lewin, 1935). For example, choosing to do what you feel like doing instead of doing work that needs to be done is why so many people procrastinate, and choosing to use a credit card to get something now instead of saving money to buy it later is why so many people pile up credit-card debt.

To be successful in the long run, you need to keep your focus on the big picture—your long-range goals and dreams that provide your motivation. At the same time, you need to focus on the details—the due dates, to-do lists, and day-to-day duties that require perspiration but keep you on track and going in the right direction.

Thus, setting an important life goal and steadily progressing toward that long-range goal requires two means of focusing. One is a narrow-focus lens that allows you to view the details immediately in front of you. The other is a wide-focus lens that gives you a big-picture view of what's further ahead of you (your long-range goal). Success involves seeing the connection between the small, short-term chores and challenges (e.g., completing an assignment that's due next week) and the large, long-range picture (e.g., college graduation and a successful future). Thus, you need to periodically shift from a wide-focus lens that gives you a vision of the bigger, more distant picture to a narrow-focus lens that shifts your attention to completing the smaller tasks immediately ahead of you and keeping on the path to your long-range goal: future success.

> "Whoever wants to reach a distant goal must take many small steps."
>
> –Helmut Schmidt, former chancellor of West Germany

Personal Story

When I was an assistant coach for a youth soccer team, I noticed that many of the less successful players tended to make one of two mistakes when they were trying to move with the ball. Some spent too much time looking down, focusing on the ball at their feet and trying to be sure that they did not lose control of it. By not lifting their head and looking ahead periodically, they often missed open territory, open teammates, or an open goal. Other unsuccessful players made the opposite mistake: They spent too much time with their heads up, trying to see saw where they were headed. By not looking down at the ball immediately in front of them, they often lost control of the ball, moved ahead without it, or sometimes stumbled over it and fell flat on their face. Successful soccer players on the team were in the habit of shifting their focus between looking down to maintain control of the ball immediately in front of them and lifting their eyes to see where they were headed.

The more I thought about how successful players alternate between handling the ball in front of them and viewing the goal further ahead, it struck me that this was a metaphor for success in life. Successful people alternate between both of these perspectives so that they don't lose sight of how completing the short-range tasks in front of them connects with the long-range goal ahead of them.

—Joe Cuseo

! Remember

Keep your future dreams and current tasks in clear focus. Integrating these two perspectives will produce an image that can provide you with the inspiration to complete your college education and the determination to complete your day-to-day tasks.

◆ Personal Character

Reaching your goals depends on acquiring and using effective strategies, but it takes something more. Ultimately, success emerges from the inside out; it flows from positive qualities or attributes found within you, which, collectively, form your personal character.

We become successful and effective humans when our actions and deeds become a natural extension of who we are and how we live. At first, developing the habits associated with achieving success and leading a productive life may require effort and intense concentration because these behaviors may be new to you. However, if these actions occur consistently enough, they're transformed into natural habits.

When you engage in effective habits regularly, they become virtues. A virtue may be defined as a characteristic or trait that is valued as good or admirable, and someone who possesses a collection of important virtues is said to be a person of character (Peterson & Seligman, 2004).

> "If you do not find it within yourself, where will you go to get it?"
>
> –Zen saying (Zen is a branch of Buddhism that emphasizes seeing deeply into the nature of things and ongoing self-awareness)

> "We are what we repeatedly do. Excellence, then, is not an act, but a habit."
>
> –Aristotle, ancient Greek philosopher

Three virtues in particular are important for success in college and beyond:

1. Wisdom
2. Integrity
3. Civility

Wisdom

When you use the knowledge you acquire to guide your behavior toward doing what is effective or good, you demonstrate wisdom (Staudinger & Baltes, 1994). For example, if you apply your knowledge of the four research-based principles found in this book (i.e., active involvement, resourcefulness, collaboration, and reflection) to guide your behavior in college, you are exhibiting wisdom.

Integrity

The word "integrity" comes from the same root as the word "integrate," which captures a key characteristic of people with integrity: their outer self is integrated or in harmony with their inner self. For example, "outer-directed" people decide on their personal standards of conduct by looking outward to see what others are doing (Riesman, Glazer, & Denney, 2001). In contrast, individuals with integrity are "inner directed"—their actions reflect their inner qualities and are guided by their conscience.

People with character are not only wise but also ethical. Besides doing what effective, they do what is good or right. They don't pursue success at any ethical cost. They have a strong set of personal values that guide them in the right moral direction.

For example, college students with integrity don't cheat and then rationalize that their cheating is acceptable because "others are doing it." They don't look to other people to determine their own values, and they don't conform to the norm if the norm is wrong; instead, they look inward and let their conscience be their guide.

Civility

People of character are personally and socially responsible. They model what it means to live in a civilized community by demonstrating civility—they respect the rights of other members of their community, including members of their college community. In exercising their own rights and freedoms, they don't step (or stomp) on the rights and freedoms of others. People with civic character not only behave civilly but also treat other members of their community in a sensitive and courteous manner and are willing to confront others who violate the rights of their fellow citizens. They are model citizens whose actions visibly demonstrate to others that they oppose any attempt to disrespect or interfere with the rights of fellow members of their community.

Insensitive Use of Personal Technology in the Classroom: A Violation of Civility

Behavior that interferes with the rights of others to learn or teach in the college classroom represents a violation of civility. Listed here are behaviors

---

Pause for Reflection

Thus far in your college experience, which of the following four principles of success have you put into practice most effectively? (Circle one.)

active involvement   resourcefulness
collaboration   reflection

Which of the four principles do you think will be the most difficult for you to put into practice? (Circle one.)

active involvement   resourcefulness
collaboration   reflection

Why?

Student Perspective

"To achieve success through deceitful actions is not success at all. In life, credibility is more important than credentials, and if honesty is not valued personally, others will not value you. Lack of self-respect results in lack of respect from others."

–First-year college student's reflection on an academic integrity violation illustrating classroom incivility that involve student use of personal technology. These behaviors are increasing in college, as is the anger of college instructors who witness them, so it is wise to avoid engaging in them.

1. **Leave your cell phone off or outside the classroom.** Keeping a cell phone on in class is a clear example of classroom incivility because if it rings it will interfere with the right of others to learn. In a study of college students who were exposed to a cell phone ringing during a class session and were later tested for their recall of information presented in class, they scored approximately 25 percent worse when attempting to recall information that was presented at the time a cell phone rang. This attention loss occurred even when the material was covered by the professor before the cell phone rang and was projected on a slide during the call. This study showed that students were further distracted when classmates frantically searched through a bag or pockets to find and silence a ringing (or vibrating) phone (Shelton, Elliot, Eaves, & Exner, 2009). These findings clearly suggest that the civil thing to do is turn your cell phone off before entering the classroom or keep it out of the classroom altogether.

2. **Save text messaging until after class.** Just as answering a cell phone during class represents a violation of civility because it interferes with the learning of other members of the classroom community, so too does text messaging. Although messaging is often viewed it as a quick and soundless way to communicate, it can momentarily disrupt learning if it takes place when the instructor is covering critical or complex information. Text messaging while driving a car can take your eyes and mind off the road, thereby putting yourself and others in danger. Similarly, messaging in the classroom takes your eyes and mind off the instructor and any visual aids being displayed at the time. It's also discourteous or disrespectful to instructors when you put your head down and turn your attention from them while they're speaking to the class. Finally, it can be distracting or disturbing to classmates who see you messaging instead of listening and learning.

"There is no pillow as soft as a clear conscience."

–French proverb

"Our character is what we do when we think no one is looking."

–Henry David Thoreau, American philosopher and lifelong abolitionist who championed the human spirit over materialism and conformity

Emollit mores nec sinit esse feros. ("Learning humanizes character and does not permit it to be cruel.")

–Motto of the University of South Carolina

Pause for Reflection

Have you observed an example of personal integrity that you thought was exceptionally admirable or particularly despicable?

What was the situation, and what was done that demonstrated integrity or an integrity violation?

Snapshot Summary

4.1

Guidelines for Civil and Responsible Use of Personal Technology in the College Classroom

- Turn your cell phone completely off or leave it out of the classroom. In the rare case of an emergency when you think you need to leave it on, inform you instructor.
- Don't check your cell phone during the class period by turning it on and off.
- Don't text message during class.
- Don't surf the Web during class.
- Don't touch your cell phone during any exam because this may be viewed by the instructor as a form of cheating.

◆ Summary and Conclusion

Goal setting only becomes meaningful if you have motivation to reach the goals you set. Motivation may be said to consist of three Ds: drive, discipline, and determination. Drive is the internal force that gives you the energy to overcome inertia and initiate action. Discipline consists of positive, personal qualities such as commitment, devotion, and dedication that enable you to sustain your effort over time. Determination enables you to relentlessly pursue your goals, persist in the face of frustration, and bounce back after any setback.

Reaching your goals requires all three Ds; it also involves the use of effective self-motivational strategies, such as:

- Visualizing reaching your long-range goals;
- Putting goals in writing;
- Creating a visual map of your goals;
- Keeping a record of your progress;
- Developing a skeletal résumé;
- Rewarding yourself for progress toward long-range goals;
- Capitalizing on available campus and social resources;
- Converting setbacks into comebacks by using positive self-talk, maintaining positive expectations, and avoiding negative self-fulfilling prophecies; and
- Keeping your eye on the long-term consequences of your short-term choices and decisions.

To reach your goals you must acquire and use effective strategies, but you also need character. Three character traits or virtues are particularly important for college and life success:

- **Wisdom.** Using knowledge to guide your behavior toward effective or good actions.
- **Integrity.** Doing what is ethical. Plagiarism, or giving readers the impression (intentionally or not) that someone else's work is your own, is a violation of academic integrity.
- **Civility.** Respecting the rights of other members of your college and larger communities. Violations of civility include insensitive use of personal technology in the classroom (e.g., using cell phones and text messaging).

Studies of highly successful people, whether scientists, musicians, writers, chess masters, or basketball stars, consistently show that achieving high levels of skill and success requires practice (Levitin, 2006). This is true even of people whose success is thought to be to be due to natural gifts or talents. For example, during the Beatles' first 4 years as a band and before they burst into musical stardom, they performed live an estimated 1,200 times, and many of these performances lasted 5 or more hours a night. They performed (practiced) for more hours during those first 4 years than most bands perform during their entire career. Similarly, before Bill Gates became a computer software giant and creator of Microsoft, he logged almost 1,600 hours of computer time during one 7-month period alone, averaging 8 hours a day, 7 days a week (Gladwell, 2008).

What these extraordinary success stories show is that it takes time and practice for effective skills to take hold and take effect. Reaching long-range goals means making small steps; they aren't achieved in one quick, quantum leap. If you are patient and persistent and consistently practice effective strategies, their positive effects will gradually accumulate and eventually have a significant impact on your success in college and beyond.

Remember

Success isn't a short-range goal; it's not a sprint but a long-distance run that takes patience and perseverance to complete. What matters most is not how fast you start but where you finish.

Learning More Through the World Wide Web

Internet-Based Resources for Further Information on Liberal Arts Education

For additional information related to the ideas discussed in this chapter, we recommend the following Web sites:

Goal Setting: www.siue.edu/SPIN/activity.html

Self-Motivational Strategies: www.selfmotivationstrategies.com

Academic Integrity and Character Development: www.academicintegrity.org/useful_links/index.php

4.1 Prioritizing Important Life Goals

Consider the following life goals. Rank them in the order of their priority for you (1 = highest, 5 = lowest).

___ Emotional well-being

___ Spiritual growth

___ Physical health

___ Social relationships

___ Rewarding career

Self-Assessment Questions

1. What were the primary reasons behind your first- and last-ranked choices?

2. Have you established any short- or mid-range goals for reaching your highest-ranked choice? If yes, what are they? If no, what could they be?

4.2 Setting Goals for Reducing the Gap Between the Ideal Scenario and the Current Reality

Think of an aspect of your life with a gap between what you hoped it would be (the ideal) and what it is (the reality). On the lines that follow, identify goals you could purse that would reduce this gap.

Long-range goal: _____

Mid-range goal: _____

Short-range goal: _____

Use the form that follows to identify strategies for reaching each of these three goals. Consider the following areas for each goal:

- Actions to be taken
- Available resources
- Possible roadblocks
- Potential solutions to roadblocks

Long-range goal: _____

- Actions to be taken:

- Available resources:

- Possible roadblocks:

- Potential solutions to roadblocks:

Mid-range goal: _____

- Actions to be taken:

- Available resources:

- Possible roadblocks:

- Potential solutions to roadblocks:

Short-range goal: _____

- Actions to be taken:

- Available resources:

- Possible roadblocks:

- Potential solutions to roadblocks:

4.3 Converting Setbacks into Comebacks: Transforming Pessimism into Optimism

In Hamlet, Shakespeare wrote: "There is nothing good or bad, but thinking makes it so." His point was that experiences have the potential to be positive or negative, depending on how people interpret them and react to them.

Listed here is a series of statements representing negative interpretations and reactions to a situation or experience:

1. "I'm just not good at this."

2. "There's nothing I can do about it."

3. "Things will never be the same."

4. "Nothing is going to change."

5. "This always happens to me."

6. "This is unbearable."

7. "Everybody is going to think I'm a loser."

8. "I'm trapped, and there's no way out."

For each of the preceding statements, replace the negative statement with a statement that represents a more positive interpretation or reaction.

No Goals, No Direction

Amy Aimless decided to go to college because it seemed like that's what she was expected to do. All of her closest friends were going and her parents have talked to her about going to college as long as she can remember.

Now that she's in her first term, Amy isn't sure she made the right decision. She has no educational or career goals, nor does she have any idea about what her major might be. None of the subjects she took in high school and none of the courses she's taking in her first term of college have really sparked her interest. Since she has no goals or sense of purpose, she's beginning to think that being in college is a waste of time and money, so she's considering withdrawing at the end of her first term.

Reflection and Discussion Questions

1. What advice would you give Amy about whether she should remain in college or withdraw?

2. What suggestion would you have for Amy that might help her find some sense of educational purpose or direction?

3. How could you counter Amy's claim that no subjects interest her as a possible college major?

4. Would you agree that Amy is currently wasting her time and her parents' money? Why?

5. Would you agree that Amy shouldn't have begun college in the first place? Why?

Your Collegiate "Bucket List"—20 Goals/Dreams

This exercise will have you create your own collegiate "Bucket List" of goals/dreams—a list of **20 dreams** you want to complete during your time at UNCG. Use this as an opportunity to put your goals and dreams on paper—THINK BIG! Challenge yourself to not only come up with your list, but provide a specific date for when you'd like to accomplish/fulfill each goal/dream. You can get it done within one semester, sophomore year, junior year, post-graduation, or at any point in your collegiate career! Think about academic, personal, and professional goals/dreams. You will utilize this list to create your Personal Success Plan. Here are some areas you might want to consider to help you get started:

Family	Career	Health	Education
Recreation	Service	Travel	Romance
Spiritual	Financial	Adventure	Relationships

Goal/Dream	When to complete? (circle or fill in blank)
1.	Sem Soph Jr. Sr. Grad or by: _____
2.	Sem Soph Jr. Sr. Grad or by: _____
3.	Sem Soph Jr. Sr. Grad or by: _____
4.	Sem Soph Jr. Sr. Grad or by: _____
5.	Sem Soph Jr. Sr. Grad or by: _____
6.	Sem Soph Jr. Sr. Grad or by: _____
7.	Sem Soph Jr. Sr. Grad or by: _____
8.	Sem Soph Jr. Sr. Grad or by: _____
9.	Sem Soph Jr. Sr. Grad or by: _____
10.	Sem Soph Jr. Sr. Grad or by: _____
11.	Sem Soph Jr. Sr. Grad or by: _____

Adapted from The "Bucket List"—20 Life-long Dreams created by William H. Johnson, Jr., Office of Life Planning & Personal Development, The University of North Carolina at Greensboro.

12.	Sem Soph Jr. Sr. Grad or by: _____
13.	Sem Soph Jr. Sr. Grad or by: _____
14.	Sem Soph Jr. Sr. Grad or by: _____
15.	Sem Soph Jr. Sr. Grad or by: _____
16.	Sem Soph Jr. Sr. Grad or by: _____
17.	Sem Soph Jr. Sr. Grad or by: _____
18.	Sem Soph Jr. Sr. Grad or by: _____
19.	Sem Soph Jr. Sr. Grad or by: _____
20.	Sem Soph Jr. Sr. Grad or by: _____

Your First Year Resources

The first year of college is an exciting and challenging time. We want you to have the best experience possible, so we've designed a website just for you. It's full of tips, tricks, and links to help you make the most of Your First Year! If you have questions or need help finding your way at UNCG, you can always email us at yfy@uncg.edu. Visit yourfirstyear.uncg.edu and the websites below for helpful resources and services about goal setting, motivation and character.

Academic Advising Centers   **Refer to Chapter 12 for comprehensive list**

Career Services Center   **336-334-5454**
http://csc.uncg.edu/

Dean of Students Office   **336-334-5514**
http://deanofstudents.uncg.edu/

Students First Office   **336-334-5730**
http://studentsfirst.uncg.edu/

Student Success Center   **336-334-3878**
http://success.uncg.edu/

Time Management

ACTIVATE YOUR THINKING | **Journal Entry** | **5.1**

Complete the following sentence with the first thought that comes to your mind:

For me, time is . . .

_____

_____

_____

LEARNING GOAL

To help you appreciate the significance of managing time and supply you with a powerful set of time-management strategies that can be used to promote your success in college and beyond.

◆ The Importance of Time Management

For many first-year students, the beginning of college means the beginning of more independent living and self-management. Even if you've lived on your own for some time, managing time is an important skill to possess because you're likely juggling multiple responsibilities, including school, family, and work.

In college, the academic calendar and your class schedule differ radically from those during high school. You have less "seat time" in class each week and more "free time" outside of class, which you have the freedom to self-manage; it is not closely monitored by school authorities or family members, and you are expected to do more academic work on your own outside of class. Time-management skills grow in importance when a person's time is less structured or controlled by others, leaving the individual with more decision-making power about how to spend personal time. Thus, it is no surprise that research shows the ability to manage time effectively as playing a crucial role in college success (Erickson, Peters, & Strommer, 2006).

Simply stated, college students who have difficulty managing their time have difficulty managing college. In one study, sophomores who had an outstanding first year in college (both academically and socially) were compared with another group of sophomores who struggled during the prior year. Interviews conducted with these students revealed one key difference between the two groups: The sophomores who experienced a successful first year repeatedly brought up the topic of time during the interviews. The successful students

Student Perspective

"The major difference [between high school and college] is time. You have so much free time on your hands that you don't know what to do for most of the time."

–First-year college student
(Erickson & Strommer, 1991)

Student Perspective

"I cannot stress enough that you need to intelligently budget your time."

–Advice to new college students from a first-year student

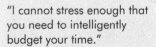

said they had to think carefully about how they spent their time and that they needed to budget their time because it was a scarce resource. In contrast, the sophomores who experienced difficulty in their first year of college hardly talked about the topic of time during their interviews, even when they were specifically asked about it (Light, 2001).

Studies also indicate that managing time plays a pivotal role in the lives of working adults. Setting priorities and balancing multiple responsibilities (e.g., work and family) that compete for limited time and energy can be a juggling act and a source of stress for people of all ages (Harriott & Ferrari, 1996).

For these reasons, time management should be viewed not only as a college-success strategy but also as a life-management and life-success skill. Studies show that people who manage their time well report they are more in control of their life and are happier (Myers, 1993). In short, when you gain greater control of your time, you become more satisfied with your life.

Personal Story

I started the process of earning my doctorate a little later in life than other students. I was a married father with a preschool daughter (Sara). Since my wife left for work early in the morning, it was always my duty to get up and get Sara's day going in the right direction. In addition, I had to do the same for me—which was often harder than doing it for my daughter. Three days of my week were spent on campus in class or in the library. (We did not have quick access to research on home computers then as you do now.) The other two days of the workweek and the weekend were spent on household chores, family time, and studying.

I knew that if I was going to have any chance of finishing my Ph.D in a reasonable amount of time and have a decent family life I had to adopt an effective schedule for managing my time. Each day of the week, I held to a strict routine. I got up in the morning, drank coffee while reading the paper, took a shower, got Sara ready for school, and took her to school. Once I returned home, I put a load of laundry in the washer, studied, wrote, and spent time concentrating on what I needed to do to be successful from 8:30 a.m. to 12:00 p.m. every day. At lunch, I had a pastrami and cheese sandwich and a soft drink while rewarding myself by watching *Perry Mason* reruns until 1:00 p.m. I then continued to study until it was time to pick up Sara from school. Each night I spent time with my wife and daughter and prepared for the next day. I lived a life that had a preset schedule. By following this schedule, I was able to successfully complete my doctorate in a decent amount of time while giving my family the time they needed. (By the way, I still watch *Perry Mason* reruns.)

—Aaron Thompson

Strategies for Managing Time

You can use a series of strategies to manage your time:

1. **Analyzing.** Breaking down time into segments and work into specific tasks;
2. **Itemizing.** Identifying what you need to accomplish and when it needs to be done;
3. **Prioritizing.** Organizing your tasks based on their importance.

The following steps can help you discover time you did not know you had and use the time you have more wisely.

1. Break down your time and become more aware about how it's spent.

Have you ever asked yourself "Where did all the time go?" or told yourself "I just can't seem to find the time"? One way to find out where your time went is by taking a time inventory (Webber, 1991). To do this, you conduct a time analysis by breaking down and tracking your time, recording what you do and when you do it. By mapping out how you spend time, you become more aware of how much total time you have available to you and how its component parts are used, including patches of wasted time in which you get little or nothing accomplished. You don't have to do this time analysis for more than a week or two. This should be long enough to give you some sense of where your time is going and allow you to start developing strategies for using your time more effectively and efficiently.

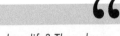

Pause for Reflection

Do you have time gaps between your classes this term? If you do, what have you been doing during those periods?

What would you say is your greatest time waster?

Do you see a need to stop or eliminate it?

If no, why not? If yes, what would you like to see yourself doing instead?

2. Identify which tasks you need to accomplish and when you need to accomplish them.

People make lists to be sure they don't forget items they need from the grocery store or people they want to be sure are invited to a party. You can use the same list-making strategy for work tasks so that you don't forget to do them or forget to do them on time. Studies of effective people show that they are list makers and they write out lists not only for grocery items and wedding invitations but also for things they want to accomplish each day (Covey, 1990).

You can itemize your tasks by listing them in either of the following time-management tools:

- **Small, portable planner.** List all your major assignments and exams for the term, along with their due dates. By pulling all work tasks from different courses in one place, it is easier to keep track of what you have to do and when you have to do it.
- **Large, stable calendar.** Record in the calendar's date boxes your major assignments for the academic term and when they are due. Place the calendar in a position or location where it's in full view and you can't help but see it every day (e.g., on your bedroom or refrigerator door). If you regularly and literally "look" at the things you have to do, you're less likely to "overlook" them, forget about them, or subconsciously push them out of your mind.

"Doesn't thou love life? Then do not squander time, for that is the stuff life is made of."

—Benjamin Franklin, eighteenth-century inventor, newspaper writer, and cosigner of the *Declaration of Independence*

© Gary Woodward, 2010. Under license from Shutterstock, Inc.

Using a personal planner is an effective way to itemize your academic commitments.

3. Rank your tasks in order of their importance.

Once you've itemized your work by listing all tasks you need to do, prioritize them—determine the order in which you will do them. Prioritizing basically involves ranking your tasks in terms of their importance, with the highest-ranked tasks appearing at the top of your list to ensure that they are tackled first. How do you determine which tasks are most important and should be ranked highest? Two criteria or standards of judgment can be used to help determine which tasks should be your priorities:

- **Urgency.** Tasks that are closest to their deadline or due date should receive high priority. For example, finishing an assignment that's due tomorrow should receive higher priority than starting an assignment that's due next month.

Personal Story

My mom was the person who ensured I got up for school on time. Once I got to school the bell would ring to let me know to move on to the next class. When I returned home I had to do my homework and chores. My daily and weekly schedules were dictated by someone else.

When I entered college, I quickly realized that I needed to develop my own system for being organized, focused, and productive without the assistance of my mother. Since I came from a modest background, I had to work my way through college. Juggling schedules became an art and science for me. I knew the things that I could not miss, such as work and school, and the things I could miss—TV and girls. (OK, TV, but not girls.)

After college, I spent 10 years in business—a world where I was measured by being on time and a productive "bottom line." It was during this time that I discovered a scheduling book. When I became a professor, I had other mechanisms to make sure I did what I needed to do when I needed to do it. This was largely based on when my classes were offered. Other time was dedicated to working out and spending time with my family. Now, as an administrator, I have an assistant who keep my schedule for me. She tells me where I am going, how long I should be there, and what I need to accomplish while I am there. Unless you take your parents with you or have the luxury of a personal assistant, it's important to determine which activities are required and to allow time in your schedule for fun. Use a planner!

—Aaron Thompson

Pause for Reflection

Do you have a calendar for the current academic term that you carry with you?

If yes, why? If no, why not?

If you carry neither a calendar nor a work list, why do you think you don't?

Student Perspective

"I like to get rid of my stress by doing what I have to do first, like if it's a paper."

–First-year college student

- **Gravity.** Tasks that carry the heaviest weight (count the most) should receive highest priority. For example, if an assignment worth 100 points and another worth 10 points are due at the same time, the 100-point task should receive higher priority. You want to be sure you invest your work time on tasks that matter most. Just like investing money, you want to invest your time on tasks that yield the greatest dividends or payoff.

One strategy for prioritizing your tasks is to divide them into A, B, and C lists (Lakein, 1973). The A list is for *essential* tasks—what you *must* do now. The B list is for *important* tasks—what you *should* do soon. Finally, the C list is for *optional* tasks—what you *could* or *might* do if there is time remaining after you've completed the tasks on the A and B lists. Organizing your tasks in this fashion can help you decide how to divide your labor in a way that ensures you put first things first. What you don't want to do is waste time doing unimportant things and deceive yourself into thinking that you're keeping busy and getting things done when actually you're doing things that just take your time (and mind) away from the more important things that should be done.

At first glance, itemizing and prioritizing may appear to be rather boring chores. However, if you look at these mental tasks carefully, they require many higher-level thinking skills, such as

1. **Analysis.** Dividing time into component elements or segments and breaking down work into specific tasks;
2. **Evaluation.** Critically evaluating the relative importance or value of tasks; and
3. **Synthesis.** Organizing individual tasks into classes or categories based on their level of priority.

Thus, developing self-awareness about how you spend time is more than a menial, clerical task; when done with thoughtful reflection, it's an exercise in higher-level thinking. It's also a good exercise in values clarification because what people choose to spend their time on is a more accurate indicator of what they truly value rather than what they say they value.

Develop a Time-Management Plan

Humans are creatures of habit. Routines help you organize and gain control of your lives. Doing things by design, rather than leaving them to chance or accident, is the first step toward making things happen for you rather than allowing them to happen you—by chance or accident. By developing an intentional plan for how you're going to spend your time, you're developing a plan to gain greater control of your life.

Don't buy into the myth that you don't have time to plan because it takes too much time that could be spent getting started and getting things done. Time-management experts estimate that the amount of time you spend planning your work reduces your total work time by a factor of three (Lakein, 1973). In other words, for every one unit of time you spend planning, you save three units of work time. Thus, 5 minutes of planning time will typically save you 15 minutes of total work time, and 10 minutes of planning time will save you 30 minutes of work time. This saving of work time probably occurs because you develop a clearer game plan or plan of attack for identifying what needs to be done and the best order in which to get it done. A clearer sense of direction reduces the number of mistakes you may make due to false starts—starting the work but then having to restart it because you started off in the wrong direction. If you have no plan of attack, you're more likely to go off track; when you discover this at some point after you've started, you're then forced to retreat and start over.

As the proverb goes, "A stitch in time saves nine." Planning your time represents the "stitch" (unit of time) that saves you nine additional stitches (units of time). Similar to successful chess players, successful time managers plan ahead and anticipate their next moves.

> "Time = Life. Therefore waste your time and waste your life, or master your time and master your life."
>
> —Alan Lakein, international expert on time management and author of the best-selling book *How to Get Control of Your Time and Your Life* (1973)

> "Failing to plan is planning to fail."
>
> —Alan Lakein

Elements of a Comprehensive Time-Management Plan

Once you've accepted the notion that taking the time to plan your time saves you time in the long run, you're ready to design a time-management plan. The following are elements of a comprehensive, well-designed plan for managing time.

1. A good time-management plan should have several time frames.

Your academic time-management plan should include:

- A *long-range* plan for the entire academic term that identifies deadline dates for reports and papers that are due toward the end of the term;

- A *mid-range* plan for the upcoming month and week; and
- A *short-range* plan for the following day.

The preceding time frames may be integrated into a total time-management plan for the term by taking the following steps:

- Identify deadline dates of all assignments, or the time when each of them must be completed (your long-range plan).
- Work backward from these final deadlines to identify dates when you plan to begin taking action on these assignments (your short-range plan).
- Identify intermediate dates when you plan to finish particular parts or pieces of the total assignment (your mid-range plan).

This three-stage plan should help you make steady progress throughout the term on college assignments that are due later in the term. At the same time, it will reduce your risk of procrastinating and running out of time.

Here's how you can put this three-stage plan into action this term

a. **Develop a long-range plan for the academic term.**
   - Review the *course syllabus (course outline)* for each class you are enrolled in this term, and highlight all major exams, tests, quizzes, assignments, and papers and the dates on which they are due.

! Remember

College professors are more likely than high school teachers to expect you to rely on your course syllabus to keep track of what you have to do and when you have to do it.

   - Obtain a *large calendar* for the academic term (available at your campus bookstore or learning center) and record all your exams, assignments, and so on, for all your courses in the calendar boxes that represent their due dates. To fit this information within the calendar boxes, use creative abbreviations to represent different tasks, such as E for exam and TP for term paper (not toilet paper). When you're done, you'll have a centralized chart or map of deadline dates and a potential master plan for the entire term.

b. **Plan your week.**
   - Make a map of your *weekly schedule* that includes times during the week when you are in class, when you typically eat and sleep, and if you are employed, when you work.
   - If you are a full-time college student, find *at least 25 total hours per week* when you can do academic work outside the classroom. (These 25 hours can be pieced together in any way you like, including time between daytime classes and work commitments, evening time, and weekend time.) When adding these 25 hours to the time you spend in class each week, you will end up with a 40-hour workweek, similar to any full-time job. If you are a part-time student, you should plan on spending at least 2 hours on academic work outside of class for every 1 hour that you're in class.
   - Make good use of your *free time between classes* by working on assignments and studying in advance for upcoming exams. See **Box 5.1** for a summary of how you can use your out-of-class time to improve your academic performance and course grades.

c. **Plan your day.**
  * Make a *daily to-do list*.

> ! **Remember**
>
> If you write it out, you're less likely to block it out and forget about it.

  * Attack daily tasks in *priority order*.

> ! **Remember**
>
> "First things first." Plan your work by placing the most important and most urgent tasks at the top of your list, and work your plan by attacking tasks in the order in which you have listed them.

  * Carry a *small calendar, planner, or appointment book* at all times. This will enable you to record appointments that you may make on the run during the day and will allow you to jot down creative ideas or memories of things you need to do—which sometimes pop into your mind at the most unexpected times.
  * Carry *portable work* with you during the day,—that is, work you can take with you and do in any place at any time. This will enable you to take advantage of "dead time" during the day. For example, carry material with you that you can read while sitting and waiting for appointments or transportation, allowing you to resurrect this dead time and convert it to "live" work time. (This isn't only a good time-management strategy; it's a good stress-management strategy because it puts you in control of "wait time," enabling you use it to save time later rather than making you feel frustrated about losing time or bored about having nothing do with your time while you're waiting.)
  * Wear a *watch* or carry a cell phone that can accurately and instantly tell you what time it is and what date it is. You can't even begin to manage time if you don't know what time it is, and you can't plan a schedule if you don't know what date it is. Set the time on your watch or cell phone slightly ahead of the actual time; this will help ensure that you arrive to class, work, or meetings on time.

2. A good time-management plan should include reserve time to take care of the unexpected.

You should always hope for the best but be prepared for the worst. Your time-management plan should include a buffer zone or safety net, building in extra time that you can use to accommodate unforeseen developments or unexpected emergencies. Just as you should plan to save money in your bank for unexpected extra costs (e.g., emergency medical expenses), you should plan to save time in your schedule for unexpected events that cost you time (e.g., dealing with unscheduled tasks or taking longer than expected to complete already-planned tasks).

Making Productive Use of Free Time Outside the Classroom

Unlike high school, homework in college often does not involve turning things in to your instructor daily or weekly. The academic work you do outside the classroom may not even be collected and graded. Instead, it is done for your own benefit as you prepare yourself for upcoming exams and major assignments (e.g., term papers or research reports). Rather than formally assigning work to you as homework, your professors expect that you will do this work on your own and without supervision. Listed here are strategies for working independently and in advance of college exams and assignments, which will increase the quality of your preparation and performance.

Independent Work in Advance of Exams

Use the following strategies to prepare for exams:

- Complete reading assignments in advance of lectures that relate to the same topic as the reading. This will make lectures easier to understand and will prepare you to ask intelligent questions and make relevant comments in class.
- Review your class notes between class periods so that you can construct a mental bridge from one class to the next and make each upcoming lecture easier to follow. When reviewing your notes before the next class, rewrite any class notes that may be sloppily written. If you find notes related to the same point all over the place, reorganize them by combining them into one set of notes. Lastly, if you find any information gaps or confusing points in your notes, seek out the course instructor or a trusted classmate to clear them up before the next class takes place.
- Review information that you have highlighted in your reading assignments to improve your memory of the information. If certain points are confusing to you, discuss them with your course instructor or a fellow classmate.
- Integrate key ideas in your class notes with information that you have highlighted in your assigned reading and that is related to the same major point or general category. In other words, put related information from your lecture notes and your reading in the same place.
- Use a part-to-whole study method whereby you study material from your class notes and reading in small parts during short, separate study sessions that take place well in advance of the exam (the parts); then make your last study session before the exam a longer review session during which you restudy all the small parts together (the whole). The belief that studying in advance is a waste of time because you will forget it all anyway is a myth. Information studied in advance of an exam remains in your brain and is still there when you later review it. Even if you cannot recall the previously studied information when you first start reviewing it, you will relearn it faster than you did the first time, thus proving that some memory of it was retained.

Independent Work in Advance of Term Papers or Research Reports

Work on large, long-term assignments by breaking them into the following smaller, short-term tasks:

1. Search for and select a topic.
2. Locate sources of information on the topic.
3. Organize the information obtained from these sources into categories.
4. Develop an outline of the report's major points and the order or sequence in which you plan to discuss them.
5. Construct a first draft of the paper (and, if necessary, a second draft).
6. Write a final draft of the paper.
7. Proofread the final draft of your paper for minor mechanical mistakes, such as spelling and grammatical errors, before submitting it to your instructor.

3. A good time-management plan should include a balance of work and recreation.

Don't only plan work time; plan time to relax, refuel, and recharge. Your overall plan shouldn't turn you into an obsessive-compulsive workaholic. Instead, it should represent a balanced blend of work and play, which includes activities that promote your mental and physical wellness—such as relaxation, recreation, and reflection. You could also arrange your schedule of work and play as a self-motivation strategy by using your play time to reward your work time.

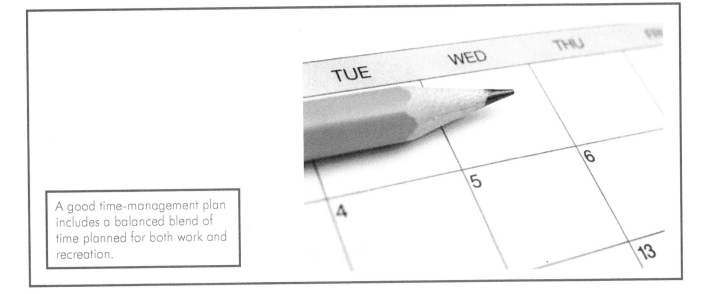

A good time-management plan includes a balanced blend of time planned for both work and recreation.

Remember

A good time-management plan should help you stress less, learn more, and earn higher grades while leaving you time for other important aspects of your life. A good plan not only enables you to get your work done on time but also enables you to attain and maintain balance in your life.

Pause for Reflection

What activities do you engage in for fun or recreation?

What do you do to relax or relieve stress?

Do you intentionally plan to engage in these activities?

4. A good time-management plan should have some flexibility.

Some people are immediately turned off by the idea of developing a schedule and planning their time because they feel it overstructures their lives and limits their freedom. It's only natural for you to prize your personal freedom and resist anything that appears to restrict your freedom in any way. A good plan preserves your freedom by helping you get done what must be done, reserving free time for you to do what you want and like to do.

A good time-management plan shouldn't enslave you to a rigid work schedule. It should be flexible enough to allow you to occasionally bend it without

"Some people regard discipline as a chore. For me, it is a kind of order that sets me free to fly."

–Julie Andrews, Academy award–winning English actress who starred in the Broadway musicals Mary Poppins and The Sound of Music

having to break it. Just as work commitments and family responsibilities can crop up unexpectedly, so, too, can opportunities for fun and enjoyable activities. Your plan should allow you the freedom to modify your schedule so that you can take advantage of these enjoyable opportunities and experiences. However, you should plan to make up the work time you lost. In other words, you can borrow or trade work time for play time, but don't "steal" it; you should plan to pay back the work time you borrowed by substituting it for a play period that existed in your original schedule.

> **! Remember**
>
> When you create a personal time-management plan, remember that it is *your* plan—you own it and you run it. It shouldn't run you.

Converting Your Time-Management Plan into an Action Plan

Once you've planned the work, the next step is to work the plan. A good action plan is one that gives you a preview of what you intend to accomplish and an opportunity to review what you actually accomplished. You can begin to implement an action plan by constructing a daily to-do list, bringing that list with you as the day begins, and checking off items on the list as you get them done. At the end of the day, review your list and identify what was completed and what still needs to be done. The uncompleted tasks should become high priorities for the next day.

At the end of the day, if you find many unchecked items remain on your daily to-do list, this could mean that you're spreading yourself too thin by trying to do too many things in a day. You may need to be more realistic about the number of things you can reasonably expect to accomplish per day by shortening your daily to-do list.

Being unable to complete many of your intended daily tasks may also mean that you need to modify your time-management plan by adding work time or subtracting activities that are drawing time and attention away from your work (e.g., taking phone calls during your planned work times).

> **Pause for Reflection**
>
> By the end of a typical day, how often do you find that you accomplished most of the important tasks you hoped to accomplish? (Circle one.)
>
> never   seldom   often   almost always
>
> Why?

◆ Dealing with Procrastination

Procrastination Defined

The word "procrastination" derives from two roots: *pro* (meaning "forward") plus *crastinus* (meaning "tomorrow.") As these roots suggest, procrastinators don't abide by the proverb "Why put off to tomorrow what can be done today?" Their philosophy is just the opposite: "Why do today what can be put off until tomorrow?" Adopting this philosophy promotes a perpetual pattern of postponing what needs to be done until the last possible moment, which results in rushing frantically to get it done (and compromising its quality), getting it only partially done, or not finishing it.

Research shows that 75 percent of college students label themselves as procrastinators (Potts, 1987), more than 80 percent procrastinate at least

A procrastinator's idea of planning ahead and working in advance often boils down to this scenario.

List of Things To Do Today	List of Things Due Today
1. Write Paper	1. Turn in Paper
2. Study for Math Test	2. Take Math Test
3. Prepare Speech	3. Deliver Speech

Next time, I'll start sooner!

occasionally (Ellis & Knaus, 1977), and almost 50 percent procrastinate consistently (Onwuegbuzie, 2000). Furthermore, the percentage of people reporting that they procrastinate is on the rise (Kachgal, Hansen, & Nutter, 2001).

Procrastination is such a serious issue for college students that some colleges and universities have opened "procrastination centers" to provide help exclusively for students who are experiencing problems with procrastination (Burka & Yuen, 1983).

Myths That Promote Procrastination

Before there can be any hope of putting a stop to procrastination, procrastinators need to let go of two popular myths (misconceptions) about time and performance.

Myth 1. "I work better under pressure" (e.g., on the day or night before something is due).

Procrastinators often confuse desperation with motivation. Their belief that they work better under pressure is often just a rationalization to justify or deny the truth, which is that they *only* work when they're under pressure—that is, when they're running out of time and are under the gun to get it done just before the deadline.

It's true that some people will only start to work and will work really fast when they're under pressure, but that does not mean they're working more *effectively* and producing work of better *quality*. Because they're playing "beat the clock," procrastinators' focus no longer is on doing the job *well* but is on doing the job *fast* so that it gets done before they run out of time. This typically results in a product that turns out to be incomplete or inferior to what could have been produced if the work process began earlier.

"Haste makes waste."

–Benjamin Franklin

© Elena Elisseeva, 2010. Under license from Shutterstock, Inc.

Although you may work quickly under pressure, you are probably not working better.

Myth 2. "Studying in advance is a waste of time because you will forget it all by test time."

The misconception that information learned early will be forgotten is commonly used to justify procrastinating with respect to preparing for upcoming exams. Studying that is distributed (spread out) over time is more effective than massed (crammed) studying. Furthermore, last-minute studying that takes place the night before exams often results in lost sleep time due to the need to pull late-nighters or all-nighters. This fly-by-night strategy interferes with retention of information that has been studied and elevates test anxiety because of lost dream sleep (a.k.a. rapid eye movement, or REM), which enables the brain to store memories and cope with stress (Hobson, 1988; Voelker, 2004). Research indicates that procrastinators experience higher rates of stress-related physical disorders, such as insomnia, stomach problems, colds, and flu (McCance & Pychyl, 2003).

Working under time pressure adds to performance pressure because procrastinators are left with no margin of error to correct mistakes, no time to seek help on their work, and no chance to handle random catastrophes that may arise at the last minute (e.g., an attack of the flu or a family emergency).

Psychological Causes of Procrastination

Sometimes, procrastination has deeper psychological roots. People may procrastinate for reasons related not directly to poor time-management habits but more to emotional issues involving self-esteem or self-image. For instance, studies show that procrastination is sometimes used as a psychological strategy to protect self-esteem, which is referred to as self-handicapping. This strategy may be used by some procrastinators (consciously or unconsciously) to give themselves a "handicap" or disadvantage. Thus, if their performance turns out to be less than spectacular, they can conclude (rationalize) that it was because they were performing under a handicap—lack of time (Smith, Snyder, & Handelsman, 1982).

For example, if the grade they receive on a test or paper turns out to be low, they can still "save face" (self-esteem) by concluding that it was because they waited until the last minute and didn't put much time or effort into it. In other words, they had the ability or intelligence to earn a good grade; they just didn't try very hard. Better yet, if they happened to luck out and get a good grade—despite doing it at the last minute—then they can think the grade just shows how intelligent they are. Thus, self-handicapping creates a fail-safe scenario that's guaranteed to protect the procrastinators' self-image: If the work performance or product is less than excellent, it can be blamed on external factors (e.g., lack of time); if it happens to earn them a high grade, then they can attribute the result to themselves—their extraordinary ability enabled them to do so well despite working at the last minute.

In addition to self-handicapping, other psychological factors have been found to contribute to procrastination, including the following:

- **Fear of failure.** Feeling that it's better to postpone the job, or not do it, than to fail at it (Burka & Yuen, 1983; Soloman & Rothblum, 1984);

Pause for Reflection

Do you tend to put off work for so long that getting it done turns into an emergency or panic situation?

If your answer is yes, why do you think you find yourself in this position? If your answer is no, what is it that prevents this from happening to you?

"We didn't lose the game; we just ran out of time."

—Vince Lombardi, football coach

"Procrastinators would rather be seen as lacking in effort than lacking in ability."

—Joseph Ferrari, professor of psychology and procrastination researcher

- **Perfectionism.** Having unrealistically high personal standards or expectations, which leads to the belief that it's better to postpone work or not do it than to risk doing it less than perfectly (Flett, Blankstein, Hewitt, & Koledin, 1992; Kachgal et al., 2001);
- **Fear of success.** Fearing that doing well will show others that the procrastinator has the ability to achieve success and will allow others to expect the procrastinator to maintain those high standards by repeating the performance (Beck, Koons, & Milgram, 2000; Ellis & Knaus, 1977);
- **Indecisiveness.** Having difficulty making decisions, including decisions about what to do or how to begin doing it (Anderson, 2003; Steel, 2003);
- **Thrill seeking.** Enjoying the adrenaline rush triggered by hurrying to get things done just before a deadline (Szalavitz, 2003).

If these or any other issues are involved, their underlying psychological causes must be dealt with before procrastination can be overcome. Because they have deeper roots, it may take some time and professional assistance to uproot them. A good place to get such assistance is the Counseling Center. Personal counselors on college campuses are professional psychologists who are trained to deal with psychological issues that can contribute to procrastination.

> "Striving for excellence motivates you; striving for perfection is demoralizing."
>
> —Harriet Braiker, psychologist and best-selling author

Pause for Reflection

How often do you procrastinate? (Circle one.)

rarely   occasionally   frequently   consistently

When you do procrastinate, what is the usual reason?

Self-Help Strategies for Beating the Procrastination Habit

Once inaccurate beliefs or emotional issues underlying procrastination have been identified and dealt with, the next step is to move from gaining self-insight to taking direct action on the procrastination habit itself. Listed here are our top strategies for minimizing or eliminating the procrastination habit.

1. Continually practice effective time-management strategies.

If effective time-management practices, such as those previously cited in this chapter, are implemented consistently, they can turn into a habit. Studies show that when people repeatedly practice effective time-management strategies these practices gradually become part of their routine and develop into habits. For example, when procrastinators repeatedly practice effective time-management strategies with respect to tasks that they procrastinate on, their procrastination tendencies begin to fade and are gradually replaced by good time-management habits (Ainslie, 1992; Baumeister, Heatherton, & Tice, 1994).

2. Make the start of work as inviting or appealing as possible.

Getting started can be a stumbling block for many procrastinators. They experience what's called "start-up stress" when they're about to begin a task they expect will be unpleasant, difficult, or boring (Burka & Yuen, 1983). If you have trouble starting your work, one way to give yourself a jump start is to arrange your work tasks in an order that allows you to start on tasks that you're likely to find most interesting or are most likely to experience success with. Once you've overcome the initial inertia and get going, you can ride the momentum you've created to attack the tasks that you find less appealing and more daunting.

> "Just do it."
>
> —Commercial slogan of Nike, the athletic equipment company named after the Greek goddess of victory

Student Perspective

"Did you ever dread doing something, then it turned out to take only about 20 minutes to do?"

—Conversation between two college students overheard in a coffee shop

You're also likely to discover that the dreaded work wasn't as difficult, boring, or time consuming as it appeared to be. When you sense that you're making some progress toward getting work done, your anxiety begins to decline. Like many experiences in life that are dreaded and avoided, the anticipation of the event turns out to be worse than the event itself. Research on students who hadn't started a project until it was about to be due indicates that these students experience anxiety and guilt about delaying their work but that once they begin working these negative emotions decline and are replaced by more positive feelings (McCance & Pychyl, 2003).

3. Make the work manageable.

Work becomes less overwhelming and less stressful when it's handled in small chunks or pieces. You can conquer procrastination for large tasks by using a "divide and conquer" strategy: Divide the large task into smaller, more manageable units, and then attack and complete them one at a time.

Don't underestimate the power of short work sessions. They can be more effective than longer sessions because it's easier to maintain momentum and concentration for shorter periods. If you're working on a large project or preparing for a major exam, dividing your work into short sessions will enable you to take quick jabs and poke small holes in it, reducing its overall size with each successive punch. This approach will also give you the sense of satisfaction that comes with knowing that you're making steady progress toward completing a big task—continually chipping away at it in short strokes and gradually taking away the pressure associated with having to go for a big knockout punch right before the final bell (deadline).

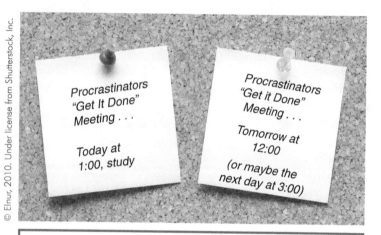

For many procrastinators, getting *started* is often their biggest obstacle.

> "To eat an elephant, first cut it into small pieces."
>
> —Author unknown

Personal Story

The two biggest projects I've had to complete in my life were writing my doctoral thesis and writing this textbook. The strategy that enabled me to keep going until I competed both of these large tasks was to make up short-term deadlines for myself (e.g., complete 5-10 pages each week). I psyched myself into thinking that these make-believe due dates were real, drop-dead deadlines and that if I didn't meet them by completing these smaller tasks on time I was going to fall so far behind that I'd never get the whole thing done. I think these self-imposed deadlines worked for me because they gave me short, more manageable tasks to work on that allowed me to make steady progress toward my larger, long-term task. It was as if I took a huge, hard-to-digest meal and broke it into small, bite-sized pieces that I could easily swallow and gradually digest over time—as opposed to trying to consume a large meal right before bedtime (the final deadline).

—Joe Cuseo

4. Understand that organization matters.

Research indicates that disorganization is a factor that contributes to procrastination (Steel, 2003). How well you organize your workplace and manage your work materials can reduce your risk of procrastination. Having the right materials in the right place at the right time can make it easier to get to and get going on your work. Once you've made a decision to get the job done, you don't want to waste time looking for the tools you need to begin doing it. For procrastinators, this time delay may be just the amount of time they need to change their mind and not start their work.

> **!**
>
> ### Remember
>
> The less effort it takes to start doing something, the more likely you are to do it.

One simple yet effective way to organize your college work materials is by developing your own file system. You can begin to create an effective file system by filing (storing) materials from different courses in different colored folders or notebooks. This will allow you to keep all materials related to the same course in the same place and give you direct and immediate access to the materials you need as soon as you need them. Such a system helps you get organized, reduces stress associated with having things all over the place, and reduces the risk of procrastination by reducing the time it takes for you to start working.

5. Recognize that location matters.

Where you work can influence when or whether you work. Research demonstrates that distraction is a factor that can contribute to procrastination (Steel, 2003). Thus, it may be possible for you to minimize procrastination by working in an environment whose location and arrangement prevent distraction and promote concentration.

Distractions tend to come in two major forms: social distractions (e.g., people nearby who are not working) and media distractions (e.g., cell phones, e-mails, text messages, CDs, and TV). Research indicates that the number of hours per week that college students spend watching TV is *negatively* associated with academic success, including lower grade point average, less likelihood of graduating with honors, and lower levels of personal development (Astin, 1993).

Pause for Reflection

List your two most common sources of distraction while working. Next to each distraction, identify a strategy that you might use to reduce or eliminate it.

Source of Distraction	Strategy for Reducing this Distraction
1.	
2.	

> **!**
>
> ### Remember
>
> Select a workplace and arrange your workspace to minimize distraction from people and media. Try to remove everything from your work site that's not directly relevant to your work.

Lastly, keep in mind that you can arrange your work environment in a way that not only disables distraction but also enables concentration. You can enable or empower your concentration by working in an environment that allows you easy access to work-support materials (e.g., class notes, textbooks,

Student Perspective

"To reduce distractions, work at a computer on campus rather than using one in your room or home."

—Advice to new college students from a first-year student

and a dictionary) and easy access to social support (e.g., working with a group of motivated students who will encourage you to get focused, stay on task, and keep on track to complete you work tasks).

6. Arrange the order or sequence of your work tasks to intercept procrastination when you're most likely to experience it.

While procrastination often involves difficulty starting work, it can also involve difficulty continuing and completing work (Lay & Silverman, 1996). As previously mentioned, if you have trouble starting work, it might be best to first do tasks that you find most interesting or easiest. However, if you have difficulty maintaining or sustaining your work until it's finished, you might try to schedule work tasks that you find easier and more interesting *in the middle or toward the end* of your planned work time. If you're performing tasks of greater interest and ease at a point in your work when you typically lose interest or energy, you may be able to sustain your interest and energy long enough to continue working until you complete them, which means that you'll have completed your entire list of tasks. Also, doing your most enjoyable and easiest tasks later can provide an incentive or reward for completing your less enjoyable tasks first.

7. Learn that momentum matters.

It's often harder to restart a task than it is to finish a task that you've already started; this occurs because you've overcome come the initial inertia associated with getting started and can ride the momentum that you've already created. Furthermore, finishing a task can give you a sense of closure—the feeling of personal accomplishment and self-satisfaction that comes from knowing that you "closed the deal." Placing a checkmark next to a completed task and seeing that it's one less thing you have to do can motivate you to continue working on the remaining tasks on your list.

◆ Summary and Conclusion

To manage time effectively, you need to

- **Analyze.** Break down time and become aware of how you spend it;
- **Itemize.** Identify the tasks you need to accomplish and their due dates; and
- **Prioritize.** Tackle your tasks in their order of importance.

Developing a comprehensive time-management plan involves long-, mid-, and short-range plans, such as

- Planning the total term (long-range);
- Planning your week (mid-range); and
- Planning your day (short-range).

A good time-management plan also has the following features:

- It sets aside time to take care of unexpected developments.
- It takes advantage of your natural peak periods and down times.

- It balances work and recreation.
- It gives you the flexibility to accommodate unforeseen opportunities.

The enemy of effective time management is procrastination, which often relies on the following myths:

- Better work occurs on the day or night before something is due.
- Advance studying wastes time because everything learned will be forgotten by test time.

Effective strategies for beating the procrastination habit include the following:

- Start with the work that is the most inviting or appealing.
- Divide a large task into manageable units.
- Organize work materials.
- Work in a location that minimizes distractions and temptations not to work.
- Intentionally arrange work tasks so that more enjoyable or stimulating tasks are the focus when you're vulnerable to procrastination.
- Maintain momentum, because it's often harder to restart a task than to finish one.

Mastering the skill of managing time is critical for success in college and in life beyond college. Time is one of the most powerful personal resources; the better use you make of it, the greater control you gain over your priorities and your life.

Learning More Through the World Wide Web

Internet-Based Resources for Further Information on Time Management

For additional information related to the ideas discussed in this chapter, we recommend the following Web sites:

Procrastination Elimination: **www.time-management-guide.com/procrastination.html**

Time-Management Strategies for All Students: **www.studygs.net/timman.htm**

Time-Management Strategies for Non-Traditional-Age Students:
www.essortment.com/lifestyle/timemanagement_sjmu.htm

5.1 Term at a Glance

Term _____ ,   Year _____

Review the syllabus (course outline) for all classes you're enrolled in this term, and complete the following information for each course.

Course ↖	Professor ↖	Exams ↖	Projects & Papers ↖	Other Assignments ↖	Attendance Policy ↖	Late & Makeup Assignment Policy ↖

Self-Assessment Questions

1. Is the overall workload what you expected? Are your surprised by the amount of work required in any particular course or courses?

2. At this point in the term, what do you see as your most challenging or demanding course or courses? Why?

3. Do you think you can handle the total workload required by the full set of courses you're enrolled in this term?

4. What adjustments or changes could you make to your personal schedule that would make it easier to accommodate your academic workload this term?

5.2 Taking a Personal Time Inventory

On the blank Week-at-a-Glance Grid that follows, map out your typical or average week for this term. Start by recording what you usually do on these days, including when you have class, when you work, and when you relax or recreate. You can use abbreviations (e.g., use J for job and R&R for rest and relaxation) or write tasks out in full if you have enough room in the box. List the abbreviations you created at the bottom of the page so that your instructor can follow them.

If you're a *full-time* student, find 25 *hours* in your week that you could devote to homework (HW). These 25 hours could be found between classes, during the day, in the evenings, or on the weekends. If you can find 25 hours per week for homework, in addition to your class schedule, you'll have a 40-hour workweek for coursework, which research has shown to result in good grades and success in college.

If you're a *part-time* student, find 2 *hours* you could devote to homework *for every hour* that you're in class (e.g., if you're in class 9 hours per week, find 18 hours of homework time).

Week-at-a-Glance Grid

	Sunday	Monday	Tuesday	Wednesday	Thursday	Friday	Saturday
7:00 a.m.							
8:00 a.m.							
9:00 a.m.							
10:00 a.m.							
11:00 a.m.							
12:00 p.m.							
1:00 p.m.							
2:00 p.m.							
3:00 p.m.							
4:00 p.m.							
5:00 p.m.							
6:00 p.m.							
7:00 p.m.							
8:00 p.m.							
9:00 p.m.							
10:00 p.m.							
11:00 p.m.							

1. Go to the following Web site: www.ulc.psu.edu/studyskills/time_management.html#monitoring_your_time

2. Complete the time management exercise at this site. The exercise asks you to estimate the hours per day or week that you spend doing various activities (e.g., sleeping, employment, and commuting). As you enter the amount of time you engage in these activities, the total number of remaining hours available in the week for academic work will be automatically computed.

3. After completing your entries, look at your week-at-a-glance grid and answer the following questions, or provide your best estimate.

Self-Assessment Questions

1. How many hours per week do you have available for academic work?

2. Do you have 2 hours available for academic work outside of class for each hour you spend in class?

3. What time wasters do you detect that might be easily eliminated or reduced to create more time for academic work outside of class?

Procrastination: The Vicious Cycle

Delilah has a major paper due at the end of the term. It's now past midterm, and she still hasn't started to work on her paper. She tells herself, "I should have started sooner."

However, Delilah continues to postpone starting her work on the paper and begins to feel anxious and guilty about it. To relieve her growing anxiety and guilt, she starts doing other tasks instead, such as cleaning her room and returning e-mails. This makes Delilah feel a little better because these tasks keep her busy, take her mind off the term paper, and give her the feeling that at least she's getting something accomplished. Time continues to pass, and the deadline for the paper is growing dangerously close. Delilah now finds herself in the position of having lots of work to do and little time in which to do it.

Source: Burka & Lenora (1983).

Reflection and Discussion Questions

1. What do you predict Delilah will do at this point?

2. Why did you make this prediction?

3. What grade do you think Delilah will receive on her paper?

4. What do you think Delilah will do on the next term paper she's assigned?

5. Other than starting sooner, what recommendations would you have for Delilah (and other procrastinators like her) to break this cycle of procrastination and prevent it from happening repeatedly?

Your First Year Resources

The first year of college is an exciting and challenging time. We want you to have the best experience possible, so we've designed a website just for you. It's full of tips, tricks, and links to help you make the most of Your First Year! If you have questions or need help finding your way at UNCG, you can always email us at yfy@uncg.edu. Visit yourfirstyear.uncg.edu and the websites below for helpful resources and services about time management.

Students First Office   **336-334-5730**
http://studentsfirst.uncg.edu/

Student Success Center   **336-334-3878**
http://success.uncg.edu/

Managing Money and Minimizing Debt

6

ACTIVATE YOUR THINKING | Journal Entry **6.1**

Complete the following sentence with the first thought that comes to your mind:

For me, financial literacy means. . .

_____

_____

_____

LEARNING GOAL

To become more self-aware, knowledgeable, and strategic with respect to managing money and financing a college education.

The beginning of college often marks the beginning of greater personal independence and greater demands for effective financial self-management and fiscal decision making. The importance of money management for college students is growing for two major reasons. The first reason is the rising cost of a college education, which has resulted in more students working more hours while they're in college (Levine & Cureton, 1998; Perna & DuBois, 2010). The rising cost of a college education is also requiring students to make more difficult decisions about what options (or combination of options) to use to meet their college expenses. Unfortunately, research indicates that many students today are not making the most effective decisions about how to finance their college education in a way that best contributes to their academic success in college and their financial success beyond college (King, 2005).

A second reason money management is growing in importance for college students is the availability and convenience of credit cards. It has never been easier for college students to get access to, use, and abuse credit cards. A college graduate today can do everything right in college, such as earn good grades, get involved on campus, and get work experience before graduating, but a poor credit history resulting from irresponsible credit card use while in college can reduce that student's chances of obtaining credit after college as well as their job prospects after graduation (Mae, 2005). Credit reporting agencies and bureaus collect information about how faithfully college students make credit-card payments and report their "credit scores" to credit-card companies and banks. Employers check these credit scores and use them as indicators or predictors of how responsible students will be as employees, because there's a statistical relationship between using credit cards responsibly and being a responsible employee (Ring, 1997; Susswein, 1995). Thus, being irresponsible with credit while you're in college can affect your ability to land a job after (or during) college. Your credit score report will also affect your likelihood of qualifying for car loans and home loans, as well as your ability to rent an apartment (Pratt, 2008).

Furthermore, research indicates that accumulating high levels of debt while in college is associated with higher levels of stress (Nelson, Lust, Story, & Ehlinger, 2008), lower academic performance (Susswein, 1995), and greater risk of withdrawing from college (Ring, 1997). On the positive side of the ledger, studies show that when students learn to use effective money-management strategies, they reduce unnecessary spending, minimize accumulation of debt, and lower their level of stress (Health & Soll, 1996; Kidwell & Turrisi, 2004; Walker, 1996).

◆ Strategies for Managing Money Effectively

Developing Financial Self-Awareness

Developing any good habit begins with the critical first step of self-awareness. The habit of effective money management begins with awareness of your *cash flow*—the amount of money you have flowing in and flowing out. As illustrated in **Figure 13.1**, you can track your cash flow by monitoring:

- The amount of money you have coming in (income) versus the amount going out (expenses or expenditures), and
- The amount of money you've earned and not spent (savings) versus the amount you've borrowed and not yet paid back (debt).

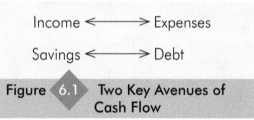

Figure **6.1** Two Key Avenues of Cash Flow

Income for college students typically comes from one or more of the following sources:

- Scholarships or grants, which don't have to be paid back
- Loans, which must be repaid
- Salary earned from part-time or full-time work
- Personal savings
- Gifts or other forms of monetary support from parents and other family members

Your sources of expenses or expenditures may be classified into three categories:

1. Basic needs or essential necessities—expenses that tend to be fixed because you cannot do without them (e.g., expenses for food, housing, tuition, textbooks, phone, transportation to and from school, and health-related costs)
2. Incidentals or extras—expenses that tend to be flexible because spending money on them is optional or discretionary, i.e., you choose to spend at your own discretion or judgment; these expenses typically include:
   a. money spent on entertainment, enjoyment, or pleasure (e.g., music, movies, and spring-break vacations), and
   b. money spent primarily for reasons of promoting personal status or self-image (e.g., buying expensive brand-name products, fashionable clothes, jewelry, and other personal accessories)

3. Emergency expenses—unpredicted, unforeseen, or unexpected costs (e.g., money paid for doctor visits and medicine needed to treat illnesses or injuries)

Developing a Money-Management Plan

Once you're aware of the amount of money you have coming in (and from what sources) plus the amount of money you're spending (and for what reasons), the next step is to develop a plan for managing your cash flow. The bottom line is to ensure that the money coming in (income) is equal to or greater than the money going out (expenses). If the amount of money going out exceeds the amount coming in, you're "in the red" or have "negative cash flow."

◆ Strategic Selection and Use of Financial Tools for Tracking Cash Flow

To track your cash flow and manage your money, there are a variety of tools available to you .These cash-flow tools include:

- Checking accounts
- Credit cards
- Charge cards
- Debit cards

What follows is a description of these different tools, along with specific strategies for using them effectively.

Checking Account

Long before credit cards were created, a checking account was the method most people used to keep track of their money. Many people still use checking accounts in addition to (or instead of) credit cards. A checking account may be obtained from a bank or credit union; its typical costs include a deposit ($20–$25) to open the account, a monthly service fee (e.g., $10), and small fees for checks. Some banks charge customers a service fee based on the number of checks written, which is a good option if you don't plan to write many checks each month. If you maintain a high enough balance of money deposited in your account, the bank may not charge any extra fees, and if you're able to maintain an even higher balance, the bank may also pay you interest—known as an interest-bearing checking account.

In conjunction with your checking account, banks usually provide you with an automatic teller machine (ATM) card that you can use to get cash. Look for a checking account that doesn't charge a separate fee for ATM transactions, but offers it as a free service along with your checking account. Also, look for a checking account that doesn't charge you if your balance drops below a certain minimum figure.

Strategies for Using Checking Accounts Effectively

Apply the following strategies to make the best use of your checking account:

- Whenever you write a check or make an ATM withdrawal, immediately subtract its amount from your *balance* (the amount of money remaining in your account) to determine your new balance.
- Keep a running balance in your checkbook; it will ensure that you know exactly how much money you have in your account at all times. This will reduce your risk of writing a check that *bounces*—a check that you don't have enough money in the bank to cover. If you do bounce a check, you'll probably have to pay a charge to the bank and possibly to the business that attempted to cash your bounced check.
- Double-check your checkbook balance with each monthly statement you receive from the bank. Be sure to include the service charges your bank makes to your account that appear on your monthly statement. This practice will make it easier to track errors—on either your part or the bank's part. (Banks can and do occasionally make mistakes.)

Advantages of a Checking Account

A checking account has several advantages:

- You can carry checks instead of cash.
- You have access to cash at almost any time through an ATM.
- It allows you to keep a visible track record of income and expenses in your checkbook.
- A properly managed checking account can serve as a good credit reference for future loans and purchases.

Credit Card (e.g., MasterCard®, Visa®, or Discover®)

A credit card is basically money loaned to you by the credit-card company that issues you the card, which you pay back to the company monthly. You can pay the whole bill or a portion of the bill each month, as long as some minimum payment is made. However, for any remaining (unpaid) portion of your bill, you are charged a high interest rate, which is usually about 18 percent.

Strategies for Selecting a Credit Card

If you decide to use a credit card, pay attention to *its annual percentage rate (APR)*—the interest rate you pay for previously unpaid monthly balances. This rate can vary from one credit-card company to the next. Credit-card companies also vary in terms of their annual service fee. You will likely find companies that charge higher interest rates tend to charge lower annual fees, and vice versa. As a rule, if you expect to pay the full balance every month, you're probably better off choosing a credit card that does not charge you an annual service fee. On the other hand, if you think you'll need more time to make the full monthly payments, you may be better off with a credit-card company that offers a low interest rate.

Another feature that differentiates one credit-card company from another is whether or not you're allowed a *grace period*—a certain period after you receive your monthly statement during which you can pay back the company without paying added interest fees. Some companies may allow you a grace

Don't let peer pressure determine your spending habits.

period of a full month, while others may provide none and begin charging interest immediately after you fail to pay on the bill's due date.

Credit cards may also differ in terms of their *credit limit* (also called a *credit line* or *line of credit*), which refers to the maximum amount of money the credit-card company will make available to you. If you're a new customer, most companies will set a credit limit beyond which no additional credit is granted.

Advantages of a Credit Card

If a credit card is used responsibly, it has some key advantages as a money-management tool, such as those listed below.

- It helps you track your spending habits because the credit card company sends you a monthly statement that provides an itemized list of all your card-related purchases. This list supplies you with a "paper trail" of what you purchased that month and when you purchased it.
- It provides the convenience of making purchases online, which can save time and money that would otherwise be spent traveling to and from stores.
- It allows access to cash whenever and wherever you need it, because any bank or ATM that displays your credit card's symbol will give you cash up to a certain limit (usually for a small transaction fee). Keep in mind that some credit card companies charge a higher interest rate for cash advances than credit card purchases.
- It enables you to establish a personal credit history. If you use a credit card responsibly, you can establish a good credit history that you can use later in life for big-ticket purchases such as a car or home. In effect, responsible use of a credit card shows others from whom you wish to seek credit (or borrow money) that you're financially responsible.

! Remember

Don't buy into the belief that the only way you can establish a good credit history is by using a credit card. It's not your only option; you can establish a good credit history through responsible use of a checking account and by paying your bills on time.

Strategies for Using Credit Cards Responsibly

While there may be advantages to using a credit card, you only reap those advantages if you use your card strategically. If not, the advantages of a credit card can be quickly and greatly outweighed by its disadvantages. Listed here are some strategies for using a credit card in a way that maximizes its advantages and minimizes its disadvantages.

1. **Use a credit card only as a convenience for making purchases and tracking the purchases you make; don't use it as a tool for obtaining a long-term loan.** A credit card's main money-management advantage is that it enables you to make purchases with plastic instead of cash. A credit card saves you the inconvenience of having to carry around cash and it provides you with a monthly statement of your purchases from the credit card company, which makes it easier for you to track and analyze your spending habits.

The credit provided by a credit card should be seen simply as a short-term loan that must be paid back at the end of every month. Do not use credit cards for long-term credit or long-term loans because their interest rates are outrageously high. Paying such a high rate of interest for a loan represents an ineffective (and irresponsible) money-management strategy.

2. **Limit yourself to one credit card.** The average college student has 2.8 credit cards (United College Marketing Service, cited in Pratt, 2008). More than one credit card just means more accounts to keep track of and more opportunities to accumulate debt. You don't need additional credit cards from department stores, gas stations, or any other profit-making business because they duplicate what your personal credit card already does (plus they charge extremely high interest rates for late payments).

3. **Pay off your balance each month in full and on time.** If you pay the full amount of your bill each month, this means that you're using your credit card effectively to obtain an interest-free, short-term (one-month) loan. You're just paying principal—the total amount of money borrowed and nothing more. However, if your payment is late and you need to pay interest, you end up paying more for the items you purchased than their actual ticket price. For instance, if you have an unpaid balance of $500 on your monthly credit bill for merchandise purchased the previous month and you are charged the typical 18 percent credit card interest rate for late payment, you end up paying $590: $500 (merchandise) + $90 (18 percent interest to the credit card company).

Credit card companies make their profit from the interest they collect from cardholders who don't pay back their credit on time. Just as procrastinating about completing schoolwork is a poor time-management habit that can hurt your grades, procrastinating about paying your credit-card bills is a poor money-management habit that can hurt your pocketbook by forcing you to pay high interest rates.

Don't allow credit card companies to make profit at your expense. Pay your total balance on time and avoid paying exorbitantly high interest rates. If you can't pay the total amount owed at the end of the month, rather than making the minimum monthly payment, pay off as much of it as you possibly can. If you keep making only the minimum payment each month, you'll begin to pile up huge amounts of debt.

Remember

If you keep charging on your credit card while you have an unpaid balance or debt, you no longer have a grace period to pay back your charges; instead, interest is charged immediately on all your purchases.

Charge Card

A charge card works similar to a credit card in that you're given a short-term loan for one month; the only difference is that you must pay your bill in full at the end of each month and you cannot carry over any debt from one month to the next. Its major disadvantage relative to a credit card is that it has less flexibility—no matter what your expenses may be for a particular month, you must still pay up or lose your ability to acquire credit for the next month. For people who habitually fail to pay their monthly credit card bills on time, this makes a charge card a smarter money-management tool than a credit card because the cardholder cannot continue to accumulate debt.

Debit Card

A debit card looks almost identical to a credit card (e.g., it has a MasterCard or Visa logo), but it works differently. When you use a debit card, money is immediately taken out or subtracted from your checking account. Thus, you're only using money that's already in your account (rather than borrowing money), and you don't receive a bill at the end of the month. If you attempt to purchase something with a debit card that costs more than the amount of money you have in your account, your card will not allow you to do so. Just like a bounced check, a debit card will not permit you to pay out any money that is not in your account. Like a check or ATM withdrawal, any purchase you make with a debit card should immediately be subtracted from your balance.

Like a credit card, a major advantage of the debit card is that it provides you with the convenience of plastic; however, unlike a credit card, it prevents you from spending beyond your means and accumulating debt. For this reason, financial advisors often recommend using a debit card rather than a credit card (Knox, 2004; Tyson, 2003).

> **Pause for Reflection**
>
> Do you have a credit card? Do you have more than one?
>
> If you have at least one credit card, do you pay off your entire balance each month?
>
> If you don't pay off your entire balance each month, what's your average unpaid balance per month?
>
> What changes would you have to make in your money-management habits to be able to pay off your entire balance each month?

> "Never spend your money before you have it."
>
> –Thomas Jefferson, third president of the United States and founder of the University of Virginia

◆ Sources of Income for Financing Your College Education

Free Application for Federal Student Aid (FAFSA)

The Free Application for Federal Student Aid (FAFSA) is the application used by the U.S. Department of Education to determine financial aid eligibility for students. A formula is used to determine each student's *estimated family contribution (EFC)*—the amount of money the government has determined a family can contribute to the educational costs of the family member who is attending college. No fee is charged to complete the application, so you should complete one every year to determine your eligibility to receive financial aid, whether you believe you're eligible or not. See the Financial Aid Office on your campus for the FAFSA form and for help in completing it.

> **Pause for Reflection**
>
> Which of the terms in Snapshot Summary 13.1 were unfamiliar to you?
>
> Which of the terms apply to your current financial situation or money-management plans?

Scholarships

Scholarships are available from many sources besides the institution you've chosen to attend. Typically, scholarships are awarded at the time of admission to college, but some scholarships may be awarded to students at a later point in their college experience. To find out about scholarships that you may still be eligible to receive, visit your Financial Aid Office. You can also conduct an Internet search to find many sites that offer scholarship information. (However, don't enter your credit card or bank account information on any site.)

Snapshot Summary

6.1

Financial Literacy: Understanding the Language of Money Management

As you can tell from the number of financial terms used in this chapter, there is a fiscal vocabulary or language that we need to master in order to fully understand our financial options and transactions. In other words, we need to become *financially literate*. As you read the financial terms listed below, place a checkmark next to any term whose meaning you didn't already know.

Account. A formal business arrangement in which a bank provides financial services to a customer (e.g., checking account or savings account).

Annual percentage rate (APR). The interest rate that must be paid when monthly credit card balances are not paid in full.

Balance. The amount of money in a person's account or the amount of unpaid debt.

Bounced check. A check written for a greater amount of money than the amount contained in a personal checking account, which typically requires the person to pay a charge to the bank and possibly to the business that attempted to cash the bounced check.

Budget. A plan for coordinating income and expenses to ensure that sufficient money is available to cover personal expenses or expenditures.

Cash flow. Amount of money flowing in (income) and flowing out (expenses). "Negative cash flow" occurs when the amount of money going out exceeds the amount coming in.

Credit. Money obtained with the understanding that it will be paid back, either with or without interest.

Credit line (a.k.a. credit limit). The maximum amount of money (credit) made available to a borrower.

Debt. Amount of money owed.

Default. Failure to meet a financial obligation (e.g., a student who fails to repay a college loan "defaults" on that loan).

Emergency student loan. Immediate, interest-free loans provided by a college or university to help financially strapped students cover short-term expenses (e.g., cost of textbooks) or deal with financial emergencies (e.g., accidents and illnesses). Emergency student loans are typically granted within 24–48 hours, sometimes even the same day, and usually need to be repaid within two months.

Deferred student payment plan. A plan that allows student borrowers to temporarily defer or postpone loan payments for some acceptable reason (e.g., to pursue an internship or to do volunteer work after college).

Estimated family contribution (EFC). The amount of money the government has determined a family can contribute to the educational costs of the family member who is attending college.

Fixed interest rate. A loan with an interest rate that will remain the same for the entire term of the loan.

Grace period. The amount of time after a monthly credit card statement has been issued during which the credit card holder can pay back the company without paying added interest fees.

Grant. Money received that doesn't have to be repaid.

Gross income. Income generated before taxes and other expenses are deducted.

Insurance premium. The amount paid in regular installments to an insurance company to remain insured.

Interest. The amount of money paid to a customer for deposited money (as in a bank account) or money paid by a customer for borrowed money (e.g., interest on a loan). Interest is usually calculated as a percentage of the total amount of money deposited or borrowed.

Interest-bearing account. A bank account that earns interest if the customer keeps a sufficiently large sum of money in the bank.

Loan consolidation. Consolidating (combining) separate student loans into one larger loan to make the process of tracking, budgeting, and repayment easier. Loan consolidation typically requires the borrower to pay slightly more interest.

Loan premium. The amount of money loaned without interest.

Merit-based scholarship. Money awarded to a student on the basis of performance or achievement that doesn't have to be repaid.

Need-based scholarship. Money awarded to a student on the basis of financial need that doesn't have to be repaid.

Net income. Money earned or remaining after all expenses and taxes have been paid.

Principal. The total amount of money borrowed or deposited, not counting interest.

Variable interest rate. An interest rate on a loan that can vary or be changed by the lender.

Yield. Revenue or profit produced by an investment beyond the original amount invested. For example, the higher lifetime income and other monetary benefits acquired from a college education that exceed the amount of money invested in or spent on a college education.

Also, keep in mind that scholarships are very competitive and deadlines are strictly enforced.

Grants

Grants are considered to be gift aid, which typically does not have to be repaid. About two-thirds of all college students receive grant aid, which, on average, reduces their tuition bills by more than half (College Board, 2009). The Federal Pell Grant is the largest grant program; it provides need-based aid to low-income undergraduate students. The amount of the grant depends on criteria such as (1) the anticipated contribution of the family to the student's education (EFC), (2) the cost of the postsecondary institution that the student is attending, and (3) the enrollment status of the student (part-time or full-time).

Loans

Student loans need to be repaid once a student graduates from college. Listed below are some of the more common student loan programs.

- **The Federal Perkins Loan** is a 5 percent simple-interest loan awarded to exceptionally needy students. The repayment for this loan begins nine months after a student is no longer enrolled at least half-time.
- **The Federal Subsidized Stafford Loan** is available to students enrolled at least half-time and has a fixed interest rate that's established each year on July 1. The federal government pays the interest on the loan while the student is enrolled. The repayment for this loan begins six months after a student is no longer enrolled half-time.
- **The Federal Unsubsidized Stafford Loan** is a loan that's not based on need and has the same interest rate as the Federal Subsidized Stafford Loan.

Students are responsible for paying the interest on this loan while they're enrolled in college. The loan amount limits for Stafford loans are based on the classification of the student (e.g., freshman or sophomore).

Keep in mind that federal and state regulations require that if you're receiving financial aid, you must maintain "satisfactory academic progress." In most cases this means you must do the following:

1. **Maintain a satisfactory GPA.** Your entire academic record will be reviewed, even if you have paid for any of the classes with your own resources.
2. **Make satisfactory academic progress.** Your academic progress will be evaluated at least once per year, usually at the end of each spring semester.
3. **Complete a degree or certificate program within an established period of time.** Check with your institution's Financial Aid Office for details.

Snapshot Summary 6.2

Federal Loan versus Private Loan: A Critical Difference

Private loans and federal loans are different, unrelated types of loans. Here are the key differences:

Federal loans have fixed interest rates that are comparatively low (currently less than 7 percent).

Private loans have variable interest rates that are very high (currently more than 15 percent) and can go higher at any time.

Note: Despite the high cost of private loans, they are the fastest-growing type of loans taken out by college students, largely because of aggressive, misleading, and sometimes irresponsible or unethical advertising on loan-shopping Web sites. Students sometimes think they're getting a federal loan only to find out later they have taken on a more expensive private loan.

"Apply for as much grant aid as possible before borrowing, and then seek lower-interest federal student loans before tapping private ones. There is a lot of student aid that can help make the expense [of college] more manageable."

–Sandy Baum, senior policy analyst, College Board (Gordon, 2009)

"Borrow money from a pessimist. He won't expect it back."

–Steven Wright, American comedian and first inductee to the Boston Comedy Hall of Fame

Source: Hamilton (2012); Kristof (2008).

> ### ❗ Remember
>
> Not all loans are created equally. Federally guaranteed student loans are relatively low-cost compared to private loans, and they may be paid off slowly after graduation. On the other hand, private lenders of student loans are like credit-card companies: they charge extremely high interest rates (that can go even higher at any time), and must be paid off as quickly as possible. They should not to be used as a primary loan to help pay for college, and they should only be used as a last resort when no other options are available for covering your college expenses.

Salary Earnings

If you find yourself relying on your salary to pay for college tuition, check with your employer to see whether the company offers tuition reimbursement. Also, check with the Billing Office on your campus to determine whether payment plans are available for tuition costs. These plans may differ in terms of how much is due, deadlines for payments, and how any remaining debt owed to the institution is dealt with at the end of the term. You may find that the college you're attending will not allow you to register for the following term until the previous term is completely paid for.

Research shows that when students work on campus (versus off campus) they're more likely to succeed in college (Astin, 1993; Pascarella & Terenzini, 1991; 2005), probably because they become more connected to the college when they work on campus (Cermak & Filkins, 2004; Tinto, 1993) and also because on-campus employers are more flexible than off-campus employers in allowing students to meet their academic commitments (Leonard, 2008). For instance, campus employers are more willing to schedule students' work hours around their class schedule and allow students to modify their work schedules when their academic workload increases (e.g., at midterm and finals). Thus, if at all possible, rather than seeking work off campus, try to find work on campus and capitalize on its proven capacity to promote college success.

◆ Money-Saving Strategies and Habits

The ultimate goal of money management is to save money and dodge debt. Here are some strategies for accomplishing this goal.

Prepare a personal budget. A budget is simply a plan for coordinating income and expenses to ensure that your cash flow leaves you with sufficient money to cover your expenses. A budget helps you maintain awareness of your financial state or condition, and enables you to be your own accountant who keeps an accurate account of your own money.

Just like managing and budgeting time, the first step in managing and budgeting money involves prioritizing. Money management requires identifying your most important expenses (indispensable necessities you can't live without) and distinguishing them from incidentals (dispensable luxuries you can live without). People can easily confuse essentials (what they need) and desirables (what they want). For instance, if a piece of merchandise happens to be on sale, it may be a desirable purchase at that time because of its reduced price, but it's not an essential purchase unless the person really needs that piece of merchandise at that particular time.

Postponing immediate or impulsive satisfaction of material desires is a key element of effective college financing and long-term financial success. We need to remain aware of whether we're spending money on impulse and out of habit or out of need and after thoughtful reflection. The truth is that humans spend money for a host of psychological reasons (conscious or subconscious), many of which are unrelated to actual need. For example, some people spend money to build their self-esteem or self-image, to combat personal boredom, or to seek an emotional "high" (Dittmar, 2004; Furnham & Argyle, 1998). Furthermore, people can become obsessed with spending money, shop compulsively, and develop an addiction to purchasing products. Just as Alcoholics Anonymous (AA) exists as a support group for alcoholics, Debtors Anonymous exists as a support group for shopaholics and includes a 12-step recovery program similar to AA.

Student Perspective

"I need to save money and not shop so much and impulse buy."

—First-year student

Personal Story

I was a student who had to manage my own college expenses, so I soon became an expert in managing small budgets. The first thing I always took care of was my tuition. I was going to go to school even if I starved. The next thing I budgeted for was my housing, food, clothing, and transportation needs. If I ran out of money, I would then work additional hours if it didn't interfere with my academics. I clearly understood that I was working to make a better future life for myself, rather than making and spending money while I was in college. To be successful, I had to be a great money manager because there was so little of it to manage. This took a lot of focus and strong will, but did it ever pay off? Absolutely.

—Aaron Thompson

Make all your bills visible and pay them off as soon as possible. When your bills remain in your sight, they remain on your mind; you're less likely to forget to pay them or forget to pay them on time. Increase the visibility of your bill payments by keeping a financial calendar on which you record key fiscal deadlines for the academic year (e.g., due dates for tuition payments, residential bills, and financial aid applications). Also, try to get in the habit of paying a bill as soon as you open it and have it in your hands, rather than setting it aside and running the risk of forgetting to pay it (or losing it altogether).

Live within your means. To state it simply: Don't purchase what you can't afford. If you're spending more money than you're taking in, it means you're living *beyond* your means. To begin living *within* your means, you have two options:

1. Decrease your expenses (reduce your spending), or
2. Increase your income (earn more money).

"We choose to spend more money than we have today. Choose debt, or choose freedom, it's your choice."

—Bill Pratt, *Extra Credit: The 7 Things Every College Student Needs to Know About Credit, Debt & Cash*

Remember

Remaining consciously aware of the distinction between **essentials** that must be purchased and **incidentals** that may or may not be purchased is an important first step toward preparing an effective budget and avoiding debt.

Since most college students are already working while attending college (Orszag, Orszag, & Whitmore, 2001) and working so many hours that it's interfering with their academic performance or progress (King, 2005), the best option for most college students who find themselves in debt is to reduce their spending and begin living within their means.

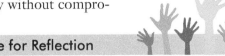

Economize. By being intelligent consumers who use critical thinking skills when purchasing products, we can be frugal or thrifty without compromising the quality of our purchases. For example, we could pay less to see the same movie in the late afternoon than we could to see it at night. Why pay more for brand-name products that are the same as products with a different name? Why pay 33 percent more for Advil or Tylenol when the same amount of pain-relieving ingredient (ibuprofen or acetaminophen) is contained in generic brands? Often, what we're paying for when we buy brand-name products is all the advertising these companies pay to the media and to celebrities to publicly promote their products.

> **Pause for Reflection**
>
> Are you working for money while attending college?
>
> If you're not working, are you sacrificing anything you want or need because you don't have the money to buy it?

If you are working:

1. How many hours per week do you currently work?
2. Do you think that working is interfering with your academic performance or progress?
3. Would it be possible for you to reduce the number of weekly hours you now work and still be able to make ends meet?

> **! Remember**
>
> Advertising creates product familiarity, not product quality. The more money manufacturers pay for advertising and creating a well-known brand, the more money we pay for the product—not necessarily because we're acquiring a product of higher quality, but more likely because we're covering its high cost of advertising.

Downsize. Cut down or cut out spending for products that you don't need. Don't engage in conspicuous consumption just to keep up with the "Joneses" (your neighbors or friends), and don't allow peer pressure to determine your spending habits. Let your spending habits reflect your ability to think critically rather than your tendency to conform socially.

Save money by living with others rather than living alone. Although you lose privacy when you share living quarters with others, you save money. Living with others also has the fringe social benefit of spending time with roommates or housemates whom you've chosen to live with and whose company you enjoy.

Give gifts of time rather than money. Spending money on gifts for family, friends, and romantic partners isn't the only way to show that you care. The point of gift giving isn't to show others you aren't cheap or show off by being a big-time spender; instead, show off your social sensitivity by doing something special or by making something meaningful for them. Gifts of time and kindness can often be more personal and more special than store-bought gifts.

Develop your own set of money-saving strategies and habits. You can save money by starting to develop little money-saving habits that eventually add up to big savings over time. Consider the following list of habit-forming tips for saving money that were suggested by students in a first-year seminar class:

- Don't carry a lot of extra money in your wallet. (It's just like food; if it's easy to get to, you'll be more likely to eat it up.)
- Shop with a list—get in, get what you need, and get out.
- Put all your extra change in a jar.

"It is preoccupation with possessions, more than anything else, that prevents us from living freely and nobly."

–Bertrand Russell, British philosopher and mathematician

"The richer your friends, the more they will cost you."

–Elisabeth Marbury, legal agent for theatrical and literary stars in the late 19th and early 20th centuries

"If you would be wealthy, think of saving as well as getting."

–Benjamin Franklin, 18th-century inventor, newspaper writer, and signer of the Declaration of Independence

When my wife (Mary) and I were first dating, I was trying to gain weight because I was on the thin side. (All right, I was skinny.) One day when I came home from school, I found this hand-delivered package in front of my apartment door. I opened it up and there was a homemade loaf of whole wheat bread made from scratch by Mary. That gift didn't cost her much money, but she took the time to do it and she remembered to do something that was important to me (gaining weight). That gift really touched me; it's a gift I've never forgotten. Since I eventually married Mary and we're still happily married, I guess you could say that inexpensive loaf of bread was a "gift that kept on giving."

—Joe Cuseo

Pause for Reflection

Do you use any of the strategies on the above list?

Have you developed any effective strategies that do not appear on the list?

"The safest way to double your money is to fold it over and put it in your pocket."

–Kin Hubbard, American humorist, cartoonist, and journalist

"Ask yourself how much of your income is being eaten up by car payments. It may be time to admit you made a mistake . . . sell it [and] replace it with an older or less sporty model."

–Bill Pratt, *Extra Credit: The 7 Things Every College Student Needs to Know About Credit, Debt & Cash*

- Put extra cash in a piggy bank that requires you to smash the piggy to get at it.
- Seal your savings in an envelope.
- When you get extra money, get it immediately into the bank (and out of your hands).
- Bring (don't buy) your lunch.
- Take full advantage of your meal plan—you've already paid for it, so don't pay twice for your meals by buying food elsewhere.
- Use e-mail instead of the telephone.
- Hide your credit card or put it in the freezer so that you don't use it on impulse.
- Use cash (instead of credit cards) because you can give yourself a set amount of cash and clearly see how much of it you have at the start of a week (and how much is left at any point during the week).

When making purchases, always think in terms of their long-term total cost. It's convenient and tempting for consumers to think in the short term ("I see it; I like it; I want it; and I want it now.") However, long-term thinking is one of the essential keys to successful money management and financial planning. Those small (monthly) installment plans that businesses offer to get you to buy expensive products may make the cost of those products appear attractive and affordable in the short run. However, when you factor in the interest rates you pay on monthly installment plans, plus the length of time (number of months) you're making installment payments, you get a more accurate picture of the product's total cost over the long run. This longer-range perspective can quickly alert you to the reality that a product's sticker price represents its partial and seemingly affordable short-term cost but its long-term total cost is much less affordable (and perhaps out of your league).

Furthermore, the long-term price for purchases sometimes involves additional "hidden costs" that don't relate directly to the product's initial price but must be paid to keep using the product. For example, the sticker price you pay for clothes doesn't include the hidden, long-term costs that may be involved if those clothes require dry cleaning. By just taking a moment to check the inside label, you can save yourself this hidden, long-term cost by purchasing clothes that are machine washable. To use an example of a big-ticket purchase, the extra money spent to buy a new car (instead of a used car) includes not only paying a higher sticker price but also paying the higher hidden costs of licensing and insuring the new car, as well as any interest fees if the new car was purchased on an installment plan. When you add in these hidden, long-term costs to a new car's total cost, buying a good used car is clearly a much more effective money-management strategy than buying a new one.

Personal Story

When I was four years old and living in the mountains of Kentucky, it was safe for a young lad to walk the railroad tracks and roads alone. So, my mother would send me on long walks to the general store to buy various small items we needed for our household. Since we had little money, she was very cautious about spending money only on the essential necessities we needed to survive. I could only purchase items from the general store that my mother strictly ordered me to purchase. Most of these items cost less than a dollar, and in many cases multiple items could be bought for a dollar in the early 1960s. At the store I would hand my mother's handwritten list to the owners. They would pick the items for me, and we would exchange the items for my money. On the checkout counter jars were different kinds of candy or gum. You could buy two pieces for a penny. As a hardworking boy who was doing a good deed for his parents, I didn't think there would be any harm in rewarding myself with two pieces of candy after doing a good deed. After all, I could devour the evidence of my disobedience on my slow walk home. Upon my return, my mother, being the protector of the vault and the sergeant-of-arms in our household, would count each item I brought home to make sure I had been charged correctly. She always found that I had either been overcharged by one cent or that I had spent one cent. In those days, parents believed in behavior modification. After she gave me a scolding, she would say "Boy, you better learn how to count your money if you're ever going to be successful in life." I learned the value of saving money and the danger of overspending at a young age!

—*Aaron Thompson*

!

Remember

Avoid buying costly items impulsively. Instead, take time to reflect on the purchase you intend to make, do a cost analysis of its hidden and long-term costs, and then integrate these invisible costs with the product's sticker price to generate an accurate synthesis and clearer picture of the product's total cost.

◆ Long-Range Fiscal Planning: Financing Your College Education

An effective money-management plan should be time-sensitive and include the following time frames:

- Short-range financial planning (e.g., weekly income and expenses)
- Mid-range financial planning (e.g., monthly income and expenses)
- Long-range financial planning (e.g., projected or anticipated income and expenses for the entire college experience)
- Extended long-range financial planning (e.g., expected income and debt after graduation, including a plan for repayment of college loans)

Thus far, our discussion has focused primarily on short-range and mid-range financial planning strategies that will keep you out of debt on a monthly or yearly basis. We turn now to issues involving long-term financial planning for your entire college experience. While no one "correct" strategy exists for financing a college education, there are some important research findings on the effectiveness of different financing strategies that you should be aware of when doing long-range financial planning for college and beyond.

"People don't realize how much work it is to stay in college. It's its own job in itself, plus if you've got another job you go to, too. I mean, it's just a lot."

–College student (quoted in Engle & Bermeo, 2006)

"I work two jobs and go to school and it's hard, real hard. I go home at like 9 or 10, and I'm too tired to do my homework."

–College student (quoted in Engle & Bermeo, 2006)

Pause for Reflection

Do you need to work part-time to meet your college expenses?

If you answered "yes" to the above question, are you working more than 15 hours per week?

If you answered "yes" to the above question, can you reduce your work time to 15 or fewer hours per week and still make ends meet?

Research shows that obtaining a student loan and working no more than 15 hours per week is an effective long-range strategy for students at all income levels to finance their college education and meet their personal expenses. Students who use this strategy are more likely to graduate from college, graduate in less time, and graduate with higher grades than students who work part-time for more than 15 hours per week while attending college full-time, or students who work full-time and attend college part-time (King, 2002; Perna & DuBois, 2010). Unfortunately, less than 6 percent of all first-year students use this strategy. Instead, almost 50 percent of first-year students choose a strategy that research shows to be least associated with college success: borrowing nothing and trying to work more than 15 hours per week. Students who use this strategy increase their risk of lowering their grades significantly and withdrawing from college altogether (King, 2005)—probably because they have difficulty finding enough time to handle the amount of academic work required by college on top of the more than 15 hours they're working per week. Thus, a good strategy for balancing learning and earning is to try to limit work for pay to 15 hours per week (or as close to 15 hours as possible). Working longer hours increases the temptation to switch from full-time to part-time enrollment, which can increase the risk of delaying graduation or not graduating at all.

Some students decide to finance their college education by working full-time and going to college part-time. These students believe it will be less expensive in the long run to attend college part-time because it will allow them to avoid any debt from student loans. However, studies show that when students use this strategy, it lengthens their time to degree completion and increases the risk that they will never complete a degree (Orszag et al., 2001).

Students who manage to eventually graduate from college but take longer to do so because they have worked more than 15 hours per week will lose money in the long run. The longer they take to graduate, the longer they must wait to "cash in" on their college degrees and enter higher-paying, full-time positions that a college diploma would qualify them to enter. The hourly pay for most part-time jobs students hold while going to college is less than half what they will earn from working in full-time positions as college graduates (King, 2005).

Furthermore, studies show that two out of three college students have at least one credit card and nearly one of every two students with credit cards carries an average balance of more than $2,000 per month (Mae, 2005). A debt level this high is likely to push many students into working more than 15 hours a week to pay it off ("I owe, I owe, so off to work I go"). This often results in their taking longer to graduate and start earning a college graduate's salary because they end up taking fewer courses per term so they can work more hours to pay off their credit card debt.

Instead of paying almost 20 percent interest to credit card companies for their monthly debt, these students would be better off obtaining a student loan at a much lower interest rate, which they will not start paying back until 6 months after graduation—when they'll be making more money in full-time positions as college graduates. Despite this clear advantage of student loans compared to credit card loans, only about 25 percent of college students who use credit cards take out student loans (King, 2002).

> **Remember**
>
> Student loans are provided by the American government with the intent of helping its citizens become better educated. In contrast, for-profit businesses such as credit-card companies lend students money with no intent of helping them become better educated, but with the clear intent of helping themselves make money—from the high rates of interest they collect from students who do not pay off their debt in full at the end of each month.

Keep in mind that not all debt is bad. Debt can be good if it represents an investment in something that will appreciate with time—i.e., something that will gain in value and eventually turn into profit for the investor. Purchasing a college education on credit is a good investment because, over time, it appreciates in the form of higher salaries for the remainder of the life of the investor (the college graduate). In contrast, purchasing a new car is a bad long-term investment because it immediately begins to depreciate or lose monetary value once it's purchased. The instant you drive that new car off the dealer's lot, you immediately become the proud owner of a used car that's worth much less than what you just paid for it.

> **Remember**
>
> What you're willing to sacrifice and save for, and what you're willing to go into debt for, say a lot about who you are and what you value.

You may have heard the expression that "time is money." One way to interpret this expression is that the more money you spend, the more time you must spend making money. If you're going to college, spending more time on earning money to cover your spending habits often means spending less time studying, learning, completing classes, and earning good grades. You can avoid this vicious cycle by viewing academic work as work that "pays" you back in terms of completed courses and higher grades. If you put in more academic time to complete more courses in less time and with higher grades, you're paid back by graduating and earning the full-time salary of a college graduate sooner—which will pay you about twice as much money per hour than you'll earn doing part-time work without a college degree (not to mention fringe benefits such as health insurance and paid vacation time). Furthermore, the time you put into earning higher grades in college should pay off immediately in your first full-time position after college, because research shows that students graduating in the same field who have higher grades receive higher starting salaries (Pascarella & Terenzini, 2005).

◆ Summary and Conclusion

The following strategies for effectively managing money were recommended in this chapter:

- **Develop financial self-awareness.** Become aware of your cash flow—the amount of money flowing in and flowing out of your hands.

"Unlike a car that depreciates in value each year that you drive it, an investment in education yields monetary, social, and intellectual profit. A car is more tangible in the short term, but an investment in education (even if it means borrowing money) gives you more bang for the buck in the long run."

–Eric Tyson, financial counselor and national bestselling author of *Personal Finance for Dummies*

"The cynic knows the price of everything and the value of nothing."

–Oscar Wilde, Irish playwright, poet, and author of numerous short stories

Pause for Reflection

In addition to college, what might be other good long-term investments you could make now in the near future?

"If a man empties his purse into his head, no one can take it away from him. An investment in knowledge always pays the best interest."

–Benjamin Franklin, 18th-century scientist, inventor, and a founding father of the United States

"I invested in myself—in study, in mastering my tools, in preparation. Many a man who is putting a few dollars a week into the bank would do much better to put it into himself."

—Henry Ford, founder of the Ford Motor Company and one of the richest people of the 20th century

- **Develop a money-management plan.** Ensure that your income is equal to or greater than your expenses.
- **Manage your money effectively.** Use available financial tools and instruments to track and maximize your cash flow, such as checking accounts, credit cards, charge cards, or debit cards.
- **Finance your education wisely.** Explore all sources of income for financing your college education, including the FAFSA, scholarships, grants, loans, monetary gifts from family or friends, salary earnings, and personal savings.
- **Prepare a personal budget.** A budget helps you keep an accurate account of your money and ensures you have sufficient money to cover your expenses.
- **Pay your bills when they arrive.** Paying bills when you first lay your hands on them serves to reduce the risk that you'll forget to pay them or pay them late.
- **Live within your means.** Don't purchase what you can't afford.
- **Economize.** Be an intelligent consumer who uses critical thinking skills to evaluate and prioritize your purchases.
- **Downsize.** Don't buy products you don't need, and don't let peer pressure determine your spending habits.
- **Live with others, rather than live alone.** The reduction in privacy can be offset by the financial savings. Living with others can also bring the fringe social benefit of having roommates or housemates whom you've chosen to live with and whose company you enjoy.
- **Work for better grades now and better pay later.** Research shows that taking out a student loan and working part-time for 15 or fewer hours per week is the most effective financial and educational strategy for students at all income levels.
- **Take full advantage of your Financial Aid Office.** Check periodically to see if you qualify for additional sources of income, such as part-time employment on campus, low-interest loans, grants, or scholarships.

Money management is a personal skill that can either support or sabotage your success in college and life beyond college. As with time management, if you effectively manage your money and gain control of how you spend it, you gain greater control over the quality of your life. Research shows that accumulating high levels of debt while in college is associated with higher levels of stress, lower academic performance, and greater risk of withdrawing from college. The good news is that research demonstrates that students who learn to use effective money-management strategies are able to reduce unnecessary spending, decrease their risk of debt and stress, and increase the quality of their academic performance.

Learning More Through the World Wide Web

Internet-Based Resources for Further Information on Money Management

For additional information related to the ideas discussed in this chapter, we recommend the following Web sites:

Fiscal Literacy and Money Management:

www.360financialliteracy.org

www.cashcourse.org

www.loveyourmoney.org

Financial Aid and Federal Funding Sources for a College Education: **studentaid.ed.gov**

6.1 Self-Assessment of Financial Attitudes and Habits

Answer the following questions as accurately and honestly as possible.

		Agree	Disagree
1.	I pay my rent or mortgage on time each month.	_____	_____
2.	I avoid maxing out or going over the limit on my credit cards.	_____	_____
3.	I balance my checkbook each month.	_____	_____
4.	I set aside money each month for savings.	_____	_____
5.	I pay my phone and utility bills on time each month.	_____	_____
6.	I pay my credit card bills in full each month to avoid interest charges.	_____	_____
7.	I believe it's important to buy the things I want when I want them.	_____	_____
8.	Borrowing money to pay for college is a smart thing to do.	_____	_____
9.	I have a monthly or weekly budget that I follow.	_____	_____
10.	The thing I enjoy most about making money is spending money.	_____	_____
11.	I limit myself to one credit card.	_____	_____
12.	Getting a degree will get me a good job and a good income.	_____	_____

Sources: Cude et al. (2006); Niederjohn (2008).

Give yourself one point for each item that you marked "agree"—except for items 7, 9, and 10. For these items, give yourself a point if you marked "disagree."

A perfect score on this short survey would be 12.

1. What was your total score?

2. Which items lowered your score?

3. Do you detect any pattern across the items that lowered your score?

4. Do you see any realistic way(s) for improving your score on this test?

6.2 Financial Self-Awareness: Monitoring Money and Tracking Cash Flow

1. Use the worksheet that follows to *estimate* your income and expenses per month, and enter them in column 2.

2. *Track* your actual income and expenses for a month and enter them in column 3. (To help you do this accurately, keep a file of your cash receipts, bills paid, and credit card or checking account records for the month.)

3. After one month of tracking your cash flow, answer the self-assessment questions.

   a. Were your estimates generally accurate?

   b. For what specific items were there the largest discrepancies between your estimated cost and the actual cost?

   c. Comparing your bottom-line totals for income and expenses, are you satisfied with how your monthly cash flow is going?

   d. What changes could you make to create more positive cash flow—i.e., to increase your income or savings and reduce your expenses or debt?

   e. How likely is it that you'll make the changes you mentioned in the previous question?

Financial Self-Awareness Worksheet

	Estimate	Actual
Income Sources		
Parents/Family		
Work/Job		
Grants/Scholarships		
Loans		
Savings		
Other:		
TOTAL INCOME		
Essentials (Fixed Expenses)		
Living Expenses: Food/Groceries		
Rent/Room & Board		
Utilities (gas/electric)		
Clothing		
Laundry/Dry Cleaning		
Phone		
Computer		
Household Items (dishes, etc.)		
Medical Insurance Expenses		
Debt Payments (loans/credit cards)		
Other:		
School Expenses: Tuition		
Books		
Supplies (print cartridges, etc.)		
Special Fees (lab fees, etc.)		
Other:		
Transportation: Public Transportation (bus fees, etc.)		
Car Insurance		
Car Maintenance		
Fuel (gas)		
Car Payments		
Other:		
Incidentals (Variable Expenses)		
Entertainment: Movies/Concerts		
DVDs/CDs		
Restaurants (eating out)		
Other:		
Personal Appearance/Accessories: Haircuts/Hairstyling		

Cosmetics/Manicures		
Fashionable Clothes		
Jewelry		
Other:		
Hobbies: Travel (trips home, vacations)		
Gifts		
Other:		
TOTAL EXPENSES		

Problems Paying for College

A college student posted the following message on the Internet:

"I went to college for one semester, failed some my classes, and ended with 900 dollars in student loans. Now I can't even get financial aid or a loan because of some stupid thing that says if you fail a certain amount of classes you can't get aid or a loan. And now since I couldn't go to college this semester they want me to pay for my loans already, and I don't even have a job. Any suggestions?"

Reflection and Discussion Questions

1. What suggestions would you offer this student? Which of your suggestions should the student do immediately? Which should the student do eventually?

2. What should the student have done to prevent this from happening in the first place?

3. Do you think that this student's situation is common or unusual? Why?

Your First Year Resources

The first year of college is an exciting and challenging time. We want you to have the best experience possible, so we've designed a website just for you. It's full of tips, tricks, and links to help you make the most of Your First Year! If you have questions or need help finding your way at UNCG, you can always email us at yfy@uncg.edu. Visit yourfirstyear.uncg.edu and the websites below for helpful resources and services about money and financial management.

Financial Aid   **336-334-5702**
http://fia.uncg.edu/

Students First Office   **336-334-5730**
http://studentsfirst.uncg.edu/

Student Success Center   **336-334-3878**
http://success.uncg.edu/

Higher-Level Thinking

Moving Beyond Factual Knowledge to Higher Levels of Critical and Creative Thinking

ACTIVATE YOUR THINKING   Journal Entry   **7.1**

To me, critical thinking means . . .

(At a later point in this chapter, we discuss critical thinking and have you flashback to the response you made here.)

_____

_____

_____

LEARNING GOAL

To increase awareness of what it means to think at a higher level and to use higher-level thinking for achieving excellence in college and beyond.

◆ What Is Higher-Level Thinking?

The term "higher-level thinking" refers to a more advanced level of thought than that used for basic learning. Higher-level thinking takes place when you reflect on the knowledge you've acquired and take additional mental action on it, such as evaluating its validity and practicality or integrating it with something else you've learned to create a more comprehensive or creative product.

Contestants performing on TV quiz shows such as *Jeopardy* or *Who Wants to Be a Millionaire?* respond with factual knowledge to questions asking for information about who, what, when, and where. If game-show contestants were to be tested for higher-level thinking, they would not be recalling facts; they would be engaged in thinking about such questions as "Why?" "How?" and "What if?" Your previous experiences in school or at work may have trained you to answer questions asked by others. However, in college, it's as important to ask the right question as it is to give the right answer.

> **Student Perspective**
>
> "To me, thinking at a higher level means to think and analyze something beyond the obvious and find the deeper meaning."
>
> —First-year college student

> "What is the hardest task in the world? To think."
>
> —Ralph Waldo Emerson, nineteenth-century American essayist and lecturer

> **!** **Remember**
>
> The focus of higher-level thinking is not just to answer questions but also to question answers.

As its name implies, higher-level thinking involves raising the bar and jacking up your thinking to levels that go beyond merely remembering, reproducing, or regurgitating factual information. "Education is what's left over after you've forgotten all the facts" is an old saying that carries a lot of truth. Studies show that students' memory of facts learned in college often fades with time (Pascarella & Terenzini, 1991, 2005). Factual information that has been memorized has a short life span; learning to think at a higher level is a durable, lifelong learning skill that you will retain and use throughout life.

Compared to high school, college courses focus less on memorizing information and more on thinking about issues, concepts, and principles (Conley, 2005). Remembering information in college may get you a C grade, demonstrating comprehension of that information may give you a B, and going beyond comprehension to demonstrate higher-level thinking should earn you an A. Simply stated, college professors are more concerned with teaching you *how* to think than with teaching you *what* to think (i.e., what facts to remember).

> **!**
>
> ### Remember
>
> Your college professors will often expect you to do more than just retain or reproduce information; they'll ask you to demonstrate higher levels of thinking with respect to what you've learned, such as analyze it, evaluate it, apply it, or connect it with other concepts that you've learned.

This is not to say that basic knowledge and comprehension are unimportant. They supply you with the raw material needed to manufacture higher-level thinking. The deep learning and broad base of knowledge you experience in college will provide the stepping stones you need to climb to higher levels of thinking (as illustrated in **Figure 7.1**).

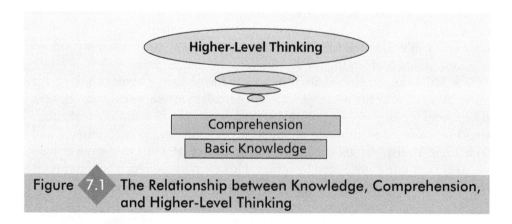

Figure 7.1 **The Relationship between Knowledge, Comprehension, and Higher-Level Thinking**

◆ Defining and Describing the Major Forms of Higher-Level Thinking

In national surveys of college professors teaching freshman- through senior-level courses in various fields, more than 95 percent of them report that the most important goal of a college education is to develop students' ability to think critically (Gardiner, 2005; Milton, 1982). Similarly, college professors who teach introductory courses to freshmen and sophomores indicate that the primary educational purpose of their courses is to develop students' critical thinking skills (Stark et al., 1990).

When your college professors ask you to "think critically," they're usually asking you to use one or more of the eight forms of thinking listed in the **Snapshot Summary 7.1**. As you read the descriptions of each form of thinking, note whether or not you've heard of it before.

Snapshot Summary  7.1

Major Forms of Higher-Level Thinking

1. Application (Applied Thinking). Putting knowledge into practice to solve problems and resolve issues;
2. Analysis (Analytical Thinking). Breaking down information to identify its key parts and underlying elements;
3. Synthesis. Building up ideas by integrating separate pieces of information into a larger whole or more comprehensive product;
4. Multidimensional Thinking. Taking multiple perspectives (i.e., viewing issues from different vantage points);

5. Inferential Reasoning. Making arguments or judgment by inferring (stepping to) a conclusion that is supported by empirical (observable) evidence or logical consistency;
6. Balanced Thinking. Carefully considering arguments for and against a particular position or viewpoint;
7. Critical Thinking. Evaluating (judging the quality of) arguments, conclusions, and ideas;
8. Creative Thinking. Generating ideas that are unique, original, or distinctively different.

Application (Applied Thinking)

When you learn something deeply, you transform information into knowledge; when you translate knowledge into action, you're engaging in a higher-level thinking process known as application. Applied thinking moves you beyond simply knowing something to actually doing something with the knowledge you possesses; you use it to solve a problem or resolve an issue. For example, when you use knowledge you've acquired in a human relations course to resolve an interpersonal conflict, you're engaging in application. Similarly, you're using applied thinking when you use knowledge acquired in a math course to solve a problem that you haven't seen before. Application is a powerful form of higher-level thinking because it allows you to transfer your knowledge to new situations or contexts and put it into practice.

Always be on the lookout for ways to apply the knowledge you acquire to your personal life experiences and current events or issues. When you use your knowledge for the practical purpose of doing something good, such as bettering yourself or fellow humans, you not only demonstrate application but also demonstrate wisdom (Staudinger & Baltes, 1994).

Pause for Reflection

Look back at the eight forms of thinking described in the Snapshot Summary 7.1. Which of these forms of thinking had you heard before? Did you use any of these forms of thinking on high school exams or assignments?

Analysis (Analytical Thinking)

The mental process of analysis is like the physical process of peeling an onion. When you analyze something, you break it down, take it apart, and identify its main points, key parts, or underlying elements. For example, if you were to analyze a textbook chapter, you would go beyond simply reading it just to cover the content; instead, you would read it to uncover the author's main ideas—finding the core ideas by separating them from background information and surface details.

You use analysis to identify the components or elements that should be examined in a work of art (e.g., its structure, texture, tone, and form). Analysis is also used to identify underlying reasons or causes, commonly referred to as causal analysis. For instance, a causal analysis of the September 11, 2001, attack on the United States would involve identifying the factors that led to the attack or the underlying reasons for which the attack took place.

Synthesis

A higher-level thinking process that's basically the opposite of analysis is synthesis. When you analyze, you break information into its parts; when you synthesize, you take parts or pieces of information and build them into an integrated whole or comprehensive product (like piecing together a puzzle). You would be engaging in synthesis if you were to connect ideas presented in different courses—for instance, if you were to integrate ethical concepts you learned in a philosophy course with marketing concepts you learned in a business course to produce a set of ethical guidelines for marketing and advertising products.

Synthesis involves more than a summary. It goes beyond just condensing information to finding and forming meaningful connections among separate pieces of information, weaving them together to form a unified picture. When you're synthesizing, you're thinking conceptually by converting isolated facts and separated bits of information and integrating them into a concept—a larger system or network of related ideas.

Although synthesis and analysis are virtually opposite thought processes, they complement each other. When you analyze, you disassemble wholes into their key parts. When you synthesize, you reassemble parts into a new whole. For instance, when writing this book, we analyzed published material in many fields (e.g., psychology, history, philosophy, and biology) and identified information from parts of these fields that were most relevant to promoting the success of beginning college students. We then synthesized or reassembled these parts to create a new whole—the textbook you're now reading.

Multidimensional Thinking

When you engage in multidimensional thinking, you view yourself and the world around you from different angles or vantage points. In particular, a multidimensional thinker is able to think from four perspectives:

1. Person (self)
2. Place

Student Perspective

"In physics, you have to be analytical and break it [the problem] down into its parts, and not look at the question all at once."

–Physics student (Donald, 2002)

Pause for Reflection

A TV commercial for a particular brand of liquor (which shall remain nameless) once showed a young man getting out of his car in front of a house where a party is going on. The driver gets out of his car, takes out a knife, slashes his tires, and goes inside to join the party. Using the higher-level thinking skill of analysis, what are the underlying or embedded messages in this commercial?

Student Perspective

"To me, thinking at a higher level is when you approach a question or topic thoughtfully, when you fully explore every aspect of that topic from all angles."

–First-year college student

3. Time
4. Culture

Multidimensional thinkers consider how these perspectives influence, and are influenced by, the issue they're discussing or debating. For example, they would ask the following questions:

- How does this issue affect me as an individual? (the perspective of person)
- What impact does this issue have on people living in different countries? (the perspective of place)
- How will future generations of people be affected by this issue? (the perspective of time)
- How is this issue likely to be interpreted or experienced by groups of people who share different social customs and traditions? (the perspective of culture)

Each of these perspectives has different elements embedded within it. The four major perspectives, along with the elements that comprise each of them, are listed and described in the **Snapshot Summary** 7.2. Note how these perspectives are consistent with those developed by the liberal arts.

Important issues, problems, and challenges do not exist in isolation but as parts of an interconnected, multiple-perspective system. For example, global warming is a current issue that involves the earth's atmosphere gradually thickening and trapping more heat due to a collection of greenhouse gases,

Snapshot Summary

7.2

Perspectives Associated with Multidimensional Thinking

Perspective 1: PERSON
Perspectives of the individual or self

Components:
- Intellectual (Cognitive). Personal knowledge, thoughts, and self-concept;
- Emotional. Personal feelings, emotional adjustment, and mental health;
- Social. Personal relationships and interpersonal interactions;
- Ethical. Personal values and moral convictions;
- Physical. Personal health and wellness;
- Spiritual. Personal beliefs about the meaning or purpose of life and the hereafter;
- Vocational (Occupational). Personal means of making a living or earning an income.

Perspective 2: PLACE
Broader perspectives representing progressively larger circles of social and spatial distance beyond the self

Components:
- Family. Parents, children, and relatives;
- Community. Local communities and neighborhoods;
- Society. Societal institutions (e.g., schools, churches, and hospitals) and groups within society (e.g., groups differing in age, gender, race, or social class);
- National. Country or place of citizenship;
- International. Different nations or countries;

- **Global.** The earth (e.g., all its life forms and natural resources);
- **Universal.** The relationship between earth and its place in a galaxy that includes planets and heavenly bodies.

Perspective 3: TIME

The chronological perspective

Components:
- **Historical.** The past;
- **Contemporary.** The present;
- **Futuristic.** The future.

Perspective 4: CULTURE

The distinctive way or style of living of a group of people who share the same social heritage and traditions

Components:
- **Linguistic (Language).** How group members communicate through written or spoken words and through nonverbal communication (body language);
- **Political.** How the group organizes societal authority and uses it to govern itself, make collective decisions, and maintain social order;
- **Economic.** How the material wants and needs of the group are met through the allocation of limited resources, and how wealth is distributed among its members;

- **Geographical.** How the group's physical location influences the nature of social interactions and affects the way group members adapt to and use their environment;
- **Aesthetic.** How the group appreciates and expresses artistic beauty and creativity through the fine arts (e.g., visual art, music, theater, literature, and dance);
- **Scientific.** How the group views, understands, and investigates natural phenomena through systematic research (e.g., scientific tests and experiments);
- **Ecological.** How the group views the interrelationship between the biological world (humans and other living creatures) and the natural world (the surrounding physical environment);
- **Anthropological.** How the group's culture originated, evolved, and developed over time;
- **Sociological.** How the group's society is structured or organized into social subgroups and social institutions;
- **Psychological.** How group members tend to think, feel, and interact, and how their attitudes, opinions, or beliefs have been acquired;
- **Philosophical.** The group's ideas or views on wisdom, goodness, truth, and the meaning or purpose of life;
- **Theological.** Group members' conception and beliefs about a transcendent, supreme being, and how they express their shared faith in a supreme being.

Pause for Reflection

Briefly explain how each of the perspectives of person, place, time, and culture may be involved in causing and solving one the following problems:

1. War and terrorism

2. Poverty and hunger

3. Prejudice and discrimination

4. Any world issue of your choice

which are being produced primarily by the burning of fossil fuels. It's theorized that the increase of manmade pollution is causing temperatures to rise (and sometimes fall) around the world and is contributing to natural disasters, such as droughts, wildfires, and dust storms (Joint Science Academies Statement, 2005; National Resources Defense Council, 2005). A comprehensive understanding and solution to this global problem involves interrelationships among many of the perspectives depicted in **Figure 7.2**. It's an issue that involves:

- **Ecology.** The interrelationship between humans and their natural environment;

- Science. The need for research and development of alternative sources of energy;
- Economics. The cost incurred by industries to change their existing sources of energy;
- National politics. Laws may need to be created to encourage or enforce changes in industries' use of energy sources; and
- International relations. The collaboration needed among all countries that are contributing to the current problem and could contribute to its future solution.

	IMPLICATION
Person	Global warming involves us on an individual level because our personal efforts at energy conservation in our homes and our willingness to purchase energy-efficient products can play a major role in solving this problem.
Place	Global warming is an international issue that extends beyond the boundaries of one's own country to all countries in the world, and its solution will require worldwide collaboration.
Time	If the current trend toward higher global temperatures caused by global warming continues, it could seriously threaten the lives of future generations of people who inhabit our planet.
Culture	The problem of global warming has been caused by industries in technologically advanced cultures, yet the problem of rising global temperatures is likely to have its most negative impact on less technologically advanced cultures that lack the resources to respond to it (Joint Science Academies Statement, 2005). To prevent this from happening, technologically advanced cultures will need to use their advanced technology to devise alternative methods for generating energy that does not continue to release heat-trapping gases into the atmosphere.

Figure 7.2

Inferential Reasoning

When people make arguments or arrive at conclusions, they do so by starting with a premise (a statement or an observation) and using it to infer (step to) a conclusion. The following sentence starters demonstrate the process of inferential reasoning:

"Because this is true, it follows that . . ."
"Based on this evidence, I can conclude that . . ."

In college, you will often be required to draw conclusions and support those conclusions with evidence. If you're asked to formulate an argument, you're being asked to use inferential reasoning to reach a conclusion and support your conclusion. In a sense, you're being asked to take on the role of a lawyer who's trying to prove a case through documentation by providing supporting arguments and evidence (e.g., exhibit A, exhibit B, and exhibit C).

The following are two major ways in which you use inferential reasoning to support your points or arguments:

1. Citing empirical (observable) evidence (e.g., specific examples, personal experiences, facts, figures, statistical data, scientific research findings, expert testimonies, supporting quotes, or statements from leading authorities in the field);
2. Using principles of logical consistency (i.e., demonstrating that your conclusion follows or flows logically from an established premise or general statement).

The following are examples of logical consistency:

- The constitution guarantees all U.S. citizens the right to vote (established premise);
- U.S. citizens include women and people of color; therefore,
- Denying women and people of color the right to vote was illogical (and unconstitutional).

Here's how these two strategies for supporting an argument have been used by some to conclude that the drinking age in the United States should be lowered to 18:

Pause for Reflection

Can you think of any arguments against lowering the drinking age to 18 that are based on empirical (observable) evidence or logical consistency?

1. **Citing empirical (observable) evidence.** In other countries where drinking is allowed at age 18, statistics show that they have fewer binge-drinking and drunk-driving problems than the United States.
2. **Using the principle of logical consistency.** The 18-year-olds in the United States are considered to be legal adults with respect to such rights and responsibilities as voting, serving on juries, joining the military, and being held responsible for committing crimes; therefore, 18-year-olds should have the right to drink.

Inferential reasoning represents the primary thought processes humans use to reach conclusions about themselves and the world around them. This is also the form of thinking that you will use to make arguments and reach conclusions about ideas presented in your college courses.

Unfortunately, errors can be made in the inferential reasoning process; these errors are often referred to as logical fallacies. Some of the more common logical fallacies are summarized in the **Snapshot Summary 7.3**. As you read each of these reasoning errors, briefly note in the margin whether you've ever witnessed it or experienced it.

Snapshot Summary

Logical Fallacies: Inferential-Reasoning Errors

- **Dogmatism.** Stubbornly clinging to a personally held viewpoint that's unsupported by evidence and remaining closed minded (nonreceptive) to other viewpoints that are better supported by evidence (e.g., believing that America's version of capitalism is the only economic system that can work in a successful democracy and refusing to acknowledge that other successful countries do not have a capitalistic economy).

> *"Facts do not cease to exist because they are ignored."*
>
> –Aldous Huxley, English writer and author of *Brave New World*.

- **Selective Perception.** Seeing only examples and instances that support a position while overlooking or ignoring those that contradict it (e.g., believing in astrology and only noticing and pointing out people whose personalities happen to fit their astrological sign, not those who don't).

> *"A very bad (and all too common) way to misread a newspaper: To see whatever supports your point of view as fact, and anything that contradicts your point of view as bias."*
>
> –Daniel Okrent, first public editor of *The New York Times* and inventor of Rotisserie League Baseball, the best-known form of fantasy baseball

- **Double Standard.** Having two sets of standards for judgment: a higher standard for judging others and a lower standard for judging oneself. This is the classic "do as I say, not as I do" hypocrisy (e.g., critically evaluating and challenging the opinions of others but not your own).
- **Wishful Thinking.** Thinking that something is true not because of logic or evidence but because the person wants it to be true (e.g., a teenage girl not wanting to become pregnant and believing that she will not even though she and her boyfriend always have sex without using a contraceptive).

> *"Belief can be produced in practically unlimited quantity and intensity, without observation or reasoning, and even in defiance of both by the simple desire to believe."*
>
> –George Bernard Shaw, Irish playwright and Nobel Prize winner for literature

- **Hasty Generalization.** Reaching a limited number of instances or experiences (e.g., concluding that people belonging to a group are all or nearly all "that way" on the basis of personal experiences with only one or two individuals).
- **Jumping to a Conclusion.** Making a leap of logic to reach a conclusion that's based on only one reason or factor while ignoring other possible reasons or contributing factors (e.g., concluding, after being rejected for a date or a job, that "I must be a real loser").

- Glittering Generality. Making a positive general statement without supplying details or evidence to back it up (e.g., writing a letter of recommendation describing someone as a "wonderful human" with a "great personality" but not providing any reasons or evidence for these claims).
- Straw Man Argument. Distorting an opponent's argument position and then attacking it (e.g., attacking an opposing political candidate for supporting censorship and restricting civil liberties when the opponent supported only a ban on violent pornography).
- Ad Hominem Argument. Aiming an argument at the person rather than the person's argument (e.g., telling a younger person, "You're too young and inexperienced to know what you're talking about," or telling an older person, "You're too old-fashioned to understand this issue"). Literally translated, the term *ad hominem* means "to the man."
- Red Herring. Bringing up an irrelevant issue that disguises or distracts attention from the real issue being discussed or debated (e.g., responding to criticism of former President Richard Nixon's involvement in the Watergate scandal by arguing, "He was a good president who accomplished many good things while he was in office"). The term "red herring" derives from an old practice of dragging a herring—a strong-smelling fish—across a trail to distract the scent of pursuing dogs. (In the example, Nixon's effectiveness as a president is an irrelevant issue or a red herring; the real issue being discussed is Nixon's behavior in the Watergate scandal.)
- Smoke Screen. Intentionally disguising or covering up true reasons or motives with reasons that are designed to confuse or mislead others (e.g., opposing gun control legislation by arguing that it is a violation of the constitutional right to bear arms without revealing that the opponent of the legislation is receiving financial support from gun manufacturing companies).
- Slippery Slope. Using a fear tactic and arguing that not accepting a position will result in a domino effect—that is, it will result in something negative happening that will inevitably lead to another negative event, and so on, like a series of falling dominoes (e.g., saying, "If someone experiments with marijuana, it will automatically lead to harder drugs, loss of motivation, withdrawal from college, and a ruined life").
- Rhetorical Deception. Using deceptive language to conclude that something is true without providing reasons or evidence (e.g., confidently making such statements as "Clearly this is . . ." "It is obvious that . . ." or "Any reasonable person can see . . ." without explaining why it's so clear, obvious, or reasonable).
- Circular Reasoning (a.k.a. "Begging the Question"). Drawing a conclusion that is merely a rewording or restatement of a position on the issue without any supporting reasons or evidence, which leaves the original question unanswered and the issue still unsolved (e.g., concluding that "Stem cell research should remain illegal because it's research that shouldn't be done").
- Appealing to Authority or Prestige. Believing that if an authority figure or celebrity says it's true then it must be true or should be done (e.g., buying product X simply because a famous actor or athlete uses it or believing that if someone in authority, such as the U.S. president, says something should be done then it must be the right or best thing to do).
- Appealing to the Traditional or the Familiar. Concluding that if something has been thought true or done the same way for a long time then it must be a valid or the best method (e.g., stating that "This is the way it's always be done, so it's the way it should be done").
- Appealing to Popularity or the Majority (a.k.a. Jumping on the Bandwagon). That if a belief is popular or is held by the majority then it must be true (e.g., arguing "So many people believe in psychics, it has to be true; they can't all be wrong").
- Appealing to Emotion. Reaching a conclusion based on the intensity of feelings experienced or expressed, rather than the quality of reasoning used to reach the conclusion (e.g., believing that "If I feel strongly about something, it must be true"). The expressions, "always trust your feelings" and "just listen to your heart" may not always lead to the most accurate conclusions and the best decisions because they are based on emotion rather than reason.

Balanced Thinking

Balanced thinking involves seeking out and carefully considering evidence for and against a particular position. The process of supporting a position with evidence is technically referred to as adduction; when you adduce, you offer reasons *for* a position. The process of arguing against a position by presenting contradictory evidence or reasons is called refutation; when you refute, you provide a rebuttal by supplying evidence *against* a particular position.

Balanced thinking involves both adduction and refutation. The goal of a balanced thinker is not to stack up evidence for one position or the other but to be an impartial investigator who looks at supporting and opposing evidence for both sides of an issue and attempts to reach a conclusion that is neither biased nor one sided. The opposing positions' stronger arguments are acknowledged, and its weaker ones are refuted (Fairbairn & Winch, 1995). Thus, your first step in the process of seeking truth should not be to immediately jump in and take an either–or (for-or-against) stance on a debatable issue. Instead, your first step should be to look at arguments for and against each position, acknowledge the strengths and weaknesses of these arguments, and identify what additional information may still be needed to make a judgment or reach a conclusion.

Balanced thinking requires more than just adding up the number of arguments for and against a position; it also involves weighing the strength of those arguments. Arguments can vary in terms of their level or degree of support. When evaluating arguments, ask yourself, "How sure am I about the conclusion made by this argument?" Determine whether the evidence is:

1. **Definitive.** So strong or compelling that a definite conclusion can be reached;
2. **Suggestive.** Strong enough to suggest that a tentative conclusion may be reached; or
3. **Inconclusive.** Too weak to reach any conclusion.

> **! Remember**
>
> A characteristic of balanced thinking is being mindful of the weight (degree of importance) you assign to different arguments and articulating how their weight has been factored into your final conclusion (e.g., in a written report or class presentation).

In some cases, after reviewing both supporting and contradictory evidence for opposing positions, balanced thinking may lead you to suspend judgment and to withhold making a firm decision that favors one position over the other. A balanced thinker may occasionally reach the following conclusions: "Right now, I can't be sure; the evidence doesn't strongly favor one position over the other" or "More information is needed before I can make a final judgment or reach a firm conclusion." This isn't being wishy-washy; it's a legitimate conclusion to draw, as long as

Pause for Reflection

Glance back at the reasoning errors summarized in the Snapshot Summary 7.2. What are two errors that you've witnessed or experienced?

What was the situation in which you saw each of these errors?

Why was each a reasoning error?

"Too often we enjoy the comfort of opinion without the discomfort of thought."

–John F. Kennedy, 35th U.S. president

Pause for Reflection

Consider the following positions:

1. Course requirements should be eliminated; college students should be allowed to choose the classes they want to take for their degree.

2. Course grades should be eliminated; college students should take classes on a pass–fail basis.

Using balanced thinking, what is at least one argument for each of these positions?

What is at least one argument against these positions?

it is an informed conclusion that's supported with sound reasons and solid evidence. In fact, it's better to hold an undecided but informed viewpoint based on balanced thinking than to hold a definite opinion that's uninformed, biased, or based on emotion—such as the opinions offered loudly and obnoxiously by people on radio and TV talk shows.

Personal Story

For years I really didn't know what I believed. I always seemed to stand in the no man's land between opposing arguments, yearning to be won over by one side or the other but finding instead degrees of merit in both. But in time I came to accept, even embrace, what I called "my confusion" and to recognize it as a friend and ally, with no apologies needed. I preferred to listen rather than to speak; to inquire, not crusade.

"In Praise of the 'Wobblies'" by Ted Gup (2005), journalist who has written for Time, National Geographic, and The New York Times

---

Remember

When you combine balanced thinking with multidimensional thinking, you become a more complex and comprehensive thinker who is capable of viewing any issue from both sides and all angles.

Student Perspective

"Critical thinking is an evaluative thought process that requires deep thinking."

–First-year college student

Pause for Reflection

Flash back to the journal entry at the start of this chapter. How does your response to the incomplete sentence compare with the definition of critical thinking we just provided?

How are they similar?

How do they differ?

(If you wrote that critical thinking means "being critical" or negatively criticizing something or somebody, don't feel bad. Many students think that critical thinking has this negative meaning or connotation.)

Critical Thinking

Critical thinking is a form of higher-level thinking that involves evaluation or judgment. The evaluation can be either positive or negative; for example, a movie critic can give a good (thumbs up) or bad (thumbs down) review of a film. However, critical thinking involves much more than simply stating, "I liked it" or "I didn't like it." Specific reasons or evidence must be supplied to support the critique (critical evaluation). Failing to do so makes the criticism unfounded (i.e., it has no foundation to support it).

Critical thinking is used to evaluate many things besides films, art, or music; it's also used to judge the quality of ideas, beliefs, choices, and decisions—whether they be your own or those of others.

Since thinking skills are so highly valued by professors teaching students at all stages in the college experience and all subjects in the college curriculum, working on these skills now should significantly improve you academic performance throughout college.

You can develop critical thinking skills by always thinking about how you may evaluate ideas and arguments with respect to the following dimensions:

1. **Validity (Truthfulness).** Is it true or accurate?
2. **Morality (Ethics).** Is it fair or just?
3. **Beauty (Aesthetics).** Is it beautiful or artistic?
4. **Practicality (Usefulness).** Can it be put to use for practical purposes?
5. **Priority (Order of Importance or Effectiveness).** Is it the best option or alternative?

When I teach classes or give workshops, I often challenge students or participants to debate me on either politics or religion. I ask them to choose a political party affiliation, a religion or a branch of religion for their debate topic, and their stance on a social issue for which there are political or religious viewpoints. The ground rules are as follows: They choose the topic for debate; they can only use facts to pose their argument, rebuttal, or both; and they can only respond in a rational manner, without letting emotions drive their answers. This exercise usually reveals that the topics people feel strongly about are often topics that they have not critically evaluated. People often say they are Democrat, Republican, independent, and so on, and argue from this position. However, few of them have taken the time to critically examine whether their stated affiliation is actually consistent with their personal viewpoints. For example, they almost always answer "no" to the following questions: "Have you read the core document (e.g., party platform) that outlines the party stance?" and "Have you engaged in self-examination of your party affiliation through reasoned discussions with others who say they have the same or a different political affiliation?"

—Aaron Thompson

Creative Thinking

To think creatively is to generate something new or different, whether it is a product, an idea, or a strategy. Creative thinking leads you to ask the question, "Why not?" (e.g., "Why not try doing it a different way?"). It could be said that when you think critically you look "inside the box" and evaluate the quality of its content. When you think creatively, you look "outside the box" to imagine other packages containing different content.

Anytime you combine two old ideas to generate a different idea or a new product, you're engaging in creative thinking. Creative thinking can be viewed as an extension or higher form of synthesis, whereby parts of separate ideas are combined or integrated, resulting in a final product that turns out to be different (and better) than what previously existed (Anderson & Krathwohl, 2001). Even in the arts, what is created isn't totally original or unique. Instead, creativity typically involves a combination or rearrangement of previously existing elements to generate a new "whole"—a final product that is distinctive or noticeably different. For instance, hard rock was created by combining elements of blues and rock and roll, and folk rock took form when Bob Dylan combined musical elements of acoustic blues and amplified rock (Shelton, 2003).

Creative and critical thinking are two of the most important forms of higher-level thinking, and they work well together. You use creative thinking to ask new questions and generate new ideas, and you use critical thinking to evaluate or critique the ideas you create (Paul & Elder, 2004). A creative idea must not only be different or original; it must also be effective (Sternberg, 2001; Runco, 2004). If critical thinking reveals that the quality of what you've created is poor, you then shift back to creative thinking to generate something new and improved. Or, you may start by using critical thinking to evaluate an old idea or approach and come to the judgment that it's not very good. This unfavorable evaluation naturally leads to and turns on the creative thinking process, which tries to come up with a new idea or different approach that is better than the old one.

Brainstorming is a problem-solving process that effectively illustrates of how creative and critical thinking complement each other. The steps or stages involved in the process of brainstorming are summarized in **Box 7.1**.

As the brainstorming process suggests, creativity doesn't just happen suddenly or effortlessly, like the so-called stroke of genius; instead, it takes

"The principle mark of genius is not perfection but originality, the opening of new frontiers."

–Arthur Koestler, Hungarian novelist and philosopher

"The blues are the roots. Everything else are the fruits."

–Willie Dixon, blues songwriter; commenting on how all forms of contemporary American music contain elements of blues music, which originated among African American slaves

"Creativity is allowing oneself to make mistakes; art is knowing which ones to keep."

–Scott Adams, creator of the Dilbert comic strip and author of *The Dilbert Principle*

The Process of Brainstorming

1. List as many ideas as you can, generating them rapidly without stopping to evaluate their validity or practicality. Studies show that worrying about whether an idea is correct often blocks creativity (Basadur, Runco, & Vega, 2000). So, at this stage of the process, let your imagination run wild; don't worry about whether the idea you generate is impractical, unrealistic, or outrageous.
2. Use the ideas on your list as a springboard to trigger additional ideas, or combine them to create new ideas.
3. After you run out of ideas, review and evaluate the list of ideas you've generated and eliminate those that you think are least effective.
4. From the remaining list of ideas, choose the best idea or best combination of ideas.

7.1

Note: The first two steps in the brainstorming process involve creative thinking that goes off in different directions to generate multiple ideas. In contrast, the last two steps in the process involve critical thinking, which focuses on and narrows down the ideas, evaluating them to identify the one that's most effective.

I'm in the middle of an intense brainstorm; ideas are pouring out of my mind at lightning speed! Write 'em down fast!!

Personal Story

Several years ago, I was working with a friend to come up with ideas for a grant proposal. We started out by sitting at his kitchen table, sipping coffee; then we both got up and began to pace back and forth, walking all around the room while bouncing different ideas off each other. Whenever a new idea was thrown out, one of us would jot it down (whoever was pacing closer to the kitchen table at the moment).

After we ran out of ideas, we shifted gears, slowed down, and sat at the table to carefully review each of the ideas we just generated during our "binge-thinking" episode. After some debate, we finally settled on an idea that we judged to be the best one of all the ideas we produced, and we used this idea for the grant proposal.

Although I wasn't fully aware of it at the time, the stimulating thought process we were using was called brainstorming, which involved creative thinking (our fast-paced walking and idea-production stage) followed by critical thinking (our slower-paced sitting and idea-evaluation stage).

—Joe Cuseo

considerable mental effort (Paul & Elder, 2004; Torrance, 1963). Although creative thinking may include some sudden breakthroughs or intuitive leaps, it also involves carefully reflecting on those leaps and critically evaluating whether any of them landed you on a good idea.

Lastly, keep in mind that creative thinking is not restricted to the arts; it can occur in all subject areas, even in fields that seek precision and definite answers. For example, in math, creative thinking may involve using new approaches or strategies for arriving at a correct solution to a problem. In science, creative thinking takes place when a scientist uses imaginative thinking to create a hypothesis or logical hunch ("What might happen if . . . ?") and then conducts an experiment and collects evidence to test whether the hypothesis is true.

> "Imagination should give wings to our thoughts, but imagination must be checked and documented by the factual results of the experiment."
>
> –Louis Pasteur, French microbiologist, chemist, and founder of pasteurization (a method for preventing milk and wine from going sour)

◆ Strategies for Developing Higher-Level Thinking Skills and Applying Them to Improve Academic Performance

Thus far, this chapter has been devoted to helping you get a clear idea about what higher-level thinking is and what its major forms are. The remainder of this chapter focuses on helping you develop habits of higher-level thinking and apply these habits to improve your performance in the first year of college and beyond.

1. Cross-reference and connect any ideas you acquire in class with related ideas you acquire from your assigned reading.

When you discover information in your reading that relates to something you've learned about in class (or vice versa), make a note of it in the margin of your textbook or your class notebook. By integrating knowledge you've obtained from these two major sources, you're using synthesis—a higher-level thinking skill, which you can then demonstrate on your course exams and assignments to improve your academic performance.

2. When listening to lectures and completing reading assignments, pay attention not only to the content but also to the thinking process being used with respect to the content.

Periodically ask yourself what form of higher-level thinking your instructors are using during major segments of a class presentation and what your textbook authors are using in different sections of a chapter. The more conscious you are of the type of higher-level thinking you're being exposed to, the better you'll be able to apply it to the material you're learning and to demonstrate it on exams and assignments.

3. Periodically pause to reflect on your own thinking process.

Ask yourself what type of thinking you are doing (e.g., analysis, synthesis, or evaluation). When you think about your own thinking, you're engaging in a mental process known as metacognition—that is, you're aware of how you are thinking while you are thinking (Flavell, 1985). Metacognition is a mental habit that's been found to promote higher-level thinking and improve problem-solving (Halpern, 2003; Resnick, 1986).

Asking yourself higher-level thinking questions during lectures should prevent you from asking questions like this one.

4. Develop habits of higher-level thinking by asking yourself higher-level thinking questions.

One simple but powerful way to think about your thinking is through self-questioning. Since questions have the power to activate and elevate your thinking and thinking often involves talking silently to yourself, make an intentional

Asking yourself a good question can stimulate your higher-level thinking about almost any experience, whether it takes place inside or outside the classroom.

effort to ask yourself good questions that can train your mind to think at a higher level. Good questions serve as spark plugs for igniting mental action and launching thinking to higher levels in a quest to answer them. The higher the level of thinking called for by the questions you regularly ask yourself, the higher the level of thinking you will display in class discussions, on college exams, and in written assignments.

In **Box 7.2**, you'll find numerous questions that have been intentionally designed to promote higher-level thinking. The questions are constructed in a way that will allow you to easily fill in the blank and apply the type of thinking called for by the question to ideas or issues being discussed in any course you may take. Considerable research indicates that students can learn to use questions such as these to improve their higher-level thinking ability in various subject areas (King, 1990, 1995).

As you read each set of trigger questions, place a check-mark next to one question in the set that could be applied to a concept or issue being covered in a course you're taking this term.

Pause for Reflection

Look back at the forms of thinking described in Box 7.2. Identify one question listed under each set of trigger questions and fill in the blank with an idea or issue being covered in a course you're taking this term.

Take Action!

7.2

Self-Imposed Questions for Triggering Forms of Higher-Level Thinking

Application (Applied Thinking). Putting knowledge into practice to solve problems and resolve issues

Trigger Questions:
☑ How can this idea be used to ____?
☑ How could this concept be implemented to ____?
☑ How can this theory be put into practice to ____?

Analysis (Analytical Thinking). Breaking down information into its essential elements or parts

Trigger Questions:
☑ What are the main ideas contained in ____?
☑ What are the important aspects of ____?
☑ What are the issues raised by ____?
☑ What are the major purposes of ____?
☑ What assumptions or biases lie hidden within ____?
☑ What were the reasons behind ____?

Synthesis. Integrating separate pieces of information to form a more complete product or pattern

Trigger Questions:
☑ How can this idea be joined or connected with ____ to create a more complete or comprehensive understanding of ____?
☑ How could these different ____ be grouped together into a more general class or category?
☑ How could these separate ____ be reorganized or rearranged to produce a more comprehensive understanding of the big picture?

Multidimensional Thinking. Thinking that involves viewing yourself and the world around you from different angles or vantage points

Trigger Questions:
☑ How would ____ affect different dimensions of myself (emotional, physical, etc.)?
☑ What broader impact would ____ have on the social and physical world around me?
☑ How might people living in different times (e.g., past and future) view ____?

☑ How would people from different cultural backgrounds interpret or react to _____?

☑ Have I taken into consideration all the major factors that could influence _____ or be influenced by _____?

Inferential Reasoning. Making arguments or judgment by inferring (stepping to) a conclusion that is supported by empirical (observable) evidence or logical consistency

Trigger Questions Seeking Empirical Evidence:

☑ What examples support the argument that _____?

☑ What research evidence is there for _____?

☑ What statistical data document that this _____ is true?

Trigger Questions Seeking Logical Consistency:

☑ Since _____ is true, why shouldn't _____ also be true?

☑ If people believe in _____, shouldn't they practice _____?

☑ To make the statement that _____, wouldn't it have to be assumed that _____?

Balanced Thinking. Carefully considering reasons for and against a particular position or viewpoint

Trigger Questions:

☑ Have I considered both sides of _____?

☑ What are the strengths or advantages and weaknesses or disadvantages of _____?

☑ What evidence supports and contradicts _____?

☑ What are the arguments for and the counterarguments against _____?

Trigger Questions for Adduction (arguing for a particular idea or position by supplying supporting evidence):

☑ What proof is there for _____?

☑ What are logical arguments for _____?

☑ What research evidence supports _____?

Trigger Questions for Refutation (arguing against a particular idea or position by supplying contradictory evidence):

☑ What proof is there against _____?

☑ What logical arguments indicate that _____ is false?

☑ What research evidence contradicts _____?

☑ What counterarguments would provide an effective rebuttal to _____.

Critical Thinking. Making well-informed evaluations or judgments

Trigger Questions for Validity (truthfulness):

☑ Is _____ true or accurate?

☑ Is there sufficient evidence to support the conclusion that _____?

☑ Is the reasoning behind _____ strong or weak?

Trigger Questions for Morality (ethics):

☑ Is _____ fair?

☑ Is _____ just?

☑ Is this action consistent with the professed or stated values of _____?

Trigger Questions for Beauty (aesthetics):

☑ What is the artistic merit of _____?

☑ Does _____ have any aesthetic value?

☑ Does _____ contribute to the beauty of _____?

Trigger Questions for Practicality (usefulness):

☑ Will _____ work?

☑ How can _____ be put to good use?

☑ What practical benefit would result from _____?

Trigger Questions for Priority (order of importance or effectiveness):

☑ Which one of these _____ is the most important?

☑ Is this _____ the best option or choice available?

☑ How should these _____ be ranked from first to last (best to worst) in terms of their effectiveness?

Creative Thinking. Generating ideas that are unique, original, or distinctively different.

Trigger Questions:

☑ What could be invented to _____?

☑ Imagine what would happen if _____?

☑ What might be a different way to _____?

☑ How would this change if _____?

☑ What would be an ingenious way to _____.

Note: Save these higher-level thinking questions so that you can use them while completing different academic tasks required by your courses (e.g., preparing for exams, writing papers or reports, and participating in class discussions or study-group sessions).

5. To stimulate creative thinking, use the following strategies.

- **Be flexible.** Think about ideas and objects in unusual or unconventional ways. The power of flexible and unconventional thinking is well illustrated in the movie *Apollo 13*, which is based on the real story of an astronaut saving his life by creatively using duct tape as an air filter. Johannes Gutenberg made his discovery of the printing press while watching a machine being used to crush grapes at a wine harvest. He thought that the same type of machine could be used to press letters onto paper (Dorfman, Shames, & Kihlstrom, 1996).

- **Be experimental.** Play with ideas, trying them out to see whether they'll work and work better than the status quo. Studies show that creative people tend to be mental risk-takers who experiment with ideas and techniques (Sternberg, 2001). Consciously resist the temptation to settle for the security of familiarity. Doing things the way they've always been done doesn't mean you're doing them the best way possible. It may mean that it's just the most habitual (and mindless) way to do them. When people cling rigidly or stubbornly to what is conventional or traditional, they may be clinging to the comfort or security of what's most familiar and predictable, which blocks originality, ingenuity, and openness to change.

- **Get mobile.** Get up and move around. By just standing up, studies show that the brain gets approximately 10 percent more oxygen than it does when a person is sitting down (Sousa, 1998). Since oxygen provides fuel for the brain, your ability to think creatively is likely to be enhanced when you think on your feet and move around rather than when you think while sitting down for extended periods.

- **Get it down.** Carry a pen and a small notepad or packet of sticky notes with you at all times because creative ideas often come to mind at the most unexpected moments. The process of creative ideas suddenly popping into your mind is sometimes referred to as incubation—like an egg, an idea can suddenly hatch and emerge from your subconscious after you've sat on it for a while. Unfortunately, however, as suddenly as ideas pop into your mind, they can just as suddenly slip out of your mind when you start thinking about something else. You can prevent this from happening by having the right equipment on hand to record your creative ideas as soon as you have them. That equipment could be pen and paper, or it could be your cell phone. You can go to Jott.com and provide your cell number and e-mail address. Whenever you get a creative idea you want to jot down, speed-dial 866-JOTT123 and you get a voice message that asks you who you want to "jott." After saying "myself," you can state your idea; within 5 minutes, it's transcribed into a typed message that appears in your e-mail inbox.

- **Get diverse.** Seek ideas from diverse sources and subjects of study. Bouncing your ideas off of different people and getting their ideas about your idea is a good way to generate energy, synergy, and serendipity (accidental discoveries). Studies show that creative people have a range of knowledge and interests, and they capitalize on their breadth to create new ideas by combining knowledge from different sources (Riquelme, 2002). They go well beyond the boundaries of their particular area of training or specialization (Baer, 1993; Kaufman & Baer, 2002). Be on the lookout to combine the knowledge and skills you acquire from different subject areas and different people to create bridges to new ideas.

> ❝
>
> *"I make progress by having people around who are smarter than I am—and listening to them. And I assume that everyone is smarter about something than I am."*
>
> —Henry Kaiser, successful industrialist, known as the father of American shipbuilding

- **Take a break.** When working on a problem that you can't seem to solve, stop working on it for a while and come back to it later. Creative solutions often come to mind after you stop thinking about the problem. When you're trying so hard and working so intensely on a problem or challenging task, your attention may become mentally set or rigidly fixed on one aspect of it (Maier, 1970). Taking your mind off of it and returning to it at a later point allows the problem to incubate in your mind at a lower level of consciousness and stress. This can sometimes give birth to a sudden solution. Furthermore, when you come back to the task later, your focus of attention is likely to shift to a different feature or aspect of the problem. This new focus may enable you to view the problem from a different angle or vantage point, which can lead to a breakthrough idea that was blocked by your previous perspective (Anderson, 2000).
- **Reorganize the problem.** When you're stuck on a problem, try rearranging its parts or pieces. Rearrangement can transform the problem into a different pattern that provides you with a new perspective. The new perspective may position you to suddenly see a solution that was previously overlooked, much like changing the order of letters in a word jumble suddenly enables you to see the hidden, scrambled word. By changing the wording of any problem you're working on, or by recording ideas on index cards (or sticky notes) and laying them out in different orders and arrangements, you may suddenly see a solution.
- If you're having trouble solving problems that involve a sequence of steps (e.g., math problems), try reversing the sequence and start by working from the end or middle. The new sequence changes your approach to the problem by forcing you to come at it from a different direction, which may provide you with an alternative path to its solution.
- **Be persistent.** Studies show that creativity takes time, dedication, and hard work (Ericsson & Charness, 1994). Creative thoughts often do not emerge in one sudden stroke of genius but evolve gradually after repeated reflection and persistent effort.

Pause for Reflection

The popularity of sticky notes is no doubt due to their versatility—you can post them on almost anything, remove them from where they were stuck (without a mess), and restick them somewhere else.

Think creatively for a minute. In what ways could college students use sticky notes to help complete the academic tasks they face in college? Think of as many ways as possible.

◆ Summary and Conclusion

Since higher-level thinking is the number one educational goal of college professors, developing this skill is crucial for achieving academic excellence. In addition improving academic performance in college, however, developing higher-level thinking skills have three other critical benefits.

1. Higher-level thinking is essential in today's "information age" in which new information is being generated at faster rates than at any other time in human history.

The majority of new workers in the information age will no longer work with their hands but will instead work with their heads (Miller, 2003), and employers will value college graduates who have inquiring minds and possess higher-level thinking skills (Harvey, Moon, Geall, & Bower, 1997).

2. Higher-level thinking skills are vital for citizens in a democracy.

Authoritarian political systems, such as dictatorships and fascist regimes, suppress critical thought and demand submissive obedience to authority. In contrast, citizens living in a democracy are expected to control their political destiny by choosing (electing) their political leaders; thus, judging and choosing wisely are crucial civic responsibilities in a democratic nation. Citizens living and voting in a democracy must use higher-level reasoning skills, such as balanced and critical thinking, to make wise political choices.

3. Higher-level thinking is an important safeguard against prejudice, discrimination, and hostility.

Racial, ethnic, and national prejudices often stem from narrow, self-centered, or group-centered thinking (Paul & Elder, 2002). Prejudice often results from oversimplified, dualistic thinking that can lead individuals to categorize other people into either "in" groups (us) or "out" groups (them). This type of dualistic thinking can lead, in turn, to ethnocentrism—the tendency to view one's own racial or ethnic group as the superior "in" group and see other groups as inferior "out" groups. Development of higher-level thinking skills, such as taking multiple perspectives and using balanced thinking, counteracts the type of dualistic, ethnocentric thinking that can lead to prejudice, discrimination, and hatred.

Learning More Through the World Wide Web

Internet-Based Resources for Further Information on Higher-Level Thinking

For additional information related to the ideas discussed in this chapter, we recommend the following Web sites:

Critical Thinking: **www.criticalthinking.org**

Creative Thinking: **www.amcreativityassoc.org**

Higher-Level Thinking Skills:
www.wcu.edu/ceap/houghton/Learner/think/thinkhigherorder.html

7.1 Self-Assessment of Higher-Level Thinking Characteristics

Listed here are four general characteristics of higher-level thinkers accompanied by a set of traits related to each characteristic. When you read the traits listed beneath each of the general characteristics, place a checkmark next to any trait that you think is true of you.

Characteristics of a Higher-Level Thinker

1. **Tolerant and Accepting**
   - ☑ Keep emotions under control when someone criticizes your viewpoint
   - ☑ Do not tune out ideas that conflict with your own
   - ☑ Feel comfortable with disagreement
   - ☑ Are receptive to hearing different points of view

2. **Inquisitive and Open Minded**
   - ☑ Are eager to continue learning new things from different people and different experiences
   - ☑ Have an inquiring mind that's genuinely curious, inquisitive, and ready to explore new ideas
   - ☑ Find differences of opinion and opposing viewpoints interesting and stimulating
   - ☑ Attempt to understand why people hold different viewpoints and try to find common ground between them

3. **Reflective and Tentative**
   - ☑ Suspend judgment until all the evidence is in, rather than making snap judgments before knowing the whole story
   - ☑ Acknowledge the complexity, ambiguity, or uncertainty of some issues, perhaps saying things like, "I need to give this more thought" or "I need more evidence before I can draw a conclusion"
   - ☑ Take time to think things through before drawing conclusions, making choices, and reaching decisions
   - ☑ Periodically reexamine personal viewpoints to see whether they should be maintained or changed as a result of new experiences and evidence

4. **Honest and Courageous**
   - ☑ Give fair consideration to ideas that other people may instantly disapprove of or find distasteful
   - ☑ Are willing to express personal viewpoints that may not conform to those of the majority
   - ☑ Are willing to change old opinions or beliefs when they are contradicted by new evidence
   - ☑ Are willing to acknowledge the limitations or weaknesses of your attitudes and beliefs

Look back at the list and count the number of checkmarks you placed in each of the four general areas:

1. Tolerant and Accepting = _____

2. Inquisitive and Open Minded = _____

3. Reflective and Tentative = _____

4. Honest and Courageous = _____

1. Under which characteristic did you have the most checkmarks?

2. Under which did you have the fewest checkmarks?

3. How would you interpret the meaning of this difference?

4. Why do you think this difference occurred?

7.2 Planning to Demonstrate Higher-Level Thinking in Your Current Courses

Look at the syllabus for three courses you're enrolled in this term and find an assignment or exam that carries the greatest weight (counts the most) toward your final course grade. (If you're taking fewer than three courses, you can choose more than one assignment or exam from the same course).

	Course	Major Assignment or Test
1.		
2.		
3.		

Using the grid that follows, place a checkmark in each box that represents the form of higher-level thinking you think will be required on each of these major assignments or tests.

	Major Assignment or Test		
	Course 1	**Course 2**	**Course 3**

Applied Thinking

Analysis

Synthesis

Multidimensional Thinking

Inferential Reasoning

Balanced Thinking

Critical Thinking

Creative Thinking

Choose one box you checked for each course, and describe how you would demonstrate that particular form of higher-level thinking on that particular assignment or test. For instance, if you checked a box indicating that you will use multidimensional thinking, describe what perspectives or factors you will take into consideration.

Course 1 exam or assignment: _____

Form of higher-level thinking required:

How I plan to demonstrate this form of thinking:

Course 2 exam or assignment: _____

Form of higher-level thinking required:

How I plan to demonstrate this form of thinking:

Course 3 exam or assignment: _____

Form of higher-level thinking required:

How I plan to demonstrate this form of thinking:

Trick or Treat: Confusing or Challenging Test?

Students in Professor Plato's philosophy course just got their first exam back and they're going over the test together in class. Some students are angry because they feel that Professor Plato deliberately made up trick questions to confuse them. Professor Plato states that his test questions were designed not to trick the class but to "challenge them to think."

Reflection and Discussion Questions

1. Why do you think that some of students thought that Professor Plato was trying to trick or confuse them on the exam?

2. What do you think the professor meant when he told his students that his test questions were designed to "challenge them to think"?

3. On future tests, what might the students do to reduce the likelihood that they will feel tricked again?

4. On future tests, what might the Professor Plato do to reduce the likelihood that students will complain about being asked trick questions?

Your First Year Resources

The first year of college is an exciting and challenging time. We want you to have the best experience possible, so we've designed a website just for you. It's full of tips, tricks, and links to help you make the most of Your First Year! If you have questions or need help finding your way at UNCG, you can always email us at yfy@uncg.edu. Visit yourfirstyear.uncg.edu and the websites below for helpful resources and services about critical and creative thinking.

Academic Advising Centers

Refer to Chapter 12 for comprehensive list

Students First Office
http://studentsfirst.uncg.edu/

336-334-5730

Student Success Center
http://success.uncg.edu/

336-334-3878

YOUR FIRST YEAR

The University of North Carolina at Greensboro

UNCG YOUR FIRST YEAR   UNCGYOURFIRSTYEAR   @UNCGYFY   1-336-541-6939

Dear First-Year Student

Learning should be a challenge you're willing to throw yourself at. It's an uphill climb toward probably another upward climb. Learning should be fun, it should be challenging, and most of all, it should be rewarding. However, just because learning should be challenging doesn't mean it should be overwhelming—it's a delicate balance between the two.

That's where this chapter (and my office) comes into the picture. How do you learn, and learn well, and how do you use your limited time efficiently to produce the best results? Your success in college really depends on a few factors; can you:

Courtesy of UNCG Relations Office

- Read deeply into complex materials,
- Take good notes in lectures,
- Prepare for and take tests well,
- Seek resources when necessary, and
- Advocate for yourself

If you're not sure of how or what to study, let me put your mind at ease—a lot of students aren't sure why they study the way they do, or don't know how to decide what to write down when taking notes. The difference between the successful student and the unsuccessful one usually boils down to strategic learning and adaptability.

After you finish this chapter, try adding some of these learning, studying, and test taking strategies to your repertoire. And, if you want more advice about how to improve your learning or studying, don't hesitate to contact the Tutoring and Academic Skills Programs (TASP) for more guidance (our website is http://success.uncg.edu). As the Assistant Director for Academic Skills at TASP, my job is to help students learn how to make studying more efficient—all you need to do is ask and we will be happy to assist or get you connected to the appropriate resources.

We hope you will take advantage of the services available at TASP and UNCG.

Sincerely,

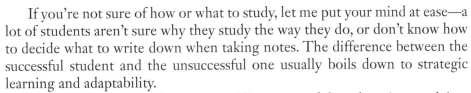

Shawn O'Neil
Assistant Director for Academic Skills
Student Success Center

Strategic Learning, Studying and Test Taking

Deep-Learning Strategies

ACTIVATE YOUR THINKING | **Journal Entry** | **8.1**

What do you think is the key difference between learning and memorizing?

_____

_____

_____

LEARNING GOAL

To develop a set of effective strategies that will enable you to learn deeply and remember longer.

◆ Stages in the Learning and Memory Process

Learning deeply, and remembering what you've learned, is a process that involves three stages:

1. **Sensory input (perception).** Taking information into the brain;
2. **Memory formation (storage).** Saving that information in the brain;
3. **Memory recall (retrieval).** Bringing information back to mind when you need it.

You can consider these stages of the learning and memory process to be similar to the way information is processed by a computer: (a) information is typed onto the screen (perceptual input), (b) the information is saved in a file (memory storage), and (c) the saved information is recalled and used when it's needed (memory retrieval).

These three stages in the learning–memory process are summarized visually in **Figure 8.1**.

This three-stage process can be used to create a systematic set of strategies for effectively using the two major routes through which you acquire information and knowledge in college:

- Taking notes as you listen to lectures, and
- Reading textbooks.

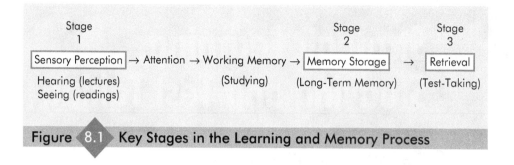

Stage 1			Stage 2	Stage 3
Sensory Perception → Attention → Working Memory →			Memory Storage →	Retrieval
Hearing (lectures) Seeing (readings)		(Studying)	(Long-Term Memory)	(Test-Taking)

Figure 8.1　**Key Stages in the Learning and Memory Process**

◆ Effective Lecture-Listening and Note-Taking Strategies

The importance of effective listening skills in the college classroom is highlighted by a study of more than 400 first-year students who were given a listening test at the start of their first term in college. At the end of their first year, 49 percent of those students who scored low on the listening test were on academic probation, compared to only 4.4 percent of students who scored high on the listening test. On the other hand, 68.5 percent of students who scored high on the listening test were eligible for the honors program at the end of their first year, compared to only 4.17 percent of those students who had low listening test scores (Conaway, 1982).

Studies show that information delivered during lectures is the number one source of test questions (and answers) on college exams (Brown, 1988; Kuhn, 1988). When lecture information appears on a test and hasn't been recorded in students' notes, it has only a 5 percent chance of being recalled (Kiewra, Hart, Scoular, Stephen, Sterup, & Tyler, 2000). When you write down information presented in lectures, rather than just listen to it, you're more likely to remember that information. For example, students who write notes during lectures achieve higher course grades than students who just listen to lectures (Kiewra, 1985), and students with a more complete set of notes are more likely to demonstrate higher levels of overall academic achievement (Johnstone, & Su, 1994; Kiewra & Fletcher, 1984).

Contrary to popular belief that writing while listening interferes with the ability to listen, students report that taking notes actually increases their attention and concentration in class (Hartley, 1998; Hartley & Marshall, 1974). Studies also show that when students write down information that's presented to them, rather than just listening to it, they're more likely to remember the most important aspects of that information when tested later (Bligh, 2000; Kiewra et al., 1991). For instance, one study discovered that successful students with grade point averages (GPAs) of 2.53 or higher record more information in their notes and retain a larger percentage of the most important information than do students with GPAs of less than 2.53 (Einstein, Morris, & Smith, 1985). These findings are not surprising when you consider that *hearing* lecture information, *writing* it, and *seeing* it while you write it lay down three different memory traces or tracks in the brain that combine to improve memory for that information.

Pause for Reflection

Do you think writing notes in class helps or hinders your ability to pay attention and learn from your instructors' lectures?

Why?

Furthermore, students with a good set of notes have a written record of that information, which can be reread and studied later.

This research suggests that you should view each lecture as if it were a test-review session during which your instructor is giving out test answers and you're given the opportunity to write all those answers in your notes. Come to class with the attitude that your instructors are dispensing answers to test questions as they speak; your purpose for being there is to pick out and pick up these answers.

> **Remember**
>
> If important points your professors make in class make it into your notes, they can become points learned, and these learned points will turn into earned points on your exams (and higher grades in your courses).

The next sections give strategies for getting the most out of lectures at three stages in the learning process: before lectures, during lectures, and after lectures.

Prelecture Strategies: What You Can Do Before Hearing Lectures

1. Check your syllabus to see where you are in the course and determine how the upcoming class fits into the total course picture.

By checking your syllabus before individual class sessions, you will strengthen your learning because you will see how each part (individual class session) relates to the whole (the entire course). This also capitalizes on the human brain's natural tendency to seek larger patterns and the "big picture." Rather than seeing things in separate parts, the brain is naturally inclined to perceive parts as interconnected and forming a meaningful whole (Caine & Caine, 1991). It looks for meaningful patterns and connections rather than isolated bits and pieces of information (Nummela & Rosengren, 1986). In **Figure 8.2**, notice how your brain naturally ties together and fills in the missing information to perceive a meaningful whole pattern.

You perceive a white triangle in the middle of this figure. However, if you use three fingers to cover up the three corners of the white triangle that fall outside the other (background) triangle, the white triangle suddenly disappears. What your brain does is take these corners as starting points and fills in the rest of the information on its own to create a complete or whole pattern that has meaning to you. (Notice also how you perceive the background triangle as a complete triangle, even though parts of its left and right sides are missing.)

Figure 8.2   Triangle Illusion

2. Get to class early so that you can look over your notes from the previous class session and from any reading assignment that relates to the day's lecture topic.

Research indicates that when students preview information related to an upcoming lecture topic it improves their ability to take more accurate and complete lecture notes (Ladas, 1980). Thus, a good strategy to help you learn from lectures is to review your notes from the previous class session and read textbook information related to an upcoming lecture topic—before hearing the lecture. This strategy will help you better understand and take more detailed notes on the lecture. Reviewing previously learned information activates your previous knowledge, enabling you to build a mental bridge from one class session to the next and connect new information to what you already know, which is the key to deep learning (Piaget, 1978; Vygotsky, 1978). Acquiring knowledge isn't a matter of simply pouring information into the brain as if it were an empty jar. It's a matter of attaching or connecting new ideas to ideas that are already stored in the brain. When you learn deeply, you make a biological connection between nerve cells in the brain (Alkon, 1992), as illustrated in **Figure 8.3.**

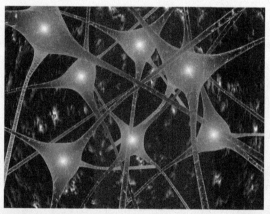

© Jurgen Ziewe, 2010. Under license from Shutterstock, Inc.

When something is learned, it's stored in the brain as a link in an interconnected network of brain cells. Thus, deep learning involves making connections between what you're trying to learn and what you already know.

Figure 8.3 Network of Brain Cells

3. Adopt a seating location that maximizes your focus of attention and minimizes sources of distraction.

Student Perspective

"I tend to sit at the very front of my classrooms. It helps me focus and take notes better. It also eliminates distractions."

–First-year college student

Studies show that students who sit in the front and center of class tend to earn higher exam scores (Rennels & Chaudhair, 1988). These results are found even when students are assigned seats by their instructor, so it's not just a matter of more motivated and studious students tending to sit in the front of the classroom; instead, the academic performance of students sitting front and center is likely higher because a learning advantage is provided by this seating location. Front-and-center seating probably aids academic performance by improving vision of the board and hearing of the instructor's words—as well as allowing better eye contact with the instructor, which increases students' attention and heightens their sense of personal responsibility in the classroom. There's another advantage to sitting up front: It increases your comfort level about speaking in class because if you ask a question or contribute a comment you will not have numerous classmates sitting in front of you who turn around to look at you when you speak.

When you enter the classroom, get in the habit of heading for a seat in the front and center of class. In large classes, it is particularly important that you get "up close and personal" with your instructors. This not only will improve your attention, note taking, and participation in class but also should improve your instructors' ability to remember who you are and how well you performed in class, which will work to your advantage when you ask for letters of recommendation.

4. Be aware of the people who sit near you.

Intentionally sit near classmates who will not distract you or interfere with the quality of your note taking. Attention comes in degrees or amounts; you can give all of it or part of it to whatever task you're performing. Trying to grasp complex information in class is a task that demands your undivided attention.

> **Student Perspective**
>
> *"[In high school] the teacher knows your name. But in college they don't know your name; they might see your face, but it means nothing to them unless you make yourself known."*
>
> —First-year college student

> **Student Perspective**
>
> *"I like to sit up front so I am not distracted by others and I don't have to look around people's heads to see the chalkboard."*
>
> —First-year college student

> **! Remember**
>
> When you enter a class, you have a choice about where you're going to sit. Choose wisely by selecting a location that will maximize your attentiveness to the instructor and the aggressiveness of your note taking.

The evolution of student attention from the back to the front of class.

5. Adopt a seating posture that screams attention.

Sitting upright and leaning forward are more likely to increase your attention because these signals of bodily alertness will reach your brain and increase mental alertness. If your body is in an alert and ready position, your mind tends to pick up these bodily cues and follow your body's lead by also becoming alert and ready (to learn). Just as baseball players assume a ready position in the field before a pitch is delivered to put their body in position to catch batted balls, learners who assume a ready position in the classroom put themselves in a better position to catch ideas batted around in the classroom. Studies show that when humans are ready and expecting to capture an idea greater amounts of the brain chemical C-kinase are released at the connection points between brain cells, which increases the likelihood that a learning connection is formed between them (Howard, 2000).

There's another advantage to being attentive in class: You send a clear message to your instructor that you're a conscientious and courteous student. This can influence your instructor's perception and evaluation of your academic performance, which can earn you the benefit of the doubt at the end of the term if you're on the border between a higher and a lower course grade.

Listening and Note-Taking Strategies: What You Can Do During Lectures

1. Take your own notes in class.

Don't rely on someone else to take notes for you. Taking your own notes in your own words ensures they make sense and have personal meaning to you. You can collaborate with classmates to compare one another's notes for completeness and accuracy or to get notes if you happen to miss class. However, do not routinely rely on others to take notes for you. Studies show that students who record and review their own notes earn higher scores on memory tests for that information than do students who review the notes of others (Fisher, Harris, & Harris, 1973). These findings point to the importance of taking and studying your own notes because they will be most meaningful to you.

Students who take notes during lectures have been found to achieve higher class grades than those who just listen.

© JupiterImages Corporation.

2. Focus your attention on important information.

Attention is the critical first step to successful learning and memory. Since the human attention span is limited, it's impossible to attend to and make note of every piece of given information. Thus, you need to use your attention *selectively* to focus on and choose the most important information. Here are some strategies for attending to and recording the most important information delivered by professors in the college classroom:

- Pay attention to information your instructors put in writing—on the board, on a slide, or in a handout. If your instructor takes the time and energy to write it out, that's usually a good clue the information is important and you're likely to see it again—on an exam.
- Pay attention to information presented during the first and last few minutes of class. Instructors are more likely to provide valuable reminders, reviews, and previews at the start and end of class.

- Use your instructor's verbal and nonverbal cues to detect important information. Don't just to tune in when the instructor is writing something down and tune out at other times. It's been found that students record almost 90 percent of information that is written on the board (Locke, 1977) but less than 50 percent of important ideas that professors state but don't write on the board (Johnstone & Su, 1994). Don't fall into the reflex-like routine of just writing something in your notes when you see your instructor writing on the board. You also have to listen actively to record important ideas in your notes that you hear your instructor saying. In **Box 8.1**, you'll find strategies for detecting important information that professors deliver orally during lectures.

3. Take organized notes.

Keep taking notes in the same paragraph if the instructor is continuing on the same point or idea. When the instructor shifts to a new idea, skip a few lines and shift to a new paragraph. Be alert to phrases that your instructor may use to signal a shift to a new or different idea (e.g., "Let's turn to . . ." or "In addition to . . ."). Use these phrases as cues for taking notes in paragraph form. By using

Take Action!

8.1

Detecting When Instructors Are Delivering Important Information During Class Lectures

1. Verbal cues
   - Phrases signal important information (e.g., "The point here is . . ." or "What's most significant about this is . . .").
   - Information is repeated or rephrased in a different way (e.g., "In other words, . . .").
   - Stated information is followed with a question to check understanding (e.g., "Is that clear?" "Do you follow that?" "Does that make sense?" or "Are you with me?").
2. Vocal (tone of voice) cues
   - Information is delivered in a louder tone or at a higher pitch than usual, which may indicate excitement or emphasis.
   - Information is delivered at a slower rate or with more pauses than usual, which may

be your instructor's way of giving you more time to write down these important ideas.

3. Nonverbal cues
   - Information is delivered by the instructor with more than the usual
     a. facial expressiveness (e.g., raised or furrowed eyebrows);
     b. body movement (e.g., more gesturing and animation); or
     c. eye contact (e.g., looking more directly and intently at the faces of students to see whether they are following or understanding what's being said).
   - The instructor moves closer to the students (e.g., moving away from the podium or blackboard).
   - The instructor's body is oriented directly toward the class (i.e., both shoulders directly or squarely face the class).

paragraphs, you improve the organizational quality of your notes, which will improve your comprehension and retention of them. Leave an extra space between successive paragraphs (ideas) to give yourself room to add information that you may have missed or to translate the professor's words into your own words, making them more meaningful to you.

Another strategy for taking organized notes, the called the Cornell Note-Taking System, is summarized in **Box 8.2.**

4. If you don't immediately understand what your instructor is saying, don't stop taking notes.

Keep taking notes, even if you are temporarily confused, because this will at least leave you with a record of the information that you can review later—when you have more time to think about it and grasp it. If you still don't understand it after taking time to review it, check it out in your textbook, with your instructor, or with a classmate.

> **Remember**
>
> Your primary goal during lectures is to get important information into your brain long enough to note it mentally and then physically by recording it in your notes. Making sense of that information often has to come later, when you have time to reflect on the notes you took in class.

Postlecture Strategies: What You Can Do After Lectures

Pause for Reflection

What do you tend to do immediately after a class session ends?

Why?

1. As soon as class ends, quickly check your notes for missing information or incomplete thoughts.

Since the information is likely to be fresh in your mind immediately after class, a quick check of your notes at this time will allow you take advantage of your short-term memory. By reviewing and reflecting on it, you can help move the information into long-term memory before forgetting takes place. This quick review can be done alone or, better yet, with a motivated classmate. If you both have gaps in your notes, check them out with your instructor before he or she leaves the classroom. Even though it may be weeks before you will be tested on the material, the quicker you address missed points and clear up sources of confusion, the better, because you'll be able to use your knowledge to help you understand and learn upcoming material. Catching confusion early in the game also enables you to avoid the last-minute, mad rush of students seeking help from the instructor just before test time. You want to reserve the critical time just before exams for studying a set of notes that you know are complete and accurate, rather than rushing around and trying to find missing information and getting fast-food help on concepts that were presented weeks ago.

2. Before the next class session meets, reflect on and review your notes to make sense of them.

Your professors will often lecture on information that you may have little prior knowledge about, so it is unrealistic to expect that you will understand

Take Action!

The Cornell Note-Taking System

1. On the page on which you're taking notes, draw a horizontal line about 2 inches from the bottom edge of the paper.
2. If there's no vertical line on the left side of the page, draw one line about 2½ inches from the left edge of the paper (as shown in the scaled-down illustration here).

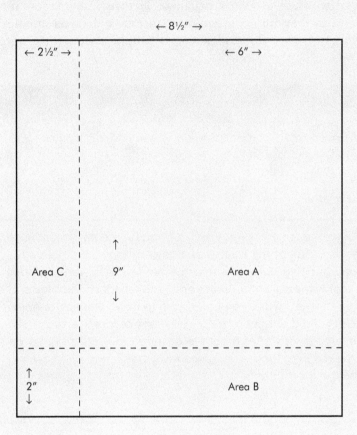

3. When your instructor is lecturing, use the large space to right of the vertical line (area A) to record your notes.
4. After a lecture, use the space at the bottom of the page (area B) to summarize the main points you recorded on that page.
5. Use the column of space on the left side of the page (area C) to write questions that are answered in the notes on the right.
6. Quiz yourself by looking at the questions listed in the left margin while covering the answers to them found in the class notes on the right.

Note: You can use this note-taking and note-review method on your own, or you could team up with two or more students and do it collaboratively.

everything that's being said the first time you hear it. Instead, you'll need to set aside time for making notes or taking notes on your own notes (i.e., rewriting them in your own words so that they make sense to you).

During this reflect-and-rewrite process, we recommend that you take notes on your notes by:

- Translating technical information into your own words to make it more meaningful to you; and
- Reorganizing your notes to get ideas related to the same point in the same place.

Studies show that when students organize lecture information into meaningful categories they show greater recall on a delayed memory test for that information than do students who simply review their notes (Howe, 1970).

> **!**
>
> ### Remember
>
> Look at note taking as a two-stage process: Stage 1 is aggressively taking notes in class (active involvement), and stage 2 occurs later—when you think about those notes more deeply (personal reflection).

Personal Story

My first year in college was mainly spent trying to manipulate my schedule to find some free time. I took all of my classes in a row without a break to save some time at the end of the day for relaxation and hanging out with friends before I went to work. Seldom did I look over my notes and read the material that I was assigned on the day I took the lecture notes and received the assignment. Thus, on the day before the test I was in a panic trying to cram the lecture notes into my head for the upcoming test. Needless to say, I did not perform well on many of these tests. Finally, I had a professor who told me that if I spent time each day after a couple of my classes catching up on reading and rewriting my notes I would retain the material longer, increase my grades, and decrease my stress at test time. I employed this system, and it worked wonderfully.

—Aaron Thompson

◆ Reading Strategically to Comprehend and Retain Textbook Information

Second only to lecture notes is information from reading assignments as a source of test questions on college exams (Brown, 1988). You're likely to find exam questions that your professors haven't talked about directly, or even mentioned, in class but that were drawn from your assigned reading. College professors often expect you to relate or connect what they are lecturing about in class with material that you've been assigned to read. Furthermore, they often deliver class lectures with the assumption that you have done the assigned reading, so if you haven't done it, you're likely to have more difficulty following what your instructor is talking about in class.

> **! Remember**
>
> Do the assigned reading and do it according to the schedule your instructor has established. It will help you better understand class lectures, improve the quality of your participation in class, and raise your overall grade in the course.

What follows is a series of strategies for effective reading at three stages in the learning process: before reading, while reading, and after reading. When completing your reading assignments, use effective reading strategies that are based on sound principles of human learning and memory, such as those listed here.

Prereading Strategies: What You Can Do Before Reading

1. Before jumping into your assigned reading, look at how it fits into the overall organizational structure of the book and course.

You can do this efficiently by taking a quick look at the book's table of contents to see where the chapter you're about to read is placed in the overall sequence of chapters, particularly in relation to chapters that immediately precede and follow the assigned chapter. This will give you a sense of how the particular part you're focusing on connects with the bigger picture. Research shows that if learners have advance knowledge of how the information they're about to learn is organized—if they see how the parts relate to the whole *before* they attempt to start learning the specifics—they're better able to comprehend and retain the material (Ausubel, 1978; Kintsch, 1994). Thus, the first step toward improving reading comprehension and retention of a textbook chapter is to see how its parts relate to the whole—before you begin to examine the chapter part by part.

Pause for Reflection

Rate yourself in terms of how frequently you use these note-taking strategies according to the following scale:

4 = always, 3 = sometimes, 2 = rarely, 1 = never

1. I take notes aggressively in class.   4 3 2 1

2. I sit near the front of the room during class.   4 3 2 1

3. I sit upright and lean forward while in class.   4 3 2 1

4. I take notes on what my instructors say, not just what they write on the board.   4 3 2 1

5. I pay special attention to information presented at the start and end of class.   4 3 2 1

6. I take notes in paragraph form.   4 3 2 1

7. I review my notes immediately after class to check that they are complete and accurate.   4 3 2 1

Pause for Reflection

When you open a textbook to read a chapter, how do you start the reading process? That is, what's the first thing you do?

2. Preview a chapter by reading its boldface headings and any chapter outline, objectives, summary, or end-of-chapter questions.

Get in the habit of previewing what's in a chapter to gain an overall sense of its organization before jumping right into the content. If you dive into details too quickly, you lose sight of how the smaller details relate to the larger picture. The brain's natural tendency is to perceive and comprehend whole patterns rather than isolated bits of information. Start by seeing how the parts of the chapter are integrated into the whole. This will enable you to better connect the separate pieces of information you encounter while you read, much like seeing the whole picture of a completed jigsaw puzzle helps you connect its separate pieces while assembling the puzzle.

3. Take a moment to think about what you already know that relates to the material in the chapter.

By thinking about knowledge you possess about the topic you're about to read, you activate the areas of your brain where that knowledge is stored, thereby preparing it to make meaningful connections with the material you're about to read.

Strategies to Use While Reading

Read Selectively to Find Important Information

Rather than jumping into reading and randomly highlighting, effective reading begins with a plan or goal for identifying what should be noted and remembered. Here are three strategies to use while reading to help you determine what information should be noted and retained.

1. **Use boldface or dark-print headings and subheadings as cues for identifying important information.** These headings organize the chapter's major points; thus, you can use them as "traffic" signs that direct you to the most important information in the chapter. Better yet, turn the headings into questions and then read to find answers to these questions. This question-and-answer strategy will ensure that you read actively and with a purpose. (You can do this when you preview the chapter by placing a question mark after each heading contained in the chapter.) Creating and answering questions while you read also keeps you motivated; the questions help stimulate your curiosity, and finding answers as you read rewards you for reading (Walter, Knudsbig, & Smith, 2003). Lastly, this strategy is an effective way to prepare for tests because you are practicing exactly what you'll be expected to do on exams—answer questions. You can quickly write the heading questions on separate index cards and use them as flash cards to review for exams. Use the question on the flash card to flashback and attempt to recall the information from the text that answers the question.

2. **Pay special attention to words that are *italicized*, underlined, or appear in boldface print.** These usually represent building-block terms whose meanings must be understood before you can grasp the meanings of higher-level ideas and more general concepts covered in the reading. Don't simply highlight these words because their special appearance suggests they are important. Read these terms carefully and be sure you understand their meaning before you continue reading.

3. **Pay special attention to the first and last sentences in each paragraph.** These sentences contain an important introduction and conclusion to the ideas covered in that passage. When reading sequential or cumulative material that requires comprehension of what was previously covered to understand what will be covered next, it's a good idea to reread the first and last sentences of each paragraph before you move on to the next paragraph.

4. **Reread the chapter after you've heard your instructor lecture on the material contained in the chapter.** You can use your lecture notes as a guide to help you focus on what information in the chapter your instructor feels is most important. If you adopt this strategy, your reading before lectures will help you understand the lecture and take better class notes, and your reading after lectures will help you locate and learn the most important information contained in your textbook.

> ### ! Remember
>
> Your goal when reading is not merely to cover the assigned pages but to uncover the most important information and ideas contained in those pages.

Take Written Notes on What You're Reading

Just as you write notes in response to your instructor's lectures in class, take notes in response to the author's words in the text. For example, write short answers to the boldface heading questions in the text itself by using its side, top, and bottom margins or in a reading journal organized by chapters or units. Writing requires more active thinking than highlighting because you're creating your own words rather than passively highlighting words written by someone else. Don't get into the habit of using your textbook as a coloring book in which the artistic process of highlighting what you're reading with spectacular kaleidoscopic colors distracts you from the more important process of learning actively and thinking deeply.

> "I would advise you to read with a pen in your hand, and enter in a little book of short hints of what you find that is curious, or that might be useful; for this will be the best method of imprinting such particulars in your memory, where they will be ready."
>
> –Benjamin Franklin, eighteenth-century inventor, newspaper writer, and cosigner of the Declaration of Independence

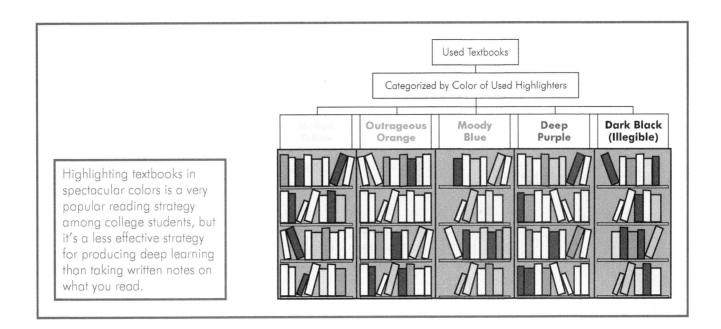

Highlighting textbooks in spectacular colors is a very popular reading strategy among college students, but it's a less effective strategy for producing deep learning than taking written notes on what you read.

Pause Periodically to Summarize and Paraphrase What You're Reading in Your Own Words

If you can express what someone else has written in words that make sense to you, this means that you understand what you're reading and can relate it to what you already know—which is a telltale sign of deep learning (Demmert & Towner, 2003). A good time to pause and paraphrase is when you encounter a boldface heading that indicates you're about to be introduced to a new concept. This may be the ideal place to stop and summarize what you read in the section you just completed.

> **Remember**
>
> Effective reading isn't a passive or mechanical process in which you just follow printed words on a page. Instead, it's a reflective process in which you actively search for and find meaning in the words you read.

Pause for Reflection

When reading a textbook, do you usually have the following tools on hand?

Highlighter:	yes	no
Pen or pencil:	yes	no
Notebook:	yes	no
Class notes:	yes	no
Dictionary:	yes	no
Glossary:	yes	no

Use the Visual Aids Included in Your Textbook

Don't fall into the trap of thinking that visual aids can or should be skipped because they're merely add-ons that are secondary to the written words of the text. Visual aids, such as charts, graphs, diagrams, and concept maps, are powerful learning and memory tools for a couple of reasons:

1. They enable you to "see" the information in addition to reading (hearing) it.
2. They organize separate pieces of information into an integrated picture.

Furthermore, visual aids allow you to periodically experience a mode of information input other than repeatedly reading words. This occasional change of pace brings variety to the reading process, which can recharge your attention and motivation to read.

Postreading Strategies: What Should Be Done After Reading

End a Reading Session With a Short Review of the Information You've Noted or Highlighted

Most forgetting that takes place after you receive and process information occurs immediately after you stop focusing on the information and turn your attention to another task (Underwood, 1983). (See **Figure 8.4**.) Taking a few minutes at the end of your reading time to review the most important information locks that information into your memory before you turn your attention to something else and forget it.

The graph in Figure 8.4 represents recall of information at different intervals after it was originally learned. As you can see, most forgetting of information occurs right after learning (e.g., after 20 minutes, the participants in the study forgot more than 60 percent of it). This suggests that reviewing information from reading or a lecture immediately after it's been acquired is an effective strategy for intercepting the forgetting curve and improving memory.

Seek Outside Help From Informed Sources

If you find you can't understand a concept explained in your text, even after rereading and repeatedly reflecting on it, try the following strategies:

1. **Look at how another textbook explains it.** Not all textbooks are created equally; some do a better job of explaining certain concepts than others. Check to see whether your library has other texts in the same subject as your course, or check your campus bookstore for textbooks in the same subject area as the course you're taking. A different text may be able to

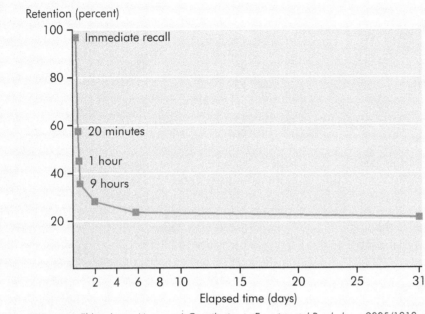

Source: Hermann Ebbinghaus, *Memory: A Contribution to Experimental Psychology*, 2885/1913

Figure 8.4   The Forgetting Curve

explain a hard-to-understand concept much better than the textbook you purchased for the course.

2. **Seek help from your instructor.** If you read carefully and made every effort to understand a particular concept but still can't grasp it, your instructor should be willing to assist you. If your instructor is unavailable or unwilling to assist you, seek help from the professionals and peer tutors in the Learning Center or Academic Support Center on campus.

Another technique for organizing and remembering strategies for improving reading comprehension and retention is the SQ3R method. See **Box 8.3** for a summary of steps involved in this reading method.

Take Action!

The SQ3R Method

SQ3R is an acronym of the five steps you can take to increase textbook-reading comprehension and retention, particularly when reading highly technical or complex material. The sequence in this method is as follows:

1. Survey
2. Question
3. Read
4. Recite
5. Review

S = *Survey: Get a preview and overview of what you're about to read.*

8.3

1. Read the title to activate your thoughts about the subject and prepare your mind to receive information related to it.
2. Read the introduction, chapter objectives, and chapter summary to become familiar with the author's purpose, goals, and most important points.
3. Note the boldface headings and subheadings to get a sense of the chapter's organization before you begin to read. It will help you understand or create a mental structure for the information to come.
4. Notice any graphics, such as charts, maps, and diagrams. They provide valuable visual support and reinforcement for the material you're reading, so don't ignore them.
5. Pay special attention to reading aids (e.g., italics and boldface font) that you can use to identify, understand, and remember key concepts.

Q = **Q**uestion: *Stay active and curious.*

As you read, use the boldface headings to formulate questions you think will be answered in that particular section. When your mind is actively searching for answers to questions, it becomes more engaged in the learning process.

As you continue to read, add any questions that you have about the reading.

R = **R**ead: *Find the answer to the question or questions.*

Read one section at a time, with your questions in mind, and search for answers to these questions. Also, keep an eye out for new questions that need to be asked.

R = **R**ecite: *Rehearse your answers.*

After you read each section, recall the questions you asked and see whether you can answer them from memory. If not, look at the questions again and practice your answers to them until you can recall them without looking. Don't move onto the next section until you're able to answer all questions in the section you've just completed.

R = **R**eview: *Look back and get a second view of the whole picture.*

Once you've finished the chapter, review all the questions you've created for different parts or sections. See whether you can still answer them all without looking. If not, go back and refresh your memory.

◆ Study Strategies for Learning Deeply and Remembering Longer

Learning gets information into your brain; the next step is to save that information in your brain (memory storage) and bring it back to mind at test time (memory retrieval). Described here is a series of effective study strategies for acquiring knowledge (learning) and keeping that knowledge in your brain (memory).

The Importance of Undivided Attention

Attention comes in a fixed amount. You only have so much of it available to you at any point in time, and you can give all or part of it to whatever task you're working on. If study time is spent on multiple tasks that provide sources of external stimulation (e.g., listening to music, watching TV, or text-messaging friends), the total attention time available for studying is subtracted and divided among the other tasks. In other words, studying doesn't receive your undivided attention.

Studies show that when people multitask they don't pay equal attention to all tasks at the same time. Instead, they divide their attention by shifting it back and forth between tasks (Howard, 2000), and their performance on the task that demands the most concentration or deepest thinking is the one that suffers the most (Crawford & Strapp, 1994). Furthermore, research shows that multitasking can increase boredom with tasks that involve concentration. One study found that with even a low level of distraction, such as a TV turned on a low volume in the next room, students were more likely to describe the mental task they were concentrating on as "boring" (Damrad-Frye & Laird, 1989).

When performing tasks that cannot be done automatically (mindlessly), including complex mental tasks, other tasks and sources of external stimulation interfere with the quiet, internal reflection needed for permanent connections to form between brain cells (Jensen, 1998)—which is what has to happen biologically for deep, long-lasting learning to take place.

Remember

Without attention first, there can be no retention later.

Meaningful Association

Relating what you're trying to learn to something you already know is a powerful learning strategy because learning is all about making connections in the brain. People tend to perceive meaningful patterns in information because knowledge is stored in the form of a connected network of brain cells (Coward, 1990).

The brain's natural tendency to seek meaningful, whole patterns applies to words, as well as images. The following passage once appeared (anonymously) on the Internet. See whether you can read it and grasp its meaning.

Pause for Reflection

Rate yourself in terms of how frequently you use these reading strategies according to the following scale:

4 = always, 3 = sometimes, 2 = rarely, 1 = never

1. I read the chapter outlines and summaries before I start reading the chapter content.   4 3 2 1

2. I preview a chapter's boldface headings and subheadings before I begin to read the chapter.   4 3 2 1

3. I adjust my reading speed to the type of subject I am reading.   4 3 2 1

4. I look up the meaning of unfamiliar words and unknown terms that I come across before I continue reading.   4 3 2 1

5. I take written notes on information I read.   4 3 2 1

6. I use the visual aids included in my textbooks.   4 3 2 1

7. I finish my reading sessions with a review of important information that I noted or highlighted.   4 3 2 1

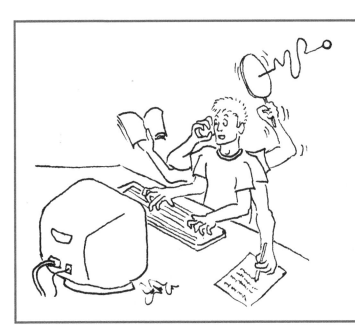

Studies show that doing challenging academic work while multi-tasking divides up attention and drives down comprehension and retention.

Aoccdrnig to rscheearch at Cmabridge Uinverstisy, it deos't mattaer in what order the ltteers in a word are, the only iprmoetnt thing is that the frist and lsat ltteer be at the rghit pclae. The rset can be a total mses and you can still raed it wouthit a porbelm. This is bcusae the human mind deos not raed ervey lteter by istlef, but the word as a wlohe. Amzanig huh?

Notice how easily you found the meaning of the misspelled words by naturally transforming them into correctly spelled words—which you knew because they were stored in your brain. Thus, whenever you learn something, you do so by connecting what you're trying to understand to what you already know.

Learning by making meaningful connections is referred to as deep learning (Entwistle & Ramsden, 1983). It involves moving beyond shallow memorization to deeper levels of understanding. This is a major a shift from the old view that learning occurs by passively absorbing information like a sponge, for example, by receiving it from the teacher or text and studying it in the same, prepackaged form as you received it. Instead, you want to adopt an approach to learning that involves actively transforming the information you receive into a form that's meaningful to you (Entwistle & Marton, 1984; Feldman & Paulsen, 1994). This enables you to move beyond surface-level memorization of information to deeper learning and acquisition of knowledge.

Before you start to repeatedly pound what you're learning into your head like a hammer hitting a nail, first look for a hook to hang it on by relating it to something you already know that's stored in your brain. It may take a little while to discover the right hook, but once you've found it, the information will store in your brain quickly and remain there a long time. For example, consider a meaningful way to learn and remember how to correctly spell one of the most frequently misspelled words in the English language: "separate" (not "seperate"). By remembering that "to par" means to divide, as in the words *par*ts or *par*tition, it makes sense that the word "separate" should be spelled se*par*ate because its meaning is "to divide into parts."

> "
>
> "The extent to which we remember a new experience has more to do with how it relates to existing memories than with how many times or how recently we have experienced it."
>
> –Morton Hunt, *The Universe Within: A New Science Explores the Human Mind*

Remember

The more meaningful you make what you're learning, the deeper you learn it and the longer you remember it.

Personal Story   Some time ago, I had to give up running because of damage to my right hip, so I decided to start riding a stationary bike instead. My wife found an inexpensive, used stationary bike at a garage sale. It was an old and somewhat rusty bike that made a repeated noise that sounded like "ee-zoh" as the wheel spun. One evening I was riding it and, after about 10 minutes, I noticed that I was hearing the words "zero," "rosy," and "Rio" off and on in my head. My brain was taking a meaningless sound ("ee-zoh"), which it apparently grew bored of hearing as the wheels spun, and transforming that sound into words that provided it with variety and meaning. Perhaps this was a classic case of how the human brain naturally prefers to seek meaning rather than mindless repetition.

—Joe Cuseo

Meaning in Academic Terms

Each academic field has specialized vocabulary that can sound like a foreign language to someone who has no experience with the subject area. Before you start to brutally beat these terms into your brain through sheer repetition, try to find some meaning in them. You can make a term more meaningful to you by looking up its word root in the dictionary or by identifying its prefix or suffix, which may give away the term's meaning. For instance, suppose you were studying the autonomic nervous system in biology, which is the part of the nervous system that operates without your conscious awareness or voluntary control (e.g., your heart beating and lungs breathing). The meaning of the phrase is given away by the prefix "auto," which means self-controlling—as in the word "automatic" (e.g., automatic transmission).

Pause for Reflection

Can you think of information you're learning in a course this term that you could form a meaningful association to remember?

What is the information you're attempting to learn?

What is the meaningful association you could use to help you remember it?

If the term's root, prefix, or suffix doesn't give away its meaning, then see whether you can make it more meaningful to you in some other way. For instance, suppose you looked up the root of the term "artery" and nothing about the origins of this term suggested its meaning or purpose. You could then create your own meaning for this term by taking its first letter (a), and have it stand for "*a*way"—to help you remember that arteries carry blood away from the heart. Thus, you've taken a biological term and made it personally meaningful (and memorable).

Compare and Contrast

When you're studying something new, get in the habit of asking yourself the following questions:

1. Is this idea similar or comparable to something that I've already learned? (Compare)
2. How does this idea differ from what I already know? (Contrast)

Research indicates that this simple strategy is one of the most powerful ways to promote learning of academic information (Marzano, Pickering, & Pollock, 2001). The power of the compare-and-contrast strategy probably stems from asking the question, "How is this similar to and different from concepts that I already know?" By working to answer this question, you make learning more personally meaningful because you are relating what you're trying to learn to what you already know.

Integration and Organization

Pull together or integrate information from your class notes and assigned reading related to the same major concept or category. For example, get this information in the same place by recording it on the same index card under the same category heading. Index cards are a good tool for such purposes; you can use each card as a miniature file cabinet for a separate category of information. The category heading on each card functions like the hub of a wheel, around which individual pieces of related information are attached like spokes. Integrating information related to the same topic in the same place and studying it at the same time

Pause for Reflection

Are you more likely to study in advance of exams or cram just before exams?

Why?

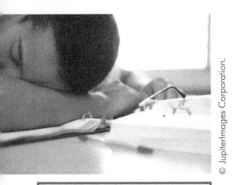

© JupiterImages Corporation.

Spreading out your studying into shorter sessions improves your memory by reducing loss of attention due to fatigue.

helps divide the total material you need to learn into more identifiable and manageable parts. In contrast, when ideas pertaining to the same point or concept are spread all over the place, they're more likely to take that form in your mind—leaving them mentally disconnected and leaving you confused (as well as feeling stressed and overwhelmed).

Divide and Conquer

Effective learning depends not only on *how* you learn (your study method); it also depends on *when* you learn (your study timing). Although cramming just before exams is better than not studying, it is far less effective than studying that's spread out across time. Rather than cramming all your studying into one long session, use the distributed practice method, which spreads study time over several shorter sessions. Research consistently shows that short, periodic practice sessions are more effective than a single marathon session.

Distributing your study time over several shorter sessions improves your learning and memory by:

- Reducing loss of attention due to fatigue or boredom; and
- Reducing mental interference by giving the brain some downtime to cool down and lock in information that it's received without being interrupted by the need to deal with additional information (Murname & Shiffrin, 1991).

If the brain's downtime is interfered with by the arrival of additional information, it gets overloaded and its capacity for handling information becomes impaired. This is what cramming does—it overloads the brain with lots of information in a limited period. In contrast, distributed study does just the opposite—it uses shorter sessions with downtime between sessions, thereby giving the brain the time and opportunity to save (retain) the information that it's processing (studying).

Another major advantage of distributed study is that it's less stressful and more motivating than cramming. Shorter sessions can be an incentive to study because you know that you're not going to be doing it for a long stretch of time or lose any sleep over it. It's easier to maintain your interest and motivation for any task that's done for a shorter rather than a longer period. Furthermore, you should feel more relaxed because if you run into difficulty understanding anything you know there's still time to get help with it before you're tested and graded on it.

The Part-to-Whole Study Method

The part-to-whole method of studying is a natural extension of the distributed practice just discussed. With the part-to-whole method, you break the material you need to study into separate parts and study those parts in separate sessions in advance of the exam. You then use your last study session just before the exam to review (restudy) all the parts that you previously studied in separate sessions. Thus, your last study session is a review session, rather than a study session, because you're not trying to learn information for the first time.

Student Perspective

"When I have to retain knowledge, I do not procrastinate; I can usually slowly remember everything. The knowledge is in [my] long-term memory, so I usually have no problems retaining it."

–First-year college student

Student Perspective

"Do not cram. If you start to prepare for a test about 3–5 days before, then you will only need to do a quick review the night before."

–Advice to new college students from an experienced student (Walsh, 2005)

Consuming large doses of caffeine or other stimulants to stay awake for all-night cram sessions is likely to maximize anxiety and minimize memory.

Don't buy into the myth that studying in advance is a waste of time because you'll forget it all by test time. This is the myth that procrastinators use to put off studying until the last moment, when they cram for their exams. Do not underestimate the power of breaking material to be learned into smaller parts and studying those parts some time before a major exam. Even if you cannot recall what you previously studied, when you start reviewing it you'll find that you will relearn it much faster than when you studied it the first time. This proves that studying in advance is not pointless, because it takes less time to relearn the material. The memory of it remains in your brain from the time you studied it earlier (Kintsch, 1994).

Reviewing

For sequential or cumulative subjects that build on understanding of previously covered material to learn new concepts (e.g., math), it's especially important to begin each study session with a quick review of what you learned in your previous study session.

Research shows that students of all ability levels learn material in college courses more effectively when it's studied in small units and when progression to the next unit takes place only after the previous unit has been mastered or understood (Pascarella & Terenzini, 1991, 2005). This strategy has two advantages: (a) it reinforces your memory for what you previously learned and (b) it builds on what you already know to help you learn new material. This is particularly important in cumulative subjects that require memory for problem-solving procedures or steps, such as math and science. By repeatedly practicing these procedures, they become more automatic and you're able to retrieve them quicker (e.g., on a timed test) and use them efficiently without having to expend a lot of mental effort and energy (Newell & Rosenbloom, 1981). This frees your working memory for more important tasks, such as critical thinking and creative problem solving (Schneider & Chein, 2003).

Variety in the Study Process

The following strategies can be used to infuse variety and a change of pace into your study routine, which can increase your concentration and motivation.

1. Periodically vary the type of academic work you do while studying.

Changing the nature of your work activities or the type of mental tasks you're performing while studying increases your level of alertness and concentration by reducing habituation—a psychological term referring to the attention loss that occurs after repeated engagement in the same type of mental task (McGuiness & Pribram, 1980). To combat attention loss due to habituation, occasionally vary the type of study task you're performing. For instance, shift periodically among tasks that involve reading, writing, studying (e.g., rehearsing or reciting), and practicing skills (e.g., solving problems).

2. Study different subjects in different places.

Studying in different locations provides different environmental contexts for learning, which reduces the amount of interference that normally builds up when all information is studied in the same place (Anderson & Bower, 1974). Thus, in addition to spreading out your studying at different times, it's a good idea to spread it out in different places. The great public speakers in ancient Greek and Rome used this method of changing places to remember long speeches by walking through different rooms while rehearsing their speech, learning each major part of their speech in a different room (Higbee, 1998).

Changing the nature of the learning task and the learning environment provides changes of pace that infuse variety into the learning process, which improves attention and concentration. Although it's useful to have a set time and place to study for getting you into a regular work routine, this doesn't mean that learning occurs best by habitually performing all types of academic tasks in the same place. Instead, research suggests that you should periodically change the learning tasks you perform and the environment in which you perform them to maximize attention and minimize interference (Druckman & Bjork, 1991).

> **!**
>
> ### Remember
>
> Change of pace and place while studying can stimulate your attention to, and your interest in, what you're studying.

3. Mix long study sessions with short study breaks that involve physical activity (e.g., a short jog or brisk walk).

Study breaks that include physical activity not only refresh the mind by giving it a rest from studying but also stimulate the mind by increasing blood flow to your brain, which will help you retain what you've already studied and regain concentration for what you'll study next.

Pause for Reflection

Would you say that you're more of a visual learner or verbal learner?

How do you think most people would answer this question?

4. Use all of your senses.

When studying, try to use as many sensory channels as possible. Research shows that information perceived through multiple sensory modalities or channels is remembered better (Bjork, 1994; Schacter, 1992) because it forms more interconnections in long-term memory areas of the brain (Zull, 2002). When a memory is formed in the brain, different sensory aspects of it are stored in different areas. For example, when your brain receives visual, auditory (hearing), and motor (movement) stimulation that accompany with what you're learning, each of these associations is stored in a different part of the brain. See **Figure 8.5** for a map of the surface of the human brain; you can see how different parts of the brain are specialized to receive input from different sensory modalities. When you use all of these sensory modalities while learning, multiple memory traces of what you're studying are recorded in different parts of your brain, which leads to deeper learning and stronger memory (Education Commission of the States, 1996).

5. Learn visually.

The human brain consists of two hemispheres (half rounds): the left and the right hemispheres (see **Figure 8.6**).

Each hemisphere of the brain specializes in a different type of learning. In most people, the left hemisphere specializes in verbal learning, dealing primarily with words. In contrast, the right hemisphere specializes in visual–spatial learning, dealing primarily with images and objects that occupy physical space. If you use both hemispheres while studying, you lay down two different memory traces in your brain: one in left hemisphere, where words are stored, and one in the right hemisphere, where images are stored. This process of laying down a double memory trace (verbal and visual) is referred to as dual

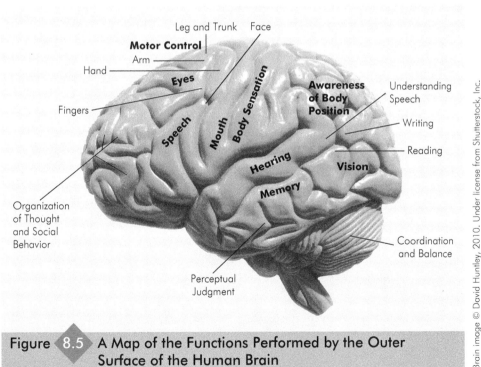

Brain image © David Huntley, 2010. Under license from Shutterstock, Inc.

Figure 8.5 **A Map of the Functions Performed by the Outer Surface of the Human Brain**

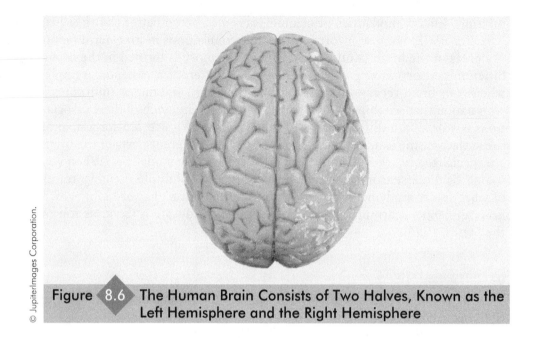

Figure 8.6 **The Human Brain Consists of Two Halves, Known as the Left Hemisphere and the Right Hemisphere**

coding (Paivio, 1990). When this happens, memory for what you're learning is substantially strengthened, primarily because two memory traces are better than one.

To capitalize on the advantage of dual coding, use any visual aids that are available to you. Use the visual aids provided in your textbook and by your instructor, or create your own by drawing pictures, symbols, and concept maps, such as flowcharts or branching tree diagrams. See **Figure 8.7** for a concept map that could be used to help you remember the parts and functions of the human nervous system.

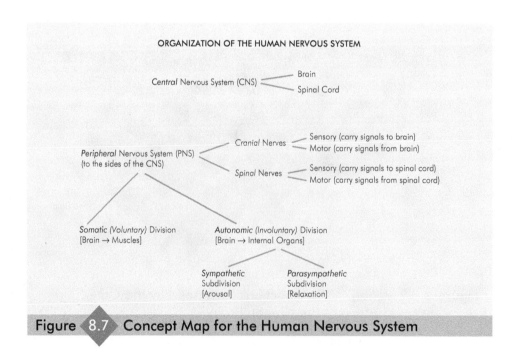

Figure 8.7 **Concept Map for the Human Nervous System**

Drawing and other forms of visual illustration are not just artistic exercises; they also can be powerful learning tools (i.e., you can draw to learn). Drawing keeps you actively involved with the material you're trying to learn. By representing the material in visual form, you're able to dual-code the information you're studying, thus doubling its number of memory traces in your brain. As the old saying goes, "A picture is worth a thousand words."

Pause for Reflection

Think of a course you're taking this term in which you're learning related pieces of information that could be joined together to form a concept map. In the space that follows, make a rough sketch of this map that includes the information you need to remember.

6. Learn by moving or using motor learning (a.k.a. muscle memory).

In addition to hearing and seeing, movement is a sensory channel. When you move, your brain receives kinesthetic stimulation—the sensations generated by your muscles when your body moves. Research shows that memory traces for movement are commonly stored in an area of your brain that plays a major role for all types of learning (Middleton & Strick, 1994). Thus, associating movement with what you're learning can improve your ability to retain it because you record an additional muscle memory trace of it to another area of your brain.

Personal Story

I was talking about memory in class one day and mentioned that when I temporarily forget how to spell a word its correct spelling comes back to me once I start to write it. One of my students raised her hand and said the same thing happens to her when she forgets a phone number—it comes back to her when she starts dialing it. In both of these cases, motor memory brings information back to mind that was temporarily forgotten, which points to the power of movement for promoting learning and memory.

—Joe Cuseo

You can use movement to help you learn and retain academic information by using your body to act out what you're studying or to symbolize it with your hands (Kagan & Kagan, 1998). For example, if you're trying to remember five points about something (e.g., five consequences of the Civil War), when you're studying these points, count them on your fingers as you try to recall each of them. Also, remember that talking involves muscle movement of your lips and tongue. Thus, by speaking aloud when you're studying, either to a friend or to yourself, your memory of what you're studying may be improved by adding kinesthetic stimulation to your brain (in addition to the auditory or sound stimulation your brain receives from hearing what you're saying).

Student Perspective

"When I have to remember something, it is better for me to do something with my hands so I could physically see it happening."

–First-year college student

7. Learn with emotion.

Information reaches the brain through your senses and can be stored in the brain as a memory trace. The same is true of emotions. Numerous connections occur between brain cells in the emotional and memory centers (Zull, 1998). For instance, when you're experiencing emotional excitement about what you are learning, adrenaline is released and is carried through the bloodstream to your brain. Once adrenaline reaches the brain, it increases blood flow and glucose production, which can stimulate learning and strengthen memory (LeDoux, 1998; Rosenfield, 1988). If you have an emotionally intense experience, such a substantial amount of adrenaline is released in your body that it can lead to immediate, long-term storage of that memory; you'll remember the experience for the rest of your life. For instance, most people remember exactly what they were doing at the time they experienced such emotionally intense events as the September 11 terrorist attack on the United States, their first kiss, or their favorite team winning a world championship.

What does this emotion–memory link have to do with helping you remember academic information that you're studying? Research indicates that emotional intensity, excitement, and enthusiasm affect memory of academic information just as they affect memory for life events and personal experiences. If you get psyched up about what you're learning, you have a much better chance of learning and remembering it. Even telling yourself that it's important to remember what you're learning can increase your memory of it (Howard, 2000; Minninger, 1984).

> ### Remember
>
> You will learn most effectively when you actively involve all your senses (including bodily movement) and when you learn with passion and enthusiasm. In other words, learning grows deeper and lasts longer when you put your whole self into it—your heart, your mind, and your body.

8. Learn with others.

> "We are born for cooperation, as are the feet, the hands, the eyelids, and the upper and lower jaws."
>
> —Marcus Aurelius, Roman emperor

One way to put the power of group learning into practice is by forming study groups. Research indicates that college students who work regularly in small groups of four to six become more actively involved in the learning process and learn more (Light, 2001).

To maximize the power of study groups, each member should study individually *before* studying in a group and should come prepared with specific information or answers to share with teammates, as well as questions or points of confusion that the team can attempt to help answer or clarify.

Personal Story

When I was in my senior year of college, I had to take a theory course by independent study because the course would not be offered again until after I planned to graduate. Another senior found himself in the same situation. The instructor allowed both of us to take this course together and agreed to meet with us every 2 weeks. My fellow classmate and I studied independently for the first 2 weeks. I prepared for the biweekly meetings by reading thoroughly, yet I had little understanding of what I had read. After our first meeting, I left with a strong desire to drop the course but decided to stick with it. Over the next 2 weeks, I spent many sleepless nights trying to prepare for our next meeting and was feeling pretty low about not being the brightest student in my class of two. During the next meeting with the instructor, I found out that the other student was also having difficulty. Not only did I notice, so did the instructor. After that meeting, the instructor gave us study questions and asked us to read separately and then get together to discuss the questions. During the next 2 weeks, my classmate and I met several times to discuss what we were learning (or attempting to learn). By being able to communicate with each other about the issues we were studying, we both ended up gaining greater understanding. Our instructor was delighted to see that he was able to suggest a learning strategy that worked for both of us.

—Aaron Thompson

Self-Monitoring Learning

Successful learners reflect and check on themselves to see whether they really understand what they're attempting to learn. They monitor their comprehension as they go along by asking themselves questions such as "Am I following this?" "Do I really understand it?" and "Do I know it for sure?"

How do you know if you really know it? Probably the best answer to this question is "I find *meaning* in it—that is, I can relate to it personally or put it in terms that make sense to me" (Ramsden, 2003). When you really understand a concept, you learn it at a deeper level than by merely memorizing it. You're also more likely to remember that concept because the deeper its roots, the more durable its memory trace that enables you to retain it long term (Kintsch, 1970).

Discussed here are some strategies for checking whether you truly understand what you're trying to learn. They help you answer the question, "How do I know if I really know it?" These strategies can be used as indicators or checkpoints for determining whether you're just memorizing information or you're learning deeply and acquiring knowledge.

- **Can you restate or translate what you're learning into your own words?** When you can paraphrase what you're learning, you're able to complete the following sentence: "In other words, . . ." If you can complete that sentence in your own words, this is a good indication that you've moved beyond memorization to comprehension because you've transformed what you're learning into words that are meaningful to you. Thus, you learn deeply not by simply stating what your instructor or textbook states but by restating the information in words that are your own.

- **Can you explain what you're learning to someone who is unfamiliar with it?** If you can explain to a friend what you've learned, this is a good sign that you've moved beyond memorization to comprehension because you are able to translate it into less technical language that someone hearing it for the first time can understand. Often, you won't realize how well you know or don't know something until you have to explain it to someone who's never heard it before (just ask any teacher). Simply put, if you can't explain it to someone else, you don't really understand it yourself. Studies show that students gain deeper levels of understanding for what they're learning when they're asked to explain it to someone else (Chi, de Leeuw, Chiu, & LaVancher, 1994). If you cannot find someone else to explain it to, then explain it aloud as if you were talking to an imaginary friend.

- **Can you think of an example of what you've learned?** If you can come up with an instance of what you're learning that is your own example—not one given by your instructor or textbook—this is a good sign that you truly comprehend it. It shows you're able to take a general, abstract concept and apply it to a specific, real-life experience (Bligh, 2000). Furthermore, a personal example is a powerful memory tool. Studies show that when people retrieve a concept from memory they first

Student Perspective

"I learn best through teaching. When I learn something and teach it to someone else, I find that it really sticks with me a lot better."

–College sophomore

Pause for Reflection

Rate yourself in terms of how frequently you use these study strategies according to the following scale:

4 = always, 3 = sometimes, 2 = rarely, 1 = never

1. I block out all distracting sources of outside stimulation when I study.   4 3 2 1

2. I try to find meaning in technical terms by looking at their prefix or suffix or by looking up their word root in the dictionary.   4 3 2 1

3. I compare and contrast what I'm currently studying with what I've already learned.   4 3 2 1

4. I organize the information I'm studying into categories or classes.   4 3 2 1

5. I integrate or pull together information from my class notes and readings that relate to the same concept or general category.   4 3 2 1

6. I distribute or spread out my study time over several short sessions in advance of the exam, and I use my last study session before the test to review the information I previously studied.   4 3 2 1

7. I participate in study groups with my classmates.   4 3 2 1

recall an example of it, which then serves a memory-retrieval cue to trigger their memory of other details about the concept, such as its definition and relationship to other concepts (Norman, 1982; Park, 1984).

- **Can you represent or describe what you've learned in terms of an analogy or metaphor that compares it to something that has similar meaning or that works in a similar way?** Analogies and metaphors are basically ways of learning something new by understanding it in terms of its similarity to something you already understand. For instance, the computer can be used as a metaphor for the human brain to get a better understanding of learning and memory as a three-stage process in which information is (a) perceived or received (through lectures and readings), (b) stored or saved (through studying), and (c) retrieved (recalled at test time). If you can use an analogy or metaphor to represent what you're learning, you're grasping it at a deep level because you're able to build a mental bridge that connects it to what you already know (Cameron, 2003).

- **Can you apply what you're learning to solve a new problem that you haven't previously seen?** The ability to use your knowledge shows deep learning (Erickson & Strommer, 2005). Learning specialists refer to this mental process as decontextualization—taking what you learned in one context (situation) and applying it to another (Bransford, Brown, & Cocking, 1999). For instance, you know that you've learned a mathematical concept when you can use that concept to solve math problems that are different from the ones initially used by your instructor or textbook to help you learn it. This is why your math instructors rarely include on exams the exact problems solved in class or in your textbook. They're not trying to trick you at test time; they're trying to test your comprehension to determine whether you've learned the concept or principle deeply or just memorized it superficially.

◆ Summary and Conclusion

Information delivered during lectures is most likely to form questions and answers on college tests. At exam time, students who did not record lectures in notes have a slim chance of recalling the information presented. Thus, effective note taking is critical to successful academic performance in college.

Information from reading assignments is the next most common source of test questions on college exams. Professors often won't discuss these assignments in detail in class and sometimes don't even bring up the information from this reading. Thus, doing the assigned reading, and doing it in a way that's most effective for promoting comprehension and retention, plays an important role in your academic success.

The most effective strategies for promoting effective classroom listening, textbook reading, and higher-level thinking are those that reflect three of the college-success principles discussed: (a) active involvement, (b) interpersonal interaction and collaboration, and (c) personal reflection and self-awareness.

Active involvement is critical for learning from lectures (e.g., actively taking notes while listening to lectures) and learning from reading (e.g., actively taking notes while reading). While active involvement is necessary for learning because it engages your attention and thus enables information to reach your brain, personal reflection is necessary for deep learning because it promotes consolidation, retaining information in your brain by locking it into long-term memory. Reflection also encourages deep learning by promoting self-awareness. By periodically pausing to reflect on whether you are truly attending to and understanding the words you're hearing in lectures and the words you're seeing while reading, you become a more self-aware learner and a more effective learner.

Lastly, learning from note taking, reading, and higher-level thinking can all be magnified if they're done collaboratively. You can collaborate with peers to take better notes in class, to identify what's most important in your assigned reading, and to ask questions of one another that promote higher-level thinking.

Learning More on Your Own Through the World Wide Web

Internet-Based Resources for Further Information on Liberal Arts Education

For additional information related to the ideas discussed in this chapter, we recommend the following Web sites:

www.Dartmouth.edu/~acskills/success/index.html

www.utexas.edu/student/utlc

www.muskingum.edu/~cal/database/general/

www.pima.edu/library/online-distance/study-guides/StudySkills.shtml

Learning Math and Overcoming Math Anxiety:

www.mathacademy.com/pr/minitext/anxiety

www.onlinemathlearning.com/math-mnemonics.html

Chapter 8 Exercises

8.1 Self-Assessment of Note-Taking and Reading Habits

Look back at the ratings you gave yourself for effective note-taking, reading, and studying strategies. Add up your total score for these three sets of learning strategies (the maximum score for each set is 28):

Note Taking = _____

Reading = _____

Studying = _____

Total Learning Strategy Score = _____

Self-Assessment Questions

1. In which learning strategy area did you score lowest?

2. Do you think that the strategy area in which you scored lowest has anything to do with your lowest course grade at this point in the term?

3. Of the seven strategies listed within the area in which you scored lowest, which ones could you immediately put into practice to improve your lowest course grade this term?

4. What is the likelihood that you will put the preceding strategies into practice this term?

8.2 Consultation with a Learning Center or Academic Development Specialist

Make an appointment to visit your Learning Center or Academic Support Center on campus to discuss the results of your note-taking, reading, and studying self-assessment in Exercise 8.1 (or any other learning self-assessment you may have taken). Ask for recommendations about how you can improve your learning habits in your lowest-score area. Following your visit, answer the following questions.

Learning Resource Center Reflection

1. Date of appointment _____

2. Who did you meet with in the Learning Center? _____

3. Was your appointment useful (e.g., did you gain any insights or acquire any new learning or test-taking strategies)?

4. What steps were recommended to you for improving your academic performance?

5. How likely is it that you will take the steps mentioned in the previous question: (a) definitely, (b) probably, (c) possibly, or (d) unlikely? Why?

6. Do you plan to visit the Learning Center again? If yes, why? If no, why not?

Too Fast, Too Frustrating: A Note-Taking Nightmare

Joanna Scribe is a first-year student who is majoring in journalism, and she's enrolled in an introductory course that is required for her major (Introduction to Mass Media). Her instructor for this course lectures at a rapid rate and uses vocabulary words that go right over her head. Since she cannot get all the instructor's words down on paper and cannot understand half the words she does manage to write down, she becomes frustrated and stops taking notes. She wants to do well in this course because it's the first course in her major, but she's afraid she will fail it because her class notes are so pitiful.

Reflection and Discussion Questions

1. Can you relate to this case personally, or do know any students who are in the same boat as Joanna?

2. What would you recommend that Joanna do at this point?

3. Why did you make the preceding recommendation?

Your First Year Resources

The first year of college is an exciting and challenging time. We want you to have the best experience possible, so we've designed a website just for you. It's full of tips, tricks, and links to help you make the most of Your First Year! If you have questions or need help finding your way at UNCG, you can always email us at yfy@uncg.edu. Visit yourfirstyear.uncg.edu and the websites below for helpful resources and services about strategic learning, studying and test-taking.

Academic Advising Centers	**Refer to Chapter 12 for comprehensive list**
Office of Accessibility Resources & Services http://ods.uncg.edu/	**336-334-5440**
Student Success Center http://success.uncg.edu/	**336-334-3878**
Students First Office http://studentsfirst.uncg.edu/	**336-334-5730**

Achieving Peak Levels of Academic Performance

Taking Tests, Writing Papers, and Making Presentations

1. In which of the following academic-performance situations do you tend to perform best? (Circle one.) In which do you perform worst? (Circle one.)

   Taking multiple-choice tests
   Taking essay tests
   Writing papers
   Making oral presentations

2. What do you think accounts for the fact you perform better in one situation than the other?

_____

_____

_____

◆LEARNING GOAL

To strengthen your performance on three tasks used to evaluate students' academic achievement in college: tests, papers, and presentations.

◆ Test-Taking Strategies

Academic learning in college involves three stages: acquiring information from lectures and readings; studying that information and storing it in your brain as knowledge; and demonstrating that knowledge on exams.

What follows is a series of strategies related to stage three of the learning: test taking. The strategies are divided into three categories:

- Strategies to use in advance of test day,
- Strategies to use during the test, and
- Strategies to use after test results are returned.

Pretest Strategies: What to Do in Advance of Test Day

Your ability to remember what you've studied will depend not only on how much and how well you studied but also on how your memory will be tested (Stein, 1978). You may be able to remember what you've studied if you are tested in one format (e.g., multiple-choice questions) but may not remember the material as well if the test is in a different format (e.g., essay questions). You need to be aware of the type of test you'll be taking and adjust your study strategy accordingly.

College test questions fall into two major categories: (1) recognition questions and (2) recall questions. Each of these types of questions requires a different type of memory and a different study strategy.

- **Recognition test questions.** Recognition questions ask you to select or choose the correct answer from choices that are provided for you. Falling into this category are multiple-choice, true–false, and matching questions. These test questions don't require you to supply or produce the correct answer on your own; instead, you're asked to recognize or pick out the correct answer—similar to picking out the "correct" criminal from a lineup of potential suspects.

Mutiple-choice questions require recognition memory similar to that used to identify the correct criminal from a line-up of possible suspects.

"It's number three, Mr. Hugo, our seventh grade teacher--the one whose exams contained questions not covered in the assigned reading."

- **Recall test questions.** Recall questions require you to retrieve information you've stored in your brain and reproduce it on your own at test time. As the word "recall" implies, you have to recall or "call back" back to mind the information you need and supply it yourself, rather than selecting it or picking it out from information that's supplied for you. Recall test questions include essay and short-answer questions, which require a written response.

Since recognition test questions ask you to recognize or identify the correct answer from among answers that are provided for you, repeatedly reading over your class and textbook notes to identify important concepts may be an effective study strategy for multiple-choice and true–false test questions. Doing so matches the type of mental activity you'll be asked to perform on the exam—read over and identify correct answers.

On the other hand, recall test questions, such as essay questions, require you to retrieve information and generate correct answers on your own. Studying for essay tests by looking over your class notes and highlighted reading will not prepare you to retrieve and recall information on your own because it does not simulate what you'll be doing on the test itself. However, if you prepare for essay tests by writing out answers on your own, you ensure that your practice (study) sessions match your performance (test) situation because you are be rehearsing what you'll be expected to do on the test—write essays.

Two strategies that are particularly effective for practicing the type of memory retrieval you will need to perform on recall tests are reciting and creating retrieval cues.

Reciting

Recitation involves saying the information you need to recall—without looking at it. Research indicates that memory for information is significantly strengthened when students study by trying to generate that information on their own, rather than reviewing or rereading it (Graf, 1982). Reciting strengthens recall memory in three ways:

- Reciting forces you to actively retrieve information, which is what you will have to do on the test, rather than passively reviewing information that's in front of you and in full view, which is not what you will do on the test.
- Reciting gives you clear feedback on whether you can recall the information you're studying. If you cannot retrieve and recite it without looking at it, you know for sure that you will not be able to recall it at test time and that you need to study it further. One way to provide yourself with this feedback is to put the question on one side of an index card and the answer on the flip side. If you find yourself flipping over the index card to look at the answer in order to state it, you clearly cannot retrieve the information on your own and need to study it further.
- Reciting encourages you to use your own words; this gives you feedback on whether you can paraphrase it. If you can paraphrase it (rephrase it in your own words), it's a good indication you really understand it; and if you really understand it, you're more likely to recall it at test time.

Reciting can be done silently, by speaking aloud, or by writing what you are saying. We recommend speaking or writing out what you're reciting because these strategies involve physical action, which keeps you more actively involved when you're studying.

Creating Retrieval Cues

Suppose you're trying to remember the name of a person you know but just cannot recall it. If a friend gives you a clue (e.g., the first letter of the person's name or a name that rhymes with it), then it may suddenly trigger your memory of the person's entire name. What your friend did was provide you with a retrieval cue. A retrieval cue is a type of memory reminder (like a string tied around your finger) that brings back to your mind what you've temporarily forgotten. Human memories are stored as parts in an interconnected network

(Pribram, 1991). If you're able to recall one piece or segment of the network (the retrieval cue), it can trigger recall of the other pieces of information linked to it in the same organizational network (Collins & Loftus, 1975).

Studies show that students who are unable to remember previously studied information are better able to recall that information if they are given retrieval cue. For instance, suppose students have studied a list of items that includes different animals (e.g., giraffe, coyote, and turkey) but are unable to recall all these animals on a later memory test. If a retrieval cue is provided at the time of the recall test (e.g., if the word "animals" is written on top of the answer sheet), the students often are able to recall many animals they couldn't name before the retrieval cue was provided (Kintsch, 1968). These research findings suggest that category names can serve as powerful retrieval cues. By taking information that you'll need to recall on an essay test and organizing it into categories, you can then use the category names as retrieval cues at the time of the test.

Another strategy for creating retrieval cues is to create catchwords or catchphrases that you can use as a net to "catch" related ideas that you need to recall. For example, an acronym can serve as a catchword, with each letter acting as a retrieval cue for a set of related ideas. Suppose you're studying for a test in abnormal psychology that is likely to include essay questions that will test your knowledge about types of mental illness. You could create the acronym SCOT as a retrieval cue to help you remember to include each of the following elements of mental illness in your answers: symptoms (S), causes (C), outcomes (O), and therapies (T).

Pause for Reflection

Think of material in a course you're taking this term that could be easily grouped into categories to help you remember that material. What is the course?

What categories could you use to organize information that's been covered in the course?

! Remember

Unlike multiple-choice questions on which you choose from answers given to you, on essay questions your mind can go blank because you're facing a blank sheet of paper that requires you to provide answers. To avoid drawing blanks on essay questions, you need to study differently—you need to recite (rehearse) your answers while studying and bring retrieval cues with you to the test.

Students can go "completely blank" on essay tests because they face a blank sheet that requires them to provide information on their own—as opposed to multiple-choice tests, which ask students to recognize or pick-out a correct answer from information that is provided for them.

"When I looked at the first essay question, my whole life flashed before my eyes, then my whole mind went totally blank!"

Strategies to Use Immediately Before the Test

1. **Before exams, take a brisk walk.** Physical activity will increase mental alertness by increasing oxygen flow to the brain; it will also decrease tension by increasing the brain's production of emotionally "mellowing" brain chemicals (e.g., serotonin and endorphins).

2. **Arrive at the test room fully equipped with all the test-taking tools you'll need.** In addition to the required supplies (e.g., No. 2 pencil, pen, blue book, Scantron, calculator, etc.), bring backup equipment in case you experience equipment failure (e.g., an extra pen in case your first one runs out of ink or extra pencils in case your original one breaks).

3. **Try to get to the test a few minutes early.** Arriving at the test ahead of time will give you a chance to review any terms, formulas, and equations you may have struggled to remember and any recall shortcuts you may have created (e.g., acronyms). You want to be sure that you have this information in your working memory when you receive the exam so that you can get it down on paper—before you forget it. Arriving early will also allow you to take a few minutes to get into a relaxed pretest state of mind by thinking positive thoughts; taking slow, deep breaths; and stretch your muscles. Try to avoid discussing the test with other students immediately before it begins because their last-minute questions, confusion, and anxiety may rub off on you. (Anxiety can be contagious.)

4. **Sit in the same seat that you normally occupy in class.** Research indicates that memory is improved when information is recalled in the same place where it was originally received or reviewed (Sprenger, 1999). Thus, taking the test in the same seat you normally occupy during lectures, which is the place where you originally heard much of the information appearing on the test, may improve your test performance.

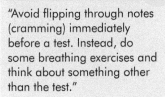

> **!**
>
> **Remember**
>
> Popular energy drinks typically contain a significant amount of caffeine, which can increase nervousness, blood pressure, and the tendency to crash (experience a sharp drop in energy) after the drink's effects wear off.

Strategies to Use During the Test

1. **As soon as you receive a copy of the test, write down key information.** Writing down any hard-to-remember terms, formulas, and equations and any memory-improvement shortcuts you may have created as soon as you start the exam will ensure that you don't forget this information once you get involved with answering test questions.

2. **Answer the easier test questions first.** As soon as you receive the test, before launching into the first question, check out the layout of the test. Note the questions that are worth the most points and the questions that you know well. One way to implement this recommendation is to first survey the test and put a checkmark by difficult questions and come back to them later—after you've answered the easier ones.

3. **Prevent "memory block" from setting in.** If you experience memory block for information that you

Pause for Reflection

During tests, if I experience memory block, I usually . . .

I am most likely to experience memory block in the following subject areas:

know you've studied and have stored in your brain, use the following strategies:

- Mentally put yourself back in the environment or situation in which you studied the information. Recreate the steps in which you learned the information that you've temporarily forgotten by mentally picturing the place where you first heard or saw it and where you studied it, including the sights, sounds, smells, and time of day. This memory-improvement strategy is referred to as guided retrieval, and research supports its effectiveness for recalling information, including information recalled by eye witnesses to a crime (Glenberg, Bradley, Kraus, & Renzaglia, 1983).

- Think of any idea or piece of information that may be related to the information you cannot remember. Studies show that when students experience temporary forgetting they're more likely to suddenly recall that information if they first recall partial information that relates to it in some way (Reed, 1996). This related piece of information may trigger your memory for the forgotten information because related pieces of information are likely to be stored as memory traces within the same network of brain cells.

- Take your mind off the question and turn to another question. This allows your subconscious to work on the problem, which may trigger your memory of the information you've forgotten. Also, by turning to other test questions, you may find some information included in those questions that can trigger memory for the information you forgot.

Strategies for Answering Multiple-Choice Questions

Multiple-choice questions are commonly used on college tests, on exams to be admitted to graduate school (e.g., for master's and doctoral degree programs) or professional school (e.g., law school and medical school), and on certification or licensing exams to practice in particular professions (e.g., nursing and teaching). Since multiple-choice tests are so common in college and beyond, this section of the text is devoted to a detailed discussion of strategies for answering such test questions.

Pause for Reflection

How would you rate your general level of test anxiety during most exams? (Circle one.)

high   moderate   low

What types of tests or subjects tend to produce the most test stress or test anxiety for you?

Why?

1. **Read all choices listed and use a process-of-elimination approach.** You can find an answer by eliminating choices that are clearly wrong and continuing doing so until you're left with one answer that seems to be the most accurate option. Keep in mind that the correct answer is often the one that has the highest probability or likelihood of being true; it doesn't have to be absolutely true—just truer than the other choices listed.

2. **Use *test-wise* strategies when you don't know the correct answer.** Your first strategy on any multiple-choice question should be to choose an answer based on your knowledge of the material, not to try to outsmart the test or the test maker by guessing the correct answer based on how the question is worded. However, if you've relied on your knowledge and used the process-of-elimination strategy to eliminate clearly wrong choices but you're still left you with two or more answers that appear to be correct, then you should turn to being test wise, which refers your ability to use the

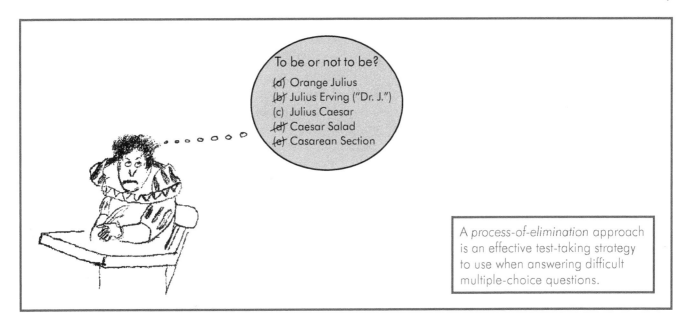

To be or not to be?
(a) Orange Julius
(b) Julius Erving ("Dr. J.")
(c) Julius Caesar
(d) Caesar Salad
(e) Casarean Section

A *process-of-elimination* approach is an effective test-taking strategy to use when answering difficult multiple-choice questions.

characteristics of the test question itself (such as its wording or format) to increase your chances of selecting the correct answer (Millman, Bishop, & Ebel, 1965). Listed here are three test-wise strategies for multiple-choice questions whose answer you don't know or can't remember:

- **Pick an answer that contains qualifying words.** Look for words such as "usually," "probably," "likely," "sometimes," "perhaps," or "may." Truth often doesn't come neatly wrapped in the form of a definitive statement, so choices that are stated as broad generalizations or absolute truths are more likely to be false. For example, answers containing words such as "always," "never," "only," "must," and "completely" are more likely to be false than true.

- **Pick the longest answer.** True statements often require more words to make them true.

- **Pick a middle answer rather than the first or last answer.** For example, on a question with four choices, select answer "b" or "c" rather than "a" or "d." Studies show that many instructors have a tendency to place correct answers as middle choices rather than as the first or last choice (Linn & Gronlund, 1995)—perhaps because they think the correct answer will be too obvious or stand out if it's listed as the beginning or end.

3. **Check that your answers are in line.** When looking over your test before turning it in, search carefully for questions you may have skipped and intended to go back to later. Sometimes you may skip a test question on a multiple-choice test and forget to skip the number of that question on the answer form, which will throw off all the other answers by one space or line. On a computer-scored test, this means that you may get multiple items marked wrong because your answers are misplaced. This can produce a domino effect of wrong answers that will severely damage your test score. As a damage-prevention measure, check all of your answers to be sure no blank lines or spaces on your answer sheet could set off this domino effect.

4. **Don't feel locked in to your answers.** When checking your answers on multiple-choice or true–false tests, don't be afraid to change an answer

after you've given it more thought. There have been numerous studies on the topic of changing answers on multiple-choice and true–false tests dating back to 1928 (Kuhn, 1988). These studies consistently show that most changed test answers go from being incorrect to correct, resulting in improved test scores (Benjamin, Cavell, & Shallenberger, 1984; Shatz & Best, 1987). In one study of more than 1,500 students' midterm exams in an introductory psychology course, it was found that when students changed their answers they went from right to wrong only 25 percent of the time (Kruger, Wirtz, & Miller, 2005). These findings probably reflect that students may catch a mistake they made when they read the question the first time or discover some information later in the test that causes them to reconsider their first answer. So, don't buy into the common belief that your first answer is always your best answer. If you have good reason to think a change should be made, don't be afraid to make it. However, if you find yourself changing many of your original answers, this may indicate that you were not well prepared for the exam and are just doing a lot of guessing (and second guessing).

Strategies for Answering Essay Questions

Along with multiple-choice questions, essay questions are among the most commonly used forms on college exams. Listed here are strategies that will help you reach peak levels of performance on essay questions.

1. **Focus on the main ideas.** Make a brief outline or list of bullet points to represent the main ideas you will include in your answers before you begin to write them. This strategy is effective for several reasons:
   - **An outline will help you remember major points.** In addition to reminding you of the points you intend to make, an outline will give you the order in which you intend to make them. This should help prevent you from forgetting the big picture and the most important concepts when you become wrapped up in the details of constructing sentences and choosing words for your answers.
   - **An outline improves your answer's organization.** One factor that instructors will consider when determining an answer's grade is its organization. (You can make your answer's organization clearer by underlining your major sections or numbering your major points.)
   - **Having an advanced idea of what you will write can reduce your test anxiety.** The outline will take care of the answer's organization in advance so that you don't have the added stress of organizing your answer and explaining it while you're writing it.
   - **An outline can add points to an incomplete answer's score.** If you run out of test time, your instructor will be able to see your outline for any questions that you didn't have time to complete. Even if you didn't have the opportunity to convert it into sentence form, your outline should earn you points because it demonstrates your knowledge of the major ideas called for by the question. In contrast, if you skip an outline and just starting writing answers to test questions one at a time, you run the risk of not getting to questions you know well before your time is up; you'll then have nothing written on your test to show what you know about those unfinished questions.

Exhibit 1

Identical twins
Adoption
Parents/family tree

$\frac{6}{6}$

1. *There are several different studies that scientists conduct, but one study that they conduct is to find out how genetics can influence human behavior in <u>identical twins</u>. Since they are identical, they will most likely end up very similar in behavior because of their identical genetic make up. Although environment has some impact, genetics are still a huge factor and they will, more likely than not, behave similarly. Another type of study is with <u>parents and their family trees</u>. Looking at a subject's family tree will alleviate why a certain person is bi-polar or depressed. It is most likely a cause of a gene in the family tree, even if it was last seen decades ago. Lastly, another study is with adopted children. If an <u>adopted child</u> acts a certain way that is unique to that child, and researchers find the parents' family tree, they will most likely see similar behavior in the parents and siblings as well.*

No freewill
No afterlife

$\frac{6}{6}$

2. *The monistic view of the mind-brain relationship is so strongly opposed and criticized because there is a belief or assumption that <u>freewill</u> is taken away from people. For example, if a person commits a horrendous crime, it can be argued "monastically" that the chemicals in the brain were the reason, and that a person cannot think for themselves to act otherwise. This view limits responsibility.*
Another reason that this view is opposed is because it has been said that <u>there is no afterlife</u>. If the mind and brain are one and the same, and there is <u>NO</u> difference, then once the brain is dead and is no longer functioning, so is the mind. Thus, is cannot continue to live beyond what we know today as life. <u>And</u> this goes against many religions, which is why this reason, in particular, is heavily opposed.

Written answers to two short essay questions given by a college sophomore, which demonstrate effective use of bulleted lists or short outlines to ensure recall of most important points.

2. **Get directly to the point on each essay question.** Avoid elaborate introductions that take up your test time (and your instructor's grading time) but don't earn you any points. For example, an answer that begins with the statement "This is an interesting question that we had a great discussion on in class . . ." is pointless because it will not add points to your test score. The time available to you on essay tests is often limited, so you can't afford flowery introductions that are pointless—both in their content and in what they would add to your score.

One effective way to focus your response is to include part of the question in the first sentence of your answer. For example, suppose the test says, "Argue for or against capital punishment by explaining how it will or will not reduce the nation's murder rate." Your first sentence could read, "Capital punishment will not reduce the murder rate for the following reasons . . ." Thus, your first sentence becomes your thesis statement, which points you directly to the major points you're going to make in your essay and to earning points for your essay.

3. **Answer all essay questions as precisely and completely as possible.** Don't assume that your instructor already knows what you're talking about or will be bored by details. Instead, take the approach that you're writing to someone who knows little or nothing about the subject—as if you're an expert teacher and the reader is a clueless student.

> **!** **Remember**
>
> As a rule, it's better to overexplain than underexplain your answers to essay questions.

4. **Support your points with evidence—facts, statistics, quotes, or examples.** When taking essay tests, take on the role of a criminal lawyer who makes a case by presenting concrete evidence (exhibit A, exhibit B, etc.). Since timed essay tests can often press you for time, be sure to prioritize and cite your most powerful points and persuasive evidence. If you have time later, you can return to add other points worth mentioning.

5. **Leave space between your answers to each essay question.** This strategy will enable you to easily add information to your original answer if you have time or if you recall something later in the test that you had originally forgotten.

6. **Proofread your test and correct grammar and spelling errors.** When checking your answers to essay questions, before turning in your test, proofread what you've written and correct any spelling or grammatical errors you find. Eliminating them is likely to improve your test score. Even if your instructor doesn't explicitly state that grammar and spelling will be counted in determining your grade, these mechanical mistakes may still subconsciously influence your professor's overall evaluation of your written work.

7. **Remember that neatness matters.** Research indicates that neatly written essays tend to be scored higher than sloppy ones, even if the answers are essentially the same (Klein & Hart, 1968). This is understandable when you consider that grading essay answers is a time-consuming task that requires your weary-eyed instructor to plod through multiple styles of handwriting whose readability may range from crystal clear to cryptic code. Thus, make a point of writing as clearly as possible, and if you finish the test with time to spare, clean up your work by rewriting any sloppily written words or sentences.

8. **Before turning in your test, carefully review and double-check your answers.** This is the critical last step in the process of effective test taking. Sometimes the rush and anxiety of taking a test can cause test takers to overlook details, misread instructions, unintentionally skip questions, or make absentminded mistakes. When you're done, take time to look over your answers to be sure you didn't make any mindless mistakes. Avoid the temptation to immediately cut out because you're pooped out or to take off on an ego trip by trying to be among the first and fastest students in class to finish their test. Instead, take the full amount of time that you have to complete the test. When you consider the amount of time and effort you put into preparing for the exam, it's foolish not to take just a few more minutes to ensure you get maximum mileage out of the time you have to complete the exam.

Pause for Reflection

Rate yourself in terms of how frequently you use these test-taking strategies according to the following scale:

4 = always, 3 = sometimes, 2 = rarely, 1 = never

1. I take tests in the same seat that I usually sit in to take class notes.   4 3 2 1

2. I answer easier test questions first.   4 3 2 1

3. I use a process-of-elimination approach on multiple-choice tests to eliminate choices until I find one that is correct or appears to be the most accurate option.   4 3 2 1

4. For essay questions, I outline or map out my ideas before I begin to write the answer.   4 3 2 1

5. I look for information included on the test that may help me answer difficult questions or that may help me remember information I've forgotten.   4 3 2 1

6. I leave extra space between my answers to essay questions in case I want to come back and add more information later.   4 3 2 1

7. I carefully review my work, double-checking for errors and skipped questions before turning in my tests.   4 3 2 1

Posttest Strategies: What to Do After Receiving Test Results

1. **Use your test results as feedback to improve your future performance.** Your test results are not just an end result; they may also be used as a means to an end—to improve your future test performances and your final course grade. Examine your tests carefully when you get them back, being sure to note any written comments your instructor may have made.

   If your test results are disappointing, don't become mad or sad; instead, get even by using the results as feedback to assess where you went wrong so that you can avoid making the same mistake again. If your test results were positive, use them to see where you went right so that you can do it the same way again.

2. **Ask for additional feedback.** In addition to using your own test results as a source of feedback, actively seek feedback from people whose judgment you trust and value. Three social resources you can use to obtain feedback on how to improve your performance are your instructors, professionals in your Learning or Academic Support Center, and your peers.

   You can make appointments with your instructors to visit them during office hours and get their feedback on how you might be able to improve your performance. You'll likely find it easier to see your instructors after a test than before it, because most students don't realize that it's just as valuable to seek feedback from instructors following an exam as it is to try and get last-minute help before it.

   Tutors and other learning support professionals on your campus can also be excellent sources of feedback about what adjustments to make in your study habits or test-taking strategies to improve your future performance.

   Also, be alert and open to receiving feedback from trusted peers. While feedback from experienced professionals is valuable, don't overlook your peers as another source of feedback on how to improve your performance. You can review your test with other students in class, particularly with students who did exceptionally well. Their tests can provide you with models of what type of work your instructor expects on exams. Also, ask successful students what they did to be successful—for example, what they did to prepare for the test that enabled them to perform so well.

   Whatever you do, don't let a bad test grade get you mad, sad, or down, particularly if it occurs early in the course when you're still learning the rules of the game. Look at mistakes in terms of what they can do for you, rather than to you. A poor test performance can be turned into a valuable learning experience by using test results as feedback or an error detector to locate the source of your mistakes.

> "People can't learn without feedback. It's not teaching that causes learning. Attempts by the learner to perform cause learning, dependent upon the quality of the feedback and opportunities to use it."
>
> —Grant Wiggins, *Feedback: How Learning Occurs*

> "When you make a mistake, there are only three things you should do about it: admit it; learn from it; and don't repeat it."
>
> —Paul "Bear" Bryant, college football coach

Remember

Your past mistakes shouldn't be ignored or neglected; they should be detected and corrected so that you don't replay them on future tests.

Strategies for Pinpointing the Reason for Lost Points on Exams

On test questions where you lost points, identify the stage in the learning process at which the breakdown occurred by asking yourself the following questions.

- **Did you have the information you needed to answer the question correctly?** If you didn't have the information, what was the source of the missing information? Was it information presented in class that didn't get into your notes? If so, look at our strategies for improving listening and note-taking habits. If the missing information was contained in your assigned reading, check whether you're using effective reading strategies.
- **Did you have the information but not study it because you didn't think it was important?** If you didn't realize which information would be on the test, then you might want to review the study strategies for finding and focusing on the most important information in class lectures and reading assignments.
- **Did you know the information but not retain it?** Not holding on information may mean one of three things:
  1. You didn't store the information adequately in your brain, so your memory trace wasn't strong enough for you to recall it at the time you took the test. This suggests that more study time needs to be spent on recitation or rehearsal.
  2. You may have tried to cram too much information in too little time just before the exam and may have not given your brain time enough to digest it and store it in long-term memory. The solution would be to distribute your study time more evenly in advance of the next exam and take advantage of the effective part-to-whole study method.
  3. You put in enough study time and didn't cram, but you didn't study effectively or strategically. For example, you may have studied for essay questions by just reading over your class and reading notes rather than by writing and rehearsing them. The solution would be to adjust your study strategy so that it better matches or aligns with the type of test you'll be taking.
- **Did you study the material but not really understand it or learn it deeply?** If deep learning didn't occur, you may need to self-monitor your comprehension more carefully while studying to track whether you truly understand the material at a deeper level.
- **Did you know the information but were not able to retrieve it during the exam?** If you had the information on the "tip of your tongue" during the exam, this indicates that you did retain it and it was stored (saved) in your brain but you couldn't get at it and get it out (retrieve it) when you needed. This error may be corrected by making better use of memory-retrieval cues.
- **Did you know the answer but just make a careless test-taking mistake?** If your mistake was careless, the solution may be simply to take more time to review your test once you've completed it and check for absent-minded errors before turning it in.

> **! Remember**
>
> Just as you learn before tests by preparing for your performance, you can learn after tests by reviewing your performance.

◆ Writing Papers and Reports

The Importance of Writing

Writing is a powerful, transferable skill that you can used to promote your success across the curriculum, including general education courses and courses in your academic major. You may have many great ideas in your head, but unless you can communicate them, your instructors will never know that you have them and you will never receive full credit for them in your college courses. Writing is a major route through which you can communicate your ideas, and it is a route of communication that your instructors will travel often to judge the extent of your knowledge and the quality of your thinking. Thus, if you improve your writing skills, you will improve your ability to demonstrate your knowledge, communicate your ideas, and elevate your grades.

Your ability to write clearly, concisely, and persuasively is a skill that not only will enable you succeed academically but also will help you succeed professionally. In one study, college alumni were asked about the importance of different skills to their current work responsibilities more than 10 years after they graduated, and more than 90 percent of the alumni ranked "need to write effectively" as a skill they considered to be of "great importance" to their current work (Worth, cited in Light, 2001). The first contact and first impression you will make on future employers is likely to be your letter of application or cover letter that you write when applying for positions. Constructing a well-written letter of application may be your first step toward converting your college experience and college degree into a future career.

> **! Remember**
>
> Writing skills will contribute to your academic success across all subjects throughout all your years in college, and they will promote your professional success in any career you may pursue after college.

Papers and Reports

Studies show that a small percentage of high school students' class and homework time is spent on writing assignments that are as lengthy and demanding as those given in college. For example, in high school, most writing assignments involve summaries or descriptive reports; in college, students are expected to engage in expository (persuasive) writing, which requires the writer to make or prove a case by supporting it with sound evidence (Applebee, 1981; Applebee, Langer, Jenkins, Mullis, & Foertsch, 1990).

Pause for Reflection

Reflect back on your high school experience, and try to recall your writing assignments. What was the longest paper you wrote in high school?

What type of thinking were you usually asked to do on your writing assignments (e.g., memorize, summarize, analyze, criticize, or compare and contrast)?

Dividing large writing assignments into smaller, manageable steps can reduce late-night frustration and the risk of permanent computer damage.

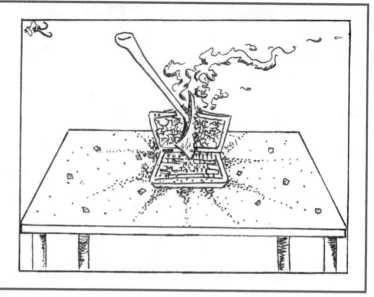

"Begin with the end in mind."

–Stephen Covey, *The Seven Habits of Highly Effective People*

Writing is a multistep process that cannot be completed in one night. Dividing the writing process into a series of shorter steps that are taken in advance of the paper's due date is an effective way to strengthen the quality of your final product.

What follows is a six-step plan for dividing your time and labor that should make the task of writing papers more manageable, less stressful, and more successful.

1. **Know the purpose or objective of the assignment.** Having a clear understanding of the purpose or goal of the writing assignment is the critical first step to completing it successfully. It helps you stay on track and moving in the right direction; it also helps you get on track in the first place, because one major cause of writer's block is uncertainty about the goal or purpose of the writing task (Rennie & Brewer, 1987).

   Before you begin to do any writing, be sure you have a clear understanding of what your instructor expects you to accomplish. You can do this by asking yourself these three questions about the writing assignment:
   - What is the objective or intended outcome of this assignment?
   - What type of thinking am I being asked to demonstrate in this assignment?
   - What criteria (judgment standards) will my instructor use to evaluate and grade my performance on this assignment?

   To help determine what particular form or forms of thinking you are expected to demonstrate in a writing assignment, make special note of any action verbs in the description of the assignment. These verbs can provide valuable clues to the type of thinking that your instructor wants you to demonstrate. Listed in **Box 9.1** are some thinking verbs that you're likely to see college writing assignments and the type of mental action typically called for by each of these verbs.

   As you read the following list, make a short note after each mental action, indicating whether or not you've been asked to use such thinking on any assignments you completed before college.

2. **Generate ideas.** At this stage of the writing process, the only thing you're concerned about is getting the ideas you have in your head out of your head and on to paper. Don't worry about how good or bad the ideas may be. Writing scholars refer to this process as focused freewriting—writing nonstop for a certain period just to generate ideas, without

9.1

Take Action!

Ten Mental-Action Verbs Commonly Found in College Writing Assignments

1. Analyze. Break it down into its key parts and evaluate those parts (e.g., strengths and weaknesses).
2. Compare. Identify the similarities and differences between major ideas.
3. Contrast. Identify the differences between ideas, particularly sharp differences and opposing viewpoints.
4. Describe. Provide details (e.g., who, what, where, and when).
5. Discuss. Analyze (break apart) and evaluate the parts (e.g., strengths and weaknesses).
6. Document. Support your judgment and conclusions with evidence.
7. Explain. Provide reasons that answer the questions "why?" and "how?"
8. Illustrate. Supply concrete examples or specific instances.
9. Interpret. Draw your own conclusion about something, and explain why you came to that conclusion.
10. Support. Back up your ideas with factual evidence or logical arguments.

worrying about writing complete or correct sentences (Bean, 2001). Remember that the act of writing itself can stimulate ideas, so if you're not sure what ideas you have, start writing because it will likely trigger ideas, which, in turn, will lead to additional ideas. One way to overcome writer's block is to start writing something (Zinsser, 1990). It could be anything, as long as it jump-starts the process.

Pause for Reflection

Which of the mental actions in the list in Box 9.1 was most often required on your high school writing assignments?

Which was least often (or never) required?

3. **Organize your ideas.** Ideas should be organized in a paper or written report in one of two ways:

- Separate pieces of specific information related to the same general idea need to be organized conceptually into the same categories.

  Strategy: Review the ideas that you've brainstormed and group together those ideas that may be classified in the same general category. For instance, if your topic is terrorism and you find three ideas on your list referring to different causes of terrorism, group those ideas together under the category of "causes." Similarly, if you find ideas on your list that relate to possible solutions to the problem of terrorism, group those ideas under the category of "solutions." (You could record your separate ideas on sticky notes and stick the notes with ideas pertaining to the same general category on index cards, with the category heading written at the top of the card.)

- General categories of ideas need to be organized sequentially into an order that flows smoothly or logically from start to finish.

  Strategy: Arrange your general categories of ideas into an orderly sequence that creates a beginning, middle, and end. Index cards come in handy when trying to find the best progression of your major ideas because the cards can be arranged and rearranged easily until you discover an order that produces the smoothest, most logical sequence. You can use your sequence of index cards to create an outline for your paper that lists the major categories of your ideas and the order in which they will appear in your paper.

Strategy: Another effective way to organize and sequence your ideas is by creating a concept map or idea map that represents your main categories of ideas in a visual–spatial format that's similar to a road map.

Figure 9.1 shows a concept map that was used to organize and sequence the main ideas on higher-level thinking. This type of concept map is called a clock map because its main ideas are organized like the numbers of a clock, beginning at the top and then moving sequentially in a clockwise direction.

4. **Write multiple drafts.** The steps in the writing process discussed thus far are referred to as prewriting because they focus on generating and organizing your ideas before communicating them to anyone else (Murray, 1993). In your first draft, you begin the formal writing process of converting your major ideas into sentences, but you do so without worrying about the mechanics of writing (e.g., punctuation, grammar, or spelling). In your first draft, the goal is to simply "talk through" your key ideas on paper.

Pause for Reflection

When you attempt to organize your ideas, are you more likely to use a map (diagram) format or an outline format—in which you list major ideas as headings (A, B, C, etc.) and related minor ideas as subheadings (1, 2, 3, etc.)?

Why do you think you tend to favor one method over the other?

Which method for organizing ideas appears more natural or comfortable to you?

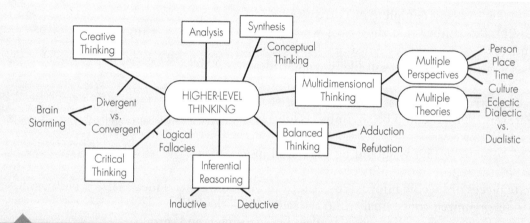

Figure 9.1 **Concept Map Used to Organize and Sequence Major Ideas Relating to Higher-Level Thinking**

"I'm not a writer; I'm a rewriter."

–James Thurber, award-winning American journalist and author

Remember

Don't expect to write a perfect draft of your paper on the first try. Even professional writers report that it takes them more than one draft (often three or four) before they produce their final draft. Although the final product of award-winning writers may look spectacular, what precedes it is a messy process that includes lots of revisions between the first try and the final product (Bean, 2001).

"End with the beginnig in mind."

–Joe Cuseo

- **In your final draft be sure that your conclusion and introduction are aligned or interrelated.** The most important sentence in your conclusion should be a restatement of your original thesis or should answer the question that was posed in your introduction. Connecting your thesis statement and concluding statement provides a pair of meaningful bookends to your paper, anchoring it at its two most pivotal points—the beginning and the end. It allows you to drive your point home at two influential points of in the communication process—the first and the last impression.

5. **Read and edit your writing.** After you complete a second draft of your paper, take your mind off it for a while and come back to it in a different role—as reader and editor. Up to now, your role has been that of a writer; at this stage, you shift roles from writer to reader; you read your own words as if they were written by someone else, and you critically evaluate the paper's ideas, organization, and writing style. If you find words and sentences that aren't clearly capturing or reflecting what you meant to say, then revision is necessary. At this stage, make sure your paper is double-spaced so that you have ample room for editing and revising.

6. **Proofread your paper carefully for clerical and technical mistakes before submitting it.** Proofreading may be said to be a micro form of editing; it shifts the focus of your editorial attention to the minute mechanics of your paper and detection of details related to referencing, grammar, punctuation, and spelling. Proofreading is a critical last step in the editorial process because small, technical errors are likely to have been overlooked during earlier stages of the writing process when your attention was focused on larger issues related to your paper's content and organizational structure.

When proofing your paper, don't forget that your computer's spell-checker doesn't check whether word are correctly spelled in the context (sentence) in which you're using them. For instance, a spell-checker would not detect the three "correctly" spelled words that are actually misspelled words in the context of the following sentence: "She *war* her high-*healed* sneakers to the *bawl*."

There is another essential element of careful proofreading: Checking to be sure that you've cited all your sources accurately and thoroughly. This will ensure that you demonstrate academic integrity and avoid plagiarism. (See **Box 9.2** for more details.)

! Remember

Careful proofreading represents the key, final step in the process of writing a high-quality paper. Earlier stages of the writing process are more mentally demanding and time consuming than proofreading, so it would be a shame to overlook this simple last step and lose points for mistakes that can be quickly detected and corrected.

◆ Public Speaking: Making Oral Presentations and Delivering Speeches
The Importance of Oral Communication

In addition to writing, the second major channel used to convey ideas and demonstrate your knowledge is oral communication. Developing your ability to speak in a clear, concise, and confident manner will strengthen your performance in college and your career. The oral communication skills you demonstrate during your job interviews are likely to play a pivotal role in determining whether you're initially hired, and your ability to speak effectively at meetings and when making professional presentations will contribute significantly

"As you move up through your career path, you're judged on your ability to articulate a point of view."

–Donald Keogh, former president of the Coca-Cola Company

Take Action!

Plagiarism: A Violation of Academic Integrity

What Is Academic Integrity?

There are ethical aspects of writing papers and reports. Academic integrity involves avoiding the unethical practice of stealing the ideas of others, whether they are the ideas of peers (e.g., not cheating on exams) or the words and ideas of authorities that have been borrowed or have influenced the writer's thoughts but for which the writer has failed to give credit. When writing papers and reports, students with academic integrity give credit where credit is due; they carefully cite and reference their sources.

What Is Plagiarism?

Plagiarism is a violation of academic integrity that involves deliberate or unintentional use of someone else's work without acknowledging it, giving the reader the impression it's original work.

Student Perspective

"My intent was not to plagiarize. I realize I was unclear [about] the policy and am actually thankful for now knowing exactly what I can and cannot do on assignments and how to prevent academic dishonesty in the future."

—First-year college student's reflection on a plagiarism violation

Various Forms of Plagiarism

1. Submitting an entire paper, or portion thereof, that was written by someone else,
2. Copying sections of someone else's work and inserting it into your own work,

3. Cutting paragraphs from separate sources and pasting them into the body of your own paper,

9.2

Student Perspective

"When a student violates an academic integrity policy no one wins, even if the person gets away with it. It isn't right to cheat and it is an insult to everyone who put the effort in and did the work, and it cheapens the school for everyone. I learned my lesson and have no intention of ever cheating again."

—First-year college student's reflection on an academic integrity violation

4. Paraphrasing (rewording) someone else's words or ideas without citing that person as a source, (For examples of acceptable paraphrasing versus plagiarism, go to www.princeton.edu/pr/pub/integrity/pages/plagiarism.html)

Note: If the source for information included in your paper is listed at the end of your paper in your reference (works cited) section but is not cited in the body of your paper, this still qualifies as plagiarism.

5. Not placing quotation marks around someone else's exact words that appear in the body of your paper,
6. Failing to cite the source of factual information included in your paper that's not common knowledge.

Sources: Academic Integrity at Princeton (2003); Pennsylvania State University (2005); Purdue University Online Writing Lab (1995–2004).

to your prospects for promotion. Research repeatedly shows that employers place high value on oral communication skills and rank them among the top characteristics they seek in prospective employees (AC Nielsen Research Services, 2000; National Association of Colleges & Employers, 2003; Conference Board of Canada, 2000).

National surveys show that fear of public speaking is extremely common among people of all ages, including adolescents and adults (Motley, 1997). Studies also show that many college students experience classroom communication apprehension—that is, they are fearful about speaking in class (Richmond & McCloskey, 1997). If you're at least somewhat nervous about public speaking, welcome to a club that has many members.

Francie reprinted by permission of Sherrie Shepherd.

Surveys reveal that fear of public speaking is very common and ranks high on the list of most intense human fears.

Strategies for Making Effective Oral Presentations and Speeches

In the following section of this chapter, you'll find strategies you can use immediately to improve your ability to make oral presentations and speeches. Since speaking and writing both involve communicating thoughts in the form of words, you'll find that many of the strategies suggested here for improving oral reports will also be useful for improving written reports. You should be able to double dip and transfer the effective strategies you learn for oral presentations to improve your written papers presentations, and vice versa.

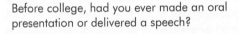

Know the purpose of your presentation. Knowing the intended outcome of your presentation is the critical first step toward making an effective presentation. You can't begin to take the right steps toward doing anything well until you know why you're doing it. If you have any doubt about what your oral presentation should accomplish, seek clarification from your instructor before proceeding.

Similar to formal papers, formal presentations usually fall into one of the following two categories, depending on their purpose or objective:

- **Informative presentations,** which are intended to provide the audience with accurate information and explanations
- **Persuasive (expository) presentations,** which are intended to persuade (convince) the audience to agree with a certain position by supporting it with solid evidence and sound arguments

In college, most of your oral presentations will fall into the persuasive category, which means that you will search for information, draw conclusions

> **Pause for Reflection**
>
> Before college, had you ever made an oral presentation or delivered a speech?
>
> Does your college include a course in speech or public speaking as a graduation requirement?
>
> If your college doesn't require it, would you consider taking an elective course in public speaking?

>
> **Student Perspective**
>
> "I was really nervous during the entire thing, but I felt so relieved and proud afterwards."
>
> –First-year college student commenting on her first public speech

about your research, and document your conclusions with evidence. Similar to writing research papers, persuasive presentations usually require you to think at a higher level, cite sources, and demonstrate academic integrity.

Strategies for Delivering Your Presentation

1. **Rehearse and revise.** Just as you should write several drafts of a paper before turning it in, your oral presentation should be rehearsed and revised before you deliver it. Rehearsal will improve your memory and increase the clarity of your presentation by reducing long pauses, the need to stop and restart, and the use of distracting fillers (e.g., "uh," "umm," "like," and "you know").

Rehearsing what you plan to say before you start to say it increases the clarity of your oral presentations by reducing the likelihood that you'll fill silent pauses with unnecessary fillers, such as "like," "kind of," and "you know."

"If somebody asked me what my like favorite class is, you know, I'd hafta go, 'Speech'."

During your presentation, you can occasionally look at your notes or slides and use them as cue cards to help you recall the key points you intend to make; however, they shouldn't be used as a script that's read verbatim.

> **Remember**
>
> An oral presentation is a form of public speaking, not a public reading.

On the other hand, a formal presentation is not an impromptu speech that's spontaneously delivered off the top of your head. Instead, it's an extemporaneous presentation, which is something between a formal reading and an impromptu speech; it involves advanced preparation and use of some notes but isn't written out entirely in advance and read (or memorized) word for word (Luotto, Stoll, & Hoglund-Ketttmann,

Take Action!

9.3

Tips for Using (Not Abusing) PowerPoint®

- List information on your slides as bulleted points, not as complete sentences. Wordiness will result in your audience spending more time reading than listening to you. You can further encourage your audience to listen by showing only one of your slide's points at a time. This will keep the audience members focused on the point you're discussing and prevent them from reading ahead.
- Avoid reading your slides. Keep eye contact primarily with your audience.

Remember

The points on the slide are meant to be quick launching pads for more elaborate ideas that you present verbally. PowerPoint should be used to reinforce your oral presentation; it shouldn't become your presentation, nor should it turn public speaking into public reading.

"A presentation is about explaining things to people that go above and beyond what they get in the slides. If it weren't, they might just as well get your slides and read them in the comfort of their own office, home, boat, or bathroom."

–Jesper Johansson, senior security strategist for Microsoft and author of *Death by PowerPoint* (personal blog) (2005)

- Limit the amount of information on a slide to three to five points. Research indicates that the number of points or bits of information that humans can hold in their short-term memory is about four (plus or minus two; Cowan, 2001).
- Use the title of the slide as a general heading to organize or connect the bullets listed on the slide.
- Use a font size of at least 18 points, or else people in the back of the room will have difficulty reading what's printed on the slide.
- Use color not to decorate or distract but to add meaning to the points on the slide. For example, use a dark or bold blue heading to represent a major category, and list the subcategories beneath it in a lighter (but still visible) shade of blue.
- Use your slides to deliver pictures or visual images that relate to and reinforce the points you're making verbally. This may be the true power of PowerPoint.

Remember

Probably the most powerful advantage of PowerPoint is its ability to enhance your verbal presentation with visual images, which can magnify the impact of your spoken message and expand the attention span of your audience.

- If you include words or an image on a slide that's not your own work, acknowledge its source at the bottom of the slide.
- Proof your slides like you would a written paper before going public with them.

Sources: Johansson (2005); Ten Commandments of PowerPoint Presentations (2005); University of Wisconsin, La Crosse (2001).

2001). Extemporaneous speaking allows you some freedom to ad lib or improvise. If you forget the exact words you intended to use, some improvising can prevent you from getting struck by silence, and it can prevent your audience from even noticing that you forgot what you were planning to say.

2. **Incorporate visual elements into your presentation.** Visual aids can be a powerful way to illustrate or reinforce your points and stimulate audience

interest. You can use pictures, images, graphs, or cartoons that are relevant to the content of your presentation. Or you can bring in objects or artifacts that relate points you'll make in your presentation.

Remember

The more organized and prepared you are for speaking in public, the less anxiety you'll experience when speaking in public.

During Delivery of Your Speech

- Don't remain motionless; move around a bit. When you're experiencing even moderate stress, your body releases adrenaline—an energy-generating hormone. Thus, it may be natural for your body to want to move during your speech, so move it. Trying to inhibit your body's natural tendency to move can increase your level of tension. Furthermore, research shows that some movement and gesticulation on the part of the speaker help hold the audience's attention and interest more effectively than standing still (Andersen, 1985). Perhaps this is because movement suggests energy, which may send the message that you're not emotionless but passionate about the topic you're talking about.
- Focus attention on the *message* you're delivering (the content of your speech), not the *messenger* who's delivering it (yourself). By remaining conscious of the ideas you're communicating to your listeners, you become less self-conscious about the impression you're making on them and their impression (evaluation) of you.
- If you continue to experience high levels of speech anxiety after implementing these strategies, seek advice and help from a professional in your Learning Center or Counseling Center.

◆ Summary and Conclusion

Improving performance on college exams involves strategies used in advance of the test, during the test, and after test results are returned. Good test performance begins with good test preparation and adjustment of your study strategy to the type of test you'll be taking (e.g., multiple-choice or essay test).

You can learn and improve your grades not only by preparing for tests but also by reviewing your tests and using them as feedback to apply as you continue in the course. Past mistakes shouldn't be ignored or neglected; they should be detected and corrected so that they're not replayed on future tests.

Since speaking and writing both involve communicating thoughts in the form of words, many of the strategies for strengthening written reports are effective for strengthening oral presentations (e.g., knowing the purpose of the presentation, revising and editing, and developing a strong introduction and conclusion).

Writing and speaking are essential skills for effective performance in all academic and professional fields. The time and energy you invest in developing these communication skills will pay huge dividends toward promoting your success in college and beyond.

Learning More Through the World Wide Web

Internet-Based Resources for Further Information on Research, Writing, and Speaking

For additional information related to ideas discussed in this chapter, we recommend the following Web sites:

Test-Taking Strategies: www.muskingum.edu/~cal/database/general/testtaking.html

Writing Strategies: www.enhancemywriting.com/

Public Speaking Skills: www.public-speaking.org

9.1 Midterm Self-Evaluation

Since you are near the midpoint of this text book, you may be near the midpoint of your first term in college. At this time of the term you are likely to experience the midterm crunch—a wave of midterm exams and due dates for certain papers and projects. This may be a good time to step back and assess your academic progress thus far.

Use the form that follows to list the courses you're taking this term and the grades you are currently receiving in each of these courses. If you do not know what your grade is, take a few minutes to check your syllabus for your instructor's grading policy and add up your scores on completed tests and assignments; this should give you at least a rough idea of where you stand in your courses. If you're having difficulty determining your grade in any course, even after checking your course syllabus and returned tests or assignments, then ask your instructor how you could estimate your current grade.

Course No.	Course Title	Instructor	Grade
1.			
2.			
3.			
4.			
5.			

Self-Assessment Questions

1. Were these the grades you were hoping for? Are you pleased or disappointed by them?

2. Were these the grades you expected to get? If not, were they better or worse than expected?

3. Do you see any patterns in your performance that suggest things you are doing well or things that you need to improve?

4. If you had to pinpoint one action you could immediately take to improve your lowest course grades, what would it be?

9.2 Calculating Your Midterm Grade Point Average

Use the information in the following box to calculate what your grade point average (GPA) would be if these grades turn out to be your final course grades for the term.

Snapshot Summary

9.1

How to Compute Your Grade-Point Average (GPA)

Most colleges and universities use a grading scale that ranges from 0 to 4.0 to represent a student's grade-point average (GPA) or quality-point average (QPA). Some schools use letter grades only, while other institutions use letter grades with pluses and minuses.

Grading System Using Letters Only

Grade = Point value

A = 4
B = 3
C = 2
D = 1
F = 0

GRADE POINTS Earned Per Course = Course Grade Multiplied by the Number of Course Credits

$$\text{GRADE POINT AVERAGE (GPA)} = \frac{\text{Total Number of Grade Points for all Courses}}{\text{Divided by Total Number of Course Units}}$$

SAMPLE/EXAMPLE

Course	Units	×	Grade	=	Grade Points
Roots of Rock 'n' Roll	3	×	C (2)	=	6
Daydreaming Analysis	3	×	A (4)	=	12
Surfing Strategies	1	×	A (4)	=	4
Wilderness Survival	4	×	B (3)	=	12
Sitcom Analysis	2	×	D (1)	=	2
Love and Romance	3	×	A (4)	=	12
	16				48

$$\text{GPA} = \frac{48}{16} = 3.0$$

1. What is your overall GPA at this point in the term?

2. When this term began, what GPA were you hoping to attain?

3. Do you think your actual GPA the end of the term will be higher or lower than it is now? Why?

Notes

It's normal for GPAs to be lower in college than they were in high school, particularly after the first of college. Here are the results of one study that compared students' high school GPAs with the GPAs after their first year of college:

- 29% of beginning college students had GPAs of 3.75 or higher in high school, but only 17% had GPAs that high at the end of their first year of college.
- 46% had high school GPAs between 3.25 and 3.74, but only 32% had GPAs that high after the first year of college (National Resource Center for the First-Year Experience and Students in Transition, 2004).

9.3 Preparing an Oral Presentation on Student Success

1. Scan this textbook and identify a chapter topic or chapter section that you find most interesting or most important.

2. Create an introduction for a class presentation on this topic that

    a. provides an overview or sneak preview of what you will cover in your presentation;

    b. grabs the attention of your audience (your classmates); and

    c. demonstrates the topic's relevance or importance for your audience.

3. Create a conclusion to your presentation that

    a. relates back to your introduction;

    b. highlights your most important point or points; and

    c. leaves a memorable last impression.

Bad Feedback: Shocking Midterm Grades

Joe Frosh has enjoyed his first weeks on campus. He has met lots of interesting people and feels that he fits in socially. He also likes that his college schedule does not require him to be in class for 5 to 6 hours per day, like it did in high school. This is the good news. The bad news is that unlike high school, where his grades were all As and Bs, his first midterm grades in college are three Cs, one D, and one F. He is stunned and a bit depressed by his midterm grades because he thought he was doing well. Since he never received grades this low in high school, he's beginning to think that he is not college material and may flunk out.

Reflection and Discussion Questions

1. What factors may have caused or contributed to Joe's bad start?

2. What are Joe's options at this point?

3. What do you recommend Joe do now to get his grades up and avoid being placed on academic probation?

4. What might Joe do in the future to prevent this midterm setback from happening again?

Crime and Punishment: Plagiarism and Its Consequences

In an article that appeared in an Ohio newspaper, titled "Plagiarism persists in classrooms," an English professor was quoted as saying: "Technology has made it easier to plagiarize because students can download papers and exchange information and papers through their computers. But technology has also made it easier to catch students who plagiarize." This professor's college now subscribes to a Web site that matches the content of students' papers with content from books and online sources. Many professors now require students to submit their papers through this Web site. If students are caught plagiarizing, for a first offense, they typically receive an F for the assignment or the course. A second offense can result in dismissal or expulsion from college, which has already happened to a few students.

Source: Mariettatimes.com (March 22, 2006).

1. Why do you think students plagiarize? What do you suspect are the primary motives, reasons, or causes?

2. What do you think is a fair or just penalty for those found guilty of a first violation plagiarism? What is fair for those who commit a second violation?

3. How do you think plagiarism could be most effectively reduced or prevented from happening?

4. What could students do to minimize or eliminate plagiarism?

5. What could professors do to minimize or eliminate plagiarism?

Your First Year Resources

The first year of college is an exciting and challenging time. We want you to have the best experience possible, so we've designed a website just for you. It's full of tips, tricks, and links to help you make the most of Your First Year! If you have questions or need help finding your way at UNCG, you can always email us at yfy@uncg.edu. Visit yourfirstyear.uncg.edu and the websites below for helpful resources and services about achieving peak levels of academic performance.

Office of Accessibility Resources & Services   336-334-5440
http://ods.uncg.edu

Student Success Center   336-334-3878
http://success.uncg.edu/

The University Speaking Center   336-256-1346
http://speakingcenter.uncg.edu/default.php

The Writing Center   336-334-3125
http://www.uncg.edu/eng/writingcenter/default.php

Students First Office   336-334-5730
http://studentsfirst.uncg.edu/

Getting Started on Your First Speech

© Ashley Whitworth, 2008. Under license from Shutterstock, Inc.

"Speech is a mirror of the soul:
as a man speaks, so is he."

—Publilius Syrus (c. 42 b.c.)

Eight Steps for Preparing to Speak

1. Decide on a Topic
2. Demonstrate Ethical Behavior Throughout the Process
3. Determine the General Purpose, Specific Purpose, and Thesis Statement
   General Purpose
   Specific Purpose
   Thesis Statement
4. Define the Audience
   What does the audience know about me?
   What does the audience know about my specific purpose?
   What are my audience's views on my topic and purpose?
   How do audience members define themselves as an audience?
   How does the setting and speech occasion influence my audience?
   What other factors may affect how the audience responds?
5. Document Ideas Through Support and Sound Reasoning
   Use Facts
   Provide Statistics
   Illustrate Using Examples
   Include Testimony
   Construct Analogies

6. Draft the Introduction, Body, and Conclusion
   Introduction
   Body
   Conclusion
7. Develop the Language of the Speech with Care
   Use Plain English
   Remember That Writing and Speaking Are Different Activities
   Relate Your Language to Your Audience's Level of Knowledge
   Use Language for Specific Effect
8. Deliver Your Speech While Making Your Tension Work for You
   Verbal and Nonverbal Delivery
   Strategies for Controlling Tension

Summary

Questions for Study and Discussion

Activities

References

For some, speaking in public can be an exciting, adrenalin-producing activity, but for others, it is a dreaded experience to be feared. Whereas some will jump at the chance to perform in public, others will do just about anything to avoid standing, let alone speaking, before a group of people. A few years ago, there was a community fundraiser at a local restaurant. People gathered for a meal, a silent auction, and some entertainment. Those in charge of entertainment thought it would be fun to select some community members to provide the group with a rendition of the song "YMCA." Wendell, an enormously successful businessman, was chosen to participate. He stood up, opened his wallet, and took out $50, stating, "I won't do it, but I'll pay my way out." His money was welcomed, and Wendell was allowed to choose the person to replace him. He chose John, another successful businessman. John stood up, opened his wallet, and shelled out $50. John then selected Bob, a restaurant owner, who opened his wallet, frowned, showed the crowd he only had $2, and said, "I guess I'm in!"

Think about your response to this situation. Some of you may have jumped at the idea of performing "YMCA." After all, most of the people knew each other, and the atmosphere was festive. But for those of you with real apprehension, the comfort of a friendly group is not good enough.

Lack of preparation time may have influenced Wendell and John's apprehension. Wendell confesses his dislike of public speaking, no matter what the circumstances. He admits that not having a college education, combined with his own poor perception of his speaking skills make public speaking one of the worst possible situations for him to endure.

Whether you embrace the opportunity for public speaking or feel the urge to run away, there are many things you can do to enhance your potential for success. Following is an overview of eight key steps you should follow when preparing and presenting a speech. This overview is particularly important for your first speech. Keep in mind that you will most likely move back and forth among the steps. The chapter ahead is designed to provide more detail so you may increase your knowledge about public speaking and your skill as a speaker and as a listener.

◆ Eight Steps for Preparing to Speak

1. Decide on a topic.
2. Demonstrate ethical behavior throughout the process.
3. Determine the general purpose, specific purpose, and thesis statement.
4. Define your audience.
5. Document your ideas through firm support and sound reasoning.
6. Draft the beginning, middle, and end.
7. Develop the language of your speech with care.
8. Deliver your speech while making your tension work for you.

1. Decide on a Topic

A difficult task for students beginning the study and practice of public speaking is to select a topic. Some instructors will give you a topic and others will provide strict limits. If you can choose, however, often the best place to begin your search for a speech topic is yourself. When the topic springs from your own interests, you bring to it personal involvement, motivation, and the information necessary for a good speech.

If you choose a speech topic that you're interested in, the audience will share in your enthusiasm.

For example, Courtney found herself preoccupied with choosing the topic for her informative speech. As she reflected on her possibilities, she thought about her two years' experience at a local day care center before college. She realized she could speak to her classmates about how working at a day care led to her decision to work with children as her vocation. She felt earning a degree in education would open more doors, and she stressed the notion of getting some experience through work or internship in one's area of interest before completing a major. Her speech was full of informative anecdotes and her enthusiasm made the speech highly effective.

Perhaps you have some interesting work experience to share with your class, or an amazing travel story, or maybe a life-changing service learning experience. In any case, if at all possible, choose your first speech topic from what you know best.

If no ideas come to you when thinking about a speech topic, try the following. Write down two or three broad categories representing subjects of interest to you, and divide the categories into parts. You might begin, for example, with the broad areas of politics and sports. From these general topics useful lists will emerge.

Politics

1. Campus politics
2. Political corruption
3. Contemporary political campaign tactics

Sports

1. Learning from participation in sports
2. The challenges facing student athletes
3. Why NASCAR races are increasingly popular

As your list of choices grows, you will probably find yourself coming back to the same topic or a variation of it. For example, "Football after college" could be added to "The challenges facing student athletes." Perhaps your brother played college football, and then attempted to join a professional football league. You could talk about his experiences, including successes and failures. Now you have your topic.

Do not assume, however, that *any* topic is relevant. Before choosing a topic, make sure you know the amount of time you have to speak, your level of knowledge about the topic, and the needs of your audience. A five-minute speech is not supposed to last ten minutes; it is not even supposed to last six. In some public situations, you may be in danger of getting cut off if your speech is too long. If you have a wealth of information, you need to determine what must be left out. If you do not have much knowledge about the topic, recognize where you need to do research, or choose another topic. If you know about the background of your audience, you can decide what information is most relevant and how much time should be spent on each point.

2. Demonstrate Ethical Behavior Throughout the Process

A consideration of ethics is important in virtually all aspects of speech development, including, but certainly not limited to, how you approach a topic, where you get information, how you edit or interpret information, word choice, and distinguishing between your own ideas and those which need to be cited. **Plagiarism,** which involves using other's work, words, or ideas without adequate acknowledgement, has never been easier than it is today, according to Plagiarism.org (p.1). Add the ability to send files and share information via computers to the overwhelming amount of information available through the Internet, and the potential for engaging in unethical behavior is enormous.

Ethics are being discussed within the context of many disciplines, including medicine, psychology, business, and communication. It is relatively easy to find stories in the newspaper concerning ethical issues. According to communication professor Bert Bradley, "Speakers have ethical responsibilities which must be accepted if rhetoric is to play its most meaningful role in communication" (Bradley 1998, 47). That said, government officials have failed to speak truthfully until forced to do so, deception continues to be uncovered in the nation's business practices, and students, when questioned anonymously, admit to what can be described as wide-spread cheating.

On August 24, 2006, the Associated Press reported that "Allegations of criminal wrongdoing and ethical lapses among lawmakers are coloring a handful of competitive House and Senate races across the country this midterm election year." In October 2004, pop culture's Ashlee Simpson was derided for using a pre-recorded vocal track for a performance on *Saturday Night Live.* Certainly, politicians and pop stars are not the only ones engaging in unethical behavior. During the early months of 2006, Oprah Winfrey brought to task James Frey, author of the book *A Million Little Pieces.* On national television, Frey admitted to making up part of his "memoir," and his publisher discussed

© Fred Prouser/Reuters/Corbis.

Ashlee Simpson's pre-recorded vocals were accidentally exposed in a performance on *Saturday Night Live.*

how the firm was duped. More than 3.5 million people bought Frey's book assuming it was non-fiction.

These abuses have heightened our sensitivity to the need for honesty from all sources, including public speakers. Speakers may have different values and beliefs based on family, cultural, and educational backgrounds, but many ethical standards are considered universal.

Freedom of speech is a fundamental right in our democracy, and implied in this freedom is the speaker's responsibility to avoid deceiving others. As you think critically about your topic, your audience, supporting material, and so on, remain concerned for the welfare of others. Use accurate and current information, rely on sound reasoning, and present a speech that is your own, based on your independent research and views. Remember to cite sources and to quote and paraphrase correctly when you present information or ideas that are not your own.

3. Determine the General Purpose, Specific Purpose, and Thesis Statement

The time you spend preparing your speech may be of little value if you do not determine what you want your speech to accomplish. At the beginning, you should clarify the general and specific purposes of your speech. Then determine which statement will be the expression of your main idea; that is the thesis statement for your speech.

General Purpose

There are three general purposes for speeches: to inform, to persuade, and to entertain or inspire. If you want to explain the differences between a scooter and a motorcycle, the general purpose of your speech would be "to inform." If you hope to make people laugh after eating a good meal, your general purpose is "to entertain." If you want people to choose a hybrid for their next car, you are attempting "to persuade."

Keep in mind, however, that it is difficult to deliver a speech that is *just* informative or *just* persuasive or *just* entertaining. Often, in the perception of listeners, the purposes may converge or overlap. For example, as a speaker informs her audience about various options for eating a healthy breakfast each day, some audience members may interpret her speech as an attempt to persuade them to change their daily behavior.

Specific Purpose

Once the general purpose is set for your speech, determine the specific purpose. This is the precise response you want from your audience. Specific purpose statements should be expressed as an infinitive phrase that includes the general purpose as well as the main thrust of your speech. The specific purpose also identifies who the audience will be. Here are two examples of specific purposes:

1. To inform the class of differences between the operations of an on-campus political club and an off-campus political party
2. To persuade the class that requiring all college students to participate in service-learning projects benefits the student, college, and community

Because the specific purpose identifies the audience who will hear your speech, it guides you in speech preparation. A speech on health care reform given before a group of college students would be different than a speech on the same topic given before an audience of retirees. Obviously, the second audience has a much more immediate need for reform than the first group of listeners. The speech would be different because the older listeners usually feel a greater overall need to deal with health issues.

Thesis Statement

While the general and specific purpose statements set the goals for your speech, the thesis statement, or your core idea, focuses on what you want to say. The thesis statement distills your speech to one sentence, summarizing your main idea. According to James Humes, a corporate speech consultant, Great Britain's Prime Minister Winston Churchill once sent back a pudding because he said it had no theme. (Kleinfield 1990). A well-defined theme is critical to your speech's success. The thesis statement is the central message you want listeners to take with them. The following examples show how one moves from a topic to the thesis statement.

Topic: Study abroad
General purpose: To inform
Specific purpose: To explain to my class what is involved in the study abroad options available to them at our university
Thesis statement: Students interested in earning college credit while studying abroad have several options that differ in terms of academic content, location, length of stay, potential number of credit hours, and cost.

Topic: Study abroad
General purpose: To persuade
Specific purpose: To convince my class that studying abroad will be a life-changing experience
Thesis statement: Studying abroad can be a life-changing experience because students gain knowledge in an academic area, face the unfamiliar, and interact with individuals from a different culture.

As you can see, although the topic is "study abroad," there are different aspects of studying abroad that one could address. The above example shows choices for an informative speech and persuasive speech. A speech with the general purpose to entertain could include humorous examples and illustrations of the trials and tribulations of studying abroad.

4. Define the Audience

As stated throughout, public speaking is an audience-centered activity. Your reason for presenting a speech is to communicate your message to others in the clearest and most convincing way. When preparing your specific purpose you must define your audience. *An effective speaker analyzes and adapts to the audience.* This involves finding out as much as possible about your audience. What are their demographics (age, race, gender, religious affiliation, political affiliation, etc.)? What is their level of knowledge about your topic? Is the audience there because they want to be? Do they lean toward your point of view, or away from it? Critical thinking skills are valuable here as you determine these parameters.

The initial way to approach your responsibility as an audience-centered speaker is to find answers to the following six pertinent questions.

What Does the Audience Know About Me?

Outside of the classroom, you may become a spokesperson for an issue, a cause, or an organization. Generally speaking, your audience will have some basic information about you. In college, characteristics such as age, gender, race, and level of education are easily known, but you may need to include relevant background information at the beginning of your speech. For example, if you wanted to talk about the problems associated with children of state and federal prisoners and your father worked in the prison system, it would be helpful to note this as you begin your speech.

What Does the Audience Know About My Specific Purpose?

The amount of supporting material you include and the extent to which you explain or elaborate are influenced by the expertise of your audience. If you are speaking to a group of cardiologists on the need to convince pregnant women to stop smoking, you can assume far greater audience knowledge than if you were to deliver the same message to a group of concerned citizens.

What Are the Audience's Views on My Topic and Purpose?

Attitudes can be more important than information in determining how your audience responds to a message. It is natural to expect some preconceived attitudes about what you are hoping to accomplish. The views of your audience should influence your choice of main points, the supporting material, and the way you develop your speech.

How Do Audience Members Define Themselves as an Audience?

Individuals who come together to listen to speeches often assume the cultural or organizational identity they share with the body of listeners. Is this a general group of college students? Conservatives? Music majors? At a city council meeting that addresses housing regulations in your community, you might be with several college students attending as tenants of rental property. At another city council meeting, you might gather with other college students because the council is discussing

It's important to consider the setting and the occasion when preparing to speak to better prepare.

changing the bar-entry age in the city. Though the same people might be in the audience, how you identify or define yourselves differs from situation to situation. In one instance, you and the other college students identify yourselves as renters. In the second situation, you are with college students who are interested in expanded entertainment options.

How Does the Setting and Occasion Influence My Audience?

The setting may be an indoor gymnasium or an outdoor stadium. The occasion may be a graduation ceremony or a funeral service. It helps a speaker to plan carefully when she or he learns in advance what the general feeling is about the setting and the occasion for the presentation. We recall when a member of the clergy drifted off from his main message and began talking about his old family gatherings during a Christmas Eve service when his audience was expecting to hear about the story of the birthday of Jesus and what this event means in our present day. The congregation grew very restless. Remember that it is harder to reach a **captive audience** (those who are required to attend) than a **voluntary audience** (those who choose to attend). Students who attend a guest lecture on campus simply to obtain extra credit to boost their grade in a class may feel somewhat indifferent, if not bored, while those who chose to attend because of a keen interest in the speech and speaker will feel much differently. As a speaker, you need to obtain some helpful information about audience attitudes toward the setting and occasion that will bring everyone together for the speech.

What Other Factors Might Affect How the Audience Responds?

Are you the first speaker of the day? The last speaker? Are you speaking at a convention in Las Vegas at 8:00 a.m.? Were the participants out late? Are you one of six students to give a speech during graduation ceremony? Are you the school board representative giving a speech at graduation? If you have knowledge of any factor that may influence your listeners' attentiveness, you can plan in advance ways to increase the likelihood that they will listen carefully. You can shorten the speech, include more vivid examples, and/or work to make your speech even more engaging.

As time goes by, you get to know your classmates and their concerns. Use that information to create interest and engage their attention. Reflect on the six questions identified above and then adapt your topic, language, support, and delivery based on what you decide.

5. Document Ideas Through Support and Sound Reasoning

Each point made before an audience should be backed up with reliable supporting information and sound reasoning. For example, if you want to persuade your audience that sales tax instead of real estate tax should be used to fund education, concrete evidence will be necessary to support your specific purpose. We want to point out five different ways that you can provide support.

Use Facts

Facts are verifiable. They hold more weight than opinions. If your specific purpose was to demonstrate how political campaigns have changed dramatically over the last several decades, you might include the following facts:

- In 1960 John Kennedy became the first presidential candidate to use his own polling specialist.
- In 1972 George McGovern pioneered mass direct-mail fundraising.
- In 1980 Jimmy Carter campaigned by conference phone calls to voters in Iowa and New Hampshire.

- In 1984 Ronald Reagan used satellite transmissions to appear at fundraisers and rallies.
- In 1988 a number of presidential hopefuls used videotapes to deliver their message to voters in the early primary states.
- In 1992 California Governor Jerry Brown introduced a 1-800 number for fundraising and answering questions.
- In 1996 candidates and prominent party supporters recorded one-minute phone calls that focused on issues believed to be important to voters.
- In 2007 Hillary Clinton established a website that included video snippets, news reports, an opportunity for blogging, and numerous ways to contribute to her presidential campaign.

© Brooks Kraft/Corbis.

These facts support the speaker's claim, and show how candidates have attempted to reach the masses over time. Keep in mind that you need to cite your sources as you provide the facts.

> For a speech on changes in political campaigns, you'd want to include the various methods Hillary Clinton implemented.

Provide Statistics

Providing statistics can offer strong support to your speech. Statistics inform, startle, and convince. In trying to convince his audience about the dramatic increase in the use of the Internet in political campaigns, one student cited the work of Bruce Bimber and Richard Davis:

> *The number of Internet sites is in the tens of millions. A 2001 survey of Internet usage found that the top ten sites together attracted just under 17 percent of all Internet traffic. Despite the undeniable clout of some key businesses in delivering content on the Internet, this is a far different media environment than when Kennedy and Nixon squared off on the three networks in 1960 (2003).*

Recognizing that Internet usage is increasing every day, a student giving a similar speech today could use statistics posted May 24, 2006 from "The Bivings Report." Survey results show that "ninety-six percent of this year's Senate candidates have active websites, while only fifty-five percent of candidates had websites in 2002" (www.bivingsreport.com). Statistics updated on June 30, 2006 reveal Internet users in the United States to be around 227,000,000, which reflects approximately seventy percent of the population (www.internetworldstats.com). These statistics provide useful support to the claim that technology has changed how candidates campaign. Keep in mind, however, that your speech should not be a laundry list of statistics.

Illustrate Using Examples

A third form of support is the use of examples to help illustrate a point or claim. Illustrations, especially detailed and current ones, help to clarify points and they may leave a lasting impression on your audience. If the purpose of your speech was "to convince the class that voters are influenced by information provided on the Internet," you might use the following illustration:

> *The use of computers by members of the general public has increased considerably in recent years. For example, my brother-in-law, Tom, and his friends pur-*

chased personal computers at some point before the last national campaign. Tom meets regularly with a group of friends who have retired after years of working in a nearby automobile plant. As they developed basic computer skills and surfed the Internet, they also began to pay attention to political news and advertisements. The information they gathered as individuals became subjects for their informal get-togethers leading up to the election. They reported to their friends and family members that the information from the Internet served as a strong influence on how they voted.

This example, along with other forms of support such as facts and statistics, can demonstrate to the audience the increasing use and effectiveness of the Internet in political campaigns. As an audience-centered speaker, you want to think of the best way to keep the attention of your audience, and provide support that is best suited to them.

Include Testimony

A fourth form of support is the use of testimony, which involves quoting someone's experience or opinion. Testimony can be a powerful form of support because everyone pays attention to an expert. Courts of law frequently call on the testimony of expert witnesses; televised news programs broadcast the observations of experts on newsworthy stories; and, from time to time, even commercials provide the endorsement of experts rather than celebrities to confirm the reliability of a product or service. So to prove, reinforce, or clarify a point, a public or presentational speaker often links his/her contention with a statement of a recognized expert on a subject.

Construct Analogies

Using analogies is a fifth form of support. This involves making comparisons to clarify or prove a point. They lend support by encouraging listeners to think in a novel way. **Figurative analogies** compare different kinds of things, and **literal analogies** compare similar categories. If you compare an argument with a sporting event, you are using a figurative analogy, but if you compare one college with another college, you are using a literal analogy. For example, in a speech about studying abroad, a student could use the following figurative analogy.

Studying abroad is like your first week in college. You're unfamiliar with the environment, you don't know the people who are around you, and you're not quite sure what to expect. But as the week goes on, you start to make friendships, your environment becomes more comfortable, and you start to get into some kind of predictable routine. Keep in mind, anytime you have a new experience, you'll experience some uncertainty.

Then, the literal analogy:

Studying abroad is similar to studying at this or any other university. You attend classes and take exams. You have a place to live, and dining options. You have to study, and you also have free time. The difference is, you're far from home, you aren't familiar with your environment, and people speak a different language.

6. Draft the Introduction, Body, and Conclusion

If you spend days researching your first speech but only a few hours organizing your ideas, the result is likely to be a speech that fails to present your message in a focused way. To be effective, speeches require an easy-to-follow organizational plan that makes it possible for others to receive and understand your message. The logical way to organize your speech is to divide it into three parts: the introduction, body, and conclusion.

As you draft your speech, lay it out into the three parts. Construct a comprehensive, full-sentence outline and work to tie the sentences into a coherent whole. Then, reduce these sentences to key words and phrases and transfer them onto speaker's notes, which will serve as your guide when you deliver your speech. A well-thought out, clearly constructed outline and speaker's notes will greatly increase the potential for success. The following paragraphs highlight important aspects to consider as you develop your first speech.

© Stephen VanHorn, 2008. Under license from Shutterstock, Inc.

Choose your words with care to convey your message in the best way possible.

Introduction

The introduction should capture the attention and interest of your audience, establish your credibility as a speaker, and preview your speech. You can accomplish these aims in many ways, such as humorous anecdotes or a dramatic or startling statement. Jonathan Esslinger, a student at the University of Wisconsin, spoke about the conditions and trends of the U.S. national parks.

In his introduction, Jonathan captures our attention through his vivid description of the landscape. He establishes credibility by using *Audubon* as supporting material, showing us he has done research. Finally, in his last sentence, he presents a preview statement, which lets his audience know what he intends to cover in the body of his speech. He accomplishes the three goals of an effective introduction.

Body

The body of your speech contains your key ideas and relevant supporting material. It is the most time-consuming aspect of speech development. Frequently, speakers work on the body before the introduction, because gaps in logic or information may be discovered as the body is developed. Main points should flow from the thesis statement. To be effective, the speech needs to follow some logical pattern. You have at least five patterns of organization to consider: chronological, topical, spatial, cause and effect, and problem-solution.

Conclusion

Your concluding remarks have three purposes: (1) to reinforce the message, (2) to summarize the main points, and (3) to provide closure in some way that relates your message to your listeners' lives. Main ideas will be summarized. Your final thought may take the form of a quotation, a statement, or a question that reinforces or even broadens the purpose of your speech. The conclusion of a persuasive speech may also describe the specific actions you want your listeners to take.

7. Develop the Language of the Speech with Care

An enthusiastic young woman looked out into the audience of almost 1,500 people on her graduation day and was overwhelmed with the spirit that marked this important occasion. A hush fell over the crowd as she began her address as president of the senior class: "You guys are all terrific! Awesome! This has been an awesome four years for us, right? Like, we have really made it! Wow!" As she proceeded, reflecting on the events of the past four years, her comments were laced with slang that may have been suitable for the coffee shop or gatherings with friends, but not for such a special occasion.

The words you choose to convey your message reflect your personality, your attitude toward your subject, occasion, and audience, and your concern for communicating effectively. Words are your primary vehicle for creating meaning. They set forth ideas, spark visions, arouse concerns, elicit emotions, but if not used carefully, produce confusion. The following four guidelines will help you choose your words with care.

Use Plain English

Let simple, direct language convey your message. Your audience should not need an interpreter. You could say "contusion" or "ecchymosis," but most audiences would find the word "bruise" clearer. Also, it is generally best to avoid the use of slang.

Remember That Writing and Speaking Are Different Activities

While in a written report the terms "edifice," "regulations," and "in the eventuality of," may be acceptable; in public speaking the words, "building," "rules," and "if," are far more effective.

Relate Your Language to Your Audience's Level of Knowledge

If you are describing drug testing in professional sports, do not assume your audience understands such terms as "false positives," "chain of custody," and "legal and individual safeguards." If you use these terms in your speech, you should define them in order to keep the message clear.

Use Language for Specific Effect

If your goal is to sensitize your audience to the plight of America's working poor, the following statement is not incorrect, but it may be ineffective: *"Although millions of Americans work a full day, they cannot pay their bills or provide for their families."*

For a more powerful effect, you might try the following alternative: *"Millions of Americans come home each day, exhausted and covered with a layer of factory filth or kitchen grease. Their backbreaking labor has given them few rewards: They cannot pay their rent, buy shoes for their children, or eat meat more than once a week."* Clearly, the second version paints memorable word pictures. Keep your audience in mind as you choose effective language for communicating your ideas.

8. Deliver Your Speech While Making Your Tension Work for You

As we noted earlier, you are not alone if you have some tension or anxiety about speaking in front of an audience. Most likely, you will engage in some in-class activities to help you feel more comfortable speaking in class. In the next several paragraphs, we first focus on delivery and then discuss how to make tension work for you.

Verbal and Nonverbal Delivery

Vocal elements of delivery include, but are certainly not limited to: volume, articulation and pronunciation, pacing, and avoiding "fillers." Nonverbal aspects include: eye contact, gestures, and movement. Your audience is not expecting perfection, but you do not want to create a situation where your lack of effective vocal and/or physical delivery keeps you from achieving your goals.

Your audience must hear you. No matter how convincing or eloquent your speech is designed to be, if you speak too softly your audience cannot hear your message and will not be able to respond. Be aware that your pace (rate of speech) may be slower in the comfort of your dorm room than it is in front of your class. Some nervous speakers unconsciously race through their speech. Normally rapid speakers should try to slow down. Varying your pace can aid in maintaining audience interest and draw attention to certain parts of your speech.

© Yuri Arcurs, 2008. Under license from Shutterstock, Inc.

Speak conversationally and use eye contact and facial expression to hold your audience's attention.

Proper **articulation**, the verbalization of distinct sounds, is important in formal speaking situations. Saying "hafta," "gonna," and "wanna" is discouraged. Also, if you have any question about the correct pronunciation of a word, check on it before your speech. When speakers mispronounce words, the audience may infer a lack of knowledge, interest, or preparation.

We also encourage you to avoid **vocal fillers.** In casual conversation, it is common to hear people say "you know," or "like," or "you know what I mean?" In front of a public audience, these pauses may be filled with "ah," or "um," or "er." Fillers can be awkward or distracting and should be reduced and, if possible, eliminated.

In addition to working on the verbal aspects of your speech, you need to tune in to the nonverbal aspects of your speech. Even if your verbal message is well developed and solidly researched, remaining frozen or slouching in front of your audience is likely to distract from what you intend to communicate. Look at your audience. Through eye contact a speaker can establish a connection with the audience. Your facial expression should match the tone of your voice. Speak conversationally, and use movement, nonverbal gestures, and appropriate facial expressions to provide meaning to your words as well as to gain and maintain your audience's attention. And do not forget, enthusiasm is contagious! For some, this is difficult, but choosing a topic that truly interests you and practicing your speech repeatedly can help greatly.

Strategies for Controlling Tension

The chances are slim of being "cured" of communication apprehension, to use an academic term. However, we can provide some help. One thing to consider is that a major symptom of "speech tension" is a physiological reaction. Most people experience three stages of physiological arousal immediately before and during the first few moments of a speech. The *anticipatory stage* takes place in the minutes before the speech—heart rates zoom from a normal testing rate of about 70 beats per minute to between 95 and 140. The *confrontational stage* is typically at the beginning of the speech, when heart rates jump to between 110 and 190 beats per minute. This stage usually lasts no more than thirty seconds and gives way to the *post-confrontational stage*. This final stage is when the pulse returns to anticipation levels or lower. Confrontation experienced in stage two is so strong that speakers may not perceive the decrease. As a nervous speaker, you may stop feeling nervous without realizing it (Motley 1988).

Most fearful speakers experience the symptoms of a dry mouth and sweaty palms, and sometimes even heavy breathing. These symptoms are the body's "fight or flight" response. People who experience speech tension often feel the urge to withdraw (Run away! Run away!). We are not always aware of this desire. Even as we convince ourselves that we are not nervous, our nonverbal behavior may reveal our unconscious discomfort. Below are several strategies for controlling tension.

Many strategies are available for reducing anxiety. Ultimately, your goal is to channel this nervous energy into public speaking with self-confidence.

1. *Focus on your message and your audience, not yourself.* Keep your mind on your message and the best way to convey it to your audience. Always think of your audience as being on your side.
2. *Prepare!* Preparation sharpens your presentation and builds confidence. Start with a sound speech plan and then rehearse the speech aloud by yourself. Then practice in front of others to get the feel and response of an audience.
3. *Take several deep breaths.* Deep breathing has a calming effect on the body and mind. We have used this technique ourselves and find our students have used it with success as well. You can do this as you are waiting to speak. It also helps to take a final deep breath after you get in front of the audience and just before you speak. Try it!
4. *Realize that you may be your own worst critic.* Studies have shown that the amount of tension a speaker reports has little relationship to the amount of nervousness an audience detects. Even listeners trained to detect tension often fail to perceive it (Motley 1988, 47).
5. *Gain proficiency and confidence by choosing to speak.* Find opportunities to speak. Give "mini speeches" at meetings or in classes when discussion is invited. A colleague of ours conquered his considerable fear of public speaking before an audience and became a successful speaker in large lecture classes by volunteering to speak whenever a situation was convenient and available.
6. *Visualize your success as a speaker.* Creating powerful mental images of skillful performances and winning competitions is a technique that has been used for years by athletes who use visualization to help them succeed. This technique can also be used in public speaking. Visualize yourself speaking with confidence and self-assurance and imagine the sound of applause after your presentation (Ayers, Hopf, and Myers 1997).

7. *Release tension through assertive and animated delivery.* Here is where a nervous speaker may be caught between a rock and a hard place. Being nervous can inhibit your delivery, but assertive and animated delivery can provide a release from pent-up tension. So, if you are prepared to speak, you have practiced speaking out loud, and you focus on your audience, you will be able to gesture, use eye contact, and move—all means for releasing nervous energy.

We encourage you to try several of these suggestions during your first speech. You may not overcome your fear of speaking, but you may reduce it, and you may use your nervous energy productively. Keep in mind, nothing substitutes for preparation and practice. Just like when getting ready for a piano recital, choral concert, or a competitive sports activity, the more you practice, the more you learn, and the greater the likelihood of success.

◆ Summary

As public speaking instructors, we would prefer to cover everything in this text *before* you give a graded speech. However, we know that is not possible. That said, this chapter was designed to help you with your first speech as well as to provide a preview of the text. We have outlined eight steps for preparing to speak; each step involves reflection and decision-making. Remember to choose a topic you care about, engage in ethical behavior, determine the purpose of your speech and, as you develop your speech, use language that is appropriate and relevant to your audience. Focus on your audience. As you practice your speech, work on nonverbal aspects of delivery, such as eye contact, gestures, and movement. Find strategies to reduce tension and project enthusiasm and self-confidence.

◆ Questions for Study and Discussion

1. What factors should you keep in mind when choosing a topic and framing a purpose for speaking?
2. Discuss with members of your class what is understood to be the relationships between a speaker's link to a topic, choice of a purpose, amount of information available, and the needs of the audience.
3. Although degrees of speech tension vary from speaker to speaker, most inexperienced speakers share common feelings of discomfort. What can you do to minimize your feelings of apprehension and make your nervous energy work *for* you rather than against you?

◆ Activities

1. Take an inventory of what you believe to be your own strengths and weaknesses as a public speaker and establish goals as well as expectations you intend to pursue as you participate in this course.
2. Make a list of the basic steps in preparing your first speech for class. Study your list to see how it relates to the steps featured in this chapter.

3. Prepare and deliver a five- to six-minute informative speech. Draw the topic from your own experiences or interests and not from one of your college courses.

◆ References

Ayers, J., T. Hopf, and D. M. Myers. 1997. Visualization and performance visualization: Application, evidence, and speculation. In J.A. Daly, J. C. McCroskey, J. Ayers, T. Hopf, and D.M. Ayers (Eds.), *Avoiding communication* (305–330). Cresskill, NJ: Hampton Press.

Bimber, B., and R. Davis. 2003. *Campaigning online: The Internet in U.S. elections.* New York: Oxford.

Bradley, B. 1988. *Fundamentals of speech communication, (5th ed.)* Dubuque, IA: Wm. C. Brown.

Esslinger, J.J. 1992. "National parks: A scenery of destruction and degradation." In *Winning orations of the interstate oratorical association.* WI: Mankato State University.

Motley, M. T. 1988. Taking the terror out of talk. *Psychology Today,* 46–49.

Your First Year Resources

The first year of college is an exciting and challenging time. We want you to have the best experience possible, so we've designed a website just for you. It's full of tips, tricks, and links to help you make the most of Your First Year! If you have questions or need help finding your way at UNCG, you can always email us at yfy@uncg.edu. Visit yourfirstyear.uncg.edu and the websites below for helpful resources and services to assist with getting started on your first speech.

Foundations for Learning Program   336-334-5730
http://studentsfirst.uncg.edu/ffl/resources.php

The University Speaking Center   336-256-1346
http://speakingcenter.uncg.edu/default.php

Educational Planning and Decision Making

Making Wise Choices About Your College Courses and College Major

Are you decided or undecided about a college major?

_____

_____

If you are undecided, what subjects might be possibilities?

_____

_____

_____

If you are decided, what is your choice and why did you choose this major?

_____

_____

_____

How sure are you about that choice? (Circle one.)

- Absolutely sure
- Fairly sure
- Not too sure
- Likely to change

LEARNING GOAL

To develop strategies for exploring different academic fields and for choosing an educational path that will enable you to achieve your personal and occupational goals.

◆ To Be or Not to Be Decided About a College Major: What the Research Shows

Whether you have or have not decided on a major, here are some research findings related to student decisions about college majors that may be worth keeping in mind:

- Less than 10 percent of new college students feel they know a great deal about the field that they intend to major in.
- As students proceed through the first year of college, they grow more uncertain about the major they chose when they began college.
- More than two-thirds of new students change their mind about their major during the first year of college.
- Only one in three college seniors eventually major in the same field that they chose during their first year of college (Cuseo, 2005).

These findings point to the conclusion that the vast majority of students entering college are truly undecided about a college major. Most students do not make definite and final decisions about their major *before* starting their college experience; instead, they make these decisions *during* the college experience. Being uncertain about a major is nothing to be embarrassed about. The terms "undecided" and "undeclared" don't mean that you have somehow failed or are lost. As a new student, you may be undecided for various good reasons. For instance, you may be undecided simply because you have interests in various subjects. This is a healthy form of indecision because it shows that you have a range of interests and a high level of motivation to learn about different subjects. You may also be undecided simply because you are a careful, reflective thinker whose decision-making style is to gather more information before making any long-term commitments.

In one study of students who were undecided about a major when they started college, 43 percent had several ideas in mind but were not yet ready to commit to one of them (Gordon & Steele, 2003). These students were not clueless; instead, they had some ideas but still wanted to explore them and keep their options open, which is an effective way to go about making decisions.

As a first-year student, it's only natural to be at least somewhat uncertain about your educational goals because you have not yet experienced the variety of subjects and academic programs that make up the college curriculum. You may encounter fields of study in college that you never knew existed. One purpose of general education is to help new students develop the critical thinking skills needed to make wise choices and well-informed decisions, such as their choice of college major. The liberal arts curriculum is also designed to introduce you to various academic subjects, and as you progress through this curriculum, you may discover subjects that captivate you and capture your interest. Some of these subjects may represent fields of study that you never experienced before, and all of them represent possible choices for a college major.

In addition to finding new fields of possible interest, as you gain experience with the college curriculum, you are likely to gain more self-knowledge about your academic strengths and weaknesses. This is important knowledge to take into consideration when choosing a major, because you want to select a field that builds on your academic abilities and talents.

> "All who wander are not lost."
>
> –J. R. R. Tolkien, *Lord of the Rings*

Student Perspective

"The best words of wisdom that I could give new freshmen [are] not to feel like you need to know what you want to major in right away. They should really use their first two years to explore all of the different classes available. They may find a hidden interest in something they never would have considered. I know this from personal experience."

–Advice to new students from a college sophomore (Walsh, 2005)

It's true that people can take too long and procrastinate on reaching decisions; however, it's also true that they can make decisions too quickly that result in premature choices made without sufficient reflection and careful consideration of all options. Judging from the large number of students who end up changing their minds about a college major, it's probably safe to say that more students make the mistake of reaching a decision about a major too quickly rather than procrastinating about it indefnitely. This may be because students hear the same question repeatedly, even before they step a foot on a college campus: "What are you going to major in when you go to college?" You probably also saw this question on your college applications, and you are likely to hear it again during your first term in college. The beginning of your college experience is when you'll meet many new people, and one of the first questions you're likely to hear from them soon after they meet you will be "What's your major?" Family members are also likely to ask you the same question, particularly if they're helping to pay the high cost of a college education, because they want some assurance that their investment will pay off and they feel more assured if they know you have a clear idea about what you're doing in college (your major) and what you'll do after college (your career).

Despite pressure you may be receiving from others to make an early decision, we encourage you not to make it an official and final commitment to a major until you gain more self-knowledge and more knowledge of your options. Even if you think you're sure about your choice of major, before you make a commitment to it, take a course or two in the major to test it out and confirm whether or not your choice is compatible with your personal interests, talents, and values.

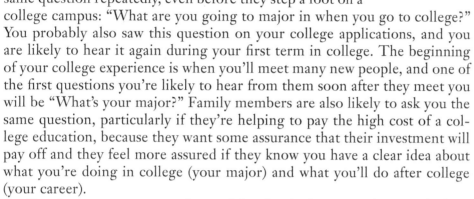

Pause for Reflection

If you have chosen a major or are considering a particular major, what or who led you to choose or consider this option?

Student Perspective

"I see so many people switch [their] major like 4 or 5 times; they end up having to take loads of summer school just to catch up because they invest time and money in classes for a major that they end up not majoring in anyway."

–College sophomore (Walsh, 2005)

◆ When Should You Reach a Firm Decision About a College Major?

It's OK to start off not knowing what your major will be and to give yourself some time and college experience before reaching a decision. You can take courses that will count toward your degree and stay on track for graduation, even if you haven't decided or declared your college major.

Similarly, if you've entered college with a major in mind, there's still time to change your mind without falling behind. If you realize that your first choice of a major wasn't a good choice, don't think that you're locked into your original plan and you're only options are to stick with it throughout college or drop out of college. Changing your original educational plans is not necessarily a bad thing. It may mean that you have discovered another field that's more interesting to you or that's more compatible with your personal interests and talents.

The only downside to changing your educational plan is that if you make that change late in your college experience it can result in more time to graduation (and more tuition) because you may need to complete additional courses for your newly chosen field. The key to preventing this scenario from happening later is to be proactive now by engaging in long-range educational planning.

"When you get to a fork in the road, take it."

–Yogi Berra, Hall of Fame baseball player

! Remember

As a rule, you should reach a fairly firm decision about your major during your second (sophomore) year in college. However, to reach a good decision within this time frame, the process of exploring and planning should begin now—during your first term in college.

◆ The Importance of Long-Range Educational Planning

College will allow you many choices about what courses to enroll in and what field to specialize in. By looking ahead and developing a tentative plan for your courses beyond the first term of college, you will position yourself to view your college experience as a full-length movie and get a sneak preview of the total picture. In contrast, scheduling your classes one term at a time just before each registration period (when everyone else is making a mad rush to get their advisor's signature for the following term's classes) forces you to view your academic experience as a series of short, separate snapshots that lack connection or direction.

Long-range educational planning also enables you to take a proactive approach to your future. Being proactive means you are taking early, preventative action that anticipates events before they sneak up on you, forcing you to react to events in your life without time to plan your best strategy. As the old saying goes, "If you fail to plan, you plan to fail." Through advanced planning, you can actively take charge of your academic future and make it happen *for* you, rather than waiting and passively letting it happen *to* you.

"When you have to make a choice and don't make it, that is in itself a choice."

–William James, philosopher and one of the founders of American psychology

> **! Remember**
>
> Any long-range plan you develop is not set in stone; it can change depending on changes in your academic interests and future plans. The purpose of long-range planning is not to lock you into a particular plan but to free you from shortsightedness, procrastination, or denial about choosing to control your future.

Don't take the denial and avoidance approach to planning your educational future.

"Education is our passport to the future, for tomorrow belongs to the people who prepare for it today."

–Malcolm X, African American Muslim minister, public speaker, and human rights activist

Factors to Consider When Choosing Your Major or Field of Study

Gaining self-awareness is the critical first step in making decisions about a college major, or any other important decision. You must know yourself before you can know what choice is best for you. While this may seem obvious, self-awareness and self-discovery are often overlooked aspects of the decision-making process. In particular, you need awareness of your

- Interests—what you like doing;
- Abilities—what you're good at doing; and
- Values—what you feel good about doing.

> **Pause for Reflection**
>
> Consider the following statement: "Choosing a major is a life-changing decision because it will determine what you do for the rest of your life."
>
> Would you agree or disagree with this statement?
>
> Why?

Furthermore, research indicates that students are more likely to continue in college and graduate when they choose majors that reflect their personal interests (Leuwerke et al., 2004).

Multiple Intelligences: Identifying Personal Abilities and Talents

One element of the self that you should be aware of when choosing a major is your mental strengths, abilities, or talents. Intelligence was once considered to be one general trait that could be detected and measured by an intelligence quotient (IQ) test. Now, the singular word "intelligence" has been replaced by the plural word "intelligences" to reflect that humans can display intelligence or mental ability in many forms other than their paper-and-pencil performance on an IQ test.

Listed in **Box 11.1** are forms of intelligence identified by Howard Gardner (1983, 1993) from studies of gifted and talented individuals, experts in different lines of work, and various other sources. As you read through the types of intelligence, place a checkmark next to the type that you think represents your strongest ability or talent. (You can possess more than one type.) Keep your type or types of intelligence in mind when you're choosing a college major. Ideally, you want to select a major that taps into and builds on your strongest skills or talents. Choosing a major that's compatible with your abilities should enable you to master the concepts and skills required by your major more rapidly and deeply. Furthermore, if you follow your academic talents, you're likely to succeed or excel in what you do, which will bolster your 'academic self-confidence and motivation.

Take Action!

Multiple Forms of Intelligence   11.1

- **Linguistic Intelligence.** Ability to communicate through words or language (e.g., verbal skills in the areas of speaking, writing, listening, or reading)
- **Logical–Mathematical Intelligence.** Ability to reason logically and succeed in tasks that involve mathematical problem solving (e.g., the skill for making logical arguments and following logical reasoning or the ability to think effectively with numbers and make quantitative calculations)
- **Spatial Intelligence.** Ability to visualize relationships among objects arranged in different spatial positions and ability to perceive or create visual images (e.g., forming mental images of three-dimensional objects; detecting detail in objects or drawings; artistic talent for drawing, painting, sculpting, and graphic design; or skills related to sense of direction and navigation)
- **Musical Intelligence.** Ability to appreciate or create rhythmical and melodic sounds (e.g., playing, writing, or arranging music)
- **Interpersonal (Social) Intelligence.** Ability to relate to others; to accurately identify others' needs, feelings, or emotional states of mind; and to effectively express emotions and feelings to others (e.g., interpersonal communication skills or the ability to accurately "read" the feelings of others or to meet their emotional needs)
- **Intrapersonal (Self) Intelligence.** Ability to self-reflect, become aware of, and understand 'your own thoughts, feelings, and behavior (e.g., capacity for personal reflection, emotional self-awareness, and self-insight into personal strengths and weaknesses)
- **Bodily–Kinesthetic (Psychomotor) Intelligence.** Ability to use 'your own body skillfully and to acquire knowledge through bodily sensations or movements (e.g., skill at tasks involving physical coordination, the ability to work well with hands, mechanical skills, talent for building models and assembling things, or skills related to technology)
- **Naturalist Intelligence.** Ability to carefully observe and appreciate features of the natural environment (e.g., keen awareness of nature or natural surroundings or the ability to understand causes or results of events occurring in the natural world)

Source: Gardner (1993).

Learning Styles: Identifying Your Learning Preferences

Your learning style is another important personal characteristic you should be aware of when choosing your major. Learning styles refer to individual differences in learning preferences—that is, ways in which individuals prefer to perceive information (receive or take it in) and process information (deal with it after taking it in). Individuals may differ in terms of whether they prefer to take in information by reading about it, listening to it, seeing an image or diagram of it, or physically touching and manipulating it. Individuals may also vary in terms of whether they like to receive information in a structured and orderly format or in an unstructured form that allows them the freedom to explore, play with, and restructure it in their own way. Once information has been received, individuals may also differ in terms of how they prefer to process or deal with it mentally. Some might like to think about it on their own; others may prefer to discuss it with someone else, make an outline of it, or draw a picture of it.

Pause for Reflection

Which type or types of intelligence listed in Box 10.1 represent you strongest area or areas?

Which majors or fields of study do you think may be the best match for your natural talents?

Personal Story

In my family, whenever there's something that needs to be assembled or set up (e.g., a ping-pong table or new electronic equipment), I've noticed that my wife, my son, and myself have different learning styles in terms of how we go about doing it. I like to read the manual's instructions carefully and completely before I even attempt to touch anything. My son prefers to look at the pictures or diagrams in the manual and uses them as models to find parts; then he begins to assemble those parts. My wife seems to prefer not to look at the manual. Instead, she likes to figure things out as she goes along by grabbing different parts from the box and trying to assemble those parts that look like they should fit together—piecing them together as if she were completing a jigsaw puzzle.

—Joe Cuseo

You can take specially designed tests to assess your particular learning style and how it compares with others. If you're interested in taking one, the Learning Center or Career Development Center are the two most likely sites on campus where you will be able to do so.

Probably the most frequently used learning styles test is the Myers-Briggs Type Indicator (MBTI; Myers, 1976; Myers & McCaulley, 1985), which is based on the personality theory of psychologist Carl Jung. The tests consists of four pairs of opposing traits and assesses how people vary on a scale (low to high) for each of these four sets of traits. The four sets of opposing traits are illustrated in **Figure 11.1**.

As you read the following four pairs of opposite traits, place a mark along the line where you think you fall with respect to each set of traits. For example, place a mark in the middle of the line if you think you are midway between these opposing traits, or place a mark at the far left or far right if you think you lean strongly toward the trait listed on either end.

Pause for Reflection

For each of the following four sets of opposing traits, make a note about where you fall—middle, far left, or far right.

	Far Left	Middle	Far Right
Extraversion–Introversion			
Sensing–Intuition			
Thinking–Feeling			
Judging–Perceiving			

What majors or fields of study do you think are most compatible with your personality traits?

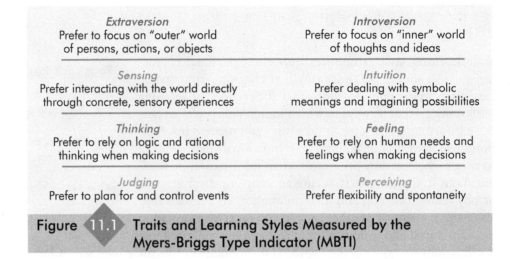

Figure 11.1   Traits and Learning Styles Measured by the Myers-Briggs Type Indicator (MBTI)

It's been found that college students who score high on the introversion scale of the MBTI are less likely to become bored than extroverts while engaging mental tasks that involve repetition and little external stimulation (Vodanovich, Wallace, & Kass, 2005). Students who score differently on the MBTI also have different learning preferences when it comes to writing and the type of writing assignments (Jensen & Ti Tiberio, cited in Bean, 2001). See **Figure 11.2** for the details on the findings.

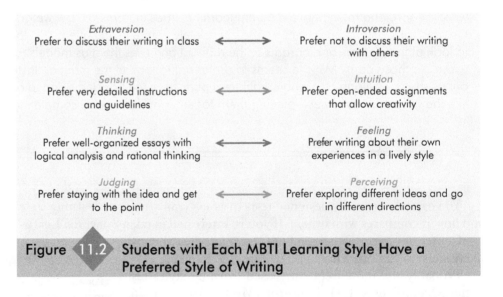

Figure 11.2   Students with Each MBTI Learning Style Have a Preferred Style of Writing

These results clearly indicate that students have different learning styles, which, in turn, influence the type of writing assignments they feel most comfortable performing. This may be important to keep in mind when choosing your major because different academic fields emphasize different styles of writing. Some fields place heavy emphasis on writing that is structured and tightly focused (e.g., science and business), while other fields encourage writing with personal style, flair, or creativity (e.g., English and art). How your writing style meshes with the style emphasized by an academic field may be an important factor to consider when making decisions about your college major.

Another popular learning styles test is the Learning Styles Inventory (Dunn, Dunn, & Price, 1990), which was originally developed by David Kolb, a professor of philosophy (Kolb, 1976, 1985). It is based on how individuals differ with respect to the following two elements of the learning process:

How Information Is *Perceived* (Taken in)

Concrete Experience

Learning through direct involvement or personal experience

Reflective Observation

Learning by watching or observing

How Information Is *Processed* (Dealt with after it has been taken in)

Abstract Conceptualization

Learning by thinking about things and drawing logical conclusions

Active Experimentation

Learning by taking chances and trying things out

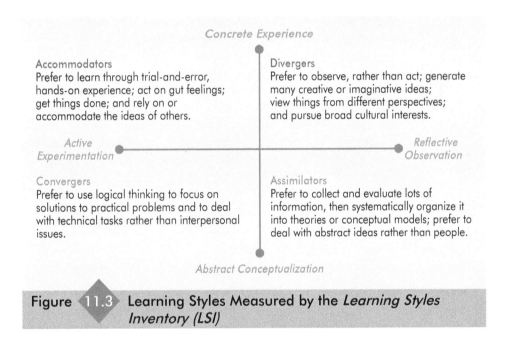

Concrete Experience

Accommodators
Prefer to learn through trial-and-error, hands-on experience; act on gut feelings; get things done; and rely on or accommodate the ideas of others.

Divergers
Prefer to observe, rather than act; generate many creative or imaginative ideas; view things from different perspectives; and pursue broad cultural interests.

Active Experimentation — *Reflective Observation*

Convergers
Prefer to use logical thinking to focus on solutions to practical problems and to deal with technical tasks rather than interpersonal issues.

Assimilators
Prefer to collect and evaluate lots of information, then systematically organize it into theories or conceptual models; prefer to deal with abstract ideas rather than people.

Abstract Conceptualization

Figure 11.3   Learning Styles Measured by the *Learning Styles Inventory (LSI)*

When these two dimensions are crisscrossed to form intersecting lines, four sectors (areas) are created, each of which represents a different learning style, as illustrated in **Figure 11.3**. As you look at the four areas (styles) in the figure, circle the style that you think reflects your most preferred way of learning.

Research indicates that students majoring in different fields tend to display differences in these four learning styles (Svinicki & Dixon, 1987). For instance, "assimilators" are more often found majoring in mathematics and natural sciences (e.g., chemistry and physics), probably because these subjects stress reflection and abstract thinking. In contrast, academic fields where "accommodators" tend to be more commonly found are business, accounting, and law, perhaps because these fields involve taking practical action and making concrete decisions. "Divergers" are more often attracted to majors in the fine arts (e.g., music, art, and drama), humanities (e.g., history and

Pause for Reflection

Which one of the four learning style appears to most closely match your learning style? (Check one of the following boxes.)

☐ Accommodator

☐ Diverger

☐ Converger

☐ Assimilator

What majors or fields of study do you think would be a good match for your learning style?

The engineering and humanities majors settle their differences in the fine arts quad!

literature), or social sciences (e.g., psychology and political science), possibly because these fields emphasize appreciating multiple viewpoints and perspectives. In contrast, "convergers" are more often found in fields such as engineering, medicine, and nursing, probably because these fields focus on finding solutions to practical and technical problems (Kolb, 1976). This same clustering of fields is found when faculty are asked to classify academic fields in terms of what learning styles they emphasize (Biglan, 1973; Carnegie Commission on Higher Education, cited in Svinicki & Dixon, 1987).

Since students have different learning styles and academic fields emphasize different styles of learning, it's important to consider how your learning style meshes with the style of learning emphasized by the field you're considering as a major. If the match seems to be close or compatible, then the marriage between you and that major could be one that leads to a satisfying and successful learning experience.

We recommend taking a trip to the Learning Center or Career Development Center on your campus to take a learning styles test, or you could try the learning styles assessment that accompanies this text (see the inside of the front cover for details). Even if the test doesn't help you choose a major, it will at least help you become more aware of your particular learning style. This alone could contribute to your academic success, because studies show that when college students gain greater

Personal Story

I first noticed that students in different academic fields may have different learning styles when I was teaching a psychology course that was required for students majoring in nursing and social work. I noticed that some students in class seemed to lose interest (and patience) when we got involved in lengthy class discussions about controversial issues or theories, while others seemed to love it. On the other hand, whenever I lectured or delivered information for an extended period, some students seemed to lose interest (and attention), while others seemed to get "into it" and took great notes. After one class period that involved quite a bit of class discussion, I began thinking about which students seemed most involved in the discussion and which seemed to drift off or lose interest. I suddenly realized that the students who did most of the talking and seemed most enthused during the class discussion were the students majoring in social work. On the other hand, most of the students who appeared disinterested or a bit frustrated were the nursing majors.

When I began to think about why this happened, it dawned on me that the nursing students were accustomed to gathering factual information and learning practical skills in their major courses and were expecting to use that learning style in my psychology course. The nursing majors felt more comfortable with structured class sessions in which they received lots of factual, practical information from the professor. On the other hand, the social work majors were more comfortable with unstructured class discussions because courses in their major often emphasized debating social issues and hearing viewpoints or perspectives.

As I left class that day, I asked myself: Did the nursing students and social work students select or gravitate toward their major because the type of learning emphasized in the field tended to match their preferred style of learning?

—Joe Cuseo

self-aware of their learning styles they improve their academic performance (Claxton & Murrell, 1988).

To sum up, the most important factor to consider when reaching decisions about a major is whether it is compatible with four characteristics of the self: your (a) learning style, (b) your abilities, (c) your personal interests, and (d) your values (see **Figure 11.4**). These four pillars provide the foundation for effective decisions about a college major.

"Minds differ still more than faces."

–Voltaire, eighteenth-century French author and philosopher

Strategies for Discovering a Major Compatible with Your Interests, Talents, and Values

If you're undecided about a major, there's no need to feel anxious or guilty. You're at an early stage in your college experience. Although you've decided to postpone your decision about a major, this doesn't mean you're a clueless procrastinator as long as you have a plan for exploring and narrowing down your options. Just be sure that you don't put all thoughts about your major on the back burner and simply drift along until you have no choice but to make a choice. Start exploring and developing a game plan now that will lead you to a wise decision about your major.

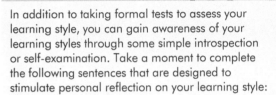

Pause for Reflection

In addition to taking formal tests to assess your learning style, you can gain awareness of your learning styles through some simple introspection or self-examination. Take a moment to complete the following sentences that are designed to stimulate personal reflection on your learning style:

I learn best if …

I learn most from …

I enjoy learning when …

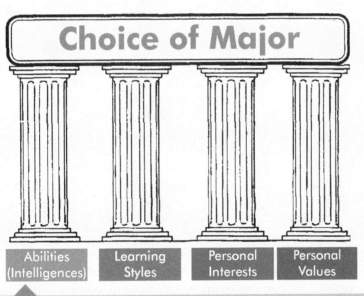

| Abilities (Intelligences) | Learning Styles | Personal Interests | Personal Values |

Figure 11.4 Personal Characteristics That Provide an Effective Foundation for Choice of a College Major

Similarly, if you've already chosen a major, this doesn't mean that you'll never have to give any more thought to that decision or that you can just shift into cruise control and motor along a mindless ride in the major you've selected. Instead, you should continue the exploration process by carefully testing your first choice, making sure it's a choice that is compatible with your abilities, interests, and values. In other words, take the approach that it's your *current* choice; whether it becomes your firm and *final* choice will depend on how well you perform, and how interested you are, in the first courses you take in the field.

To explore and identify majors that are compatible with your personal strengths and interests, use the following strategies.

1. Use past experience to help you choose a major.

Think about the subjects that you experienced during high school and your early time in college. As the old saying goes, "Nothing succeeds like success itself." If you have done well and continue to do well in a certain field of study, this may indicate that your natural abilities and learning style correspond well with the academic skills required by that particular field. This could translate into future success and satisfaction in the field if you decide to pursue it as a college major.

You can enter information about your academic performance with high school courses at a Web site (www.mymajors.com), which will analyze it and provide you with college majors that may be a good match for you (based on your academic experiences in high school).

2. Use your elective courses to test your interests and abilities in subjects that you might consider as a major.

As its name implies, "elective" courses are those that you elect or choose to take. In college, electives come in two forms: free electives and restricted electives. Free electives are courses that you may elect (choose) to enroll in; they count toward your college degree but are not required for general education or your major. Restricted electives are courses that you must take, but you choose them from a restricted list of possible courses that have been specified by your college as fulfilling a requirement in general education or your major. For example, your campus may have a general education requirement in social or behavioral sciences that requires you to take two courses in this field, but you're allowed to choose those two courses from a menu of options in the field, such as anthropology, economics, political science, psychology, or sociology. If you're considering one of these subjects as a possible major, you can take an introductory course in this subject and test your interest in it while simultaneously fulfilling a general education requirement needed for graduation. This strategy will allow you to use general education as the main highway for travel toward your final destination (a college degree) and give you the opportunity to explore potential majors along the way.

You can also use your free electives to select courses in fields that you are considering as possible majors. By using some of your free and restricted electives in this way, you can test your interest and ability in these fields; if you find one that is a good match, you may have found yourself a major.

Naturally, you don't have to use all your electives for the purpose of exploring majors. As many as one-third your courses in college may be electives. This leaves you with a great deal of freedom to shape your college experience in a way that best meets your personal needs and future interests. For suggestions on how to make the best use of your free electives, see **Box 11.2.**

Top 10 Suggestions for Making the Most of Your College Electives

At most colleges and universities, approximately one of every three or four courses will be a free elective—your choice of the many courses that are listed in your college catalog. Your elective courses give you academic freedom and personal control of your college coursework. You can exercise this freedom strategically by selecting electives in a way that enables you to make the most of your college experience and college degree. Listed below are 10 suggestions for making strategic use of your college electives. As you read them, identify two suggestions that would be of most interest or use to you.

You can use your electives for the following purposes:

1. Complete a minor or build an area of concentration. Your electives can complement and strengthen your major or allow you to pursue a field of interest other than your major.
2. Help you choose a career path. Just as you can use electives to test your interest in a college major, you can use them to test your interest in a career. For instance, you could enroll in
   - career planning or career development courses; and
   - courses that involve internships or service learning experiences in a field that you're considering as a possible career (e.g., health, education, or business).
3. Strengthen your skills in areas that may appeal to future employers. For example, courses in foreign language, leadership development, and argumentation or debate develop skills that are attractive to future employers and may improve your employment prospects.
4. Develop practical life skills that you can use now or in the near future. You could take courses in managing personal finances, marriage and family, or child development to help you manage your money and your future family.
5. Seek balance in your life and develop yourself as a whole person. You can use your electives strategically to cover all key dimensions of self-development. For instance, you could

take courses that promote your emotional development (e.g., stress management), social development (e.g., interpersonal relationships), mental development (e.g., critical thinking), physical development (e.g., nutrition, self-defense), and spiritual development (e.g., world religions or death and dying).

11.2

Remember

Choose courses that contribute not only to your major and career but also to your quality of life.

6. Make connections across different academic disciplines (subject areas). Courses designed specifically to integrate two or more academic disciplines are referred to as interdisciplinary courses. For example, psychobiology is an interdisciplinary course that combines or integrates the fields of psychology (focusing on the mind) and biology (focusing on the body) and thus helps you see how the mind influences the body, and vice versa. Making connections across subjects and seeing how they can be combined to create a more complete understanding of a subject or issue can be a stimulating mental experience. Furthermore, the presence of interdisciplinary courses on your college transcript may be attractive to future employers because responsibilities and issues in the work world are not neatly packaged into separate majors; they require the ability to combine skills acquired from different fields of study.
7. Help you develop broader perspectives on life and the world in which we live. You can take courses that progressively widen your perspectives. For example, you could select courses that provide you with a societal perspective (e.g., sociology), a national perspective (e.g., political science), an international perspective (e.g., cultural geography), and a global perspective (e.g., ecology). These broadening perspectives widen your scope of knowledge and deepen your understanding of the world.
8. Appreciate different cultural viewpoints and improve your ability to communicate with people from diverse cultural backgrounds. You could take courses related to differences across nations (international diversity), such

as international relations, and you could take courses related to ethnic and racial differences in America (domestic diversity).

9. Stretch beyond your familiar or customary learning style to experience different ways of learning or develop new skills. Your college curriculum is likely to include courses that were never previously available to you and that focus on skills you've never had the opportunity to test or develop. These courses can stretch your mind and allow you to explore new ideas and acquire new perspectives.

10. Learn something about which you were always curious or simply wanted to know more about. For instance, if you've always been curious about how members of the other sex think and feel, you could take a course on the psychology of men and women. Or if you've always been fascinated by movies and how they are made, you might elect to take a course in filmmaking or cinematography.

> **! Remember**
>
> Your elective course in college will give you the opportunity to shape and create an academic experience that is uniquely your own. Seize this opportunity, and exercise your freedom responsibly and reflectively. Don't make your elective choices randomly, or solely on the basis of scheduling convenience (e.g., choosing courses to create a schedule with no early morning or late afternoon classes). Instead, make strategic choices of courses that will contribute most to your educational, personal, and professional development.

3. Be sure you know the courses that are required for the major you're considering.

In college, it's expected that students may know the requirements for the major they've chosen. These requirements vary considerably from one major to another. Review your college catalog carefully to determine what courses are required for the major you're considering. If you have trouble tracking down the requirements in your college catalog, don't become frustrated. These catalogs are often written in a technical manner that can sometimes be hard to interpret. If you need help identifying and understanding the requirements for a major that you are considering, don't be embarrassed about seeking assistance from a professional in your school's Academic Advisement Center.

Pause for Reflection

What were the two primary strategies you selected from the list in Box 10.2?

Write a short explanation about why you chose each of these strategies.

4. Keep in mind that college majors often require courses in fields outside of the major, which are designed to support the major.

For instance, psychology majors are often required to take at least one course in biology, and business majors are often required to take calculus. If you are interested in majoring in particular subject area, be sure you are fully aware of such outside requirements and are comfortable with them.

Once you've accurately identified all courses required for the major you're considering, ask yourself the following two questions:

1. Do the course titles and descriptions appeal to my interests and values?
2. Do I have the abilities or skills needed to do well in these courses?

5. Look over an introductory textbook in the field you're considering as a major.

Find an introductory book in a major that you're considering, review its table of contents, and ask yourself whether the topics are compatible with your academic interests and talents. Also, read a few pages of the text to get some sense of the writing style used in the field and how comfortable you are with it. You should find introductory textbooks for all courses in your college bookstore, in the college library, or with a faculty member in that field.

6. Talk with students majoring in the field you are considering and ask them about their experiences.

Try to speak with several students in the field so that you get a balanced perspective that goes beyond the opinion of one individual. A good way to find students in the major you're considering is to visit student clubs on campus related to the major (e.g., psychology club or history club). You could also check the class schedule to see when and where classes in you major are meeting and then go the classroom where these classes meet and speak with students about the major, either before class begins or after class lets out. The following questions may be good ones to ask students in a major that you're considering:

- What first attracted you to this major?
- What would you say are the advantages and disadvantages of majoring in this field?
- Knowing what you know now, would you choose the same major again?

Also, ask students about the quality of teaching and advising in the department. Studies show that different departments within the same college or university can vary greatly in terms of the quality of teaching, as well as their educational philosophy and attitude toward students (Pascarella & Terenzini, 1991).

Choosing courses that best enable you to achieve your long-term educational and personal goals should take precedence over creating a class schedule that leaves your Fridays free for three-day weekends.

Speaking with students majoring in the discipline you are considering is a good way to get a balanced perspective.

© Jaimie Duplass, 2010. Under license from Shutterstock, Inc.

7. Sit in on some classes in the field you are considering as a major.

If the class you want to visit is large, you probably could just slip into the back row and listen. However, if the class is small, you should ask the instructor's permission. When visiting a class, focus on the content or ideas being covered in class rather than the instructor's personality or teaching style. (Keep in mind that you're trying to decide whether you will major in the subject, not in the teacher.)

8. Discuss the major you're considering with an academic advisor.

It's probably best to speak with an academic advisor who advises students in various majors rather than to someone who advises only students in their particular academic department or field. You want to be sure to discuss the major with an advisor who is neutral and will give you unbiased feedback about the pros and cons of majoring in that field.

9. Speak with faculty members in the department that you're considering as a major.

Consider asking the following questions:

- What academic skills or qualities are needed for a student to be successful in your field?
- What are the greatest challenges faced by students majoring in your field?
- What do students seem to like most and least about majoring in your field?
- What can students do with a major in your field after college graduation?
- What types of graduate programs or professional schools would a student in your major be well prepared to enter?

10. Visit your Career Development Center.

See whether information is available on college graduates who've majored in the field you're considering and what they've gone on to do with that major after graduation. This will give you an idea about the type of careers the major can lead to or what graduate and professional school programs students often enter after completing a major in the field that you're considering.

11. Surf the Web site of the professional organization associated with the field that you're considering as a major.

For example, if you're thinking about becoming anthropology major, check out the Web site of the American Anthropological Association. If you're considering history as a major, look at the Web site of the American Historical Association. The Web site of a professional organization often contains useful information for students who are considering that field as a major. For example, the Web site of the American Philosophical Association contains information about nonacademic careers for philosophy majors, and the American Sociological Association's Web site identifies various careers that sociology majors are qualified to pursue after college graduation. To locate the professional Web site of the field that you might want to explore as a possible major, ask a faculty member in that field or complete a search on the Web by simply entering the name of the field followed by the word "association."

12. Be sure you know what academic standards must be met for you to be accepted for entry into a major.

Because of their popularity, certain college majors may be impacted or over-subscribed, which means that more students are interested in majoring in these fields than there are openings for them. For instance, preprofessional majors that lead directly to a particular career are often the ones that often become oversubscribed (e.g., accounting, education, engineering, premed, nursing, or physical therapy). On some campuses, these majors are called restricted majors, meaning that departments control their enrollment by limiting the number of students they let into the major. For example, departments may restrict entry to their major by admitting only students who have achieved an overall GPA of 3.0 or higher in certain introductory courses required by the majors, or they may take all students who apply for the major, rank them by their GPA, and then count down until they have filled their maximum number of available spaces (Strommer, 1993).

13. Be sure you know whether the major you're considering is impacted or oversubscribed and whether it requires certain academic standards to be met before you can be admitted.

As you complete courses and receive grades, check to see whether you are meeting these standards. If you find yourself failing to meet these standards, you may need to increase the amount of time and effort you devote to your studies and seek assistance from your campus Learning Center. If you're working at your maximum level of effort and are regularly using the learning assistance services available on your campus but are still not meeting the academic standards of your intended major, consult with an academic advisor to help you identify an alternative field that may be closely related to the restricted major you were hoping to enter.

Pause for Reflection

Do you think that the major you're considering is likely to be oversubscribed (i.e., there are more students wanting to major in the field than there are openings in the courses)?

14. Consider the possibility of a college minor in a field that complements your major.

A college minor usually requires about half the number of credits (units) required for a major. Most campuses allow you the option of completing a minor with your major. Check with your academic advisor or the course catalog if your school offers a minor that interests you, find out what courses are required to complete it.

If you have strong interests in two different fields, a minor will allow you to major in one of these fields while minoring in the other. Thus, you can pursue two fields that interest you without having to sacrifice one for the other. Furthermore, a minor can be completed at the same time as most college majors without delaying your time to graduation. (In contrast, a double major will typically lengthen your time to graduation because you must complete the separate requirements of two different majors.) You can also pursue a second field of study alongside your major without increasing your time to graduation by completing a cognate area—a specialization that requires fewer courses to complete than a minor (e.g., four to five courses instead of seven to eight courses). A concentration area may have even fewer requirements (only two to three courses).

Taking a cluster of courses in a field outside your major can be an effective way to strengthen your résumé and increase your employment prospects because it demonstrates your versatility and allows you to gain experience in areas that may be missing or underemphasized in your major. For example, students majoring in the fine arts (e.g., music or theater) or humanities (e.g., English or history) may take courses in the fields of mathematics (e.g., statistics), technology (e.g., computer science), and business (e.g., economics)—all of which are not emphasized by their major.

◆ Summary and Conclusion

Here is a snapshot of the points that were made in this chapter:

* Changing your educational goal is not necessarily a bad thing; it may represent your discovery of another field that's more interesting to you or that's more compatible with your personal interests and talents.

- Several myths exist about the relationship between college majors and career that need to be dispelled:

  - **Myth 1.** When you choose your major, you're choosing your career.
  - **Myth 2.** After a bachelor's degree, any further education must be in the same field as your college major.
  - **Myth 3.** You should major business because most college graduates work in business settings.
  - **Myth 4.** If you major in a liberal arts field, the only career available is teaching.
  - **Myth 5.** Specialized skills are more important for career success than general skills.

- You should be aware of two important elements when choosing your major: your form or forms of multiple intelligence (your mental strengths or talents) and your learning style (your preferred way of learning).
- Strategically select your courses in a way that contributes most to your educational, personal, and professional development. Choose your elective courses with one or more of the following purposes in mind:

  - Choose a major or confirm whether your first choice is a good one.
  - Acquire a minor or build a concentration that will complement your major.
  - Broaden your perspectives on the world around you.
  - Become a more balanced or complete person.
  - Handle the practical life tasks that face you now and in the future.
  - Strengthen your career development and employment prospects after graduation.

Higher education supplies you with a higher degree of freedom of choice and a greater opportunity to determine your own academic course of action. Employ it and enjoy it—use your freedom strategically to make the most of your college experience and college degree.

Internet-Based Resources for Further Information on Educational Planning and Decision Making

For additional information related to the ideas discussed in this chapter, we recommend the following Web sites:

Identifying and Choosing College Majors:

www.mymajors.com

www.princetonreview.com/majors.aspx

Careers for Liberal Arts Majors:

www.eace.org/networks/liberalarts.html

11.1 Planning for a College Major

1. Go to your college catalog and use its index to locate pages containing information related to the major you have chosen or are considering. If you are undecided, select a field that you might consider as a possibility. To help you identify possible majors, you can use your catalog or go online and complete the short interview at the www.mymajors.com Web site. (Your learning-style assessment results from Figure 10.1 may also help you identify possibilities.)

   The point of this exercise is not to force you to commit to a major now but to familiarize you with the process of developing a plan, thereby putting you in a position to apply this knowledge when you reach a final decision about the major you intend to pursue. Even if you don't yet know what your final destination may be with respect to a college major, creating this educational plan will keep you moving in the right direction.

2. Once you've selected a major for this assignment, look at you college catalog and identify the courses that are required for the major you have selected. Use the form that follows to list the number and title of each course required by the major.

   You'll find that you must take certain courses for the major; these are often called core requirements. For instance, at most colleges, all business majors must take microeconomics. You will likely discover that you can choose other required courses from a menu or list of options (e.g., "choose any three courses from the following list of six courses"). Such courses are often called restricted electives in the major. When you find restricted electives in the major you've selected, read the course descriptions and choose those courses from the list that appeal most to you. Simply list the numbers and titles of these courses on the planning form. (You don't need to write down all choices listed in the catalog.)

   College catalogs can sometimes be tricky to navigate or interpret, so if you run into any difficulty, don't panic. Seek help from an academic advisor. Your campus may also have a degree audit program available, which allows you to track major requirements electronically. If so, take advantage of it.

Major Selected: _____

Core Requirements in the Major
(Courses in your major that you must take)

Course #	Course Title	Course #	Course Title

Restricted Electives in the Major
(Courses required for your major that you choose to take from a specified list)

Course #	Course Title	Course #	Course Title

Self-Assessment Questions

1. Looking over the courses required for the major you've selected, would you still be interested in majoring in this field?

2. Were there courses required by the major that you were surprised to see or that you did not expect would be required?

3. Are there questions that you still have about this major?

11.2 Developing a Comprehensive Graduation Plan

A comprehensive, long-range graduation plan includes all three types of courses you need to complete a college degree:

1. General education requirements

2. Major requirements

3. Free electives

In Chapter 1 you planned for your required general education courses and required courses in your major. The third set of courses you'll take in college that count toward your degree consists of courses are called free electives—courses that are not required for general education or your major but that you freely choose from any of the courses listed in your college catalog. By combining your general education courses, major courses, and free-elective courses, you can create a comprehensive, long-range graduation plan.

- Use the "long-range graduation planning form" to develop this complete educational plan. Use the slots to pencil in the general education courses you're planning to take to fulfill your general education requirements, your major requirements, and your free electives. (For ideas on choosing your free electives, see Box 10.2.) Since this may be a tentative plan, it 's probably best to use a pencil when completing it in case you need to make modifications to it.

Notes

1. If you have not decided on a major, a good strategy might be to concentrate on taking liberal arts courses to fulfill your general education requirements during your first year of college. This will open more slots in your course schedule during your sophomore year. By that time, you may have a better idea of what you want to major in, and you can fill these open slots with courses required by your major. This may be a particularly effective strategy if you choose to major in a field that has many lower-division (first year and sophomore) requirements that must be completed before you can take upper-division (junior and senior) courses in the major. (These lower-division requirements are often referred to as premajor requirements.)

2. Keep in mind that the course number indicates the year in the college experience that the course is usually taken. Courses numbered in the 100s (or below) are typically taken in the first year of college, 200-numbered courses in the sophomore year, 300-numbered courses in the junior year, and 400-numbered courses in the senior year. Also, be sure to check whether the course you're planning to take has any prerequisites—courses that need to be completed before you can enroll in the course you're planning to take. For example, if you are planning to take a course in literature, it is likely that you cannot enroll in it until you have completed at least one prerequisite course in writing or English composition.

3. To complete a college degree in 4 years, you should complete about 30 credits each academic year.

> **Remember**
>
> Unlike high school, summer school in college isn't something you do to make up for courses that were failed, or should have been taken during the "regular" school year (fall and spring terms). Instead, it's an additional term that you can use to make further progress toward your college degree and reduce the total time it takes to complete your degree. Adopt the attitude that summer term is a regular part of the college academic year, and make strategic use of it to keep you on a four-year timeline to graduation.

4. Check with an academic advisor to see whether your college has developed a projected plan of scheduled courses, which indicates the academic term when courses listed in the catalog are scheduled to be offered (e.g., fall, spring, or summer) for the next 2 to 3 years. If such a long-range plan of scheduled courses is

available, take advantage of it because it will enable you to develop a personal educational plan that includes not only what courses you will take, but also when you will take them. This can be an important advantage because some courses you may need for graduation will not be offered every term. We strongly encourage you to inquire about and acquire any long-range plan of scheduled courses that may be available, and use it when developing your long-range graduation plan.

5. Don't forget to include out-of-class learning experiences as part of your educational plan, such as volunteer service, internships, and study abroad.

Your long-range graduation plan is not something set in stone that can never be modified. Like clay, its shape can be molded and changed into a different form as you gain more experience with the college curriculum. Nevertheless, your creation of this initial plan will be useful because it will provide you with a blueprint to work from. Once you have created slots specifically for your general education requirements, your major courses, and your electives, you have accounted for all the categories of courses you will need to complete to graduate. Thus, if changes need to be made to your plan, they can be easily accommodated by simply substituting different courses into the slots you've already created for these three categories.

Remember

The purpose of this long-range planning assignment is not to lock you into a rigid plan but to give you a telescope for viewing your educational future and a map for reaching your educational goals.

Graduation Planning Form

STUDENT: ID NO:

MAJOR: MINOR:

TERM:		TERM:		TERM:		TERM:	
Course	Units	Course	Units	Course	Units	Course	Units
TOTAL		TOTAL		TOTAL		TOTAL	

TERM:		TERM:		TERM:		TERM:	
Course	Units	Course	Units	Course	Units	Course	Units
TOTAL		TOTAL		TOTAL		TOTAL	

TERM:		TERM:		TERM:		TERM:	
Course	Units	Course	Units	Course	Units	Course	Units
TOTAL		TOTAL		TOTAL		TOTAL	

TERM:		TERM:		TERM:		TERM:	
Course	Units	Course	Units	Course	Units	Course	Units
TOTAL		TOTAL		TOTAL		TOTAL	

		COCURRICULAR EXPERIENCES	SERVICE LEARNING AND INTERNSHIP EXPERIENCES
Advisor's Signature	Date:		
Student's Signature	Date:		
Notes:			

Self-Assessment Questions

1. Do you think this was a useful assignment? Why or why not?

2. Do you see any way in which this assignment could be improved or strengthened?

3. Did completing this long-range graduation plan influence your educational plans in any way?

Whose Choice Is It Anyway?

Ursula, a first-year student, was in tears when she showed up at the Career Center. She had just returned from a weekend visit home, where she informed her parents that she was planning to major in art or theater. When Ursula's father heard about her plans, he exploded and insisted that she major in something "practical," like business or accounting, so that she could earn a living after she graduates. Ursula replied that she had no interest in these majors, nor did she feel she had the skills needed to complete the level of math required by them, which included calculus. Her father shot back that he had no intention of "paying 4 years of college tuition for her to end up as an unemployed artist or actress!" He went on to say that if she wanted to major in art or theater she'd "have to figure out a way to pay for college herself."

Reflection and Discussion Questions

1. What options (if any) do you think Ursula has now?

2. If Ursula were your friend, what would you recommend she do?

3. Do you see any way or ways in which Ursula might pursue a major that she's interested in and, at the same time, ease her father's worries that she will end up jobless after college graduation?

Your First Year Resources

The first year of college is an exciting and challenging time. We want you to have the best experience possible, so we've designed a website just for you. It's full of tips, tricks, and links to help you make the most of Your First Year! If you have questions or need help finding your way at UNCG, you can always email us at yfy@uncg.edu. Visit yourfirstyear.uncg.edu and the websites below for helpful resources and services about educational planning and decision making.

Academic Advising Centers   **Refer to Chapter 12 for comprehensive list**

Career Services Center   336-334-5454
http://csc.uncg.edu/

The Dean of Students Office   336-334-5514
http://sa.uncg.edu/dean/

Degree Evaluation
http://reg.uncg.edu/degree-evaluation/

Students First Office   336-334-5730
http://studentsfirst.uncg.edu/

Student Success Center   336-334-3878
http://success.uncg.edu/

Undergraduate Bulletin
http://uncg.smartcatalogiq.com/2015–2016/Undergraduate-Bulletin

University Registrar's Office   336-334-5946
http://reg.uncg.edu/catalog/

Dear First-Year Student

My name is Elena Medeiros and I serve as the Coordinator of Academic Outreach in the Students First Office at UNCG. I wear multiple hats here at the university, including assisting students who are considering withdrawing from the university, providing academic support and outreach to students who are in academic distress, and coordinating Starfish (UNCG's early alert and student success software). First and foremost, however, I am an academic advisor. Each semester I meet with students who are seeking guidance related to some aspect of their academic journey and if there is one thing I have learned from this work so far, it is the importance of building a strong working relationship between students and their advisors.

Courtesy of UNCG Relations Office

In this chapter, you will find valuable information about various academic policies and requirements that you will be required to know throughout your time here at UNCG. It is entirely possible (perhaps even expected) that you will read through this chapter and feel a bit overwhelmed by all the information you are expected to retain. Before you begin your mental archiving, I would like to remind you that you have someone to help you navigate this new terrain: your academic advisor. I don't think that it is possible to overstate the importance of getting to know an academic advisor to whom you can turn for support, guidance, and understanding. It is a common misconception that your advisor is simply the person to help you register for your next semester of coursework. In reality this covers only a small portion of the assistance your advisor can provide. Advisors are here to talk with you about your goals, your strengths, your anxieties, and your questions. They will celebrate with you in your successes and guide you in times of hardship or academic uncertainty. I hope that you will make the most out of your advising relationship by taking the steps to get connected with your advisor as soon as possible.

Speaking of getting connected, I want to take a brief moment to introduce you to Starfish, the student success software and early alert system that UNCG utilizes to enhance connectedness between students, instructors, and advisors. You will find Starfish very useful because its online scheduling features allow you to schedule appointments with your instructors and advisors when it is most convenient for you. Starfish also has early alert features to keep you informed of your academic progress and can help you find the resources you need to be successful in your courses. Your instructors can raise flags when they are concerned about your academic performance and *kudos* to recognize your great work. Starfish is a tool that allows you to remain more easily connected to your instructors, advisors, and other UNCG staff who are here to support you.

I hope that you will find some of this information useful to you as you continue your academic journey with UNCG. On behalf of the Students First Office, I'd like to welcome you to UNCG and wish you a prosperous semester!

Sincerely,

Elena Medeiros

Elena Medeiros
Coordinator of Academic Outreach
Students First Office

Courtesy of The University of North Carolina at Greensboro

The Academic Advising Experience at UNCG

12

Heather Kern
With Contributions by Holly Hebard and
Jalonda Thompson

THOUGHT STARTERS

1. What does the word *advising* mean to you?

2. What do you envision your interaction with your academic advisor at UNCG will be like?

◆ What Is Academic Advising?

Few experiences in your academic career have as much potential for influencing your collegiate experience as academic advising. Much more than getting your advising code and selecting courses, developing a professional relationship with your academic advisor will help you make informed choices and decisions about your education and future career. Academic advisors often serve as mentors, coaches, or teachers when helping students with academic, social, and personal matters. Regardless of the nature of the meeting, perhaps one of the most important things to remember is that the academic advising process is a collaborative process. As a student, it is important that you are prepared and play an active role in every advising appointment. This chapter will serve as an introduction to how academic advising works at UNCG and a variety of academic policies that you may find beneficial. You will also:

1. Become familiar with the academic advising process at UNCG and your expectations as an advisee.
2. Learn how to prepare for meetings with your academic advisor.
3. Gain an understanding of the registration process and ways to stay on track in fulfilling the requirements for a degree at UNCG.

◆ Academic Advising at UNCG

Academic advising for undergraduates at UNCG is coordinated within one of the University's academic units where you will be advised according to your selected academic major. Regardless of where you are advised, you will

285

collaborate with your advisor to plan personal, educational, and career goals, learn the information and skills needed for academic success, and access a variety of campus resources. Next, you will find a comprehensive list of the seven advising centers at UNCG.

College or School	Advising Center	Website	Location
College of Arts and Sciences	CASA	uncg.edu/casa	103 Foust Building
Bryan School of Business & Economics	Undergraduate Student Services	bae.uncg.edu/advise	301 Bryan Building
School of Education	Office of Student Services	oss.uncg.edu	142 School of Education Building
School of Health and Human Sciences	HHS Student Advising Center	uncg.edu/hhs/student-advising-center	221 McIver Building
School of Music, Theatre, and Dance	Student Resources	performingarts.uncg.edu	220 Music Building
School of Nursing	Advising Center	nursing.uncg.edu/undergraduate/advising	123 Moore Nursing Building
Exploratory Majors	Students First Office	studentsfirst.uncg.edu	061 McIver Building

Planning

Many students arrive at UNCG feeling like the four years ahead of them will last an eternity, only to find that time often passes more quickly than they expect. If you do not make plans and take control of your college experience and educational path, it can pass you by! Your academic advisor is here to help you in planning your personal, educational, and career goals as well as helping you figure out how you can accomplish your goals.

Academic Success

You have most likely already discovered that college is not as similar to high school as you originally thought. Achieving success in college requires honing skills you already have as well as learning new strategies. You will find that faculty and staff members at UNCG are committed to your academic success and want to see you accomplish your goals. Academic advisors are prepared to equip you with the skills necessary to keep you on the right track.

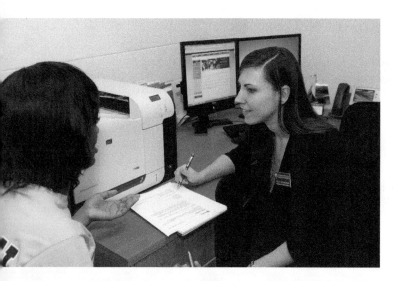

Resources

There are a variety of campus resources and services available to support you while you are at UNCG, as well as many organizations to get involved in. However, there may be times during your academic career when you find yourself wondering where you can go for help or how to make connections at UNCG. Your academic advisor is a valuable resource to help you access these organizations and support offices on campus. The *Getting Connected at UNCG* chapter in this book also includes information about what UNCG has to offer; however, you will find that discussing your options with your academic advisor will be especially beneficial.

◆Advising Policies and Resources at UNCG

As you are preparing to embark on your academic journey at UNCG, it is important to be aware of advising policies as well as the resources that are available to assist you. While you will have an academic advisor to help along the way, you are ultimately responsible for understanding your degree requirements and monitoring your academic progress. In this section, you will learn some of the key policies and tools that will be most helpful when meeting with your academic advisor.

Semester Hour Limit

You will be considered a full-time student if you are enrolled in a minimum of *12 semester hours* in the fall or spring terms. However, on average, students typically enroll in 15–17 semester hours so that they can stay on track to graduate in four years. UNCG also offers classes during summer session and winter session. Remember, if you register for winter-term courses, they will be included in your hour total for the spring semester. Keep in mind that academic excellence requires a significant amount of time spent reading, researching, and preparing for class. For every hour you are in class, you can expect to devote two to three hours of additional work outside of class.

Students are limited to a maximum of 18 semester hours each fall and spring term and 14 semester hours in the summer term (7 semester hours per session). Students occasionally request to exceed the semester hour limit so they can sign up for more than the maximum number of semester hours. If this is something you would be interested in doing, you must first receive approval from the Students First Office by filling out a **Course Overload Request Form**. This form is available online at studentsfirst.uncg.edu/advising/overload and also in room 061 of the McIver Building. Please note that approval of your request requires an institutional GPA of at least 3.00 and/or anticipated graduation within one or two terms. Course overload approvals or surpassing 14 hours in the summer are rare; however, the Students First Office welcomes all requests.

Undergraduate Bulletin

The **Undergraduate Bulletin** is one of your most valuable academic resources. It contains degree requirements for every undergraduate academic program that is offered at UNCG as well as descriptions of courses and current academic policies. The current Undergraduate Bulletin can be accessed at reg. uncg.edu/catalog/.

Degree Works

Another important tool for understanding degree requirements is **Degree Works**, which provides multiple features to help you understand curriculum requirements:

1. Degree Works Evaluation: This online degree audit is a customized report listing all the requirements you must fulfill in order to earn your degree. You will be able to see the courses you have already taken and are currently registered for, along with outstanding requirements that you have not yet completed. In addition, progress bars will display the percentage of both overall hours and specific degree requirements you have met.

2. **Academic Planner:** As you progress toward your undergraduate degree, you will find that it is particularly important to plan ahead. Degree Works offers an interactive planning tool that will be extremely beneficial in helping you organize and map your outstanding degree requirements, while also taking into account course prerequisites, scheduled course offerings, and other important information specific to your academic major. You will be able to choose from a recommended four-year template for your major and customize it to fit your needs.

3. **Interactive "What-if" Scenarios:** While you are a student at UNCG, you may consider changing your major or adding an additional major or minor to your academic plan. The What-if feature in Degree Works gives you a sneak peak at what your degree requirements would look like if you decide to officially proceed with these changes. This also provides you an opportunity to become familiar with various scenarios prior to making a commitment.

You can access Degree Works at any time through UNCGenie in order to track your progress toward graduation but it will be especially beneficial for you to view an updated audit before you meet with your advisor prior to registration. If you find that you need assistance understanding your degree evaluation or using any of the Degree Works tools, visit reg.uncg.edu/degree-evaluation/ for step-by-step assistance.

Degree Works Access

1. Click the *UNCGenie* link from the UNCG home page.
2. Click on *Enter Secure Area* and log in using your University ID and PIN.
3. Click on the *Student* tab.
4. Click on *Student Records*.
5. Click on the *Degree Works* link.

UNCGenie Class Schedule

You can find a comprehensive online list of all courses that are offered for a particular term by clicking on **Class Schedule** via the UNCGenie home page. You can select the upcoming term and search either by Course Subject or by General Education Curriculum (GEC) requirements. You can also look back at previous semesters' course offerings to plan for future terms. While it is not a guarantee that the same courses will be offered every semester, course offerings typically follow similar trends. As you are searching for courses to add to your schedule each semester, you will want to make special note of the following items:

1. Course name and number
2. Day and time the course is scheduled
3. The Course Reference Number (CRN)—this five-digit code can be used to quickly register for all of your courses at the same time.
4. GEC, CAR, and GE marker requirements the course will fulfill

Starfish

Starfish is located within Canvas and provides two valuable tools for UNCG:

1. Starfish EARLY ALERT: Through Starfish, instructors can raise flags to let students know that they may need additional support in the class. These flags are notifications to help ensure your academic success. They are not permanent records and will not appear on your UNCG transcript. In addition, instructors can raise *kudos* to congratulate students on their academic success. Be on the lookout for emails from the Starfish Outreach Team in the Students First Office to provide information on your flags and kudos!
2. Starfish CONNECT: Starfish also provides an easy and efficient way to schedule appointments with instructors and advisors. You can schedule appointments through Starfish by logging in to Canvas, clicking on your name in the top right toolbar, then selecting Starfish from the bottom of the menu on the left side of the page, and finding the individual's name in your My Success Network on the home page.

Selecting/Changing Your Major

Many students declare their majors when they apply to the University or during Spartan Orientation, Advising, and Registration (SOAR). However, with so many different academic programs offered at UNCG, many students begin college still trying to narrow down the direction of their educational plan. The Students First Office advises all Exploratory Majors and is available to discuss the self, major, and career exploration process with all students at the University. In addition, Peer Exploratory Coaches (PECs) in the Students First Office are student volunteers who can assist with pre-advising prior to meeting with your assigned academic advisors. Whether you arrive at UNCG with a major in mind or are eager to explore many options, you are free to change your major at any time to ensure that you are pursuing the educational path that is the right fit for you. However, it is recommended that all students finalize their major selection by the time they earn 45 semester hours (or at the end of their third semester at UNCG) in order to complete their degrees in four years. In addition, if you choose to change your major mid-semester, it is best to do so before the end of September during the fall term or by the end of February during the spring term to ensure the best possible advising. Changing your major by the previously listed times will allow you to be assigned a new academic advisor in your new department before the advising and registration period begins.

Adding or changing a major or minor is sometimes as simple as filling out the **Change of Major/Minor Form**, which can be found on the University Registrar's Office website by visiting uncg.edu/reg and clicking on Major Changes. Periodically, additional steps may be necessary, particularly if you are interested in pursuing one of the professional programs that have additional admission criteria. If so, please contact the designated academic department advising office to find out what steps to take next.

Academic Deadlines

Finally, it is very important to be aware of the University's academic deadlines at all times, particularly those pertaining to the date your hours lock for the semester and the last day to withdraw from a course without academic penalty. Specific dates can be found on UNCG's Academic Calendar, located on the University Registrar's Office website at www.uncg.edu/reg/Calendar/.

◆ Preparing to Meet with Your Academic Advisor

The policies and procedures discussed will be helpful as you prepare for every academic advising appointment. As emphasized earlier, academic advising is a crucial piece of your experience at UNCG and building a relationship with your academic advisor can be one of your most rewarding and beneficial experiences as you progress through your college years.

Locating Your Academic Advisor

You can find with the contact information for your assigned academic advisor in UNCGenie by following the instructions for academic advisor lookup:

Academic Advisor Lookup

- Go to the main UNCGenie page.
- Click on *Enter Secure Area* and log in using your University ID and PIN.
- Click on the *Student* tab.
- Click on the *Registration* option.
- Click on the *Look up Advisor* link.
- Select the current term and click on the *View Advisor* button.

Scheduling Your Advising Appointment

Prior to the advising and registration period each semester, the University Registrar's Office (URO) will send an electronic registration message to your UNCG email account. This email will include information about how to look up your registration window and your assigned academic advisor. In addition, you may receive email communication directly from your academic advisor with specific instructions regarding when and how to schedule your advising appointment. It is essential to check your UNCG email frequently to make sure you do not miss this important communication.

Once you receive email communication from either your assigned academic advisor or the Registrar's Office, you will need to schedule an appointment as soon as possible. Depending on what your academic advisor prefers, appointments can be made via Starfish, a sign-up sheet on their office door, or via email. Feel free to email your academic advisor or call them directly if you are unsure of their individual preference for scheduling appointments.

Preparing for Your Appointment

A positive academic advising experience depends on you taking an active role in the process. Particularly during peak advising and registration periods, you will only have a short amount of time with your advisor and likely a significant amount of information to cover.

Prior to meeting with your academic advisor, be sure to prepare in the following ways to help maximize your appointment time.

1. Review your online Degree Works Evaluation.
2. Based on the information presented on your audit, you may find it helpful to begin developing a Graduation Plan. Not only will this serve as a guide for what classes to take and when to take them over the next several years, but it will also help you in establishing short- and long-term goals related to your academic success. Students can use the interactive academic planning feature in Degree Works to begin working on your plan along with Exercise 4 at the end of this chapter. If you need additional assistance in developing your plan, schedule an appointment with an advisor in the Students First Office, 061 McIver Building.
3. Use the class schedule in UNCGenie to check course availability for the upcoming semester. Typically, the course schedule becomes available in mid-October and mid-March so that you can begin planning for the next term.
4. Using the information from your degree evaluation, the UNCGenie Class Schedule, and the Undergraduate Bulletin, create a sample schedule to discuss with your advisor. In addition to your ideal schedule, have two or three alternative choices in case class sections close before your registration window opens.
5. Write down a list of questions you want to ask your advisor or other topics you may want to discuss. These can include questions about transfer credit, adding a major or minor, requesting a course overload, your GPA, academic good standing, or any other questions that are on your mind!

◆ Registration Procedures

Adding Courses

Registration is completed online through UNCGenie. To register for courses, or to withdraw from a course at any point in the semester, you will need your **UNCG Advising Code**. This code is unique to you (no other student has the same code) and changes each semester, so you must meet with your assigned academic advisor to get your new code. Be sure to write your advising code down after you register in case you need it to make schedule adjustments in the future. If you forget or misplace your code, contact the Students First Office in room 061 of the McIver Building for assistance. Please be aware that SFO is not at liberty to distribute advising codes to students who do not have proof that they have already met with their assigned academic advisor.

Students (particularly in their first year) may become frustrated when they find that the classes they want/need are full. If this is the case, you may be given the option to be put on a **Course Waitlist**. If you choose to join the waitlist, you will be notified via email if a seat in the course opens. You will then have an allotted amount of time to confirm that you still want the spot. Because this is time-sensitive information, you will want to check your UNCG email frequently to avoid missing your opportunity.

Sometimes you do not have the option to join a waitlist. Additionally, some classes offered at UNCG require **"Written Permission Only"** and cannot be added through UNCGenie. When this happens, you will need to ask the professor of the course to be added to the class. If permitted, the instructor

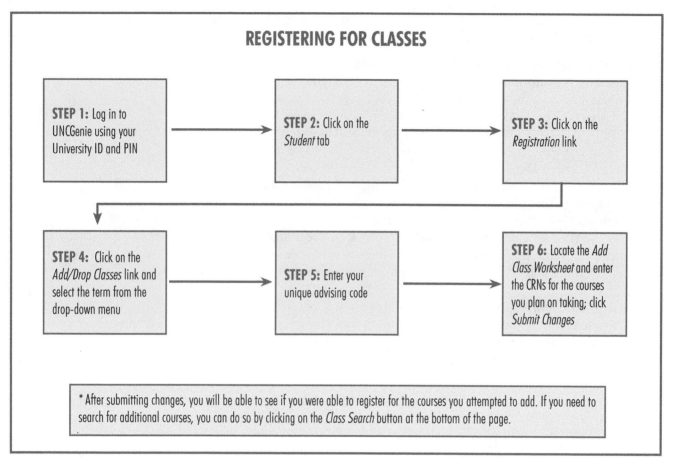

REGISTERING FOR CLASSES

STEP 1: Log in to UNCGenie using your University ID and PIN

STEP 2: Click on the *Student* tab

STEP 3: Click on the *Registration* link

STEP 4: Click on the *Add/Drop Classes* link and select the term from the drop-down menu

STEP 5: Enter your unique advising code

STEP 6: Locate the *Add Class Worksheet* and enter the CRNs for the courses you plan on taking; click *Submit Changes*

* After submitting changes, you will be able to see if you were able to register for the courses you attempted to add. If you need to search for additional courses, you can do so by clicking on the *Class Search* button at the bottom of the page.

must sign the **UNCG Drop/Add Permission Form**. This form can be found on the University Registrar Office website, in the Registrar's Office, or in the Students First Office. Once you have completed the form and have received the instructor's authorization, you must turn your form in to the University Registrar's Office, in room 180 of the Mossman Building.

Schedule Adjustment

Students may adjust their schedules during the schedule adjustment (drop/add) period, which takes place throughout the first week of each term. If you signed up for a course but decide to drop it during the schedule adjustment period, the course will be deleted from your record permanently and will *not* show up on your transcript. It is important to make all necessary changes during the schedule adjustment period because at 11:59 p.m. on the last day of schedule adjustment, your schedule will be locked. Your locked schedule will be used to determine your total hours for billing and Satisfactory Academic Progress calculations, which are used to determine your academic standing and financial aid eligibility. In addition, your locked hours will also appear on your transcript. Courses requested to be added after this period ends will only be accepted by the University Registrar's Office under extraordinary circumstances.

Course Withdrawal

Beginning Fall 2014, undergraduate students will be limited to withdrawing from a maximum of 16 semester hours throughout the duration of their academic career. This 16-hour limitation does ***not*** include the following:

* Course withdrawals that took place *prior* to Fall 2014
* Course withdrawals that take place during the schedule adjustment period each term (*within the first five days in fall and spring terms and within the first two days in summer sessions*)
* Total withdrawal from all courses prior to the term's last day to withdraw without academic penalty
* Course withdrawals that were awarded as a result of an approved Course Withdrawal Request *For students who have encountered extenuating circumstances only. Please see studentsfirst.uncg.edu/appeals/coursewithdrawal for additional information.*

Students are able to withdraw from a course in UNCGenie until the last day to withdraw from classes without academic penalty. While this date is typically the Friday of the eighth week of classes in the fall and spring semesters, students should refer to the current Academic Calendar for specific dates. Courses that you choose to withdraw from during this eight-week period will appear on your transcript as a WX, which means that it *will* count toward your 16-hour limit but it *will not* impact your GPA. While WX grades do not negatively impact your GPA, it is important to make sure you are aware of the potential consequences for withdrawing from a class. Following is a list of things to consider prior to withdrawing from a course:

* Refer to the Academic Calendar in the Undergraduate Bulletin for current semester deadlines. Courses withdrawn *after* the last day to withdraw without academic penalty will result in a WF on your transcript and ***will*** factor into your GPA.
* Academic Standing at UNCG is determined by both cumulative GPA *and* Satisfactory Academic Progress (completing 67% of your hours each term). You will want to make sure withdrawing from a course will not put you in jeopardy of falling out of Academic Good Standing.
* Students who receive financial aid should consult with the Financial Aid Office since future financial aid eligibility is also based on Satisfactory Academic Progress (completing 67% of your locked hours).
* Student athletes should consult with the Academic Enhancement Program.

If you have additional questions about if withdrawing from a course is the best plan of action, contact your academic advisor or an advisor in the Students First Office. If you do decide to withdraw from a course, make sure you print an updated copy of your schedule for your records.

◆ Requirements for Earning a Bachelor's Degree

Hour Requirement

Undergraduate majors at UNCG require students to complete between 122 and 128 hours of coursework to earn a degree. The exact number specific to your chosen degree program can be found on your Degree Works evaluation and in the Undergraduate Bulletin.

General Education Curriculum

With more than 100 different undergraduate programs at UNCG, there will be many course options, majors, and academic fields for you to explore. Regardless of which academic unit you choose to be part of, all students at UNCG also participate in the University's General Education Program, or what is more commonly referred to as the General Education Core (GEC). Central to the UNCG General Education Core is a focus on the liberal arts. Essentially, this means that by the time you graduate, you will have a broad knowledge of a variety of different academic fields (beyond your chosen major) that enables you to think critically and creatively about yourself, your peers, and the world in which you live.

With this at the forefront, UNCG embraces the mission and goals of the General Education Program as follows:

> The faculty and staff of The University of North Carolina at Greensboro embrace student learning as its highest priority. Our General Education Program provides students with the foundational knowledge, skills, and values necessary to be critical and creative thinkers; ethical decision-makers, effective communicators, and collaborative and engaged global citizens. The breadth of General Education empowers our students to thrive as lifelong learners who lead personally fulfilling lives. The mandate to foster an educated person belongs to the entire university, not to a single department, unit, or cocurricular program. Thus, the General Education Program provides foundations and alternative perspectives for the more specialized knowledge gained in the major. Likewise, the major builds upon and integrates knowledge, skills, and attitudes learned in General Education courses and the cocurriculum.

During your freshman and sophomore years, the majority of your classes will likely focus on the core areas within the general education curriculum. While there are eight different liberal arts categories within the program (outlined in the following chart), you will have numerous courses to choose from based on your personal interests.

GEC Core Categories and Abbreviations

GFA	Fine Arts
GHP	Historical Perspectives
GLT	Literature
GMT	Mathematics
GNS	Natural Sciences
GPR	Philosophical/Religious/Ethical Perspectives
GRD	Reasoning and Discourse
GSB	Social and Behavioral Sciences

In addition to the aforementioned categories, UNCG has also identified four core competencies or "markers" that are expected of all university graduates. To develop skills in these areas, all students will also take classes that focus on the following competencies:

General Education Markers and Abbreviations

GL	Global Perspectives
GN	Global Non-Western Perspectives
SI	Speaking Intensive
WI	Writing Intensive

Finally, if you are pursuing a major in the College of Arts and Sciences, you will have a few additional requirements beyond that of the UNCG General Education Core. These are intended to help you more deeply explore the liberal arts perspective, a philosophy that is central to each of the academic programs in the College.

College Additional Requirements (CAR) and Abbreviations

GFL   Foreign Language
GLS   Natural Sciences—Life Science
GMO   Historical Perspectives—Modern
GPM   Historical Perspectives—Premodern
GPS   Natural Sciences—Physical Science

With guidance from your academic advisor, you will be able to select classes that interest you, challenge you to think in new ways, and provide you with the foundational knowledge to be successful as you advance toward the coursework in your academic major. By the time you complete the General Education Core, the University intends for you to have attained the following goals:

> **LG1. Foundational Skills:** *Think critically, communicate effectively, and develop appropriate fundamental skills in quantitative and information literacies.*

> **LG2. The Physical and Natural World:** *Understand fundamental principles of mathematics and science, and recognize their relevance in the world.*

> **LG3. Knowledge of Human Histories, Cultures, and the Self:** *Describe, interpret, and evaluate the ideas, events, and expressive traditions that have shaped collective and individual human experience through inquiry and analysis in the diverse disciplines of the humanities, religions, languages, histories, and the arts.*

> **LG4. Knowledge of Social and Human Behavior:** *Describe and explain findings derived from the application of fundamental principles of empirical scientific inquiry to illuminate and analyze social and human conditions.*

> **LG5. Personal, Civic, and Professional Development:** *Develop a capacity for active citizenship, ethics, social responsibility, personal growth, and skills for lifelong learning in a global society. In so doing, students will engage in free and open inquiry that fosters mutual respect across multiple cultures and perspectives.*

Academic Standing

Students must be in **Academic Good Standing** to graduate from UNCG. Your Academic Standing will be closely monitored throughout your time at UNCG to make sure you accomplish this task; however, it is ultimately *your* responsibility to make sure you are in Academic Good Standing at all times. Beginning Fall 2014, undergraduate students' academic standing will be based on both grade point average (GPA) and Satisfactory Academic Progress (percentage of hours completed each term). You can find more information about the Academic Standing policy at UNCG at studentsfirst.uncg.edu/standing and in the Undergraduate Bulletin.

Academic Good Standing

All undergraduate students must continually meet the following requirements to remain in Academic Good Standing:

- Maintain a minimum cumulative GPA of 2.00.
- Earn a minimum 67% of their semester hours each term.

Failure to meet *any* of these requirements each term will result in Academic Warning or Academic Probation, which can have an additional impact on your academic plan or your ability to continue your enrollment at UNCG. The following chart outlines the various academic recovery programs for students who fall on Academic Warning, Academic Probation, Academic Suspension, and Academic Dismissal. For assistance calculating your semester or cumulative GPA, refer to the GPA Worksheet in Exercise 3 or use the GPA Calculator located on the Students First Office website. Your academic advisor and advisors in the Students First Office are also available to assist you with understanding the Academic Standing policy.

Student Guide to Academic Recovery at UNCG			
Academic Standing	**Student Population**	**Academic Recovery Program**	**Academic Recovery Program Description**
Academic Warning	Students in their first term who earn a 2.00 GPA or higher, but only earn 50–66.9% of their semester hours are required to participate in the ARK program.	Academic Resources and Knowledge (ARK)	This program consists of a series of three required workshops that students must attend before the end of the semester. The workshops will be offered at a variety of days/times and will include an online option for distance learners. Workshops focus on self-advocacy, academic and campus resources, and goal-setting strategies.
Academic Probation	Students who do not earn both a 2.00 GPA and 67% of their semester hours are required to participate in the FFL 115 program.	FFL 115: Reclaim, Regain, Recover	FFL 115 is a zero-credit, online, fully automated course module that guides students in developing and applying constructive academic recovery behaviors and skills. Students will be auto-enrolled in this course by SFO staff since it is online, is worth zero credit, and will not interfere with other course times or max credit hours. Components of the program focus on academic recovery strategies related to university policies, academic and campus resources, communication techniques, emotional intelligence, and goal setting.
Academic Suspension	Students returning to UNCG after being placed on Academic Suspension or receiving approval of an Academic Suspension appeal are required to participate in the ACE program.	Academic Connections in Education (ACE)	During the first semester back at UNCG, students participating in ACE will engage in two Bounce Back workshops, two one-hour sessions with a cohort of up to 10 other students, and two one-on-one sessions with an Academic Recovery Specialist.

			Components of the program focus on academic recovery strategies such as faculty connections, University resources, and peer support. The academic community students build together during the semester will be a valuable component to their individual UNCG support network and a critical part of their academic recovery journey.
Academic Dismissal	Students returning to UNCG after receiving approval of an Academic Dismissal appeal or a Returning from Dismissal appeal are required to participate in the ACT program.	Academic Coaching for Transitions (ACT)	Students will be assigned an ACT Coach with whom they have shared experiences or interests. Students will meet with their ACT Coach a minimum of seven times to receive ongoing, individualized support toward achieving student's academic goals at UNCG. In addition to supporting student's transition back to the University, ACT Coach will assist students with reconnecting to University resources, utilizing University policies, building a professional and academic support network, and developing an academic recovery plan.

Financial Aid Satisfactory Academic Progress

All students at UNCG are expected to make progress toward earning their degrees. As you learned previously in this chapter, your Satisfactory Academic Progress affects your Academic Standing *and* financial aid (if you are receiving financial aid). Students who are receiving financial aid must be in compliance with *all* of the following components of the SAP Policy to maintain eligibility to receive financial aid:

1. Students' Academic Standing must meet University standards to continue enrollment at UNCG.
2. Students must earn **66.5%** of their locked hours each term.
3. Students must maintain a minimum of **66.5%** cumulative completion rate.
4. Students must complete their degree within the Maximum Time Frame they are allowed to receive financial aid. Students are expected to graduate after completing no more than 150% of the hours needed to earn the degree. The set maximum at UNCG is **180 *attempted* hours** (regardless of major). It is important to remember that **W's *do* count toward students' attempted hours.**

◆Support

Academic advising will play a crucial role in your collegiate experience while you are at UNCG. Having a foundational knowledge of the academic policies and registration procedures you must adhere to throughout your educational career will not only help you capitalize on time spent with your academic advisor, but also help you make the most of your time at UNCG. If you encounter questions about advising, the registration process, academic policy, or GPA calculation, please contact the Students First Office, 061 McIver Building, at (336) 334-5730 or visit us online at http://studentsfirst.uncg.edu.

Courtesy of UNCG

12.1 Advising Preparation Worksheet—Fall 2015

Advisor Information

Advisor		Phone Number	
Location		Email	

Questions for Your Advisor

_____

_____

_____

Ideal Course Schedule

Using the resources from this chapter, prepare an ideal schedule to share with your advisor.

Course	Day and Time	Instructor	GEC	CRN

Alternate Courses

In the event that some of your ideal courses are unavailable when you register, plan a couple alternates.

Course	Day and Time	Instructor	GEC	CRN

Registration Window:_____ Advising Code: _____

12.2 Advising Preparation Worksheet—Spring 2016

Advisor		Phone Number	
Location		Email	

Questions for Your Advisor

_____

_____

_____

Ideal Course Schedule

Using the resources from this chapter, prepare an ideal schedule to share with your advisor.

Course	Day and Time	Instructor	GEC	CRN

Alternate Courses

In the event that some of your ideal courses are unavailable when you register, plan a couple alternates.

Course	Day and Time	Instructor	GEC	CRN

Registration Window:_____ Advising Code: _____

12.3 GPA Calculation Worksheet

Quality Points: Each letter grade you receive has a numerical equivalent called Quality Points.

Letter Grade	A+	A	A−	B+	B	B−	C+	C	C−	D+	D	D−	F/WF
Quality Points per Hour of Credit	4.3	4.0	3.7	3.3	3.0	2.7	2.3	2.0	1.7	1.3	1	.07	0

In order to calculate your *total* quality points, you will multiply the quality points earned for each course by the number of credit hours the course is worth. Use the following chart to calculate your total quality points.

Course	Grade	Quality Point Equivalent		Number of Credit Hours		Total Quality Points Earned per Course
			×		=	
			×		=	
			×		=	
			×		=	
			×		=	
			×		=	
			×		=	
		Total Credit Hours:				**Total Quality Points:**

Complete the following formula to determine your semester GPA:

Total Quality Points _____ ÷ Total Credit Hours Attempted _____ = Term GPA _____

12.4 Graduation Plan

Name: _____   ID #: _____

Major: _____   Anticipated Graduation Date: _____

Fall _____			Spring _____			Summer _____		
Course	GEC*	S.H.*	Course	GEC	S.H.	Course	GEC	S.H.
EXAMPLE: ENG 104	GLT	3	HIS 212	WI	3	(Session 1)		
						(Session 1)		
						(Session 1)		
						(Session 2)		
						(Session 2)		
						(Session 2)		
Total _____			**Total** _____			**Total** _____		

Fall _____			Spring _____			Summer _____		
Course	GEC	S.H.	Course	GEC	S.H.	Course	GEC	S.H.
						(Session 1)		
						(Session 1)		
						(Session 1)		
						(Session 2)		
						(Session 2)		
						(Session 2)		
Total _____			**Total** _____			**Total** _____		

Fall _____			Spring _____			Summer _____		
Course	GEC	S.H.	Course	GEC	S.H.	Course	GEC	S.H.
						(Session 1)		
						(Session 1)		
						(Session 1)		
						(Session 2)		
						(Session 2)		
						(Session 2)		
Total _____			**Total** _____			**Total** _____		

Fall _____			Spring _____			Summer _____		
Course	GEC	S.H.	Course	GEC	S.H.	Course	GEC	S.H.
						(Session 1)		
						(Session 1)		
						(Session 1)		
						(Session 2)		
						(Session 2)		
						(Session 2)		
Total _____			**Total** _____			**Total** _____		

*GEC=general education categories   *S.H.=semester hours

Comments: _____

_____

Student Signature: _____   Advisor Approval _____

Print Name   Signature   Department

Date _____

Your First Year Resources

The first year of college is an exciting and challenging time. We want you to have the best experience possible, so we've designed a website just for you. It's full of tips, tricks, and links to help you make the most of Your First Year! If you have questions or need help finding your way at UNCG, you can always email us at yfy@uncg.edu. Visit yourfirstyear.uncg.edu and the websites below for helpful resources and services strategic learning, studying and test taking.

Academic Advising Centers   **Refer to Chapter 12 for comprehensive list**

Degree Evaluation
http://www.uncg.edu/reg/capp/Deg_Eval.pdf

Students First Office   **336-334-5730**
http://studentsfirst.uncg.edu/

Undergraduate Bulletin
http://uncg.smartcatalogiq.com/2015-2016/Undergraduate-Bulletin

Diversity

13

Learning About and from Human Differences

ACTIVATE YOUR THINKING | Journal Entry **13.1**

Complete the following sentence:

When I hear the word "diversity," the first thoughts that come to my mind are . . .

LEARNING GOAL

To help you appreciate the value of human differences and acquire skills for making the most of diversity in college and beyond.

The Spectrum of Diversity

The word "diversity" derives from the Latin root *diversus*, meaning "various." Thus, human diversity refers to the variety of differences that exist among the people who comprise humanity (the human species). In this chapter, we use "diversity" to refer primarily to differences among the major groups of people who, collectively, comprise humankind or humanity. The relationship between diversity and humanity is represented visually in **Figure 13.1**.

The relationship between humanity and human diversity is similar to the relationship between sunlight and the spectrum of colors. Just as the sunlight passing through a prism is dispersed into all groups of colors that make up the visual spectrum, the human species that's spread across the planet is dispersed into all groups of people that make up the human spectrum (humanity).

As you can see in Figure 13.1, groups of people differ from one another in numerous ways, including physical features, religious beliefs, mental and physical abilities, national origins, social backgrounds, gender, and sexual orientation.

Since diversity has been interpreted (and misinterpreted) in different ways by different people, we begin by defining some key terms related to diversity that should lead to a clearer understanding of its true meaning and value.

" "

"We are all brothers and sisters. Each face in the rainbow of color that populates our world is precious and special. Each adds to the rich treasure of humanity."

–Morris Dees, civil rights leader and cofounder of the Southern Poverty Law Center

What Is Race?

A racial group (race) is a group of people who share some distinctive physical traits, such as skin color or facial characteristics. The U.S. Census Bureau (2000) identifies three races: White, Black, and Asian. However, as Anderson

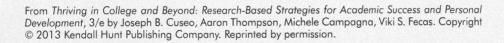

SPECTRUM
of
DIVERSITY

HUMANITY →

Gender (male-female)
Age (stage of life)
Race (e.g., White, Black, Asian)
Ethnicity (e.g., Native American, Hispanic, Irish, German)
Socioeconomic status (job status/income)
National *citizenship* (citizen of U.S. or another country)
Native (first-learned) *language*
National *origin* (nation of birth)
National *region* (e.g., raised in north/south)
Generation (historical period when people are born and live)
Political ideology (e.g., liberal/conservative)
Religious/spiritual beliefs (e.g., Christian/Buddhist/Muslim)
Family status (e.g., single-parent/two-parent family)
Marital status (single/married)
Parental status (with/without children)
Sexual orientation (heterosexual/homosexual/bisexual)
Physical ability/disability (e.g., able to hear/hearing impaired)
Mental ability/disability (e.g., mentally able/challenged)
Learning ability/disability (e.g., absence/presence of dyslexia)
Mental health/illness (e.g., absence/presence of depression)

_ _ _ _ _ _ = dimension of diversity

*This list represents some of the major dimensions of human diversity; it does not represent a complete list of all possible forms of human diversity. Also, disagreement exists about certain dimensions of diversity (e.g., whether certain groups should be considered races or ethnic groups).

Figure 13.1   Humanity and Diversity

Pause for Reflection

Look at the diversity spectrum in Figure 13.1 and look over the list of groups that make up the spectrum. Do you notice any groups that are missing from the list that should be added, either because they have distinctive backgrounds or because they have been targets of prejudice and discrimination?

and Fienberg (2000) caution, racial categories are social–political constructs (concepts) that are not scientifically based but socially determined. There continues to be disagreement among scholars about what groups of people constitute a human race or whether distinctive races exist (Wheelright, 2005). No genes differentiate one race from another. In other words, you couldn't do a blood test or any type of internal genetic test to determine a person's race. Humans have simply decided to categorize people into races on the basis of certain external differences in physical appearance, particularly the color of their outer layer of skin. The U.S. Census Bureau could just as easily have divided people into categories based on such physical characteristics as eye color (blue, brown, and green) or hair texture (straight, wavy, curly, and frizzy).

The differences in skin color that now occur among humans are likely due to biological adaptations that evolved over long periods among

Personal Experience   My mother was from Alabama and was dark in skin color, with high cheek bones and long curly black hair. My father stood approximately 6 feet and had light brown straight hair. His skin color was that of a Western European with a slight suntan. If you did not know that my father was of African American descent, you would not have thought of him as Black. All of my life I have thought of myself as African American, and all of the people who are familiar with me thought of me as African American. I have lived half of a century with that as my racial description. Several years ago, after carefully looking through records available on births and deaths in my family history, I discovered that fewer than 50 percent of my ancestors were of African lineage. Biologically, I am no longer Black. Socially and emotionally, I still am. Clearly, race is more of a social concept than a biological fact.

—Aaron Thompson

groups of humans who lived in regions of the world with different climatic conditions. For instance, darker skin tones developed among humans who inhabited and reproduced in hotter regions nearer the equator (e.g., Africans), where darker skin enabled them to adapt and survive by providing their bodies with better protection from the potentially damaging effects of the sun (Bridgeman, 2003) and allowing their bodies to better use the vitamin D supplied by sunlight (Jablonski & Chaplin, 2002). In contrast, lighter skin tones developed over time among humans inhabiting colder climates that were farther from the equator (e.g., Scandinavia) to enable their bodies to absorb greater amounts of sunlight, which was in shorter supply in their region of the world.

While humans may display diversity in skin color or tone, the biological reality is that all members of the human species are remarkably similar. More than 98 percent of the genes that make up humans from different racial groups are the same (Bridgeman, 2003; Molnar, 1991). This large amount of genetic overlap among humans accounts for the many similarities that exist, regardless of what differences in color appear at the surface of skin. For example, all people have similar external features that give them a human appearance and clearly distinguish people from other animal species, all humans have internal organs that are similar in structure and function, and regardless of the color of their outer layer of skin, when it's cut, all humans bleed in the same color.

What Is Culture?

"Culture" may be defined as a distinctive pattern of beliefs and values learned by a group of people who share a social heritage and traditions. In short, culture is the whole way in which a group of people has learned to live (Peoples & Bailey, 1998); it includes style of speaking (language), fashion, food, art, music, values, and beliefs.

Cultural differences can exist within the same society (multicultural society), within a single nation (domestic diversity), or across different nations (international diversity).

Pause for Reflection

What race do you consider yourself to be? Would you say you identify strongly with your race, or are you rarely conscious of it?

I was proofreading this chapter while sitting in a coffee shop in the Chicago O'Hare airport. I looked up from my work for a second and saw what appeared to be a while girl about 18 years old. As I lowered by head to return to my work, I did a double-take to look at her again because something about her seemed different or unusual. When I looked at her more closely the second time, I noticed that although she had white skin, the features of her face and hair appeared to be those of an African American. After a couple of seconds of puzzlement, I figured it out: she was an albino African American. That satisfied me for the moment, but then I began to wonder: Would it still be accurate to say that she is Black even though her skin is white? Would her hair and facial features be sufficient for her to be considered or classified as Black? If yes, then what about someone who had a black skin tone but did not have the typical hair and facial features characteristic of Black people? Is skin color the defining feature of being African American, or are other features equally important? I was unable to answer these questions, but I found it amusing that these thoughts were taking place while I was working on a book dealing with diversity. Later, on the plane ride home, I thought again about that albino African American girl and realized that she was a perfect example of how classifying people into races is based not on objective, scientifically determined evidence but on subjective, socially constructed categories.

—Joe Cuseo

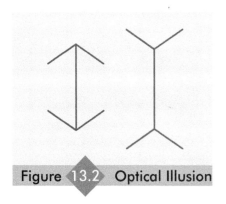

Figure 13.2 Optical Illusion

A major advantage of culture is that it helps bind its members together into a supportive, tight-knit community; however, it can blind them to other cultural perspectives. Since culture shapes the way people think, it can cause groups of people to view the world solely through their own cultural lens or frame of reference (Colombo, Cullen, & Lisle, 1995). Optical illusions are a good illustration of how cultural perspectives can blind people, or lead them to inaccurate perceptions. For instance, compare the lengths of the two lines in **Figure 13.2**.

If you perceive the line on the right to be longer than the line on the left, welcome to the club. Virtually all Americans and people from Western cultures perceive the line on the right to be longer. Actually, both lines are equal in length. (If you don't believe it, take out a ruler and check it out.) Interestingly, this perceptual error is not made by people from non-Western cultures who live in environments populated with circular structures rather than structures with linear patterns and angled corners, like Westerners use (Segall, Campbell, & Herskovits, 1966).

The key point underlying this optical illusion is that cultural experiences shape and sometimes distort perceptions of reality. People think they are seeing things objectively or as they really are, but they are often seeing things subjectively from their limited cultural vantage point. Being open to the viewpoints of diverse people who perceive the world from different cultural vantage points widens the range of perception and helps people overcome their cultural blind spots. As a result, people tend to perceive the world around them with greater clarity and accuracy.

"We see what is behind our eyes."

–Chinese proverb

Remember

One person's reality is not everyone's reality; current perceptions of the outside world are shaped (and sometime distorted) by prior cultural experiences.

What Is an Ethnic Group?

An ethnic group (ethnicity) is a group of people who share the same culture. Thus, culture refers to what an ethnic group has in common and an ethnic group refers to people who share the same culture. Unlike a racial group, whose members share physical characteristics that they are born with and that have been passed on biologically, an ethnic group's shared characteristics have been passed on through socialization—that is, their common characteristics have been learned or acquired through shared social experiences.

© JupiterImages Corporation.

Culture is a distinctive pattern of beliefs and values that develop among a group of people who share the same social heritage and traditions.

Major ethnic groups in the United States include the following:

- Native Americans (American Indians)
  - Cherokee, Navaho, Hopi, Alaskan natives, Blackfoot, etc.
- African Americans (Blacks)
  - People who have cultural roots in the continent of Africa, the Caribbean islands, etc.
- Hispanic Americans (Latinos)
  - People who have cultural roots in Mexico, Puerto Rico, Central America, South America, etc.
- Asian Americans
  - Cultural descendents from Japan, China, Korea, Vietnam, etc.
- European Americans (Whites)
  - Descendents from Scandinavia, England, Ireland, Germany, Italy, etc.

Currently, European Americans are the majority ethnic group in the United States because they account for more than 50 percent of the American population. Native Americans, African Americans, Hispanic Americans, and Asian Americans are considered to be ethnic minority groups because each of these groups represents less than 50 percent of the American population.

As with the concept of race, whether a particular group of people is defined as an ethnic group can be arbitrary, subjective, and interpreted differently by different groups of people. Currently, the only races recognized by the U.S. Census Bureau are White, Black, and Asian; Hispanic is not defined as a race but is classified as an ethnic group. However, among those who checked "some other race" in the 2000 Census, 97 percent were Hispanic. This fact has been viewed by Hispanic advocates as a desire for their ethnic group to be reclassified as a racial group (Cianciotto, 2005).

This disagreement illustrates how difficult it is to conveniently categorize groups of people into particular racial or ethnic groups. The United States will continue to struggle with this issue because the ethnic and racial diversity of its population is growing and members of different ethnic and racial groups are forming cross-ethnic and interracial families. Thus, it is becoming progressively more difficult to place people into distinct categories based on their race or ethnicity. For example, by 2050, the number of people who will identify themselves as being of two or more races is projected to more than triple, growing from 5.2 million to 16.2 million (U.S. Census Bureau, 2008).

Pause for Reflection

Which ethnic group or groups do you belong to or identify with?

What are the most common cultural values shared by your ethnic group or groups?

Student Perspective

"I'm the only person from my 'race' in class."

—Hispanic student commenting on why he felt uncomfortable in his Race, Ethnicity, & Gender class

As the child of a Black man and a White woman, someone who was born in the racial melting pot of Hawaii, with a sister who's half Indonesian but who's usually mistaken for Mexican or Puerto Rican and a brother-in-law and niece of Chinese descent, with some blood relatives who resemble Margaret Thatcher and others who could pass for Bernie Mac, family get-togethers over Christmas take on the appearance of a UN General Assembly meeting. I've never had the option of restricting my loyalties on the basis of race, or measuring my worth on the basis of tribe.

—Barack Obama (2006)

Pause for Reflection

List three human experiences that you think are universal—that is, they are experienced by all humans in all cultures:

1.

2.

3.

What Is Humanity?

It is important to realize that human variety and human similarity coexist and complement each other. Diversity is a "value that is shown in mutual respect and appreciation of similarities and differences" (Public Service Enterprise Group, 2009. Experiencing diversity not only enhances appreciation of the unique features of different cultures but also provides a larger perspective on the universal aspects of the human experience that are common to all humans, no matter what their particular cultural background may be. For example, despite racial and cultural differences, all people express the same emotions with the same facial expressions (see **Figure 13.3**).

Other human characteristics that anthropologists have found to be shared across all groups of people in every corner of the world include storytelling, poetry, adornment of the body, dance, music, decoration of artifacts, families, socialization of children by elders, a sense of right and wrong, supernatural beliefs, explanations of diseases and death, and mourning of the dead (Pinker, 1994). Although different ethnic groups may express these shared experiences in different ways, these universal experiences are common to all humans.

! **Remember**

Diversity represents variations on the common theme of humanity. Although people have different cultural backgrounds, they are still cultivated from the same soil—they are all grounded in the common experience of being human.

"We are all the same, and we are all unique."

-Georgia Dunston, African American biologist and research specialist in human genetics

Thus, different cultures associated with different ethnic groups may be viewed simply as variations on the same theme: being human. You may have heard the question, "We're all human, aren't we?" The answer to this important question is "yes and no." Yes, humans are all the same, but not in the same way.

A good metaphor for understanding this apparent contradiction is to visualize humanity as a quilt in which we are all joined by the common thread of humanity—by the common bond of being human. Yet the different patches that make up the quilt represent diversity—the distinctive or unique cultures

Humans all over the world display the same facial expressions when experiencing certain emotions. See if you can detect the emotions being expressed in the following faces. (To find the answers, turn your book upside down.)

Answers: The emotions shown. Top, left to right; anger, fear, and sadness. Bottom, left to right; disgust, happiness, and surprise.

All images © JupiterImages Corporation.

Figure 13.3

that comprise our common humanity. The quilt metaphor acknowledges the identity and beauty of all cultures. It differs from the old American melting pot metaphor, which viewed differences as something that should be melted down or eliminated, or the salad bowl metaphor, which suggested that America is a hodgepodge or mishmash of cultures thrown together without any common connection. In contrast, the quilt metaphor suggests that the cultures of different ethnic groups should be recognized and celebrated. Nevertheless, differences can be woven together to create a unified whole—as in the Latin expression *E pluribus unum* ("Out of many, one"), the motto of the United States, which you will find printed on all U.S. coins.

To appreciate diversity and its relationship to humanity is to capitalize on the power of differences (diversity) while still preserving collective strength through unity (humanity).

> "We have become not a melting pot but a beautiful mosaic."
>
> –Jimmy Carter, 39th president of the United States and winner of the Nobel Peace Prize

> **!** **Remember**
>
> By learning about diversity (differences), people simultaneously learn about their commonality (shared humanity).

Personal Experience

When I was 12 years old and living in New York City, I returned from school one Friday afternoon and my mother asked me if anything interesting happened at school that day. I mentioned to her that the teacher went around the room, asking students what we had eaten for dinner the night before. At that moment, my mother began to become a bit agitated and nervously asked me, "What did you tell the teacher?" I said, "I told her and the rest of the class that I had pasta last night because my family always eats pasta on Thursdays and Sundays." My mother exploded and fired back at me, "Why couldn't you tell her that we had steak or roast beef!" For a moment, I was stunned and couldn't figure out what I had done wrong or why I should have lied about eating pasta. Then it suddenly dawned on me: My mother was embarrassed about being an Italian American. She wanted me to hide our family's ethnic background and make it sound like we were very "American." A few moments later, it also became clear to me why her maiden name was changed from the Italian-sounding DeVigilio to the more American-sounding Vigilis, and why her first name was changed from Carmella to Mildred (and why my father's first name was also changed from Biaggio to Blase). Their generation wanted to minimize discrimination and maximize their assimilation (absorption) into American culture.

I never forgot this incident because it was such an emotionally intense experience. For the first time in my life, I became aware that my mother was ashamed of being a member of the same group to which every other member of my family belonged, including me. After her outburst, I felt a combined rush of astonishment and embarrassment. However, these feelings eventually faded and my mother's reaction ended up having the opposite effect on me. Instead of making me feel inferior or ashamed about being Italian American, her reaction that day caused me to become more aware of, and take more pride in, my Italian heritage.

Student Perspective

When you see me, do not look at me with disgrace.
Know that I am an African-American
Birthed by a woman of style and grace.
Be proud
    To stand by my side.
Hold your head high Like me.
Be proud.
    To say you know me.
Just as I stand by you, proud to be me.

—Poem by Brittany Beard, first-year student

As I grew older, I also grew to understand why my mother felt the way she did. She grew up in America's melting pot era—a time when different American ethnic groups were expected to melt down and melt away their ethnicity. They were not to celebrate diversity; they were to eliminate it.

—Joe Cuseo

What Is Individuality?

It's important to keep in mind that the individual differences within the same racial or ethnic group are greater than the average differences between two different groups. For example, although you live in a world that is conscious of differences among races, differences in physical attributes (e.g., height and weight) and behavior patterns (e.g., personality characteristics) among individuals within the same racial group are greater than the average differences among various racial groups (Caplan & Caplan, 1994).

As you proceed through this chapter, keep in mind the following distinctions among humanity, diversity, and individuality:

- **Diversity.** We are all members of *different groups* (e.g., different gender and ethnic groups).
- **Humanity.** We are all members of the *same group* (the human species).
- **Individuality.** Each of us is a *unique person* who is different from any person in any group to which we may belong.

◆ Major Forms or Types of Diversity

International Diversity

Moving beyond your particular country of citizenship, you are also a member of an international world that includes multiple nations. Global interdependence and international collaboration are needed to solve current international problems, such as global warming and terrorism. Communication and interaction across nations are now greater than at any other time in world history, largely because of rapid advances in electronic technology (Dryden & Vos, 1999; Smith, 1994). Economic boundaries between nations are also breaking down due to increasing international travel, international trading, and development of multinational corporations. Today's world really is a small world after all, and success in it requires an international perspective. By learning from and about different nations, you become more than a citizen of your own country; you become cosmopolitan—a citizen of the world.

Taking an international perspective allows you to appreciate the diversity of humankind. If it were possible to reduce the world's population to a village of precisely 100 people, with all existing human ratios remaining the same, the demographics of this world village would look something like this:

> 60 Asians, 14 Africans, 12 Europeans, 8 Latin Americans, 5 from the United States and Canada, and 1 from the South Pacific.
> 51 males, 49 females
> 82 non-Whites, 18 Whites
> 67 non-Christians, 33 Christians
> 80 living in substandard housing
> 67 unable to read
> 50 malnourished and 1 dying of starvation
> 33 without access to a safe water supply
> 39 who lack access to improved sanitation
> 24 without any electricity (and of the 76 who do have electricity, most would only use it for light at night)
> 7 with access to the Internet
> 1 with a college education
> 1 with HIV
> 2 near birth; 1 near death
> 5 who control 32 percent of the entire world's wealth; all 5 would be citizens of the United States
> 33 who receive and attempt to live on just 3 percent of the world village's income

Source: Family Care Foundation (2005).

Ethnic and Racial Diversity

America is rapidly becoming a more racially and ethnically diverse nation. In 2008, the minority population in the United States reached an all-time high of 34 percent of the total population. The population of ethnic minorities is now growing at a much faster rate than the White majority. This trend is expected to continue, and by the middle of the twenty-first century, the minority population will have grown from one-third of the U.S. population to more than one-half (54 percent), with more than 60 percent of the nation's children expected to be members of minority groups (U.S. Census Bureau, 2008).

By 2050, the U.S. population is projected to be more than 30 percent Hispanic (up from 15 percent in 2008), 15 percent Black (up from 13 percent), 9.6 percent Asian (up from 5.3 percent), and 2 percent Native Americans (up from 1.6 percent). The native Hawaiian and Pacific Islander population is expected to more than double between 2008 and 2050. In the same time frame, the percentage of Americans who are White will drop from 66 percent (2008) to 46 percent (2050). As a result of these population trends, ethnic and racial minorities will become the new majority because they will constitute the majority of Americans by the middle of the twenty-first century. (See **Figure 13.4**.)

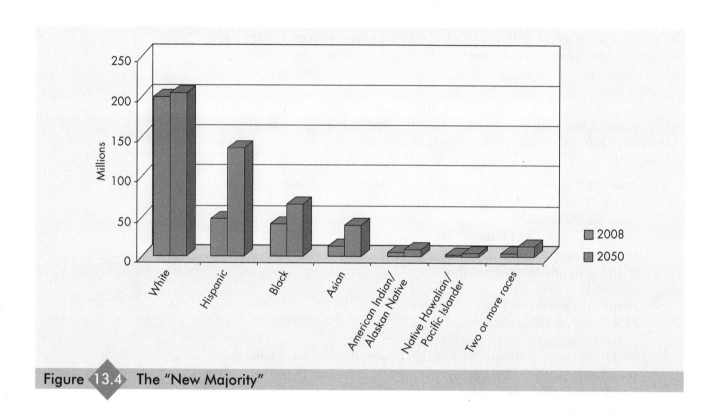

Figure **13.4** The "New Majority"

Generational Diversity

Humans are also diverse with respect to the generation in which they grew up. "Generation" refers to individuals born during the same historical period and may have developed similar attitudes, values, and habits based on the similar events that took place in the world during their formative years of development. Each generation experiences different historical events, so it's likely that generations will develop different attitudes and behaviors as a result.

Snapshot Summary 13.1 provides a brief summary of the major generations, the key historical events that occurred during the formative periods of the people in each generation, and the personal characteristics that have been associated with a particular generation (Lancaster & Stillman, 2002).

Snapshot Summary

13.1

Generational Diversity

- The Traditional Generation, a.k.a. the Silent Generation **(born 1922–1945).** This generation was influenced by events such as the Great Depression and World Wars I and II. Characteristics associated with this generation include loyalty, patriotism, respect for authority, and conservatism.
- The Baby Boomer Generation (born 1946–1964). This generation was influenced by events such as the Vietnam War, Watergate, and the human rights movement. Characteristics associated with this generation include idealism, personal fulfillment, and a concern for equal rights.
- Generation X (born 1965–1980). This generation was influenced by Sesame Street, the creation of MTV, AIDS, and soaring divorce rates that produced the first generation of latchkey children, who let themselves into their home after school (with their own key) because their parents, or their single parent, would be out working. Characteristics associated with this generation include self-reliance, resourcefulness, and being comfortable with change.

- Generation Y, a.k.a. Millennials (born 1981–2002). This generation was influenced by the September 11, 2001, terrorist attack on the United States, the shooting of students at Columbine High School, and the collapse of the Enron Corporation. Characteristics associated with this generation include a preference for working and playing in groups, being technologically savvy, and a willingness to provide volunteer service in their community (the civic generation). They are also the most ethnically diverse generation, which may explain why they are more open to diversity and see it as a positive experience.

"I don't even know what that means."

–Comment made by 38-year-old basketball coach after hearing one of his younger players say, "I'm trying to find my mojo and get my swag back."

Source: Lancaster & Stillman (2002).

◆ Diversity and the College Experience

There are more than 3,000 public and private colleges in the United States. They vary in size (small to large) and location (urban, suburban, and rural), as well as in their purpose or mission (research universities, comprehensive state universities, liberal arts colleges, and community colleges). This variety makes the American higher-education system the most diverse and accessible in the world. The diversity of educational opportunities in American colleges and universities reflects the freedom of opportunity in the United States as a democratic nation (American Council on Education, 2008).

Pause for Reflection

Look back at the characteristics associated with your generation. Which of these characteristics most accurately reflect your attitudes, values, or personality traits?

Which clearly do not?

America's system of higher education is also becoming more diverse with respect to the variety of people enrolled in it. College students in the United States are growing more diverse with respect to age; almost 40 percent of all undergraduate students in America are 25 years of age or older, compared to 28 percent in 1970 (U.S. Department of Education, 2002). The ethnic and racial diversity of students in American colleges and universities is also rapidly rising. In 1960, Whites made up almost 95 percent of the total college population; in 2005, that percentage had decreased to 69 percent. At the same time, the percentage of Asian, Hispanic, Black, and Native American students attending college increased (Chronicle of Higher Education, 2003).

Pause for Reflection

1. What diverse groups do you see represented on your campus?

2. Are there groups on your campus that you did not expect to see or to see in such large numbers?

3. Are there groups on your campus that you expected to see but do not see or see in smaller numbers than you expected?

◆ The Benefits of Experiencing Diversity

Diversity Promotes Self-Awareness

Learning from people with diverse backgrounds and experiences sharpens your self-knowledge and self-insight by allowing you to compare and contrast your life experiences with life experiences of others that differ sharply from your own. This comparative perspective gives you a reference point for viewing your own life, which places you in a better position to see more clearly how your unique cultural background has influenced the development of your personal beliefs, values, and lifestyle. By viewing your life in relation to the lives of others, you see more clearly what is distinctive about yourself and how you may be uniquely advantaged or disadvantaged.

When students around the country were interviewed about their diversity experiences in college, they reported that these experiences often helped them learn more about themselves and that their interactions with students from different races and ethnic groups produced unexpected or jarring self-insights (Light, 2001).

Student Perspective

"I remember that my self-image was being influenced by the media. I got the impression that women had to look a certain way. I dyed my hair, wore different clothes, more makeup . . . all because magazines, TV, [and] music videos 'said' that was beautiful. Luckily, when I was 15, I went to Brazil and saw a different, more natural beauty and came back to America more as myself. I let go of the hold the media image had on me."

—First-year college student

Remember

The more opportunities you create to learn from others who are different from yourself, the more opportunities you create to learn about yourself.

Diversity Enriches a College Education

Diversity magnifies the power of a college education because it helps liberate you from the tunnel vision of ethnocentricity (culture-centeredness) and egocentricity (self-centeredness), enabling you to get beyond yourself and your own culture to see yourself in relation to the world around you. Just as the various subjects you take in the college curriculum open your mind to multiple perspectives, so does your experience with people from varied backgrounds; it equips you with a wide-focus lens that allows you to take a multicultural perspective. A multicultural perspective helps

"Without exception, the observed changes [during college] involve greater breadth, expansion, and appreciation for the new and different."

—Ernest Pascarella and Pat Terenzini, *How College Affects Students* (xxxx)

you become aware of cultural blind spots and avoid the dangers of group think—the tendency for tight groups of people to think so much alike that they overlook flaws in their thinking that can lead to poor choices and faulty decisions (Janis, 1982).

Diversity Strengthens Learning and Critical Thinking

Research consistently shows that people learn more from those who are different from them than from those who are similar to them (Pascarella, 2001; Pascarella & Terenzini, 2005). When your brain encounters something that is unfamiliar or different from what you're accustomed to, you must stretch beyond your mental comfort zone and work harder to understand it because doing so forces you to compare and contrast it to what you already know (Acredolo & O'Connor, 1991; Nagda, Gurin, & Johnson, 2005). This mental stretch requires the use of extra psychological effort and energy, which strengthens and deepens learning.

> "When all men think alike, no one thinks very much."
>
> –Walter Lippmann, distinguished journalist and originator of the term "stereotype"

A good example of how "group think" can lead to ethnocentric decisions that are ineffective (and unjust).

Diversity Promotes Creative Thinking

Experiences with diversity supply you with broader base of knowledge and wider range of thinking styles that better enable you to think outside your own cultural box or boundaries. In contrast, limiting your number of cultural vantage points is akin to limiting the variety of mental tools you can use to solve new problems, thereby limiting your creativity. When like-minded people only associate with other like-minded people, they're unlikely to think outside the box.

Drawing on different ideas from people with diverse backgrounds and bouncing your ideas off them is a great way to generate energy, synergy, and serendipity—unanticipated discoveries and creative solutions.

>
>
> "When the only tool you have is a hammer, you tend to see every problem as a nail."
>
> –Abraham Maslow, humanistic psychologist, best known for his self-actualization theory of achieving human potential

Diversity Enhances Career Preparation and Success

Learning about and from diversity has a practical benefit: It better prepares you for the world of work. Whatever career you choose to pursue, you are likely find yourself working with employers, employees, co-workers, customers, and clients from diverse cultural backgrounds. America's workforce is now more diverse than at any other time in the nation's history, and it will grow ever more diverse. For example, the percentage of America's working-age population that represents members of minority groups is expected to grow from 34 percent in 2008 to 55 percent in 2050 (U.S. Bureau of Labor Statistics, 2009).

In addition to increasing diversity in America, today's work world is characterized by a global economy. Greater economic interdependence among nations, more international trading (imports and exports), more multinational corporations, and almost-instantaneous worldwide communication increasingly occur—thanks to advances in the World Wide Web (Dryden & Vos, 1999; Smith, 1994). Because of these trends, employers of college graduates now seek job candidates with the following skills and attributes: sensitivity to human differences, the ability to understand and relate to people from different cultural backgrounds, international knowledge, and foreign language skills (Fixman, 1990; National Association of Colleges & Employers, 2003; Office of Research, 1994; Smith, 1997). In one national survey, policymakers, business leaders, and employers all agreed that college graduates should be more than just aware or tolerant of diversity; they should have experience with diversity (Education Commission of the States, 1995).

> "Empirical evidence shows that the actual effects on student development of emphasizing diversity and of student participation in diversity activities are overwhelmingly positive."
>
> –Alexander Astin, *What Matters in College* (1993)

> **! Remember**
>
> The wealth of diversity on college campuses today represents an unprecedented educational opportunity. You may never again be a member of a community that includes so many people from such a rich variety of backgrounds. Seize this opportunity! You're now in the right place at the right time to experience the people and programs that can infuse and enrich the quality of your college education with diversity.

Pause for Reflection

Have you ever been stereotyped, such as based on your appearance or group membership? If so, how did it make you feel and how did you react?

Have you ever unintentionally perceived or treated someone in terms of a group stereotype rather than as an individual? What assumptions did you make about that person? Was that person aware of, or affected by, your stereotyping?

◆ Stumbling Blocks and Barriers to Experiencing Diversity

Stereotypes

The word "stereotype" derives from a combination of two roots: *stereo* (to look at in a fixed way) and *type* (to categorize or group together, as in the word "typical"). Thus, stereotyping is viewing individuals of the same type (group) in the same (fixed) way.

In effect, stereotyping ignores or disregards a person's individuality; instead, all people who share a similar group characteristic (e.g., race or gender) are viewed as having the same personal characteristics—as in the expression, "You know what they are like; they're all the same." Stereotypes involve bias, which literally means "slant." A bias can be either positive or negative. Positive bias results in a favorable stereotype (e.g., "Italians are great lovers"); negative bias produces an unfavorable stereotype (e.g., "Italians are in the Mafia"). **Box 13.1** lists some common stereotypes.

Take Action!

Examples of Common Stereotypes

Muslims are terrorists.
Whites can't jump (or dance).
Blacks are lazy.
Asians are brilliant in math.
Irish are alcoholics.
Gay men are feminine; lesbian women are masculine.
Jews are cheap.
Hispanic men are abusive to women.
Men are strong.
Women are weak.

Whether you are male or female, don't let gender stereotypes limit your career options.

Personal Experience   When I was 6 years old, I was told by another 6-year-old from a different racial group that all people of my race could not swim. Since I could not swim at that time and she could, I assumed she was correct. I asked a boy, who happened to be of the same racial group as that little girl, if that statement were true; he responded: "Yes, it is true." Since I was from an area where few other African Americans were around to counteract this belief about Blacks, I bought into this stereotype until I finally took swimming lessons as an adult. I am now a lousy swimmer after many lessons because I did not even attempt to swim until I was an adult. The moral of this story is that group stereotypes can limit the confidence and potential of individuals who are members of the stereotyped group.

—Aaron Thompson

Prejudice

If virtually all members of a stereotyped group are judged or evaluated in a negative way, the result is prejudice. (The word "prejudice" literally means to "pre-judge.") Technically, prejudice may be either positive or negative; however, the term is most often associated with a negative prejudgment or stigmatizing—associating inferior or unfavorable traits with people who belong to the same group. Thus, prejudice may be defined as a negative

"*Let us all hope that the dark clouds of racial prejudice will soon pass away and the deep fog of misunderstanding will be lifted from our fear-drenched communities, and in some not too distant tomorrow the radiant stars of love and brotherhood will shine over our great nation.*"

—Martin Luther King Jr., civil rights activist and clergyman

"'See that man over there?'
'Yes.'
'Well, I hate him.'
'But you don't know him.'
'That's why I hate him.'"

–Gordon Allport, *The Nature of Prejudice* (1954)

"A lot of us never asked questions in class before—it just wasn't done, especially by a woman or a girl, so we need to realize that and get into the habit of asking questions and challenging if we want to—regardless of the reactions of the profs and other students."

–Adult female college student (Wilkie & Thompson, 1993)

"The best way to beat prejudice is to show them. On a midterm, I got 40 points above the average. They all looked at me differently after that."

–Mexican American college student (Nemko, 1988)

Pause for Reflection

Prejudice and discrimination can be subtle and only begin to surface when the social or emotional distance among members of different groups grows closer. Rate your level of comfort with the following situations:

Someone from another racial group

1. going to your school;   high   moderate   low
2. working in your place of employment;   high   moderate   low
3. living on your street as a neighbor;   high   moderate   low
4. living with you as a roommate;   high   moderate   low
5. socializing with you as a personal friend;   high   moderate   low
6. being your most intimate friend or romantic partner; or   high   moderate   low
7. being your partner in marriage.   high   moderate   low

For any item you rated "low," what do you think was responsible for the low rating?

judgment, attitude, or belief about another person or group of people, which is formed before the facts are known. Stereotyping and prejudice often go hand in hand because individuals who are placed in a negatively stereotyped group are commonly prejudged in a negative way.

Someone with a prejudice toward a group typically avoids contact with individuals from that group. This enables the prejudice to continue unchallenged because there is little chance for the prejudiced person to have positive experiences with a member of the stigmatized group that could contradict or disprove the prejudice. Thus, a vicious cycle is established in which the prejudiced person continues to avoid contact with individuals from the stigmatized group, which, in turn, continues to maintain and reinforce the prejudice.

Discrimination

Literally translated, the term "discrimination" means "division" or "separation." Whereas prejudice involves a belief or opinion, discrimination involves an action taken toward others. Technically, discrimination can be either negative or positive—for example, a discriminating eater may be careful about eating only healthy foods. However, the term is most often associated with a negative action that results in a prejudiced person treating another person, or group of people, in an unfair way. Thus, it could be said that discrimination is prejudice put into action. Hate crimes are examples of extreme discrimination because they are acts motivated solely by prejudice against members of a stigmatized group. Victims of hate crimes may have their personal property damaged or they may be physically assaulted, sometimes referred to as gay bashing if the victim is a homosexual. Other forms of discrimination are more subtle and may take place without people being fully aware that they are discriminating. For example, evidence shows that some White, male college professors tend to treat female students and students from ethnic or racial minority groups differently from the way they treat males and nonminority students. In particular, females and minority students in classes taught by White, male instructors tend to:

- Receive less eye contact from the instructor;
- Be called on less frequently in class;
- Be given less time to respond to questions asked by the instructor in class; and
- Have less contact with the instructor outside of class (Hall & Sandler, 1982, 1984; Sedlacek, 1987; Wright, 1987).

In most of these cases, the discriminatory treatment received by these female and minority students was subtle and not done consciously or deliberately by the instructors (Green, 1989). Nevertheless, these unintended actions are still discriminatory, and they may send a message to minority and female students that their ideas are not worth hearing or that they are not as capable as other students (Sadker & Sadker, 1994).

Snapshot Summary

13.2

Stereotypes and Prejudiced Belief Systems About Group Inferiority

- **Ethnocentrism.** Considering one's own culture or ethnic group to be central or normal, and viewing different cultures as deficient or inferior. For example, people who are ethnocentric might claim that another culture is weird or abnormal for eating certain animals that they consider unethical to eat, even though they eat certain animals that the other culture would consider unethical to eat.

- **Racism.** Prejudice or discrimination based on skin color. For example, Cecil Rhodes (Englishman and empire builder of British South Africa), once claimed, "We [the British] are the finest race in the world and the more of the world we inhabit the better it is for the human race." Currently, racism is exemplified by the Ku Klux Klan, a domestic terrorist group that believes in the supremacy of the White race and considers all other races to be inferior.

"The Constitution of the United States knows no distinction between citizens on account of color."

–Frederick Douglass, abolitionist, author, advocate for equal rights for all people, and former slave

- **Classism.** Prejudice or discrimination based on social class, particularly toward people of low socioeconomic status. For example, a classicist might focus only on the contributions made by politicians and wealthy industrialists to America, ignoring the contributions of poor immigrants, farmers, slaves, and pioneer women.

- **Nationalism.** Excessive interest and belief in the strengths of one's own nation without acknowledging its mistakes or weaknesses, the needs of other nations, or the common interests of all nations. For example, blind patriotism blinds people to the shortcomings of their own nation, causing patriots to view any questioning or criticism of their nation as disloyalty or unpatriotic (as in the slogans "America: right or wrong" and "America: love it or leave it!")

- **Regionalism.** Prejudice or discrimination based on the geographical region of a nation in which an individual has been born and raised. For example, a Northerner might think that all Southerners are racists.

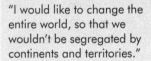

Student Perspective

"I would like to change the entire world, so that we wouldn't be segregated by continents and territories."

–College sophomore

- **Religious Bigotry.** Denying the fundamental human right of other people to hold religious beliefs or to hold religious beliefs that differ from one's own. For example, an atheist might force nonreligious (secular) beliefs on others, or a member of a religious group may believe that people who hold different religious beliefs are immoral or sinners.

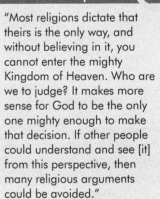

Student Perspective

"Most religions dictate that theirs is the only way, and without believing in it, you cannot enter the mighty Kingdom of Heaven. Who are we to judge? It makes more sense for God to be the only one mighty enough to make that decision. If other people could understand and see [it] from this perspective, then many religious arguments could be avoided."

–First-year college student

- **Xenophobia.** Extreme fear or hatred of foreigners, outsiders, or strangers. For example, someone might believe that all immigrants should be kept out of the country because they will increase the crime rate.

- **Anti-Semitism.** Prejudice or discrimination toward Jews or people who practice the religion of Judaism. For example, someone could claim to hate Jews because they're the ones who "killed Christ."
- **Genocide.** Mass murdering of one group by another group. An example is the Holocaust during World War II, in which millions of Jews were murdered. Other examples include the murdering of Cambodians under the Khmer Rouge, the murdering of Bosnian Muslims in the former country of Yugoslavia, and the slaughter of the Tutsi minority by the Hutu majority in Rwanda.
- **Terrorism.** Intentional acts of violence against civilians that are motivated by political or religious prejudice. An example would be the September 11, 2001, attacks on the United States.
- **Ageism.** Prejudice or discrimination based on age, particularly prejudice toward the elderly. For example, an ageist might believe that all elderly people are bad drivers with bad memories.

- **Ableism.** Prejudice or discrimination toward people who are disabled or handicapped—physically, mentally, or emotionally. For example, someone shows ableism by avoiding interaction with handicapped people because of anxiety about not knowing what to say or how to act around them.
- **Sexism.** Prejudice or discrimination based on sex or gender. For example, a sexist might believe that no one should vote for a female running for president because she would be too emotional.
- **Heterosexism.** Belief that heterosexuality is the only acceptable sexual orientation. For example, using the slang "fag" or "queer" as an insult or put down or believing that gays should not have the same legal rights and opportunities as heterosexuals shows heterosexism.
- **Homophobia.** Extreme fear or hatred of homosexuals. For example, people who engage in gay bashing (acts of violence toward gays) or who create and contribute to antigay Web sites show homophobia.

Pause for Reflection

Have you ever held a prejudice against a particular group of people?

If you have, what was the group, and how do you think your prejudice developed?

Student Perspective

"I grew up in a very racist family. Even just a year ago, I could honestly say 'I hate Asians' with a straight face and mean it. My senior AP language teacher tried hard to teach me not to be judgmental. He got me to be open to others, so much so that my current boyfriend is half Chinese!"

—First-year college student

The following practices and strategies may be used to accept and appreciate individuals from other groups toward whom you may hold prejudices, stereotypes, or subtle biases that bubble beneath the surface of your conscious awareness.

1. Consciously avoid preoccupation with physical appearances.

Go deeper and get beneath the superficial surface of appearances to judge people not in terms of how they look but in terms of whom they are and how they act. Remember the old proverb "It's what's inside that counts." Judge others by the quality of their personal character, not by the familiarity of their physical characteristics.

2. Perceive each person with whom you interact as having a unique personal identify.

Make a conscious effort to see each person with whom you interact not merely as a member of a same group but as a unique individual. Form your impressions of each person case by case rather than by using some rule of thumb.

This may seem like an obvious and easy thing to do, but research shows that humans have a natural tendency to perceive and conceive of individuals who are members of unfamiliar groups as being more alike (or all alike) than members of their own group (Taylor, Peplau, & Sears, 2006). Thus, you may have to consciously resist this tendency to overgeneralize and lump together individuals into homogenous groups; instead, make an intentional attempt to focus on treating each person you interact with as a unique human.

> ! **Remember**
>
> While it is valuable to learn about different cultures and the common character-istics shared by members of the same culture, differences exist among individuals who share the same culture. Don't assume that all individuals from the same cultural background share the same personal characteristics.

Interacting and Collaborating with Members of Diverse Groups

Once you overcome your biases and begin to perceive members of diverse groups as unique individuals, you are positioned to take the next step of interacting, collaborating, and forming friendships with them. Interpersonal contact between diverse people takes you beyond multicultural awareness and moves you up to a higher level of diversity appreciation that involves intercultural interaction. When you take this step to cross cultural boundar-ies, you transform diversity appreciation from a value or belief system into an observable action and way of living.

Your initial comfort level with interacting with people from diverse groups is likely to depend on how much experience you have had with diversity before college. If you have had little or no prior experience interacting with members of diverse groups, it may be more challenging for you to initiate interactions with diverse students on campus.

However, if you have had little previous experience with diversity, the good news is that you have the most to gain from interacting and collaborating with those of other ethnic or racial groups. Research consistently shows that when humans experience social interaction that differs radically from their prior experiences they gain the most in terms of learning and cognitive development (Acredolo & O'Connor, 1991; Piaget, 1985).

Meeting and Interacting with People from Diverse Backgrounds

1. Intentionally create opportunities for interaction and conversation with individuals from diverse groups.

Consciously resist the natural tendency to associate only with people who are similar to you. One way to do this is by intentionally placing yourself in situations where individuals from diverse groups are nearby and potential interaction can take place. Research indicates that meaningful interactions and friendships are more likely to form among people who are in physical

> "The common eye sees only the outside of things, and judges by that. But the seeing eye pierces through and reads the heart and the soul, finding there capacities which the outside didn't indicate or promise."
>
> —Samuel Clemens, a.k.a. Mark Twain; writer, lecturer, and humorist

> "Stop judging by mere appearances, and make a right judgment."
>
> —Bible, John 7:24

> "You can't judge a book by the cover."
>
> —Title of the 1962 hit song by Elias Bates, a.k.a. Bo Diddley (Note: A bo diddley is a one-stringed African guitar)

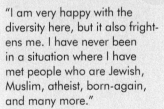

Student Perspective

"I am very happy with the diversity here, but it also fright-ens me. I have never been in a situation where I have met people who are Jewish, Muslim, atheist, born-again, and many more."

—First-year college student (Erickson, Peters, & Strommer, 2006)

proximity to one another (Latané, Liu, Nowak, Bonevento, & Zheng, 1995). Studies show that stereotyping and prejudice can be sharply reduced if contact between members of different racial or ethnic groups is frequent enough to allow time for the development of friendships (Pettigrew, 1998). You can create this condition in the college classroom by sitting near students from different ethnic or racial groups or by joining them if you are given the choice to select whom you will work with in class discussion groups and group projects.

Pause for Reflection

Rate the amount or variety of diversity you have experienced in the following settings:

1. The high school you
   attended   high moderate low

2. The college or university
   you now attend   high moderate low

3. The neighborhood in
   which you grew up   high moderate low

4. Places where you have
   worked or been employed   high moderate low

Which setting had the most and which had the least diversity?

What do you think accounts for this difference?

2. Take advantage of the Internet to chat with students from diverse groups on your campus or with students in different countries.

Electronic communication can be a more convenient and more comfortable way to initially interact with members of diverse groups with whom you have had little prior experience. After you've communicated successfully *online*, you may then feel more comfortable about interacting with them *in person*. Online and in-person interaction with students from other cultures and nations can give you a better understanding of your own culture and country, as well as increase awareness of its customs and values that you may have taken for granted (Bok, 2006).

3. Seek out the views and opinions of classmates from diverse backgrounds.

For example, during or after class discussions, ask students from different backgrounds if there was any point made or position taken in class that they would strongly question or challenge. Seeking out divergent (diverse) viewpoints has been found to be one of the best ways to develop critical thinking skills (Kurfiss, 1988).

4. Join or form discussion groups with students from diverse backgrounds.

You can gain exposure to diverse perspectives by joining or forming groups of students who differ from you in terms of such characteristics as gender, age, race, or ethnicity. You might begin by forming discussion groups composed of students who differ in one way but are similar in another way. For instance, form a learning team of students who have the same major as you do but who differ with respect to race, ethnicity, or age. This strategy gives the diverse

! Remember

Including diversity in your discussion groups not only provides social variety but also promotes the quality of the group's thinking by allowing its members to gain access to the diverse perspectives and life experiences of people from different backgrounds.

members of your team some common ground for discussion (your major) and can raise your team's awareness that although you may be members of different groups you can, at the same time, be similar with respect to your educational goals and life plans.

5. Form collaborative learning teams.

A learning team is more than a discussion group or a study group. It moves beyond discussion to collaborative learning—in other words, members of a learning team "co-labor" (work together) as part of a joint and mutually supportive effort to reach the same goal. Studies show that when individuals from different ethnic and racial groups work collaboratively toward the attainment of a common goal it reduces racial prejudice and promotes interracial friendships (Allport, 1954; Amir, 1976). These positive findings may be explained as follows: If individuals from diverse groups work on the same team, no one is a member of an "out" group (them); instead, all are members of the same "in" group (us; Pratto et al., 2000; Sidanius et al., 2000).

◆ Summary and Conclusion

Diversity refers to differences among groups of people who, together, comprise humanity. Experiencing diversity increases appreciation of the features unique to different cultures, and it gives a wider perspective on aspects of the human experience that are common to all people, regardless of their particular cultural background.

Culture is formed by the beliefs and values of a group with the same traditions and social heritage. It helps bind people into supportive, tight-knit communities. However, it can also lead people to view the world solely through their own cultural lens, known as ethnocentrism, which can blind them to other cultural perspectives. Ethnocentrism can contribute to stereotyping—viewing individual members of the same group in the same way and as having similar personal characteristics.

Evaluating members of a stereotyped group negatively results in prejudice—a negative prejudgment about another person or group of people, which is formed before the facts are known. Stereotyping and prejudice often go hand in hand because if the stereotype is negative, individual members of the stereotyped group are then prejudged negatively. Discrimination takes prejudice one step further by converting the negative prejudgment into action that results in unfair treatment of others. Thus, discrimination is prejudice put into action.

If stereotyping and prejudice are overcome, you are then positioned to experience diversity and reap its multiple benefits, which include sharpened self-awareness, social stimulation, broadened personal perspectives, deeper learning, higher-level thinking, and career success.

The increasing diversity of students on campus, combined with the wealth of diversity-related educational experiences found in the college curriculum and cocurriculum, presents you with an unprecedented opportunity to infuse diversity into your college experience. Seize this opportunity and capitalize on the power of diversity to increase the quality of your college education and your prospects for future success.

Internet-Based Resources for Further Information on Diversity

For additional information related to the ideas discussed in this chapter, we recommend the following Web sites:

www.tolerance.org

www.amnesty.org

Chapter 13 Exercises

13.1 Self-Awareness of Multigroup Identities

You can be members of multiple groups at the same time, and your membership in these overlapping groups can influence your personal development and self-identity. In the figure that follows, consider the shaded center circle to be yourself and the six nonshaded circles to be six groups you belong to that you think have influenced your personal development or personal identity.

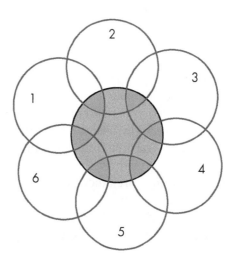

Fill in the nonshaded circles with the names of groups to which you belong that have had the most influence on your personal development. You can use the diversity spectrum that appears on the second page of this chapter to help you identify different groups. Do not feel you have to come up with six groups and fill all six circles. What is more important is to identify those groups that have had a significant influence on your personal development or identity.

Self-Assessment Questions

1. Which one of your groups has had the greatest influence on your personal identity, and why?

2. Have you ever felt limited or disadvantaged by being a member of any group or groups?

3. Have you ever felt that you experienced advantages or privileges because of your membership in any group or groups?

13.2 Intercultural Interview

Find a student, faculty member, or administrator on campus whose cultural background is different from yours, and ask if you could interview that person about his or her culture. Use the following questions in your interview:

1. How is "family" defined in your culture, and what are the traditional roles and responsibilities of different family members?

2. What are the traditional gender (male vs. female) roles associated with your culture? Are they changing?

3. What is your culture's approach to time (e.g., Is there an emphasis on punctuality? Is doing things quickly valued or frowned upon?)

4. What are your culture's staple foods or favorite foods?

5. What cultural traditions or rituals are highly valued and commonly practiced?

6. What special holidays are celebrated?

13.3 Hidden Bias Test

Go to www.tolerance.org/activity/test-yourself-hidden-bias and take one or more of the hidden bias tests on the Web site. These tests assess subtle bias with respect to gender, age, Native Americans, African Americans, Asian Americans, religious denominations, sexual orientations, disabilities, and body weight. You can assess whether you have a bias toward any of these groups.

Self-Assessment Questions

1. Did the results reveal any bias that you were unaware of?

2. Did you think the assessment results were accurate or valid?

3. What do you think best accounts for or explains your results?

4. If your parents and best friends took the test, how do you think their results would compare with yours?

Hate Crime: A Racially Motivated Murder

Jasper County, Texas, has a population of approximately 31,000 people. In this county, 80 percent of the people are White, 18 percent are Black, and 2 percent are of other races. The county's poverty rate is considerably higher than the national average, and its average household income is significantly lower. In 1998, the mayor, president of the Chamber of Commerce, and two councilmen were Black. From the outside, Jasper appeared to be a town with racial harmony, and its Black and White leaders were quick to state that there was racial harmony in Jasper.

However, on June 7, 1998, James Byrd Jr., a 49-year-old African American male, was walking home along a road one evening and was offered a ride by three White males. Rather than taking Byrd home, Lawrence Brewer (age 31), John King (age 23), and Shawn Berry (age 23), three individuals linked to White-supremacist groups, took Byrd to an isolated area and began beating him. They then dropped his pants to his ankles, painted his face black, chained Byrd to their truck, and dragged him for approximately 3 miles. The truck was driven in a zigzag fashion to inflict maximum pain on the victim. Byrd was decapitated after his body collided with a culvert in a ditch alongside the road. His skin, arms, genitalia, and other body parts were strewn along the road, while his torso was found dumped in front of a Black cemetery. Medical examiners testified that Byrd was alive for much of the dragging incident.

While in prison awaiting trial, Brewer wrote letters to King and other inmates. In one letter, Brewer wrote: "Well, I did it and am no longer a virgin. It was a rush and I'm still licking my lips for more." Once the trials were completed, Brewer and King were sentenced to death. Both Brewer and King, whose bodies were covered with racist tattoos, had been on parole before the incident, and they had previously been cellmates. King had spent an extensive amount of time in prison, where he began to associate with White males in an environment in which each race was pitted against the other.

As a result of the murder, Byrd's family created the James Byrd Foundation for Racial Healing in 1998. On January 20, 1999, a wrought iron fence that separated Black and White graves for more than 150 years in Jasper Cemetery was removed in a special unity service. Members of the racist Ku Klux Klan have since visited the gravesite of Byrd several times, leaving racist stickers and other marks that have angered the Jasper community and Byrd's family.

Sources: Houston Chronicle (June 14, 1998); San Antonio Express News (September 17, 1999); Louisiana Weekly (February 3, 2003).

Reflection and Discussion Questions

1. What factors do you think were responsible for causing this incident to take place?

2. Could this incident have been prevented? If yes, how? If no, why not?

3. What do you think will be the long-term effects of this incident on the town?

4. How likely do you think it is that an incident like this could take place in your hometown or near your college campus?

5. If this event took place in your hometown, how would you and members of your family and community react?

Your First Year Resources

The first year of college is an exciting and challenging time. We want you to have the best experience possible, so we've designed a website just for you. It's full of tips, tricks, and links to help you make the most of Your First Year! If you have questions or need help finding your way at UNCG, you can always email us at yfy@uncg.edu. Visit yourfirstyear.uncg.edu and the websites below for helpful resources and services about diversity and human differences.

Associated Campus Ministries at UNCG   **336-334-4266**
http://sa.uncg.edu/acm/

Campus Activities & Programs   **336-334-5800**
http://cap.uncg.edu/

International Programs Center   **336-334-5404**
http://www.uncg.edu/ipg/

Office of Accessibility Resources & Services   **336-334-5440**
http://ods.uncg.edu/

Office of Leadership & Service-Learning   **336-256-0538**
http://olsl.uncg.edu/

The Office of Intercultural Engagement   **336-334-5090**
http://oma.uncg.edu/

SafeZone Training, The Wellness Center   **336-334-3190**
http://www.uncg.edu/shs/wellness/

Epilogue

A Matter of Principles and Character

◆ Principles of College Success

In the first chapter of this text, we mentioned that research on human learning and student development pointed to four powerful principles of college success:

1. *active involvement,*
2. *utilizing resources,*
3. *interpersonal interaction* and *collaboration,* and
4. *self-reflection.*

These principles form the four major bases or cornerstones of college. We will conclude this text by showing how these four bases contribute to college success and demonstrating how they can also promote development of character—a lifelong quality that is essential for personal success beyond college.

Active Involvement

This principle rests on a solid foundation of research, which indicates that success in college depends on students becoming *active agents* in the learning process who are willing to invest a significant amount of *time*, *effort*, and *energy* in the college experience.

The importance of this principle emerged at the very start of this book when we noted that the positive impact of college is magnified when students become actively involved in planning their course work and participating in campus life. We saw this principle in action again in the chapters on learning and memory, where it was shown that deep, long-lasting learning involves active construction (building) of knowledge and *transformation* of information into a form that has personal meaning to the learner.

In short, the principle of active involvement suggests that students maximize their learning and development when they get "into" the college experience and do it with passion and enthusiasm. Actively involved students do not hold back or do college half-heartedly; they do it whole-heartedly—by putting their whole "heart and soul" into it.

> "
> *It is not so much what the individual thinks or feels, but what the individual does, how he or she behaves, that defines and identifies involvement.*
>
> –Alexander Astin, Professor Emeritus, UCLA; identified as the "most frequently cited author" in higher education and the person "most admired for creative insightful thinking."

Social Interaction/Collaboration

A large body of research indicates that learning is significantly strengthened when it takes place in a social context that involves human *interaction* and interpersonal *collaboration* (Cuseo, 1996; 2002). You can embrace this inter-active and collaborative spirit by seeking input and support from others, and by being open to the ideas of others. As we pointed out in Chapter 12 (Diversity), interaction and collaboration with individuals from diverse cul-tural backgrounds is one particular form of interpersonal interaction that has especially powerful effects on promoting deep learning, higher-level thinking, and social development.

You can also capture the spirit of collaboration by building *success-sup-porting* social networks, surrounding yourself with other success-seeking and high-achieving students. In addition, be on the lookout for more experienced students, college alumni, and career professionals, all of whom can serve as potential mentors or supportive role models.

Last, and perhaps most important, studies show that people who have strong social support networks are happier (Myers, 1993), healthier (Maddi, 2002), and live longer (Giles, et al., 2005).

Utilizing Resources

Success results from a combination of what students do for themselves and how effectively they capitalize on the multiple resources that their college pro-vides them. Studies show that students who utilize campus resources report higher levels of satisfaction with the college experience and get more out of their college experience (Pascaralla & Terenzini, 1991, 2005). Typically, suc-cessful students are *resourceful* students who seek out and take full advantage of their resources to help them develop academically, emotionally, physically, and spiritually.

Self-Reflection

Self-awareness is an essential pre-requisite for success. "Know thyself" is among the most frequently cited goals of higher education and one of the cardinal characteristics of a highly educated person. Effective learning not only requires action, it also requires *reflection*. Humans do not learn deeply by engaging in mindless repetition and memorization, but by thoughtful *reflection* and *connection* of what they're learning to what they already know.

Effective learning also involves periodically pausing to reflect on whether you truly *understand* or *comprehend* what you're attempting to learn and whether you are using effective learning strategies. Reflection ensures that you "watch yourself" while you learn, which enables you to maintain self-awareness of your learning habits and allows you to "know yourself" as a learner.

Deepening your self-awareness also puts you in a better position to select and pursue a career path that's true to yourself—a path that is truly compat-ible with your personal interests, values, and talents. Furthermore, maintaining awareness of your developing skills and personal qualities will put you in a bet-ter position to successfully present your strengths to future employers.

Last and perhaps most important, taking time for internal reflection is par-ticularly important in today's high-tech world that bombards us with multiple modes of communication, massive loads of information, and endless amounts of external stimulation. We need to make a conscious effort to call "time out" and turn off all this sensory stimulation from the outside world, and "tune into" the inner world of personal reflection if we hope to find meaning and direction in our life.

> "
> *Learning occurs best in a cultural context that provides both enjoyable interaction and substantial personal support.*
>
> —Peter Ewell, nationally known author and speaker on higher education

> "
> *Successful students know a lot about themselves.*
>
> —Claire Weinstein & Debra Meyer, Profes-sors of Educational Psychology, University of Texas

In sum, success in college and beyond is more likely to be achieved by students who are:

1. Actively involved,
2. Interactive and collaborative,
3. Resourceful, and
4. Reflective.

These four principles represent more than just college-specific tips or strategies; they are *lifelong-learning* skills and *life-success* principles that can be applied to all aspects of life throughout life. These principles may also be represented as four bases in a diamond of *personal* success:

The Diamond of Personal Success: Four Core Principles

Interpersonal *Interaction/Collaboration*

Self-*Reflection*   PERSONAL SUCCESS   Utilizing *Resources*

Active Involvement

☐ = Supporting Bases of Personal Success
▼ = Primary ("Home") Base of Personal Success

THINK ABOUT IT   **Journal Entry**   **E.1**

Thus far in your college experience, which of the four principles of success do you think you have most consistently put into practice?

_____

_____

Which of the four personal-success principles do you think you need to devote more attention to than you have thus far in your college experience?

_____

_____

_____

◆ Personal Character

While success in college and beyond cannot happen without both awareness and use of effective learning and living principles, it takes something more. Ultimately, success emerges from the inside out. Effective actions and good deeds emerge from positive attributes found within us; when they are combined, they form our personal *character*.

Success stems from something larger than the application of principles and strategies. We become successful human beings when our effective actions become a natural extension of who we are and how we live. At first, practicing strategies for doing well in college and leading a productive life may require deliberate concentration and conscious effort because these behaviors may be new to you. However, if these effortful actions occur frequently enough, they become transformed into regular and natural habits.

When we engage in good habits in this regular fashion, they become personal virtues. A *virtue* may be defined as a characteristic or trait that is valued as good or admirable, and a person who possesses a collection of important virtues is said to be a person of *character* (Peterson & Seligman, 2004).

Research suggests that the following five virtues are especially important for success in college and in life after college:

1. Wisdom,
2. Initiative,
3. Motivation,
4. Integrity, and
5. Civic Responsibility.

We'll turn now to a discussion of each of these key virtues and highlight their relevance for success in college and beyond.

Wisdom

When we use knowledge to guide our actions to do what is good or excellent, we are demonstrating *wisdom* (Staudinger & Baltes, 1994). The four research-based principles of success that provide the foundation of this book (i.e., involvement, collaboration, resourcefulness, and reflection) are grounded in a large body of knowledge on educational and personal success. If you use these four knowledge-based principles to inform and guide your behaviors, you are acting wisely or exhibiting wisdom.

Initiative

When you take charge of your life by attempting to gain control over the outcomes and events in your life, you are demonstrating *initiative*. In contrast, lack of initiative stems from feeling powerless and allowing things to happen to us passively, without making an effort to change them.

People with personal initiative have what psychologists call an *internal locus of control*—they believe that the source (locus) of control over events and outcomes in their life resides primarily within them, i.e., control is "internal" rather than being determined by "external" factors beyond their control—such as luck, chance, or fate (Rotter, 1966).

If you do not find it within yourself, where will you go to get it?

–Zen saying (Zen is a branch of Buddhism that emphasizes seeing deeply into the nature of things and ongoing self-awareness)

We are what we repeatedly do. Excellence, then, is not an act, but a habit.

–Aristotle, influential ancient-Greek philosopher, 384–322 BC

Sow an act and you reap a habit; sow a habit and you reap a character; sow a character and you reap a destiny.

–Frances E. Willard, 19th-century American educator and woman's rights activist

Mere knowledge is not power; it is only possibility. Action is power; and its highest manifestation is when it is directed by knowledge.

–Francis Bacon (1561–1626), English philosopher, lawyer, and champion of modern science

Research indicates that individuals with a strong internal locus of control display the following characteristics:

a. Greater independence and self-direction (Van Overwalle, Mervielde, & De Schuyer, 1995),
b. More accurate self-assessment (Hashaw, Hammond, & Rogers, 1990; Lefcourt, 1982),
c. Higher levels of learning and academic performance (Wilhite, 1990), and
d. Better physical health (Maddi, 2002; Seligman, 1991).

An internal locus of control also contributes to the development of another positive trait, which psychologists call *self-efficacy*—the belief that we have the capacity or power to produce positive outcomes in our life (Bandura, 1994). A strong sense of self-efficacy increases our motivation by increasing our willingness to initiate action, to put forth effort, and to persist or persevere in the face of setbacks and adversity (Bandura, 1997; 1986). Students with a strong sense of *academic* self-efficacy have been found to

a. Put forth great effort in their studies,
b. Use active-learning strategies,
c. Capitalize on campus resources, and
d. Persist in the face of obstacles (Multon, Brown, & Lent, 1991; Zimmerman, 1995).

Individuals with initiative do not have a false sense of entitlement; they don't feel they are "entitled to" or are "owed" anything without taking the personal initiative to attain it. For example, studies show that college graduates who successfully convert their college degree into successful career entry are individuals who take the initiative to become actively involved in the job-hunting process and use multiple job-search strategies (Brown & Krane, 2000). They do not take a passive approach that assumes a good position will be handed to them or will just fall into their lap, nor do they feel that they are owed a good job simply because they have a college degree.

> *What lies behind us and what lies in front of us are small matters compared to what lies within us.*
>
> –Ralph Waldo Emerson, 19th-century philosopher, author, and abolitionist

> *Man who stand on hill with mouth open will wait long time for roast duck to drop in.*
>
> –Confucius, famous Chinese philosopher who emphasized sincerity and social justice

THINK ABOUT IT   Journal Entry   E.2

In what area(s) of your life do you feel that you have been able to exert the most control and are producing the most positive results?

_____

_____

_____

What area(s) of your life do you wish you had more control over and were producing better results?

_____

_____

_____

Motivation

The word motivation derives from the Latin "movere," which means "to move." Success comes to those who truly want it and who exert effort to move in the direction of success. Having an arsenal of effective strategies at your disposal, such as those provided in this text, provides only the potential for success. Realizing this potential requires personal motivation to put these strategies into actual practice. As the old saying goes, "You can lead a horse to water, but you can't make him drink." In other words, if there's no will, there's no way.

Motivation consists of different elements or components that may be referred to as the "three Ds" of motivation:

a. Drive,
b. Dedication, and
c. Determination.

Drive

Drive is the force within us that provides us with the energy needed to overcome inertia and initiate action. People who possess drive make a forceful effort to convert their goals and dreams into concrete actions and behaviors.

They are not "dreamers" who simply dream; they are "doers" who take action on their dreams and strive to transform the ideal into the real. People with drive will hustle—they go all out, all the time; they give 100%, 100% of the time; they are willing to go "beyond the call of duty" and go "the extra mile" to achieve their dreams.

Dedication

Dedication includes such positive qualities as commitment, devotion, and diligence. These motivational qualities enable us to keep going, steadily sustaining our effort and our endurance over an extended period of time. Dedicated people are willing to "grind it out," to take all the small steps and to diligently do all the little things that need to be done, which gradually build up and add up to a big accomplishment.

People with dedication put in the day-to-day perspiration needed to attain their future aspirations. They are truly committed to their goals and are willing to undergo needed short-term strain and pain for long-term gain. They possess the self-control and self-restraint to resist giving in to impulses for immediate gratification or the temptation to do what they "feel like" doing at the moment or in the short run.

They have the dedication and self-discipline to sacrifice their short-term needs or desires and get done what must be done in order to get them where they want to be in the long run.

Studies show that individuals with commitment—who become deeply involved and dedicated to what they do—are more likely to be healthy and happy (Maddi, 2002).

Determination

People who are determined show a relentless tenacity in pursuit of their goals. They have the fortitude to persist in the face of frustration and they have the resilience to bounce back after setbacks. When the going gets tough, they keep

In the arena of human life, the honors and rewards fall to those who show their good qualities in action.

–Aristotle, ancient Greek philosopher; student of Plato and teacher of Alexander the Great

I long to accomplish some great and noble task, but it is my chief duty to accomplish small tasks as if they were great and noble.

–Helen Keller, seeing- and hearing-impaired author and activist for the rights of women and the handicapped

Student Perspective

"Why is it so hard when I have to do something and so easy when I want to do something?"

–First-year student

going. If they encounter something on the road to their goal that's hard to do, they work harder to do it; they don't give up or give in, they dig deeper and give more.

In fact, people who are determined often seek out *challenges*. Rather than remaining stagnant and simply doing what's safe, secure, or easy, they "stay hungry" and display an ongoing commitment to personal growth and development; they keep striving and driving to be the best they can possibly be in all aspects of their life.

Research indicates that people who seek challenges and continual self-development throughout life are more likely to be happy (Myers, 1993) and healthy (Maddi, 2002).

Integrity

In addition to pursuing performance excellence, people of character also pursue ethical excellence. They not only do what is smart; they also do what is *good* or *right*. People with integrity possess a strong set of personal values, which serves to guide them in the right moral direction.

The term *value* derives from the Latin root "valere," meaning to be of "worth" or to be "strong" (as in the words, "valuable" and "valor"). This is a particularly important virtue for college students to possess because the freedom of college brings with it new freedom to make personal choices and decisions about what life path to pursue and what people to associate with, which often serve as a test of their true priorities and values.

Individuals with integrity are "inner-directed"—their actions reflect their inner conscience; when they are unsure about what choice or decision to make, they look inward and let their own conscience guide their action. They are not "outer-directed" people whose personal standards of conduct are determined by looking outward to see what others are doing (Riesman, Glazer, & Denney, 2001). For example, college students with integrity do not cheat and rationalize their cheating as being acceptable because "other people are doing it." They don't look to others to determine their own values and they don't conform to the norm if the norm is wrong.

Unlike a chameleon, which changes its color to fit the environment it happens to be in, the behavior of people with integrity is not determined by their social environment—by the reactions or approval of others around them. Instead, their sense of self-respect, self-worth, and self-satisfaction come from within—from the internal feeling of pride that comes from knowing they did what was right and what they should have done.

People with integrity display *honesty*. They admit when they're wrong or when they haven't done what they should have done. They feel remorse or guilt when they haven't lived up to their own ethical standards, and they use this guilt productively to motivate them to do what's right in the future. When they are wrong, they don't play the role of victim and look for something or someone else to blame; they're willing to accept the blame or "take the heat" when they're wrong and to take responsibility for making it right.

People with integrity also possess *authenticity*—they are genuine or "real"—how they appear to be is who they really are. It's noteworthy that the word "integrity" comes from the same word root as "integrate." This captures the idea that people with integrity have an integrated or unified sense of self. Their "outer" self—how they appear to others, is in harmony with their inner self—who they really are.

Self-discipline is the ability to make yourself do the thing you have to do, when it ought be done, whether you like it or not.

–Thomas Henry Huxley, influential 19th-century English biologist

SUCCESS is peace of mind which is a direct result of self-satisfaction in knowing you made the effort to become the best that you are capable of becoming.

–John Wooden, legendary college basketball coach and author of the "Pyramid of Success"

In matters or principle, stand like a rock; in matters of taste, swim with the current.

–Thomas Jefferson, 3rd U.S. President and principal author of the Declaration of Independence (1776)

Be who you are; say what you feel; because those who mind, don't matter, and those who matter, don't mind.

–Theodore Seuss Giesel (a.k.a., "Dr. Seuss"), famous author of children's books such as, The Cat in the Hat

Our character is what we do when we think no one is looking.

–Henry David Thoreau, American philosopher and lifelong abolitionist who championed the human spirit over materialism and conformity

There is no pillow as soft as a clear conscience.

–French proverb

How you see yourself is your *self-concept* or *personal identity* which derives from the Latin "identitas" for "being the same" (as in the words "identical" and "identify"). In contrast, your *personality* is how others see you. Personality originates from the Latin "persona," which was a mask worn by actors in ancient Greek and Roman plays who portrayed fictional characters. People of integrity don't wear masks or play roles. Their public persona or outer personality is consistent with their private self or inner identity.

Said in another way, people with integrity have "got it together"; they are individuals whose inner character and outer personality come together to form an integrated and unified human being.

People with integrity also integrate their professed or stated values and their actual behavior. Their convictions and actions are aligned or in sync; they are models of consistency rather than hypocrisy. They say what they mean and they mean what they say. They don't give lip service to their values by just stating or announcing them; they embody them and live by them.

People with integrity not only "talk the talk," they also "walk the talk" by practicing what they preach and remaining truthful to their values. Their actions and commitments are consistent with their ideals and convictions.

Student Perspective

"I value authenticity in people's actions. I believe in genuine motives [and] none of that ulterior or deceitful stuff."

—First-year student

If you don't live it, it won't come out of your horn.

—Charlie "Bird" Parker, famed African-American jazz saxophonist, composer, and originator of Bebop

Put your creed into your deed.

—Ralph Waldo Emerson

Happiness is when what you think, what you say and what you do are in harmony.

—Mahatma Gandhi, non-violent civil rights leader who led struggle to free India from colonial rule

---

THINK ABOUT IT   **Journal Entry**   **E.3**

Since beginning college, have you observed any instances or examples of personal integrity that you thought were admirable?

_____

_____

_____

What were the situations and what was done in these situations to demonstrate integrity?

_____

_____

_____

Student Perspective

"I understood what I did was morally wrong and now I have to overcome it and move on living morally and ethically. It's really amazing that integrity is in everything we do in our lives."

—First-year student's reflection on academic integrity violation

---

Student Perspective

"To achieve success through deceitful actions is not success at all. In life, credibility is more important than credentials, and if honesty is not valued personally, others will not value you. Lack of self-respect results in lack of respect from others."

—First-year student's reflection on academic integrity violation

---

Civic Responsibility

People of character are good *citizens*. They model what it means to live in a civilized community by displaying *civility*—they are respectful of and sensitive to the rights of others. In exercising their own rights and freedoms, they do not step on (or stomp on) the rights and freedoms of others.

Civically responsible people treat their fellow citizens in a humane and compassionate manner, and they are also willing to confront others who violate the rights of their fellow citizens. People with civic character are model citizens whose actions visibly demonstrate to others that they actively oppose any attempts to disrespect or dehumanize fellow members of their community.

Civic character is also demonstrated through *civic engagement*. Civically minded and civically responsible people are actively engaged in their community, trying to make it the best it can be by partaking in the democratic process and participating in its governance.

Civically responsible people show civic concern by stepping beyond their individual interests to actively promote the welfare of others in their community. They show kindness and commitment to their community by selflessly volunteering their time and energy to help fellow citizens, particularly those who are in need.

When people give to others and contribute to the good of the larger group of which they are a part, they experience a sense of self-satisfaction and personal reward. Studies show that individuals who go beyond themselves to focus on the needs of others are more likely to report feeling "happy" (Myers, 1993). Furthermore, when we contribute to the lives of others, we're more likely to feel that we're doing something meaningful with our own life.

Five Virtues Possessed by People with Character: A Visual Summary

◆ Conclusion and Farewell

It is our hope that the ideas presented in this book will enable you to get off to a good start in college, as well as contribute to your success throughout your college years and beyond. We recommend that you save this book, use its recommended strategies beyond the first year of college, and continue to use whabits to take hold and take effect. If you remain patient and continue to use effective strategies consistently, their positive effects will begin to accumulate and their power will increase with the passage of time.

Finally, don't forget that graduation is also known as *commencement*, which means to start or begin. College graduation doesn't represent the end of your education; instead, it is the beginning of a life of ongoing learning and development. The skills you acquire by the time you graduate will continue to be used to further promote your growth and development throughout the remaining years of your life. It could be said that your growth after college is likely to follow a pattern similar to that of the Chinese bamboo tree. The first four years of this tree's growth takes place underground, after which it emerges from the ground and grows as high as 80 feet (Covey, Merrill, & Merrill, 1996). Similarly, your four academic years in college will provide the underlying roots for lifelong growth. We hope that you will continue to grow until you achieve and exceed your highest dreams.

All the best,
Joe Cuseo
Viki Sox Fecas
Aaron Thompson

P.S.: We would love to receive any feedback you can provide us about this book. We'd like to learn about your general reaction to the text and if you successfully applied any of the strategies we've recommended. We would also be interested in your ideas about what we should continue to include in future editions of this text and what we should change to improve it. You can be assured that any feedback you provide us will be taken seriously. Please send us any ideas you may have for us to this e-address (website):

www.kendallhunt.com/cuseo

We'll be sure to read your comments and write back to you.

Glossary

Ability (Aptitude) the capacity to do something well or to have the potential to do it well.

Academic Advisor a professional who advises college students on course selection, helps students understand college procedures, and helps guide their academic progress toward completion of a college degree.

Academic Dismissal denying a student continued college enrollment because of a cumulative GPA that remains below a minimum level (e.g., below 2.0).

Academic Probation a period (usually one term) during which students with a GPA that is too low (e.g., less than 2.0) are given a chance to improve their grades; if the student's GPA does not meet or exceed the college's minimum requirement after this probationary period, that student may be academically dismissed from the college.

Academic Support Center the place on campus where students can obtain individual assistance from professionals and trained peers to support and strengthen their academic performance.

Administrator someone whose primary responsibility is the governance of the college or a unit within the college, such as an academic department or student support service.

Career the sum total of vocational experiences throughout an individual's work life.

Career Advancement working up the career ladder to higher levels of decision-making responsibility and socioeconomic status.

Career Development Center a key campus resource for learning about the nature of different careers and strategies on how to locate career-related work experiences.

Career Development Course a college course that typically includes self-assessment of career interests, information about different careers, and strategies for career preparation.

Career Entry gaining entry into a career and beginning a career path.

Citation an acknowledgment of the source of any piece of information included in a written paper or oral report that doesn't represent original work or thoughts.

Cocurricular Experience the learning and development that occur outside the classroom.

Communication Skills skills necessary for accurate comprehension and articulate expression of ideas, which include reading, writing, speaking, listening, and multimedia skills.

Commuter Student a college student who does not live on campus.

Concentration a cluster of approximately three courses in the same subject area.

Concept a larger system or network of related ideas.

Concept (Idea) Map a visual diagram that represents or maps out main categories of ideas and their relationships in a visual–spatial format.

Cooperative Education (Co-op) Program a program in which students gain work experience relating to their college major, either by stopping their coursework temporarily to work full time at the co-op position or by continuing to take classes while working part time at the co-op position.

Core Course a course required of all students, regardless of their particular major.

Cover (Application) Letter a letter written by an applicant who is applying for an employment position or admission to a school.

Cramming packing study time into one session immediately before an exam.

Creative Thinking a form of higher-level thinking that involves producing a new and different idea, method, strategy, or work product.

Critical Thinking a form of higher-level thinking that involves making well-informed evaluations or judgments.

Culture a distinctive way or style of living that characterizes a group of people who share the same social system, heritage, and traditions.

Cum Laude graduating with honors (e.g., achieving a cumulative GPA of at least 3.3).

Cumulative Grade Point Average a student's GPA for all academic terms combined.

Curriculum the total set of courses offered by a college or university.

Dean's List achieving an outstanding GPA for a particular term (e.g., 3.5 or higher).

Diversity interacting with and learning from peers of varied backgrounds and lifestyles.

Diversity Appreciation becoming interested in and valuing the experiences of different groups of people and willingness to learn more about them.

Diversity (Multicultural) Course a course designed to promote diversity awareness and appreciation of multiple cultures.

Documentation information sources that serve as references to support or reinforce conclusions in a written paper or oral presentation.

Elective a course that students are not required to take but that they elect or choose to take.

Experiential Learning out-of-class experiences that promote learning and development.

Faculty the collection of instructors on campus whose primary role is to teach courses that comprise the college curriculum.

Free Elective a course that students may elect to enroll in, which counts toward a college degree but is not required for either general education or academic major.

Freshman 15 a phrase commonly used to describe the 15-pound weight gain that some students experience during their first year of college.

Graduate Assistant (GA) a graduate student who receives financial assistance to pursue graduate studies by working in a university office or college professor.

Grade Points the amount of points earned for a course, which is calculated by multiplying the course grade by the number of credits carried by the course.

Grade Point Average (GPA) the translation of students' letter grades into a numerical system, whereby the total number of grade points earned in all courses is divided by total number of course units.

Graduate School a university-related education pursued after completing a bachelor's degree.

Grant money received that does not have to be repaid.

Greek Life a term that refers to both fraternities (usually all male) and sororities (usually all female).

Hazing a rite of induction to a social or other organization, most commonly associated with fraternities.

Higher-Level Thinking thinking at a higher or more complex level than merely acquiring factual knowledge or memorizing information.

Holistic (or Whole-Person) Development the development of the total self, which includes intellectual, social, emotional, physical, spiritual, ethical, vocational, and personal development.

Human Diversity the variety of differences that exist among people who comprise humanity (the human species).

Humanity common elements of the human experience that are shared by all humans.

Hypothesis an informed guess that might be true but still needs to be tested to confirm or verify its truth.

Illustrate to provide concrete examples or specific instances.

Independent Study a project that allows a student to receive academic credit for an in-depth study of a topic of his or her choice by working independently with a faculty member without enrolling in a formal course that meets in a classroom according to a set schedule.

Information Interview an interview with a professional working in a career to obtain inside information on what the career is like.

Information Literacy the ability to find, evaluate, and use information.

Intellectual (Cognitive) Development acquiring knowledge and learning how to learn and how to think deeply.

Interdisciplinary courses or programs that are designed to help students integrate knowledge from two or more academic disciplines (fields of study).

Interest something someone likes or enjoys doing.

International Student a student attending college in one nation who is a citizen of a different nation.

International Study (Study Abroad) Program doing coursework at a college or university in another country that counts toward graduation, and which is typically done for one or two academic terms.

Internship a work experience related to a college major for which students receive academic credit and, in some cases, financial compensation.

Interpret to draw a conclusion about something and support that conclusion with evidence.

Job Shadowing a program that allows a student to follow (shadow) and observe a professional during a typical workday.

Justify to back up arguments and viewpoints with evidence.

Leadership the ability to influence people in a positive way (e.g., motivating peers to do their best) or the ability to produce positive change in an organization or institution (e.g., improving the quality of a school, business, or political organization).

Leadership Course a course in which students learn how to advance and eventually assume important leadership positions in a company or organization.

Learning Community a program offered by some colleges and universities in which the same group of students takes the same block of courses together during the same academic term.

Learning Style the way in which individuals prefer to perceive information (receive or take it in), and process information (deal with it once it has been taken in).

Liberal Arts the component of a college education that provides the essential foundation or backbone for the college curriculum and is designed to equip students with a versatile set of skills to promote their success in any academic major or career.

Lifelong Learning Skills skills that include learning how to learn and how to continue learning that can be used throughout the remainder of personal and professional life.

Magna Cum Laude graduating with high honors (e.g., achieving a cumulative GPA of at least 3.5).

Major the academic field students choose to specialize in while in college.

Mentor someone who serves as a role model and personal guide to help students reach their educational or occupational goals.

Merit-Based Scholarship money awarded on the basis of performance or achievement that does not have to be repaid.

Metacognition thinking about the process of thinking.

Midterm the midpoint of an academic term.

Minor a second field of study that is designed to complement and strengthen a major, which usually consists of about half the number of courses required for a college major (e.g., six to seven courses are usually needed for a minor).

Mnemonic Device (Mnemonics) a specific memory-improvement method designed to prevent forgetting, which often involves such memory-improvement principles as meaning, organization, visualization, or rhythm and rhyme.

MLA Style a style of citing references in a research report that is endorsed by the Modern Language Association and is commonly used by academic fields in the humanities and fine arts (e.g., English and philosophy).

Multicultural Competence the ability to understand cultural differences and to interact effectively with people from multiple cultural backgrounds.

Multidimensional Thinking a form of higher-level thinking that involves taking multiple perspectives and considering multiple theories.

Multiple Intelligences the notion that humans display intelligence or mental skills in many other forms besides their ability to perform on intellectual tests such as IQ and SAT tests.

Need a key element of life planning that represents something stronger than an interest and makes a person's life more satisfying or fulfilling.

Need-Based Scholarship money awarded to students on the basis of financial need that does not have to be repaid.

Netiquette applying the principles of social etiquette and interpersonal sensitivity when communicating online.

Online Resource a resource that can be used to search for and locate information, including online card catalogs, Internet search engines, and electronic databases.

Oral Communication Skills the ability to speak in a concise, confident, and eloquent fashion.

Oversubscribed (Impacted) Major a major that has more students interested in it than there are openings for students to be accepted.

Paraphrase restating or rephrasing information in original words.

Part-to-Whole Method a study strategy that involves dividing study time into smaller parts or units and then learning these parts in several short, separate study sessions in advance of exams.

Persuasive Speech an oral presentation intended to persuade or convince the audience to agree with a certain conclusion or position by providing supporting evidence.

Plagiarism the deliberate or unintentional use of someone else's work without acknowledging it, giving the impression that it is original work.

Portfolio a collection of work materials or products that illustrates an individual's skills and talents or demonstrates that individual's educational and personal development.

Prewriting an early stage in the writing process where the focus is on generating and organizing ideas rather than expressing or communicating ideas to someone else.

Primary Source the information obtained from a firsthand source or original document.

Process-of-Elimination Method a multiple-choice test-taking strategy that involves weeding out or eliminating choices that are clearly wrong and continuing to do so until the choices are narrowed down to one answer that seems to be the best choice available.

Procrastination the tendency to postpone making a decision or taking action until the last moment.

Professional School a formal education pursued after a bachelor's degree in school that prepare students for an "applied" profession (e.g., pharmacy, medicine, or law).

Prerequisite Course a course that must be completed before students can enroll in a more advanced course.

Proofreading a final microscopic form of editing that focuses on detecting mechanical errors relating to such things as referencing, grammar, punctuation, and spelling.

Recall Test Question a type of test question that requires students to generate or produce the correct answer on their own, such as a short-answer question or an essay question.

Recitation (Reciting) a study strategy that involves verbally stating information to be remembered without looking at it.

Recognition Test Question a type of test question that requires students to select or choose a correct answer from answers that are provided to them (e.g., multiple-choice, true-false, and matching questions).

Reconstruction a process of rebuilding a memory part by part or piece by piece.

Reentry Student a student who matriculated as a traditional (just out of high school) student but who left college to meet other job or family demands and has returned to complete a degree or obtain job training.

Reference (Referral) Letter a letter of reference typically written by a faculty member, advisor, or employer for students who are applying for entry into positions or schools after college or for students during the college experience when they apply for special academic programs, student leadership positions on campus, or part-time employment.

Reflection a thoughtful, personal review of what a person has already done, is in the process of doing, or is planning to do.

Research Skills the ability to locate, access, retrieve, organize, and evaluate information from various sources, including library- and technology-based (computer) systems.

Restricted Elective a course that falls into an area of study students must complete but can be chosen from a restricted set or list of possible courses that have been specified by the college.

Résumé a written summary or outline that effectively organizes and highlights an individual's strongest qualities, personal accomplishments, and skills, as well as personal credentials and awards.

Rough Draft an early stage in the writing process whereby a first (rough) draft is created that converts the writer's major ideas into sentences, without worrying about the mechanics of writing (e.g., punctuation, grammar, or spelling).

Scholarly a criterion or standard for critically evaluating the quality of an information source; typically, a source is considered to be scholarly if it has been reviewed by a panel or board of impartial experts in the field before being published.

Secondary Source a publication that relies on or responds to a primary source that has been previously published (e.g., a textbook that draws its information from published research studies or an article that critically reviews a published novel or movie).

Self-Assessment the process of evaluating personal characteristics, traits, or habits and their relative strengths and weaknesses.

Self-Monitoring the ability to watch yourself and maintain self-awareness of how you're learning, what you're learning, and whether you're learning.

Semester (Term) Grade Point Average a GPA for one semester or academic term.

Senior Seminar (Capstone) Course course designed to put a cap or final touch on the college experience, helping seniors to tie ideas together in their major, make a smooth transition from college to life after college, or both.

Service Learning a form of experiential learning in which students serve or help others while they acquire skills through hands-on experience that can be used to strengthen their résumé and explore fields of work that may relate to their future career interests.

Sexually Transmitted Infections (STIs) a group of contagious infections that are spread through sexual contact.

Shadow Majors students who have been admitted to their college or university but have not yet been admitted to their intended major.

Shallow (Surface-Oriented) Learning an approach to learning in which students spend most of their study time repeating and memorizing information in the exact form that it was presented to them.

Student Development (Cocurricular) Transcript an official document issued by the college that validates a student's cocurricular achievements which the student can have sent to prospective employers or schools.

Summa Cum Laude graduating with highest honors (e.g., achieving a cumulative GPA of at least 3.8).

Syllabus an academic document that serves as a contract between instructor and student, which outlines course requirements, attendance policies, grading scale, course topic outlines by date, dates of tests and for completing reading and other assignments, and information about the instructor (e.g., office location and office hours).

Synthesis a form of higher-level thinking that involves building up ideas by integrating (connecting) separate pieces of information to form a whole or more comprehensive product.

Teaching Assistant (TA) a graduate student who receives financial assistance to pursue graduate studies by teaching undergraduate courses, leading course discussions, and helping professors grade papers or conduct labs.

Test Anxiety a state of emotional tension that can weaken test performance by interfering with memory and thinking.

Test Wise the ability to use the characteristics of the test question itself (such as its wording or format) to increase the probability of choosing the correct answer.

Theory a body of related concepts and general principles that help a student organize, understand, and apply knowledge that has been acquired in a particular field of study.

Thesis Statement an important sentence in the introduction of a paper that is a one-sentence summary of the key point or main argument a writer intends to make, and support with evidence, in the body of the paper.

Transferable Skills skills that can be transferred or applied across a range of subjects, careers, and life situations.

Values what a person strongly believes in and cares about or feels is important to do and should be done.

Visual Aids charts, graphs, diagrams, or concept maps that improve learning and memory by enabling the learner to visualize information as a picture or image and connect separate pieces of information to form a meaningful whole.

Visual Memory the type of memory that relies on the sense of vision.

Visualization a memory-improvement strategy that involves creating a mental image or picture of what is to be remembered or imagining it being placed at a familiar site or location.

Vocational (Occupational) Development exploring career options, making career choices wisely, and developing skills needed for career success.

Waive to give up a right to access information (e.g., waiving the right to see a letter of recommendation).

Wellness a state of optimal health, peak performance, and positive well-being that is produced when different dimensions of the self (body, spirit and mind) are attended to and effectively integrated.

Work–Study Program a federal program that supplies colleges and universities with funds to provide on-campus employment for students who are in financial need.

Written Communication Skills the ability to write in a clear, creative, or persuasive manner.

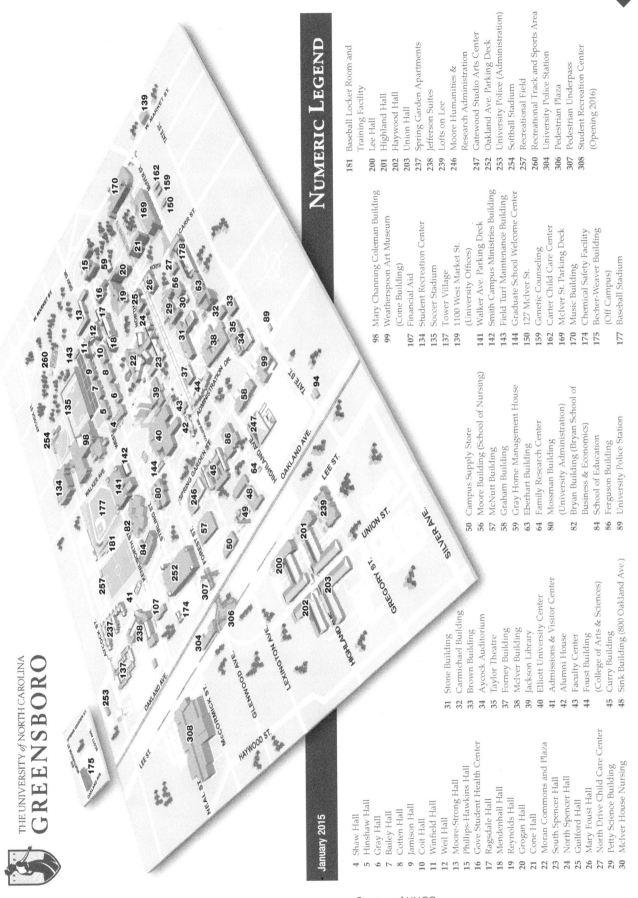

THE UNIVERSITY of NORTH CAROLINA
GREENSBORO

January 2015

NUMERIC LEGEND

4 Shaw Hall
5 Hinshaw Hall
6 Gray Hall
7 Bailey Hall
8 Cotten Hall
9 Jamison Hall
10 Coit Hall
11 Winfield Hall
12 Weil Hall
13 Moore-Strong Hall
15 Phillips-Hawkins Hall
16 Gove Student Health Center
17 Ragsdale Hall
18 Mendenhall Hall
19 Reynolds Hall
20 Grogan Hall
21 Cone Hall
22 Moran Commons and Plaza
23 South Spencer Hall
24 North Spencer Hall
25 Guilford Hall
26 Mary Foust Hall
27 North Drive Child Care Center
29 Petty Science Building
30 McIver House Nursing

31 Stone Building
32 Carmichael Building
33 Brown Building
34 Aycock Auditorium
35 Taylor Theatre
37 Forney Building
38 McIver Building
39 Jackson Library
40 Elliott University Center
41 Admissions & Visitor Center
42 Alumni House
43 Faculty Center
44 Foust Building
(College of Arts & Sciences)
45 Curry Building
48 Sink Building (800 Oakland Ave.)

50 Campus Supply Store
56 Moore Building (School of Nursing)
57 McNutt Building
58 Graham Building
59 Gray Home Management House
63 Eberhart Building
64 Family Research Center
80 Mossman Building
(University Administration)
82 Bryan Building (Bryan School of
Business & Economics)
84 School of Education
86 Ferguson Building
89 University Police Station

98 Mary Channing Coleman Building
99 Weatherspoon Art Museum
(Cone Building)
107 Financial Aid
134 Student Recreation Center
135 Soccer Stadium
137 Tower Village
139 1100 West Market St.
(University Offices)
141 Walker Ave. Parking Deck
142 Smith Campus Ministries Building
143 Field Turf Maintenance Building
144 Graduate School Welcome Center
150 127 McIver St.
159 Genetic Counseling
162 Carter Child Care Center
169 McIver St. Parking Deck
170 Music Building
174 Chemical Safety Facility
175 Becher-Weaver Building
(Off Campus)
177 Baseball Stadium

181 Baseball Locker Room and
Training Facility
200 Lee Hall
201 Highland Hall
202 Haywood Hall
203 Union Hall
237 Spring Garden Apartments
238 Jefferson Suites
239 Lofts on Lee
246 Moore Humanities &
Research Administration
247 Gatewood Studio Arts Center
252 Oakland Ave. Parking Deck
253 University Police (Administration)
254 Softball Stadium
257 Recreational Field
260 Recreational Track and Sports Area
304 University Police Station
306 Pedestrian Plaza
307 Pedestrian Underpass
308 Student Recreation Center
(Opening 2016)

Courtesy of UNCG